CW01390891

International Film Guide

2012

the definitive annual review of world cinema

edited by Ian Haydn Smith

48th edition

now online! www.internationalfilmguide.com

International Liaison

Algeria: Maryam Touzani
Argentina: Alfredo Friedlander
Armenia: Susana Harutyunyan
Australia: Peter Thompson
Austria: Gunnar Landsgesell
Belgium: Erik Martens
Bolivia: José Sanchez-H.
Bosnia and Herzegovina: Rada Sesić
Brazil: Helen Beltrame
Bulgaria: Pavlina Jeleva
Burkina Faso: Honoré Essoh
Cambodia: Michelle Vachon
Cameroon: Honoré Essoh
Canada: Tom McSorely
Chad: Agnes Thomasi
Chile: Hugo Díaz Gutierrez
China: Luna Lin
Colombia: Pedro Adrián Zuluaga
Costa Rica: Maria Lourdes Cortés
Croatia: Tomislav Kurulec
Cuba: Jorge Yglesias
Cyprus: Ninos Fenek-Mikelidis
Czech Republic: Jana Záhorková
Denmark: Christian Monggaard
Ecuador: Gabriela Aleman
Egypt: Sherif Awad
Estonia: Jaan Ruus
Finland: Antii Selkokari

France: Michel Ciment
Gabon: Agnes Thomasi
Georgia: Nino Ekvtimishvili
Germany: Andrea Dittgen
Greece: Ninos Fenek-Mikelidis
Guatemala: Maria Lourdes Cortés
Hong Kong: Tim Youngs
Hungary: John Cunningham
Iceland: Eddie Cockrell
India: Uma Da Cunha
Iran: Amir Esfandiari and Kamyar
    Mohsenin
Iraq: Sherif Awad
Israel: Dan Fainaru
Italy: Lorenzo Codelli
Ivory Coast: Honoré Essoh
Japan: Katsuta Tomomi
Kazakhstan: Gulnara Abikeyeva
Kyrgyzstan: Gulnara Abikeyeva
Lebanon: Sherif Awad
Lithuania: Auksė Kancerevičiūtė
Malaysia: Norman Yusoff
Mali: Honoré Essoh
Mauritania: Agnes Thomasi
Mexico: Carlos Bonfil
Morocco: Maryam Touzani
Netherlands: Leo Bankersen
Nepal: Prabesh Subedi

New Zealand: Peter Calder
Nigeria: Steve Ayorinde
Norway: Trond Olav Svendsen
Pakistan: Aijaz Gul
Palestine: Sherif Awad
Poland: Barbara Hollender
Portugal: Martin Dale
Qatar: Sherif Awad
Romania: Cristina Corciovescu
Russia: Kirill Razglov
Senegal: Honoré Essoh
Serbia: Goran Gocic
Singapore: Yvonne Ng
Slovakia: Miro Ulman
South Africa: Martin P. Botha
South Korea: Nikki J. Y. Lee
Spain: Jonathan Holland
Sweden: Gunnar Rehlin
Switzerland: Marcy Goldberg
Taiwan: Luna Lin
Tajikistan: Gulnara Abikeyeva
Thailand: Anchalee Chaiworaporn
Tunisia: Maryam Touzani
Turkey: Atilla Dorsay
Ukraine: Volodymyr Voytenko
United Kingdom: Jason Wood
United States: Curtis Woloschuk
Uzbekistan: Gulnara Abikeyeva

Credits

International Film Guide
4 Eastern Terrace Mews
Brighton
BN2 1EP
tel: +44 (0)1349 854931

info@cinephilia.co.uk
www.internationalfilmguide.com

ISBN 978-1-908215-01-7

A catalogue record for this book is
available from the British Library

© 2012 Cinephilia Services Ltd

Printed and bound in Poland
by Hussar Books & POZKAL

For information on sales and distribution in all territories worldwide,
please contact info@cinephilia.co.uk

Editor
Ian Haydn Smith

Publisher
Yoram Allon, Cinephilia Services Ltd

Founding Editor
Peter Cowie

Consultant Editor
Daniel Rosenthal

Selected Contributors
Eddie Cockrell, Ian Haydn Smith,
Erik Martens, Hannah Patterson,
Gunnar Rehlin, Jason Wood

Design
Elsa Mathern

Production Manager
Tom Cabot

Photo Consultants
The Kobal Collection
www.picturedesk.com

International Business Manager
Sara Tyler
Europe, Film Festivals
tel: +44 (0)1349 854931
saraifg@aol.com

International Sales Consultants
Sherif Awad
Egypt, Iran, Turkey
Tel: +20 12 0827398
sherif_awad@link.net

Anita Lewton
Belgium, France, Republic of Ireland,
United Kingdom
Tel: +44 (0)7866 294766
anita.lewton@googlemail.com

Lisa Ray
India, Italy, Middle East,
South East Asia, South Africa
Tel: +44 (0)7798 662955
l.ray@hotmail.co.uk

Front Cover
Jean Dujardin and Bérénice Bejo are the silent stars of Michel Hazanavicius's glorious homage to the golden age of Tinseltown, **The Artist** (courtesy of Momentum Pictures).

Contents

cineuropa has a new look
discover it

News   Films   Interviews   Videos

Industry   Services   Calendar

● THE SITE FOR EUROPEAN CINEMA

CINEUROPA.org
THE ONLY PORTAL DEDICATED TO
THE EUROPEAN FILM INDUSTRY
IN FOUR LANGUAGES

EUROPE LOVES CINEMA

Cineuropa.org is an initiative co-financed by the MEDIA Programme of the European Commission, the Italian Ministry of Culture, Cinema Centre of the Ministry of French Community of Belgium, Swiss Films, Federal Cinema Office of Switzerland, Centre National de la Cinématographie, ICAA - Institute of Cinematography and Audiovisual Arts, German Films, Luxembourg Film Fund, Filmunio, Czech Film Centre, Slovenian Film Fund, Malta Film Commission, the Irish Film Board

Notes from the Editor

The last year witnessed a series of events and incidents that sent ripples around the world, not just politically and economically, but also socially and culturally. From the continuing melée surrounding the faltering financial markets to the overthrow of military regimes and a series of devastating national disasters, few countries were left untouched by the end of the year.

This edition of the *International Film Guide* details how these circumstances impacted on national film industries. Many have seen a reduction in funding or a slackening in production. The spectre of piracy remains a problem in many countries, while others have questioned the advantages of recent technological innovations. There is also the ongoing drive towards a universal cultural hegemony, which some markets have found difficult to resist.

What many of the events over the course of the last year have shown is that easy access to filmmaking equipment has allowed people the chance to record these events, giving audiences around the world the opportunity to witness them first hand.

If the Arab Spring brought with it some hope and a chance for change, the cessation of studio and mainstream production during the chaos gave way to more independent films seeing the light of day. Cannes was the first major festival to screen films emerging from the affected countries, which documented what had been happening. These were not official stories of the revolutions, but on-the-ground accounts of how ordinary people were facing the challenge of opposing established regimes.

Likewise, the economic crisis found ordinary people clamouring for a voice amidst the

Ian Haydn Smith

bureaucracy of the markets, and politicians jockeying for advantage over their rivals. Nowhere is this more keenly felt than in the crowd-sourced Greek film *Debtocracy*. A viral sensation when it premiered online, it has now been seen by more than a million people in Greece and countless others around the world. Moving its focus away from the ineptitude of governments, the film focuses on the plight of everyday Greeks, even proffering alternative solutions to the EU's vacillations.

A number of countries reported a more positive year for their cinemas. As 2010 drew to a close, Tim Youngs saw a shift in the Hong Kong film market. For years, the industry paid no attention to its audience. As a result, Chinese productions gained a sizable foothold. However, even if the mainland still manages to attract a healthy revenue share, there is more evidence that local filmmakers are trying their damndest to win back audiences. The result has made for a more vibrant scene than Hong Kongers have seen for some time.

Record box-office figures do not always translate into a successful year. Turkey, along with Switzerland and a number of other countries, performed well for the cinemas in terms of takings, but the domestic share of the box office fell. Meanwhile, Luna Lin writes that although China celebrated a record year in terms of revenue, there was a significant reduction in audience numbers. The introduction of surcharges for 'extras', such as 3D, has massaged figures so that they offer a more promising reflection of the market than its actual state. How long 3D will continue to be seen as the saviour of cinema remains to be seen. For every *Pina*, *Cave of Forgotten Dreams* or *Hugo*, there is a *Clash of the Titans* – a cynical attempt by studios to cash in on a format that is often little more than a money-making gimmick.

Like China, India has also witnessed a reduction in its audience. Nowhere is the notion of a global market more relevant than in this country's vast industry. The models of old – the archetypal Bollywood extravaganza – have become increasingly unfashionable in recent years and although 2011 was an improvement on the previous year's dismal record, there is an awareness that drastic changes need to be made. Uma Da Cunha believes that investment in other countries' cinemas and an acknowledgement of the financial importance of the Indian Diaspora has helped speed up these changes.

To its neighbours, Indian exports remain a problem. Both Pakistan and Nepal have experienced trouble in attracting audiences to local films when bigger-budget Indian productions are also available. As Prabesh Subedi writes, Nepal in particular has suffered as a result of India's dominance, although there are plans to invest more money in local production to entice audiences back to films made by local filmmakers.

Pakistan also continues to suffer from piracy. However, it is nothing compared to the problem faced by Spain. As Jonathan Holland

notes, 77 per cent of all digital content is downloaded illegally. The result is disastrous in terms of the home entertainment market and the availability of pirated features before the originals are even released in cinemas.

Other factors affecting the year in film were more elemental. Japan's year in cinema – both in terms of production and exhibition – was almost halted, first by the tsunami that hit the coastline and then the meltdown of the Fukushima nuclear power plant. Likewise, the unprecedented weather that caused massive flooding in Thailand halted production and saw many of the country's cinemas closed for a prolonged period.

For all the problems faced by countries around the world over the last year, 2011 remained a buoyant one in terms of the quality of films. Documentary in particular has witnessed an incredible year. The best of these, which included *The Interrupters*, *Senna*, *Dreams of a Life*, *Pina*, *Bill Cunningham New York*, *Fire in Babylon*, *Blood in the Mobile*, *Wiebo's War*, *Gasland* and *Cave of Forgotten Dreams*, underpinned how documentary has become such a central part of contemporary cinema.

As for the best films of the year, it has been a difficult task narrowing down just five films. *A Separation*, *Le Havre* and *Oslo, August 31* each show how universal films can be, no matter what country they come from. And the sheer ambition of the two American titles – which were a long time in arriving on our screens and divided audiences as to their merits when they did – showed just what a magnificent medium cinema still can be.

Films of the Year – Editor's Choice
The Tree of Life (Terrence Malick)
Margaret (Kenneth Lonergan)
A Separation (Asghar Farhadi)
Oslo, August 31 (Joachim Trier)
Le Havre (Aki Kaurismäki)

Directors of the Year

Tomas Alfredson by Gunnar Rehlin

Growing up on film sets made young Tomas aware of all the possibilities of the medium. 'I was a young expert on everything', he said. 'Thinking how I would do it. It was a little bit like backseat driving in silence. I realised early in school that I had the ability to tell stories. I could imagine a beginning, middle and end, and throw myself out into that world. I think that I have a special ability to find images in reality. I can cut out a picture from reality, I can stimulate myself to see, for instance, how a building will look if you regard it from ten meters up in the air. And this I could do early.'

As with most aspiring filmmakers, Alfredson started out making shorts. He also had plans to become a pop musician and played drums in a band. This did not lead to a career but was a perfect stepping stone towards a career as a music video director. It is a period the director still views as useful in his career. As he says, 'I can use my musical side in the editing room – there's rhythm and timing'.

After working on a TV series aimed at young children, Alfredson directed the TV series *Bert*, which led to his feature debut, *Bert: The Last Virgin*. Both were based on a series of books written by Mikael Hjorth and Anders Jakobsen, detailing the coming-of-age story of Bert, a boy

There was little doubt over whether Tomas Alfredson was going to be a film director. The question was more when he was going to take the final step. His father is Hans Alfredson, one of Sweden's most beloved actors and directors, and young Tomas spent every summer on his father's sets, often playing bit roles in productions. 'It was a way of keeping the family together. It's difficult in this profession,' he said.

Hans Christian Tomas Alfredson, the director of *Let the Right One In* and *Tinker Tailor Soldier Spy*, was born in April 1965. At the time, his father was one member of the comedy duo Hasseåtage. The other was the tall, red-haired Tage Danielsson. For decades they made features, TV programmes, performed stand-up routines and stage shows that combined hilarious humour with serious commentary on society and all its ills. Tomas's older brother is Daniel Alfredson, the director of *The Girl Who Played with Fire* and *The Girl Who Kicked the Hornet's Nest*, the second and third films in the Stieg Larsson Millennium trilogy.

Bert: The Last Virgin

in his early teens. The film shows all the signs of having been made by someone who is young, enthusiastic and inexperienced. It was a sizable commercial success, selling more than 800,000 tickets which made it one of the bigger domestic hits of the year. Today, its interest lies in seeing how much the young director accomplished over the course of the next decade.

Having worked together with author Klas Östergren on the TV series *Victims and Culprits* ('my first production for adults'), in 1999 the comedy group Killinggänget approached Alfredson with the idea of collaboration. The group had been commissioned to make a TV series but were unsure what to do. Alfredson stepped in, chose their best ideas and turned them into four one-hour films. (included was 'Gunnar Rehlin – a short film about hurting someone', a satirical sideswipe against the author of this profile). The films became a critical and popular success, achieving cult status in Sweden.

Eight years had passed between Alfredson's debut and the hugely impressive *Let the Right One In*. His second feature, *Office Times*, was a commercial and critical disaster. The film was intended to be a satire on big business. The main protagonists, Lotta and Pernille, are two friends who work for the same company. The women have similar positions, but are very different as personalities, Pernille being orderly and methodical, while Lotta is careless. When two consultants start planning a re-organisation at the firm, Lotta moves up, only because she is louder than her colleague, highlighting the inequalities of the business world.

Office Times is neither funny nor satirical enough. There were also casting problems, with seasoned performers such as Thommy Berggren outshining other actors in the film. Though its intentions were fine, the film failed to work, resulting in Alfredson's first outright failure.

Fortunately, Alfredson's collaboration with Killinggänget on *Four Shades of Brown* achieved greater success and, considering its

length – coming in at around three hours – it did well at the box office. It has also become a cult hit on DVD in the US. The film opens with a series of shots from a helicopter, showing different Swedish landscapes. It then divides into four separate stories. What links the tales, aside of members of Killingganget playing a number of roles throughout, is the air of tragedy that the film exudes.

Four Shades of Brown

The first story, set in Dalarna, centres on a young man who comes home for the funeral of his father, a wealthy and powerful man, who is also the film's omniscient narrator. As the story unfolds, it becomes clear why the son had every reason to hate his father. The second story, set in the southern county of Skane, features Christer, a man in a loveless marriage, whose incommunicative son is doing badly at school. To encourage the boy, Christer takes him to his work, where the son causes an accident that leaves the father's face badly scarred. The third story takes place in Hotel Brunna, on Sweden's western coast. The owners, Richard and his wife Tove, are awaiting the arrival of Richard's

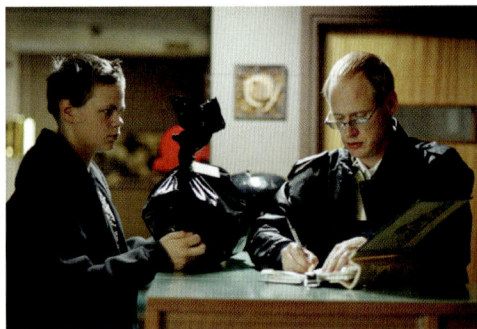

Four Shades of Brown

parents. What they don't know is that *en route* Richard's mother has picked up another man as her lover. In the final story, a group of people gather together for a cookery course that has transformed into a series of therapy sessions. As the confessions become more revealing, it turns out that some of the characters knew each other years ago. This revelation draws out a secret that they have all tried to bury.

The narrative moves effortlessly between the four stories, becoming darker and more tragic as the film progresses, with one story featuring a surprising final twist. The film was later edited into separate, one-hour television episodes. However, in this format they lacked focus.

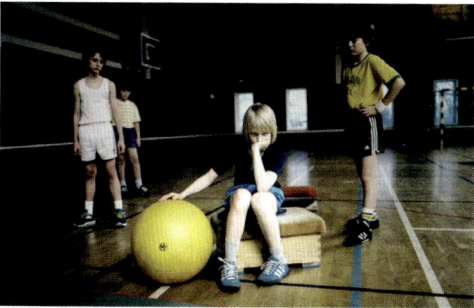

Let the Right One In

In 2008 Alfredson directed what was to become his international breakthrough, *Let the Right One In*. It was based on the bestselling novel by John Ajvide Lindqvist, a former stand-up comedian. The novel was an instant hit with its impressive combination of horror and love story. The portrait of Oskar, a young bullied boy, was partly based on the author's own experiences, being bullied during his youth in Blackeberg, the Stockholm suburb where the story unfolds.

Oskar lives with his single mother and is bullied on a daily basis by a group of boys at school. One day, an old man and a young girl, Eli, move into an apartment in the same building as Oskar. It is winter, with snow on the ground and a chill in the air, but the strange little girl walks barefoot through the snow. Gradually, the two loners become friends and Oskar discovers that Eli is a vampire. Incredibly old, she relies on

Let the Right One In

the old man to supply her with blood, finding victims amongst the run-down residential blocks. When he is hurt and hospitalised, Eli is forced to roam the neighbourhood herself to find blood. As Oskar starts to help her, so Eli protects her friend from the bullies.

Although the film has its unnerving and violent moments, Alfredson approaches it more as a love story – the tale of two outcasts forming a pact in order to survive. It is a very stylish film, efficiently employing the harsh Swedish winter as a backdrop. The acting is impeccable, particularly newcomers Kåre Hedebrandt and Lina Leandersson.

For his first non-Swedish film, *Tinker Tailor Soldier Spy* was a bold move for the director. Produced by Working Title, the adaptation of John Le Carré's celebrated novel about the hunt for a mole at the very top of Britain's secret service gave Alfredson the chance to work with Gary Oldman, John Hurt, Colin Firth and Tom Hardy. The result was one of the best films of 2011, rightfully earning laurels and award nominations around the world.

Tinker Tailor Soldier Spy

Tinker Tailor Soldier Spy

Working abroad and with actors that could easily intimidate a newcomer, Alfredson carries off his assignment with aplomb. His attention to detail is extraordinary. The film evokes, in image and mood, the drabness of Britain in the early 1970s. He is helped in no small by Gary Oldman's remarkable central performance as George Smiley, a role that had previously been assumed by Alec Guinness. Oldman's interpretation is markedly different, whilst remaining faithful to the novel.

Alfredson's film is that rare example of art and entertainment combining to create the perfect work. It is thrilling without resorting to the staple elements of the genre (all the action takes place in cramped rooms, not with car chases or shoot outs) and demands attention because of the density of its compelling narrative. Alfredson and his leading actor have both expressed an interest in continuing together, on an adaptation of Le Carré's sequel to *Tinker Tailor Soldier Spy*, 'Smiley's People'.

GUNNAR REHLIN is a Swedish journalist and critic, who works for several international media organisations, including Swedish news agency TT Spektra, Norwegian magazine *Film & Kino* and *Variety*.

Tomas Alfredson filmography

[feature film directing credits only]

1995
BERT: THE LAST VIRGIN
Script: Michale Hjorth, Anders Jacobsson, Sören Olsson and Tomas Tivemark. Photography: Leif Benjour. Production Design: Björn Nerdenhagen. Music: Michael B. Tretow. Players: Martin Andersson (Bert Ljung), Cajsa-Lisa Ejemyr (Victoria), Ing-Marie Carlsson (Madde Ljung), Johan Ulveson (Frederik Ljung), Yvonne Lombard (Svea Olsson), Povel Ramel (Henry Hoffmann). Produced by Johan Mardell. 100 mins.

2003
OFFICE TIMES
Script: Sofia Fréden. Photography: Olof Johnson. Production Design: Peter Bävman. Music: Commy Bloom and Benneth Fagerlund. Players: Ulrika Hansson (Lotta), Daniela Svensson (Pernilla), Thommy Berggren (Bill),

Sven Ahlström (Erik), Sten Elfström (Jörgen), Sanna Mari Patjas (Anna-Karin), Thomas Holmin (Magnus), Matteus Sillvel (Joppe). Produced by Anna Croneman. 104 mins.

2004
FOUR SHADES OF BROWN
Script: Tomas Alfredson, Robert Gustafsson, Jonas Inde, Andres Lokko, Martin Luuk, Johan Rheborg and Henrik Schyffert. Photography: Leif Benjour. Production Design: Eva Norén. Players: Robert Gustafsson (Christer/Johan), Maria Kulle (Anna), Jonas Inde (Ray/Tony), Johan Rheborg (Kjell Levrén/Ernst), Karin Holmberg (Arbetsterapeuten), Vikto Frieberg (Jan). Produced by Caisa Westling. 192 mins.

2008
LET THE RIGHT ONE IN
Script: John Ajvide Lindqvist (based on his novel). Photography: Hoyte Van Hoytema. Production Design: Eva Norén. Editing: Tomas Alfredson and Dino Jonsäter. Music: Johan

Söderqvist. Players: Kåre Hedebrant (Oskar), Lina Leandersson (Eli), Per Ragnar (Håkan), Henrik Dahl (Erik), Karin Bergquist (Yvonne), Peter Carlberg (Lacke), Ika Nord (Virginia). Produced by Carl Molinder and John Nordling. 115 mins.

2011
TINKER TAILOR SOLDIER SPY
Script: Peter Straughan and Bridget O'Connor (based on the novel by John Le Carré). Photography: Hoyte Van Hoytema. Production Design: Maria Djurkovic. Editing: Dino Jonsäter. Music: Alberto Iglesias. Players: Gary Oldman (George Smiley), Colin Firth (Bill Haydon), Tom Hardy (Ricki Tarr), John Hurt (Control), Toby Jones (Percy Alleline), Mark Strong (Jim Prideaux), Benedict Cumberbatch (Peter Guillam), Ciarán Hinds (Roy Bland), David Dencik (Toby Esterhase), Kathy Burke (Connie Sachs). Produced by Tim Bevan, Eric Fellner and Robyn Slovo. 127 mins.

Jean-Pierre and Luc Dardenne by Erik Martens

In 1996 two brothers, Jean-Pierre and Luc Dardenne, made a film called *The Promise* (*La Promesse*) in which they discovered a new way of filming that would place them squarely on the map of world cinema. Since then, they have become regular favourites at Cannes. At last year's festival *The Kid with a Bike* (*Le gamin au vélo*) was in the running to win an historic third Palme d'Or. It didn't, but the directors nevertheless went home with the prestigious Jury Prize.

What has happened to the Dardenne brothers is unique in the history of Belgian cinema. There has always been a film industry, but it has remained small and financially weak. The cinema of the Dutch-speaking part of Belgium (Flanders) was popular at home, at least intermittently. The French-speaking part (Wallonia and Brussels) offered a less popular cinema, but often more ambitious. It's more powerful sibling, French cinema, was something of a mixed blessing, providing a natural hinterland for French-speaking prod-uctions, but the sheer size and productivity of the industry there made it a tough competitor.

Over the years a handful of Belgian filmmakers achieved international acclaim in specialised markets (André Delvaux, documentary filmmaker Henri Storck, animation filmmaker Raoul Servais and Jaco Van Dormael), but they rarely broke into the mainstream or achieved the kind of international status that would put Belgium on the map of world cinema. However, with the release of *The Promise*, the brothers have raised the country's profile no end at festivals and cinemas around the globe. As Italians have Fellini, the Germans have Fassbinder, the Belgians now have Jean-Pierre and Luc Dardenne.

Their success was not immediate, instead developing over a lengthy period. At the end of the 1970s, when they first broke into filmmaking, the Dardennes were making documentaries about workers' issues. The lonesome labourer and his fellow workers were central to the struggle between the solidarity of the workforce and the behemoth of international capitalism. The films they made captured the countercultural movement of the times, with a rise in politicisation amongst the populace. The brothers also made the most of the then-innovative video technology, drawing inspiration from the work of Armand Gatti.

These early documentaries are, first and foremost, a remarkable record of the times. The hazy, low resolution of the first

The Kid With a Bike

Falsch

video cameras is part of the experience of discovering the first steps the brothers took. A recent DVD collection of these early works allowed audiences to see these hitherto rarely viewed gems.

From experimental and activist documentary they evolved towards narrative cinema to which they would become associated. However, the journey was not without a degree of pain on their part. Their feature debut *Falsch* (1987) draws on the Brechtian theatre tradition and was shot in a large airport terminal. It centres on Joe Falsch who is visited by different ghosts from his past, which goes all the way back to Berlin in 1938. Although the film displays a distinct style, it fails to come to life dramatically.

Their next feature *You're On My Mind* (*Je pense à vous*, 1992), was a more conventional approach to narrative cinema, but failed both artistically and commercially. Fabrice and Céline are a happily married couple who are

You're On My Mind

constructing a house on the banks of the Meuse, a physical feature that plays such an important role throughout the Dardennes' work. (It even gave name to their production company: Les Films du Fleuve – The Films of the River.) When the steel plant closes down and Fabrice loses his job, his self-confidence, self-respect and sanity are soon threatened. If the concept was interesting, characterisation and plotting, as well as the film's performances, were too artificial to be credible.

The Promise

The release of *The Promise* changed everything. It dominated the local festival awards in 1997: Brussels, Namur and Ghent. In the same year the film was awarded a César in France for Best Foreign Film. And it would go on to win awards at festivals around the world. Of particular importance were the press awards in the US: the National Society of Film Critics Award and the Los Angeles Film Critics Association Award.

And then there is Cannes. From 1999 onwards all of the brothers' films have been selected for official competition. That year the brothers won their first Palme d'Or for *Rosetta*. First time actress Emilie Duquenne was also awarded with the Best Actress prize. In 2002, with the entry of *The Son* (*Le fils*), Olivier Gourmet picked up the Best Actor award. And in 2005 *The Child* (*L'enfant*) won the brothers their second Palme d'Or. Three years later, *Lorna's Silence* (*Le silence de Lorna*) won the Best Screenplay award and finally, last year, *The Kid with a Bike* walked away with another major prize.

Rosetta

The strange love affair between the Dardenne brothers and the Cannes Film Festival is somewhat odd when you consider how different the world depicted in these film is compared to the champagne and red carpet glamour of the festival arena. Cyril is a child abandoned by his father (*The Kid with a Bike*), Lorna a young Albanian immigrant fighting to survive in a criminal environment (*Lorna's Silence*). Bruno and Sonia are two young street criminals who don't have a clue what to do with their newborn baby (*The Child*). Rosetta is desperately unemployed; Francis is a teenager just released from prison (*The Son*). Igor lives with a father, who earns a living by renting semi-slum housing to illegal immigrants (*The Promise*). All of these stories are unfold in the underbelly of society, where the social fabric is in a state of decay, or perhaps never existed. The criminal activity featured in these films is not so much the staple of a specific genre. It is matter-of-fact. Everyday. Ironically, it is the kind of reality most audiences seek to escape from when they go to see a movie.

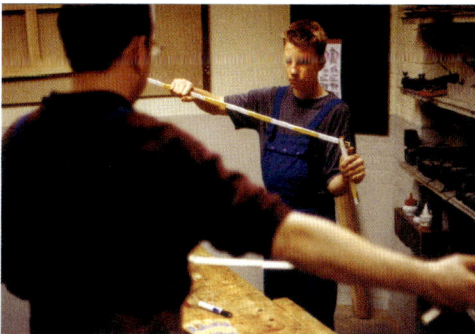

The Son

In order to understand the Dardennes' cinema it is useful to understand what happened in the crucial period 1992–96. What were the issues that led them to create the films that would attract such acclaim?

Although elements of the style of *You're On My Mind* were retained in their subsequent films, what shifted was an interest in the daily life of ordinary people. It was a return to a similar subject covered in the early documentaries, but with what could be argued is a Neorealist approach. No longer the rich, but the other end of the spectrum: the working individual or the individual who no longer has any work. They are stories about people who lose everything and do what they can to survive. Work, or the absence of it, remains the defining characteristic of this world. You are what you do for a living. It is a view of society from a leftist, if not Marxist, point of view.

The Child

Unlike the brothers' early work, whose key focus was on organised labour and the collective struggle of workers to defend their rights, the films from *The Promise* on dealt with individuals' place in the world. The protagonists no longer have relationships, or even family to take care of them. They are on their own in a consumerist world. As such it is not only the angle of the films that changed, it is also the world.

In these films, the main character often attempts to develop surrogate family relations. Lorna is in the business of false marriages.

Lorna's Silence

In *The Kid with a Bike*, Samantha is a kind of mother for Cyril. While titles as *The Child* and *The Son* speak for themselves.

'Suppose every one of us would have a price on his head', commented Luc Dardenne. 'Just suppose. No doubt you'd have to conclude that prices have gone down in recent times.' Life has become cheaper, Luc Dardenne said in the TV- documentary *Goldfish* produced by Flemish public Television VRT. Money and easy profit seem to be the only values that have survived the twentieth century. The opposite is true for the Dardennes' films. Here, young people are confronted with moral choices. Will they take responsibility; will they choose for the good and difficult or for the easy way out at the expense of their fellow man? The choice is not a frivolous matter. What is at stake here is their humanity.

It is interesting to see that in their most recent film *The Kid with a Bike*, the moral issues cover a new area. The bleak social context, which seemed to define all the earlier films, has become lighter and more colourful. And

Jean-Pierre and Luc Dardenne filmography

[feature film directing credits only]

1987
FALSCH
Script: Jean-Pierre Dardenne, Luc Dardenne and René Kalisky. Photography: Walther van den Ende. Editing: Denise Vindevogel. Art Direction: Wim Vermeylen. Music: Jean-Marie Billy and Jan Franssen. Players: Bruno Cremer (Joe), *Jacqueline Bollen* (Lilli), *Nicole Colchat* (Mina), *Christian Crahay* (Gustav), *Millie Dardenne* (Bela), *Bérangère Dautun* (Rachel), *John Dobrynine* (Georg). *82 mins.*

1992
YOU'RE ON MY MIND
Script: Jean-Pierre Dardenne, Luc Dardenne and Jean Gruault. Photography: Giorgos Arvanitis. Production Design: Yves Brover. Editing: Ludo Troch and Denise Vindevogel. Music: Wim Mertens. Players: Robin Renucci (Fabrice), *Fabienne Babe* (Céline), *Tolsty* (Marek), *Gil Lagay* (Renzo), *Pietro*

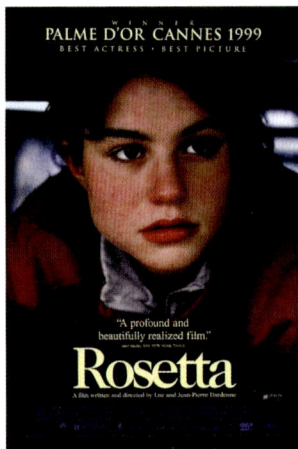

Pizzuti (Laurent). *Produced by Jean-Pierre Dardenne, Luc Dardenne, Dirk Impens, Jean-Luc Ormières and Claude Waringo. 95 mins.*

1996
THE PROMISE
Script: Hassen Daldoul, Luc Dardenne and Claude Waringo. Photography: Alain Marcoen. Editing: Marie-Hélène Dozo. Music: Jean-Marie Billy and Denis M'Punga. Players: Jérémie

Renier (Igor), *Olivier Gourmet* (Roger), *Assita Ouedraogo* (Assita). *Produced by Jean-Pierre Dardenne and Luc Dardenne. 92 mins.*

1999
ROSETTA
Script: Jean-Pierre Dardenne and Luc Dardenne. Photography: Alain Marcoen. Editing: Marie-Hélène Dozo. Production Design: Igor Gabriel. Music: Jean-Pierre Coco. Players: Émilie Dequenne (Rosetta), *Fabrizio Rongione* (Riquet), *Anna Yernaux* (The Mother), *Olivier Gourmet* (The Boss), *Bernard Marbaix* (The Campground Manager), *Frédéric Bodson* (The Head of Personnel), *Florian Delain* (The Boss's Son), *Christiane Dorval* (First Daleswoman), *Mireille Bailly* (Second Saleswoman). *Produced by Jean-Pierre Dardenne, Luc Dardenne, Laurent Pétin and Michele Pétin. 95 mins.*

2002
THE SON
Script: Jean-Pierre Dardenne and Luc Dardenne. Photography: Alain

with Belgian film star Cécile de France in the lead role, it is the first time the brothers cast someone from outside their natural environment. Their films have always created their own stars, like the two Cannes awards for Olivier Gourmet and Emily Duquenne, but also Jérémie Renier and Déborah François.

The Kid With a Bike

And all of them speak highly of the sense of respect and confidence that is invested in the filmmaking process. At the same time, the creative environment is securely guarded from the outside world. It is well known that Jean-Pierre and Luc Dardenne demand full control of all aspects of their productions.

Each of their films also needs the time to develop, taking three years or so. Attaining genuine authenticity requires delicate fostering; only devotion and the right peace of mind can make a film succeed. It is an art that Jean-Pierre and Luc Dardenne have mastered to perfection.

ERIK MARTENS is editor of DVD releases at the Royal Belgian Film Archive and a freelance film critic for different media outlets.

Marcoen. Editing: Marie-Hélène Dozo. Production Design: Igor Gabriel. Players: Olivier Gourmet (Olivier), Morgan Marinne (Francis), Isabelle Soupart (Magali), Nassim Hassaïni (Omar), Kevin Leroy (Raoul), Félicien Pitsaer (Steve), Rémy Renaud (Philippo). Produced by Jean-Pierre Dardenne, Luc Dardenne and Denis Freyd. 103 mins.

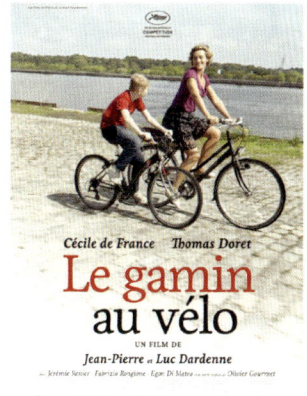

2005
THE CHILD
Script: Jean-Pierre Dardenne and Luc Dardenne. Photography: Alain Marcoen. Editing: Marie-Hélène Dozo. Production Design: Igor Gabriel. Players: Jérémie Renier (Bruno), Déborah François (Sonia), Jérémie Segard (Steve), Fabrizio Rongione (Jeune Bandit), Olivier Gourmet (Police Officer). Produced by Jean-Pierre Dardenne, Luc Dardenne and Denis Freyd. 95 mins.

2008
LORNA'S SILENCE
Script: Jean-Pierre Dardenne and Luc Dardenne. Photography: Alain Marcoen. Editing: Marie-Hélène Dozo. Production Design: Igor Gabriel. Players: Arta Dobroshi (Lorna), Jérémie Renier (Claudy Moreau), Fabrizio Rongione (Fabio), Alban Ukaj (Sokol), Morgan Marianne (Spirou), Olivier Gourmet (L'inspecteur), Anton Yakovlev (Andrei). Produced by Jean-Pierre Dardenne, Luc Dardenne and Denis Freyd. 105 mins.

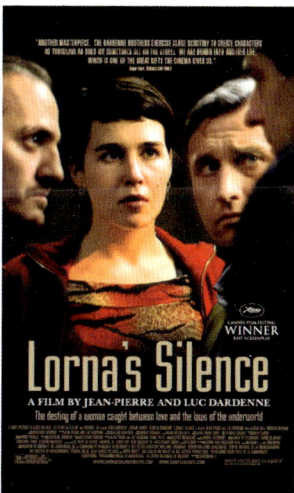

2011
THE KID WITH A BIKE
Script: Jean-Pierre Dardenne and Luc Dardenne. Photography: Alain Marcoen. Editing: Marie-Hélène Dozo. Production Design: Igor Gabriel. Players: Thomas Doret (Cyril Catoul), Cécile De France (Samantha), Jérémie Renier (Guy Catoul), Fabrizio Rongione (Le libraire), Egon Di Mateo (Wes), Olivier Gourmet (Le Patron du bar), Anton Yakovlev (Andrei). Produced by Jean-Pierre Dardenne, Luc Dardenne and Denis Freyd. 87 mins.

Terence Davies by Jason Wood

Though laying claim to a mere six features over the last four decades, Terence Davies is one of Britain's most uniquely gifted filmmakers. Noted for his recurring themes of emotional and physical endurance, and the potentially crippling effects of dogmatic religiosity on the emotional life of individuals and societies, Davies has also frequently focused on the influence of memory on everyday life.

Stylistically, Davies' works are notable for their symmetrical compositions, attentiveness to music and carefully calibrated pace. The sole screenwriter on all of all his films, Davies may have suffered debilitating funding issues and seen his output curtailed (as Davies comments, 'I didn't work for eight years and I genuinely thought, "That's it. It's over"') but there is an unparalleled richness and perfection to Davies' slim filmography.

Born in Liverpool in November 1945, Davies was the youngest in a large working-class family. Adored by his mother but frequently a target for his gruff father, Davies sought sanctuary in culture. The discovery of the cinema was as much a watershed moment for him as was his later struggles with sexuality

in the face of the staunch Catholicism in which he was raised. Davies was educated at Catholic primary and secondary schools in Liverpool, followed by work in accounting and bookkeeping. From 1965 to 1973 he also gained amateur acting experience. Finally leaving the drudgery of full-time employment behind, Davies enrolled at the Coventry School of Drama in 1973 and during that period had a number of short stories and other pieces broadcast on radio, directed a stage play and had a one-act play performed at Manchester University. From 1977 to 1980 Davies was a student at the National Film and Television School. He has also produced two works for radio, *A Walk to the Paradise Gardens*, an original radio play broadcast on BBC Radio 3 in 2001, and a two-part radio adaptation of Virginia Woolf's *The Waves*, broadcast on BBC Radio 4 in 2007. In 1984 Davies also published a novel, *Hallelujah Now*, based on his early life.

Completed with funding from the British Film Institute, it was with *Children* (1976) that Terence Davies announced his unique poetic lyricism to the world. A drama about social and domestic violence and its effects on Robert Tucker, a bullied young pupil at a Catholic boys' school in Liverpool, the film is told in a series of extended flashbacks, with

Children

Davies intercutting Robert's troubled childhood with scenes from his adolescence, including a brief sexual encounter with another man. Semi-autobiographical, it heralded a non-linear approach to the representation of memory and the passage of time.

Madonna and Child

Madonna and Child (1980), the second film in what came to be termed *The Terence Davies Trilogy*, returns to a middle-aged Robert, caught in a struggle between Catholicism and his sexuality, as he tries to reconcile his public and private personae and his love for his elderly, ailing mother in the cramped Liverpool council flat they share. Completed as Davies' graduation work from the National Film and Television School, it again embraces the interplay between past and present, taking an imprecise approach to time's passing. Both harrowing and tender, the film concludes with an astonishing vision in which Robert imagines he is dying and brought to God's judgement.

Completed with funding from the British Film Institute and a grant from the Greater London Arts Association, Davies concluded the trilogy with *Death and Transfiguration* (1983). Now an old man on the brink of death, Robert Tucker spends his final Christmas Eve reminiscing on some of the events of his life from his hospital bed, whilst also allowing himself a few sensuous flights of fancy. Robert recalls his beloved mother's funeral and his part as an angel in a school nativity play, before a nurse comforts him in his dying moments, the screen becoming bathed in white light

as his final breath departs his body. Offering evidence of the director's increasingly assured visual sense and use of fluid tracking shots, *Death and Transfiguration* also makes poignant use of Doris Day's *It All Depends On You*, the use of popular pastime songs becoming another of the defining signatures of Davies' work. A thoroughly remarkable achievement suffused with longing, loneliness and joy, *The Trilogy*, which was nominated for a Grierson Award, placed Davies at the forefront of a new generation of British filmmaking artists.

Death and Transfiguration

Further sharpening the experience of remembering and the development of a very personal and unique cinematic language, *Distant Voices, Still Lives* (1988) is undoubtedly Terence Davies' masterpiece. One of the finest features ever produced in this country, it's a highly distinctive marriage of style and content, combining the social concerns of much British cinema (in this case, life in a working-class Liverpool Catholic family) with formal and existential preoccupations more readily associated with European art cinema. Derek Malcolm described the film as '*Coronation Street* directed by Robert Bresson'.

An autobiographical work, the film examines the life of a working-class family in Liverpool, encompassing the wedding of the elder daughter, the christening of the younger daughter's infant child and the secondment into the armed forces of the family's son. Communal pub ditties are also recorded, providing a rich evocation of lives lived through the war years. Presiding over the family is the sadistic father (Pete Postlethwaite), who is always too quick with his fists, and the long-suffering, perennially loving mother (Freda Dowie).

Unfolding as a series of meticulously constructed vignettes told from the perspectives of different members of the same family (more than mere reminiscance, this is a film about the actual act of remembering), *Distant Voices, Still Lives* is rich in poetry, emotion and performance. An incredibly affecting work in which ordeal and sufferance are brilliantly juxtaposed with passages of intense happiness and communal spirit, it is also the film with which Davies established his ability to write incredible female characters and moderate their position in a patriarchal society. The director's sense of time and place is also acute, with 1940s Liverpool being incredibly well rendered by the use of a muted but never brackish colour palette that gives certain frames the look of having been hand-tinted. The director's visual aesthetic is all the more impressive given the film's modest budget.

Distant Voices, Still Lives

Awarded the International Critics Prize at Cannes, *Distant Voices, Still Lives* introduced Davies to a wider audience who immediately hailed him as one of the true poets of his medium.

Extending Davies' autobiographical memoirs from the 1940s to the 1950s, *The Long Day Closes* (1992) is another lyrical hymn to the director's childhood. Eleven-year-old Bud (a heartbreaking performance from Leigh McCormack) finds escape from the greyness of 1950s Britain through trips to the cinema, Christmases, birthdays and the protective love of his doting mother. But as Bud gets older, the agonies of the adult world, the casual cruelty of bullying, the tyranny of school and the dread of religion (coupled with an increasing uncertainty concerning sexual identity) begin to invade his life. Time and memory blend and blur through Davies' fluid and incredibly expressive camerawork; slow tracking shots, pans and dreamlike dissolves combine to create the world of Bud's imagination and the lost paradise of his bittersweet childhood.

The Long Day Closes

Adopting its protagonist as our eyes and ears, the film skilfully avoids the pitfalls of nostalgia. Pain, bitterness and resentment frequently disrupt the equilibrium and the use of dialogue from Hollywood films of the 1950s and a constant soundtrack of popular songs of the period only serve to highlight the fact that happiness and contentment are temporary states to which we can only intermittently return. The film's opening and closing images set the tone beautifully, the use of Boccherini's 'Minuet in G' lending the images a transcendental quality that from the very first frame suggest that the viewer is in the presence of greatness. Selected for Official Competition at Cannes and winner of the Best Screenplay at the 1993 Evening Standard Film Awards, *The Long Day Closes* defined a directorial style that quietly and adroitly defied classification.

The Neon Bible

Davies' first literary adaptation and his first film set in a foreign country, *The Neon Bible* (1994), is based on John Kennedy Toole's coming of age story set in the 1930s and 1940s American Bible belt. Retaining an interest in memory, reflection and recollection, the film unfolds as a series of remembrances by 15-year-old David (Jacob Tierney), who cogitates on the subject of his troubled childhood while riding a train to an unknown future. As a small boy, David (Drake Bell) was a friendless outcast who watched his father, Frank (Denis Leary in an early dramatic role) vent the frustration of their poverty by beating his wife, Sarah (Diana Scarwid). Left alone with his increasingly unstable mother after Frank enlists in the army and is swallowed up by World War II, David finds sanctuary following the arrival of the glamorous Aunt Mae (Gena Rowlands in formidable form). A lively big band singer who regales David with stories of her days on stage, Mae is however ultimately unable to shield David from the unavoidable horrors of adolescence.

Rich in atmosphere and visually resplendent (it was the director's first foray into widescreen), the film's slow pace and elliptical style was not to all tastes and it was given a hostile and chastening reception in Cannes by critics who perceived the film as suffering from the application of by now familiar concerns – church, childhood, domestic strife and the sanctuary of culture – to unfamiliar characters and landscapes. A transitional work that sometimes awkwardly straddles the experimentation of early Davies with a drive towards more conventional narratives, *The Neon Bible* remains under-seen and woefully neglected.

A sumptuous adaptation of Edith Wharton's novel which follows the fortunes – or lack of – of an ambitious but financially imperilled young woman looking for a rich husband in early twentieth-century New York, *The House of Mirth* faithfully captures the turbulence of Wharton's privileged society. Davies' furthest departure yet from his childhood obsessions, the film proved perhaps more successful than *The Neon Bible* in terms of it's director connecting more fully with the feelings and struggles of his characters.

Lily Bart (Gillian Anderson) is a ravishing socialite at the height of her success who quickly discovers the precariousness of her position when her beauty and charm attract unwelcome interest and jealousy. Torn between her heart and her head, Lily always seems to do the right thing at the wrong time.

The House of Mirth

She seeks a wealthy husband and in trying to conform to social expectations misses her chance for real love with Lawrence Selden (Eric Stolz). Lily's quest for a husband comes to a scandalous end when she is falsely accused of having an affair with a married man and is rejected by society and her friends, finally sinking into the mire of genteel poverty.

The House of Mirth

Sumptuously drawing on John Singer Sargeant, James Tissot and Johannes Vermeer, Davies' epic and beautifully cast production (Anderson has never been better served in film by her director) perceptively hones in on the cruelties of the social rituals of the privileged whilst delivering a tragic treatise on injustice, solitude and love given, but not necessarily returned. Resolutely unsentimental, the pacing is exactly right with the director perfectly treading the line between Merchant-Ivory and the more metaphorical, expressionist style of his earlier works.

Shown to acclaim at Cannes, *Of Time and the City* marked a welcome return for Terence Davies after a prolonged period of inactivity following the failure of numerous projects to materialise. Seemingly cut adrift from the UK film industry, for Davies, a deeply sensitive man, the sense of vindication following the reception of this impassioned documentary about his Liverpool birthplace must have been pronounced.

Created as part of Digital Departures, set up by North West Vision and Media to tie in with Liverpool's City of Culture status, this idiosyncratic and personal paean to Davies' hometown blends a poetic verbal account of Davies' early life with footage of the city. A eulogy that also weaves together the themes that define the auteur's early narrative works (homosexuality, Catholicism, death, loss and the power of cinema), *Of Time and the City* also expresses great anger and regret. This is particularly evident in the heartbreaking black and white images, many of which are reproduced from Nick Broomfield's *Who Cares* and *Behind the Rent Strike*, of the post-1945 slum clearance programme which saw the working-class communities relocated to purpose-built flats on the outskirts of the city. It is also present in the contemporary footage showing the Liverpool of today as a place of relative loneliness and desolation, a place where alcohol is pedalled to young teenagers and where the costly makeover and regeneration initiatives have come at the expense of a distillation of personality and identity.

Narrated in Davies' distinctive voice with a frequently playful sense of humour (the audio clips of *Around the Horn* are pregnant with innuendo), the film has been deliberately structured as a work of fiction so as to act as a fascinating, if largely memory-driven and non-linear portrait of a place to which there was always so much more than football and the Beatles. Of equal note to the images are the sounds, with Davies drawing together a rhapsodic collection of music including Handel, John Tavener, Liszt and Mahler.

Of Time and the City

The Deep Blue Sea

Named after the dilemma of choosing between two equally undesirable situations, *The Deep Blue Sea* is adapted by Davies from Terence Rattigan's play, which initially shocked with its frank exposure of British insecurities about sex and class. In the hands of Davies – whose adaptation was endorsed by the Rattigan estate – the story of a destructive love triangle also reflects the state of early 1950s Britain, a country in the throes of post-war rationing whose sense of power, worth, wealth and identity has been eroded.

Hester Collyer (Rachel Weisz) leads a privileged life in 1950s London. The beautiful wife of passionless but doting high court judge Sir William Collyer (Simon Russell Beale), Hester, in a material sense at least, wants for nothing. To the shock and dismay of those around her Hester walks out on her marriage and life of permanence and luxury to move in with a dashing young ex-RAF pilot, Freddie Page (Tom Hiddleston). Finding herself emotionally stranded and physically isolated, Hester feels Freddie drifting away from her, and in an attempt to win him back attempts suicide. Succeeding only in estranging her further, Hester is forced to confront all too clearly the foibles of the human heart.

Post-war Britain has been very much a vital and recurring setting for Davies. Stripping away much of Rattigan's exposition and many of the extraneous characters that inhabited the original production, Davies, a scholarly aficionado of the melodrama (he tips a number of nods to David Lean's *Brief Encounter*), gives contemporary audiences an almost unbearably moving and assiduously non-judgemental story about women's lives and desires. By extension, the film also looks in a wider sense at the quest, frequently fruitless or at best fleeting, for individual fulfilment and freedom.

Handsomely designed, the sets and costumes are impeccable, and luminously shot by Florian Hoffmeister, *The Deep Blue Sea* also makes characteristically exceptional and resonant use of music. 'When music is used correctly in film it really is absolutely thrilling. It's like being bathed in the most gorgeous joy', comments Davies. A recurring leitmotif, Samuel Barber's *Violin Concerto* gently underscores the emotions and, alongside the terrific and incredibly subtle performance of Rachel Weisz, is one of the films most fundamental and essential components. The raucous communal pub sing-alongs, an abiding memory of the director's childhood, again feature, also performing a wide function as the backdrop to a venomous row between Hester and Freddie initially conducted in front of a gallery of onlookers. Hester's forcing Freddie outside to conclude the spat is an important detail, revealing her disregard for convention and the director's attentive eye for the period and for detail in general.

Embraced by an adoring British press and opening to record box-office numbers for a Terence Davies film, *The Deep Blue Sea* offers numerous reminders of why Davies is a director to be embraced and positively cherished. With a proposed adaptation of Lewis Grassic Gibbon's 1932 novel *Sunset Song* in the works, it would seem that the director's career is enjoying a very successful second act.

JASON WOOD is a film programmer and contributor to *Sight and Sound* and the *Guardian*. He has also published several books on cinema.

Terence Davies filmography

[feature film directing credits only]

1976
CHILDREN

Script: Terence Davies. Photography: William Diver. Editing: Sarah Ellis and Digby Rumsey. Players: Philip Mawdsley (Robert Tucker, aged 14), Nick Stringer (Robert's Father), Valerie Liley (Robert's Mother), Robin Hooper (Robert, aged 23), Colin Hignet (Bully), Robin Bowen (Bully), Harry Wright (Teacher), Philip Joseph (Teacher). Produced by Peter Shannon. 43 mins.

1980
MADONNA AND CHILD

Script: Terence Davies. Photography: William Diver. Editing: Mick Audsley. Players: Terry O'Sullivan (Robert Tucker, middle age), Sheila Raynor (Robert's Mother), Gypsey Dave Cooper (Man with a Tattoo), Paul Barber, John Meynell, Brian Ward, Mark Walton. Produced by Mike Maloney. 30 mins.

1984
DEATH AND TRANSFIGURATION

Script: Terence Davies. Photography: William Diver. Editing: William Diver. Art Director: Miki van Zwanenberg. Players: Iain Munroe (Robert, aged 8), Terry O'Sullivan (Robert, middle age), Wilfred Brambell (Robert, elderly), Jean Doree (Mother). Produced by Claire Barwell. 23 mins.

1988
DISTANT VOICES, STILL LIVES

Script: Terence Davies. Photography: William Diver. Editing: William Diver. Production Design: Miki van Zwanenberg and Jocelyn James. Players: Freda Dowie (Mother), Pete Postlethwaite (Father), Angela Walsh (Eileen), Dean Williams (Tony),

Lorraine Ashbourne (Maisie), Sally Davies (Eileen as a child), Nathan Walsh (Tony as a child), Susan Flanagan (Maisie as a child), Michael Starke (Dave), Vincent Maguire (George), Antonia Mallen (Rose), Debbie Hones (Micky), Chris Darwin (Red), Marie Jelliman (Jingles), Andrew Schofield (Les). Produced by Jennifer Howarth. 95 mins.

1992
THE LONG DAY CLOSES

Script: Terence Davies. Photography: Michael Coulter. Editing: William Diver. Production Design: Christopher Hobbs. Music: Bob Last and Robert Lockhart. Players: Marjory Yates (Mother), Leigh McCormack (Bud), Anthony Watson (Kevin), Nicholas Lamont (John), Ayse Owens (Helen), Tina Malone (Edna), Jimmy Wilde (Curly), Mr Nicholls (Robin Polley), Peter Ivatts (Mr Bushell), Joy Blakeman (Frances). Produced by Olivia Stewart. 85 mins.

1994
THE NEON BIBLE

Script: Terence Davies (Based on the novel by John Kennedy Toole). Photography: Michael Coulter. Editing: Charles Rees. Production Design: Christopher Hobbs. Music: Robert Lockhart. Players: Jacob Tierney (David, aged 15), Drake Bell (David, aged 10), Gena Rowlands (Mae Morgan), Diana Scarwid (Sarah), Denis Leary (Frank). Produced by Elizabeth Carlsen and Olivia Stewart. 91 mins.

2008
THE HOUSE OF MIRTH

Script: Terence Davies. Photography: Remy Adefarasin. Editing: Michael Parker. Production Design: Don Taylor. Players: Gillian Anderson (Lily Bart), Dan Aykroyd (Augustus 'Gus' Trenor), Eleanor Bron (Mrs

Julia Peniston), Terry Kinney (George Dorset), Anthony LaPaglia (Sim Rosedale), Laura Linney (Bertha Dorset), Jodhi May (Grace Julia Stepney), Elizabeth McGovern (Mrs Carry Fisher), Eric Stoltz (Lawrence Seldon), Penny Downey (Judy Trenor). Produced by Olivia Stewart. 140 mins.

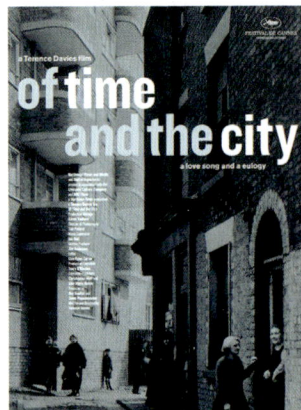

2008
OF TIME AND THE CITY

Script: Terence Davies. Director of Photography: Tim Pollard. Editing: Liza Ryan-Carter. Archive Producer: Jim Anderson. Produced by Solon Papadopoulos and Roy Boulter. 74 mins.

2011
THE DEEP BLUE SEA

Script: Terence Davies (adapted from the play by Terence Rattigan). Photography: Florian Hoffmeister. Editing: David Charap. Production Design: James Merifield. Players: Rachel Weisz (Hester Collyer), Tom Hiddleston (Freddie Page), Simon Russell Beale (William Collyer), Ann Mitchell (Mrs Elton), Karl Johnson (Miller), Harry Haddon-Patton (Jackie Jackson), Sarah Kants (Liz Jackson). Produced by Sean O'Connor and Kate Ogborn. 98 mins.

Terrence Malick by Ian Haydn Smith

Few films screening in the main competition at last year's Cannes Film Festival were as talked about as *The Tree of Life*. Terrence Malick's ambitious fifth feature is the culmination of over three decades of thought and enquiry into the nature of existence, the power of faith and our place in a world. It divided audiences. Some dismissed it as quasi-Christian nonsense or vacuous cinematic grandstanding. Others saw it as the work of a director willing to grapple with larger themes. Whatever one's opinion of Malick's work, there is no doubting his position as a unique filmmaker, distinct from all others in American cinema.

Malick was reportedly born in the milieu in which *The Tree of Life* unfolds (and if it is true that he harks from Waco, Texas – like much of his early life, such information is nebulous at best – then it was very close to where the 1950s-set sequences were filmed). He studied philosophy at Harvard, graduating *summa cum laude* and *phi beta kappa* in 1965, before becoming a Rhodes Scholar at Magdalene College, Oxford, but left before earning his doctorate. 'The Essence of Reasons', Malick's translation of Heidegger's 'Vom Wesen des Grundes', was published in 1969 and many critics have viewed Malick's work through the prism of the German philosopher's worldview.

After teaching philosophy at the Massachusetts Institute of Technology and freelancing as a journalist, Malick took an MFA at the AFI Conservatory, graduating with the short *Lanton Mills*. Through his association with classmate Mike Medavoy, who would become one of Hollywood's most powerful producers, Malick worked on a number of scripts, including Stuart Rosenberg's *Pocket Money* and early drafts of *Dirty Harry* and *Great Balls of Fire*. When his script for *Deadhead Miles* was deemed un-releasable by its studio, Malick decided to take on the role of director for his next project.

The Tree of Life

Badlands (1973) is regarded by many as the finest debut by any American director and frequently appears on many critics' 'best of' lists; yet this is perhaps a backhanded compliment that negates Malick's subsequent films. Based on the Charlie Starkweather killings of the 1950s, the film hints at Malick's fascination with humanity's relationship to nature. Narrated by Sissy Spacek's naïf, who takes up with Martin Sheen's charming serial killer, we follow the couple as they attempt to create a romantic idyll on the fringes of Montana's great wilderness, only to be stymied by Kit's uncontrollable violent urges.

Badlands

The film is also an astute critique of the growing role of celebrity in American society. It predated films such as Martin Scorsese's *The King of Comedy* and Jonathan Demme's *Melvin and Howard*, which are also regarded as prescient harbingers of a fame-obsessed society. Malick's approach is arguably subtler, as evidenced in the film's final scenes, where the State Troopers are momentarily star-struck by Kit's magnetic personality.

Some critics objected to the way Malick used actors. Pauline Kael in particular was puzzled by his tendency to distance characters emotionally from the audience. It is a criticism that has been levelled at his subsequent work, on occasion by the actors themselves. In a press conference following the premiere of *The Tree of Life*, Sean Penn expressed

The Tree of Life

puzzlement over his role, stating: 'I didn't at all find on the screen the emotion of the script, which is the most magnificent one that I've ever read. A clearer and more conventional narrative would have helped the film without, in my opinion, lessening its beauty and its impact. Frankly, I'm still trying to figure out what I'm doing there and what I was supposed to add in that context! What's more, Terry himself never managed to explain it to me clearly.' However, as the *New Yorker*'s Richard Brody recently pointed out, Malick's style of filmmaking doesn't allow for conventional acting technique. Instead, what surfaces are glimpses of an actor's persona, the familiarity of their face, or a momentary expression that captures the tenet of a story's meaning, or a scene's mood. Both Martin Sheen and Sissy Spacek perfectly embody Malick's approach, which allows us the distance to observe their actions, whilst gradually drawing us in to their attempts to forge an unattainable utopia.

Badlands

There was little criticism of the film's look. Beginning a career-long collaboration with designer Jack Fisk, *Badland*'s beguilingly stark visuals complemented the minimalism of Malick's script. Shot by Tak Fujimoto, Stevan Larner and Bryan Probyn, the vast landscapes add a Biblical dimension to the film, which would be further explored in the director's next feature.

The use of voiceover in the film is also unique. A central component of Malick's work, it is frequently employed as a counterpoint to the action on screen, or to embellish themes tangential to the plot. Often richly lyrical – few filmmakers would boldly open a film about a conflict between men with the line 'What is this war at the heart of nature?' as Malick does in the pastoral prologue to *The Thin Red Line* – it is anathema to many films' use of voiceover: commonly a lazy device that compensates for undernourished dialogue or as a way of papering over plot holes.

Days of Heaven

Voiceover was even more essential in the sublimely beautiful *Days of Heaven* (1978). A love triangle that unfolds in the Texas Panhandle in the early days of the twentieth century, the film is a paean to rural life. Here, nature becomes increasingly entwined with the lives and actions of the central characters. The ravages of weather and – in true Old Testament style – a swarm of locusts, reflect the emotional turbulence that has invaded the life of a young, but ailing, landowner (Sam Shepard), in the form of lovers Bill and Abbey (Richard Gere and Brooke Adams).

Days of Heaven

Their actions are watched over by Linda (Linda Manz), the film's gravelly-voiced narrator, whose mix of innocence and weariness mirrors the schizophrenic make-up of this world; the contrast between the beauty of the landscape and the tortured lives that play out upon it.

Days of Heaven won Néstor Almendros an Academy Award for his cinematography, and is regarded as one of the most beautiful films ever made. It was mostly shot at the 'magic hour – the last hour of the setting sun, giving the landscape a golden glow. However, such perfectionism tried the patience of certain crew-members, making for a fractious shoot, possibly one of the reasons why Malick disappeared from cinema for twenty years. Whatever the cause, his return was one of the most heralded cinematic events of the 1990s.

The Thin Red Line (1998) is both a unique and compelling take on military life during World War II. It stands in stark contrast to Steven Spielberg's impressive *Saving Private Ryan*, which was released the same year. The two directors were in contact with each

The Thin Red Line

The Thin Red Line

other during production, with many props and vehicles passing between them, due to the sheer scale of both films and the limited amount of actual equipment from that period. If Spielberg's film dealt with the horrors of war, Malick showed more interest in the nature of it. His focus is on the violence that exists in the world at large and whether nature is a cruel or benevolent force. It is a theme he returns to in *The Tree of Life*, which opens by asking if we live in a state of nature or grace.

In terms of physical production, this film is Malick's most expansive, with a multitude of characters populating the many narrative strands. They all orbit Private Witt's (Jim Caviezel) Christ-like character, another innocent set forth into the world. It best exemplifies Malick's approach to filmmaking, with many hours of footage shot and assembled through a lengthy editing process. Since *Days of Heaven*, the gestation period between a production wrapping and the completed film premiering has been a long one. In the case of *The Thin Red Line*, some actors were surprised to see how much their role had diminished in the edit, while others, such as Caviezel and Ben Chaplin, became more pivotal. There were also a host of actors, including Billy Bob Thornton, Martin Sheen, Gary Oldman, Bill Pullman, Viggo Mortensen and Mickey Rourke, who didn't even make the final cut.

Malick's use of voiceover is at its most complex in this film. No longer attributed to one character, this becomes a chorus of the shared experience of men in combat. Their

philosophical ruminations on the nature of conflict is powerfully contrasted with some of the film's brutal imagery; none more so than the attack on the Japanese army's encampment, filmed in a series of long tracking shots and accompanied by Hans Zimmer's 'Journey to the Line', the most prominent track of his moving and elegiac score. John Toll's cinematography captures the beauty and horror of this world in equal measure, adding to the richness of Malick's vision.

The New World

After the level of attention and praise lavished on *The Thin Red Line*, the response to *The New World* (2005) was underwhelming. At the film's premiere in Cannes, critics were mystified by the director's interest in the British arrival on the shores of America and John Smith's encounter with Pocahontas. Multiple voiceovers are once again employed to emphasise the shared experience of the explorers, while Pocahontas's narration is more attuned to the role of nature. Opening to the strains 'Vorspiel' from Wagner's 'Das Rheingold', with a camera moving swiftly beneath the water's surface, before meeting the British fleet as it approaches the American shoreline, the stately pace of this scene sets the tone for the film – one of wonderment at this unfettered world and the resilience of the people who have lived off it.

Initially, the story appears to be John Smith's (Colin Farrell); it is through his eyes that we see this 'new' world. However, his abrupt departure at the film's mid-point caused

The New World

confusion for some. It becomes clear that he was merely a conduit, an accessible point of entry, for our immersion into Pocahontas's culture and, subsequently, her story. The film's title not only refers to the land encountered by British troops in 1607, it is also the strange land – England – that Pocahontas visits towards the end of her life. And moving beyond the physical, the title also suggests the worlds we encounter through our senses and emotions.

Like *Days of Heaven*, which was also met with incredulity by many critics, attitudes to *The New World* have shifted markedly since it was released. For some, such as the *Guardian*'s John Patterson, it is the moment when 'cinema has reached its culmination, its apotheosis. It is both ancient and modern, cinema at its purest and most organic, its simplest and most refined.'

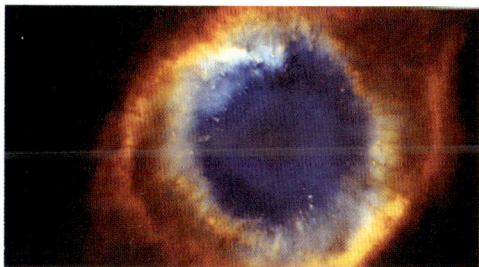

The Tree of Life

After Malick completed *Days of Heaven*, he began writing *Q*, intending to explore the origins of life on Earth. It took over three decades for the idea to be realised, becoming

The Tree of Life in the process. When the finished film was unveiled at Cannes, it was greeted with a mixture of hostility, confusion and the kind of admiration normally reserved for religious works of art. It has been seen by some as a companion to Stanley Kubrick's *2001: A Space Odyssey*, particularly the twenty-minute sequence that proffers nothing less than the creation of the universe; unsurprisingly, both films employed the skills of special effects expert Douglas Trumbull. However, Malick's vision of the universe is far removed from Kubrick's clinical approach.

The Tree of Life

The Tree of Life can be seen as a Judao-pantheistic symphony or an attempt to come to terms with the very idea of faith; yet the director's enquiry into the nature of existence is open to numerous interpretations. Structuring the film the way he has, Malick also draws a fascinating parallel between the immensity of the universe and the importance of each life within it. With pitch-perfect performances by Brad Pitt – casting aside any lingering doubts as to his skills as an actor – Jessica Chastain and Hunter McKracken, the film is a beautifully realised family drama, whose snapshots of family life in 1950s Texas are imbued with greater significance because of – not in contrast to – the film's grander vision of how our world was formed. It may not be to all tastes and some may balk at the much-derided final sequence, but it is a defining statement by Terrence Malick, a filmmaker whose originality and vision mark him out as a very rare presence in contemporary world cinema.

Terrence Malick filmography

[feature film directing credits only]

1973
BADLANDS

Script: Terrence Malick. Photography: Tak Fujimoto, Steven Larner and Brian Probyn. Editing: Robert Estrin. Art Direction: Jack Fisk. Players: Martin Sheen (Kit), Sissy Spacek (Holly), Warren Oates (Father), Ramon Bieri (Cato), Alan Vint (Deputy), Gary Littlejohn (Sheriff), John Carter (Rich Man), Bryan Montgomery (Boy), Gail Threkeld (Girl), Terrence Malick (caller). Produced by Terrence Malick. 94 mins.

1978
DAYS OF HEAVEN

Script: Terrence Malick. Photography: Néstor Almendros. Editing: Billy Weber. Production Design: Jack Fisk. Music: Ennio Morricone. Players: Richard Gere (Bill), Brooke Adams (Abbey), Linda Manz (linda), Sam Shepard (The Farmer), Robert Wilke (The Farm Foreman). Produced by Bert Schneider and Harold Schneider. 94 mins.

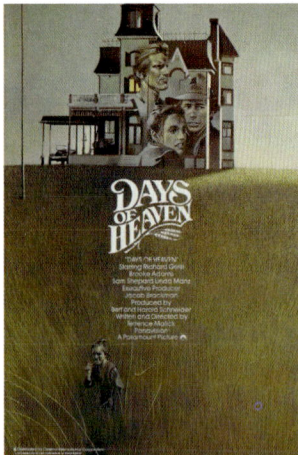

1998
THE THIN RED LINE

Script: Terrence Malick (based on the novel by James Jones). Photography: John Toll. Editing: Billy Weber, Saar Klein and Leslie Jones. Production Design: Jack Fisk. Music: Hans Zimmer. Players: Nick Nolte (Lt. Col. Gordon Tall), Jim Caviezel (Pvt. Witt), Sean Penn (1st Sgt. Welsh), Elias Koteas (Capt. James 'Bugger' Staros), Ben Chaplin (Pvt. Bell), Dash Mihok (Pfc. Doll), John Cusack (Capt. John Gaff), Adrien Brody (Cpl. Fife), John C. Reilly (Sgt. Storm), Woody Harrelson (Sgt. Keck), Miranda Otto (Marty Bell), Jared Leto (2nd Lt. Whyte), John Travolta (Brig. Gen. Quintard), George Clooney (Capt. Charles Boshe), Nick Stahl (Pfc - Beade), Thomas Jane (Pvt. Ash), John Savage (Sgt. McCron). Produced by Grant Hill and John Roberdeau. 170 mins.

2005
THE NEW WORLD

Script: Terrence Malick. Photography: Emmanuel Lubezki. Editing: Richard Chew, Hank Corwin, Saar Kleinand Mark Yoshikawa. Production Design: Jack Fisk. Music: James Horner. Players: Colin Farrell (John Smith), Q'orianka

Kilcher (Pochahontas), *Christopher Plummer* (Captain Newport), *Christian Bale* (John Rolfe), *August Schellenberg* (Powhatan), *Wes Studi* (Opechancanough), *David Thewlis* (Wingfield), *Yorick van Wageningen* (Captain Argall), *Raoul Trujillo* (Tomocomo), *Michael Greyeyes* (Rupwew), *Kalani Queypo* (Parahunt), *Ben Mendelsohn* (Ben), *Noah Taylor* (Selway), *Brian F. O'Byrne* (Lewes), *Ben Chaplin* (Robinson), *Jamie Harris* (Emery), *Eddie Marsan* (eddie). *Produced by Sarah Green. 135 mins.*

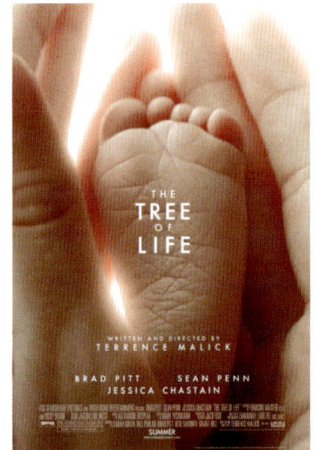

2011
THE TREE OF LIFE

Script: Terrence Malick. Photography: Emmanuel Lubezki. Editing: Hank Corwin, Jay Rabinowitz, Daniel Rezende, Billy Weber and Mark Yoshikawa. Production Design: Jack Fisk. Music: Alexandre Desplat. Players: Brad Pitt (Mr O'Brien), Sean Penn (Jack), Jessica Chastain (Mrs O'Brien), Hunter McCracken (Young Jack), Laramie Eppler (R.L.), Tye Sheridan (Steve), Fiona Shaw (Grandmother). Produced by Dede Gardner, Sarah Green, Grant Hill and Brad Pitt. 135 mins.

Nicolas Winding Refn by Eddie Cockrell

Nicolas Winding Refn doesn't have a licence, yet his latest film, the muscular neo-noir thriller *Drive*, earned him the best directing award at the 2011 Cannes Film Festival. 'I find driving so sexual and exciting', he recently told the *L.A. Times* with typical candour, 'and I'm very much aroused by speed. So I will never control a machine.'

At once fiercely independent and markedly ambitious, Refn makes movies about outsiders that thrum with the passion of violent and impulsive men making split-second decisions that more often than not prove to be the wrong ones. These violent stories of survival and retribution form the spine of the eight major features in his distinctive career to date.

The 41-year-old Copenhagen-born director is a dyed-in-the-wool movie geek. But what sets Refn apart is the size of the canvas on which he paints: from the jittery Copenhagen underworld of the *Pusher* trilogy and *Bleeder*, he has exported his narrative concerns to the American Midwest for the underrated *Fear X* (though it was shot in Canada), the surrealistic East Midlands of *Bronson*, the windswept moors of Scotland for *Valhalla Rising* and the schizophrenic Los Angeles of neon-lit nights punctuated by brutally bright days in his breakthrough feature, *Drive*.

Refn's involvement in that film came about when Ryan Gosling, who had seen all of the director's films, phoned him to gauge his interest in directing an adaptation of James Sallis's novel. As both men remember, Refn was stoned on American flu medication when they met over dinner in Los Angeles and little conversation was forthcoming. As Gosling drove him home ('I didn't want to pay for a taxi'), Refn began singing boisterously to R.E.O Speedwagon's 'I Can't Fight This Feeling Anymore' and weeping uncontrollably.

Drive

The film that's put him on the map, *Drive*, is a thriller-cum-love-story – though the director actually sees it the other way around – starring the suddenly white-hot Gosling as a taciturn cypher, a Los Angeles auto mechanic who moonlights as a getaway driver and has ambitions to race stock cars in partnership with his boss, played by *Breaking Bad* star Bryan Cranston. When he embarks on an intense but strictly platonic relationship with a young mother living next door, played by Carey Mulligan, his honest efforts to help her ex-con husband out of a spot runs him afoul of a pair of very bad men played by Ron Perlman and, in a shrewd bit of stunt casting, filmmaker and comedian Albert Brooks.

Drive

In a marketplace largely bereft of original ideas on screen – fourteen of the top twenty North American summer box-office hits were sequels or franchise pictures – critics and audiences are responding to the originality of Refn's throwback blend of method and material.

It is thus no coincidence that, when asked about his relationship with Gosling, Refn compares the star's insistence on having him in *Drive*'s driver's seat to Steve McQueen demanding Peter Yates for *Bullitt* and Lee Marvin insisting on John Boorman for *Point Blank*. The taciturn nature of Gosling's performance has also drawn comparisons to Clint Eastwood's flawed, silent heroes, while the movie itself summons memories of such influential genre touchstones as Walter Hill's ice-cool *The Driver* and William Friedkin's bravura *To Live and Die in L.A.* Brash analogies to be sure, but Refn walks it like he talks it.

Yet for the amount of light and heat surrounding this distinctive genre picture and it's equally original raconteur of a director, Refn is no overnight sensation. That particular phase of his life happened sixteen years ago, with the release of *Pusher* in 1996.

Nicolas Winding Refn was born in September 1970 in Copenhagen, Denmark, to local arts royalty. His father is filmmaker and editor Anders Refn, whose latter credits include the Lars von Trier films *Breaking the Waves* and *Antichrist*, as well as Fridrich Thor Fridricksson's *Mamma Gogo*. His mother, Vibeke Winding, is a noted cinematographer.

When Refn was ten, his family relocated to New York City and the boy became a denizen of the now long-gone Times Square B-movie picture palaces that forged his broad yet determinedly eclectic cinematic tastes. Thrown out of the American Academy of Dramatic Arts for throwing a chair at a wall during class, he returned to the land of his birth, intending to study at the Danish Film School. Before the semester had even begun, he was approached by a producer who had seen one of his short films.

Refn consciously fashioned his debut, *Pusher*, after the work of two of his heroes, John Cassavetes and Martin Scorsese. Indeed, more than one critic has noted the similarities of Refn's ease in Copenhagen's rough-and-tumble Vesterbro district to the Little Italy in which *Mean Streets* is set. And in debuting young actor Mads Mikkelsen, Refn found an expressive screen presence to whom he would return in subsequent years.

Pusher

He cemented his reputation with *Bleeder* (1999) which reunited most of the *Pusher* cast in a stand-along story about various hard-luck Danes whose tumultuous lives are led in the shadow of an urban video shop. 'For my mum', reads the dedication.

Taking aim on the American art-house market, Refn's next film was the Lynchian Danish-Canadian-British thriller *Fear X* (2003), starring John Turturro as a Midwestern shopping mall security guard trying to solve the murder of his wife. Co-written by Hubert

Fear X

Selby Jr. and scored by Brian Eno, the film premiered to considerable anticipation at that year's Sundance festival but landed with a resounding thud. Nevertheless, Refn sent a strong, uncompromising signal that he was a director of distinctive obsessions but a flexible approach; with it's claustrophobic open spaces, neat-as-a-pin interiors and deliberately somnambulant acting – Turturro was made for this kind of part – nothing else in the Refn canon to date looks or feels quite like the Lynchian world of Fear X.

With Blood On My Hands: Pusher II

Seriously in debt, Refn directed two Pusher sequels back to back in 2005. He did so with typical intensity. In With Blood On My Hands: Pusher II, nothing the dim-witted ex-con Tonny (Mads Mikkelsen) can do will win him the approval of his father. The more he tries to make things right, the more wrong his choices become. Tellingly, Tonny is surprisingly tender with the son he only recently knew he had.

But it is the recovering addict, career criminal and put-upon drug kingpin Milo (Zlatko Buric), a lesser presence in the first Pusher shoved to centre-stage in the third, who embodies the best of Refn's skills in I'm the Angel of Death: Pusher III.

I'm the Angel of Death: Pusher 3

Despite his initial reticence towards the films, the gambit worked, and the trilogy has become a cult favourite after being showcased at the 2006 Toronto Film Festival. The DVD box set includes a commercially released documentary feature about Refn, by now a star in his own right in Denmark, and his struggles to stave off the bankruptcy eventually negated by the trilogy. It is called, fittingly, Gambler.

Refn would continue to hone his visual style with two films, shot back-to-back, that have very different emotional temperatures. According to production executive-turned-screenwriter Brock Norman Brock, the emotional and chaotic prison world of Bronson (2008) is a deliberate tribute to the overheated nightclub world brought vividly to life in Bob

Bronson

Fosse's *Lenny*. And Tom Hardy's throat-grabbing performance as the cheerfully self-destructive career criminal who yearns to be famous from behind bars is every bit as bold as Dustin Hoffman's Lenny Bruce, who came to see fame as shackling his freedom of speech.

It is telling that Refn, who made significant structural and tonal changes to Brock's original script, pulls off the neat trick of preserving the writer's intent while still imbuing the film with his own voice and interests: read enough interviews with the director, and it becomes clear that, as with his countryman and rival Lars von Trier, he has no six-second delay between thought and expression – regardless of the fallout.

Valhalla Rising

Almost immediately after wrapping *Bronson*, he returned to the thoughtful, wide-screen compositions of *Fear X* in *Valhalla Rising* (2009). Starring long-time Refn cohort Mads Mikkelsen as the mute warrior One Eye, this gorgeous, brooding film (it was shot by Morton Sorborg, who photographed *I'm the Angel of Death*) is a proud anti-action film that eschews set pieces and movement – but not brutal violence – in favour of the kind of stoic introspection all too rare in the Viking genre.

Filtered through Refn's previous work, *Drive* feels both a summation and a new beginning. It has the charged silences of *Valhalla Rising*, the eccentric recidivists of *Bronson*, the piquant underworld milieu of the *Pusher* trilogy and the langourous inevitability of *Fear X*.

Unlike more discrete filmmakers, Refn isn't afraid to name names of those he encountered during his struggles to find a toe-hold in Hollywood. He has expressed comical exasperation at Harrison Ford for backing out of the Paul Schrader-scripted *The Dying of the Light* after realising his character actually had to die, and is philosophical over losing, over scheduling issues, a chance to direct Keanu Reeves in a fresh take on Robert Louis Stevenson's 'The Strange Case of Dr Jekyll and Mr Hyde'.

With *Drive* strengthening his hand considerably, he'll tell anyone who'll listen he'd like to make a studio tentpole *Wonder Woman* movie with *Mad Men* co-star Christina Hendricks, who has a brief but pivotal role in his new film. He also fantasises about shooting an Alesteir Crowley biography that would reunite him with *Bronson* star Hardy.

Christina Hendricks in **Drive**

With Gosling, he'll next make the long-nursed crime thriller *Only God Forgives*. After that, it's back to Hollywood for a remake of the 1970s science fiction film *Logan's Run*, also to star Ryan Gosling.

'In L.A. you wait a lot and I don't wanna wait,' he told one interviewer. 'Life is too short, you know.' Just what you'd expect to hear from a filmmaker as driven as Nicolas Winding Refn. In a career with a fair share of rough roads and abrupt turns, it seems he may, for a time, finally be comfortably in the driver's seat.

EDDIE COCKRELL is a freelance film critic and consulting programmer.

Nicolas Winding Refn filmography

[feature film directing credits only]

1996
PUSHER

Script: Nicolas Winding Refn. Photography: Morten Søborg. Production Design: Kim Lovetand Juleæk. Editing: Anne Østerud. Music: Povl Kristian and Peter Peter. Players: Kim Bodnia (Frank), *Zlatko Buric* (Milo), *Laura Drasbæk* (Vic), *Slavko Labovic* (Radovan), *Mads Mikkelson* (Tonny), *Peter Andersson* (Hasse), *Vanja Bajicic* (Branko), *Lisbeth Rasmussen* (Rita), *Levino Jensen* (Mike), *Thomas Bo Larsen* (Junkie). *Produced by Henrik Danstrup. 105 mins.*

1999
BLEEDER

Script: Nicolas Winding Refn. Photography: Morten Søborg. Production Design: Peter De Neergaard. Editing: Anne Østerud. Music: Peter Peter. Players: Kim Bodnia (Leo), *Mads Mikkelson* (Lenny), *Zlatko Buric* (Kitjo), *Liv Corfixen* (Lea), *Levino Jensen* (Louis), *Rikke Louise Anderson* (Louise), *Claus Flygare* (Joe). *Produced by Henrik Danstrup, Thomas Falck and Nicolas Winding Refn. 98 mins.*

2003
FEAR X

Script: Nicolas Winding Refn and Hubert Selby Jr. Photography: Larry Smith. Production Design: Peter De Neergaard. Editing: Anne Østerud, Music: Brian Eno, Deun Landon and J. Peter Schwain. Players: John Tuturro (Harry), *Deborah Kara Unger* (Kate), *Stephen McIntyre* (Phil), *William Allen Young* (Agent Lawrence), *Eugene M. Davis* (Ed), *Mark Houghton* (Diner Cop), *Jacqueline Ramel* (Claire), *James Remar* (Lt. Peter Northrup), *Nadia Litz* (Ellen). *Produced by Henrik Danstrup. 91 mins.*

2005
WITH BLOOD ON MY HANDS: PUSHER II

Script: Nicolas Winding Refn. Photography: Morten Søborg. Production Design: Ramus Thjellesen. Editing: Janus Billeskov Jansen and Anne Østerud. Music: Peter Peter. Players: Mads Mikkelson (Tonny), *Jesper Salomonsen* (Indsat #5), *Leif Sylvester* (Smeden), *Anne Sørensen* (Charlotte), *Kurt Nielsen* (Kusse-Kurt), *Øyvind Hagen-Traberg* (Ø), *Dan Dommer* (Den Gamle), *Karsten Schrøder* (Røde), *Maria Erwolter* (Gry), *Zlatko Buric* (Milo). *Produced by Henrik Danstrup and Nicolas Winding Refn. 100 mins.*

2005
I'M THE ANGEL OF DEATH: PUSHER III

Script: Nicolas Winding Refn. Photography: Morten Søborg. Production Design: Ramus Thjellesen. Editing: Miriam Nørgaard and Anne Østerud. Music: Peter Peter. Players: Zlatko Buric (Milo), *Marina Dekic* (Milena), *Slavko Labovic* (Radovan), *Ramadan Huseini* (Rexho), *Ilyas Agac* (Lille Mohammed), *Kujtim Loki* (Luan), *Vanja Bajicic* (Branko), *Levino Jensen* (Mike), *Marek Magierecki* (Mitja), *Svend Erik Eskelund Larsen* (Svend). *Produced by Henrik Danstrup. 90 mins.*

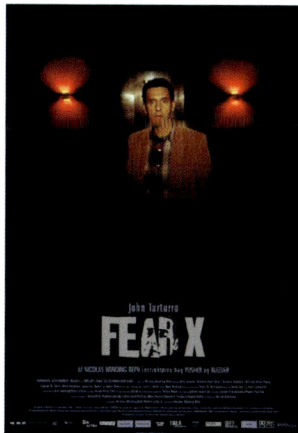

2008
BRONSON

Script: Brock Norman Brock and Nicolas Winding Refn. Photography: Larry Smith. Production Design: Adrian Smith. Editing: Mat Newman. Players: Tom Hardy (Charles Bronson/Michael Peterson), *Kelly Adams* (Irene), *Matt King* (Paul Daniels), *James Lance* (Phil), *Katy Barker* (Julie), *Amanda Burton* (Charlie's Mum), *Jonny Phillips* (Prison Govervor), *Luing Andrews* (Hysterical Screw). *Produced by Daniel Hansford and Rupert Preston. 92 mins.*

2009
VALHALL RISING

Script: Nicolas Winding Refn and Roy Jacobsen. Photography: Morten Søborg. Production Design: Kim Lovetand Juleæk. Editing: Anne Østerud. Music: Povl Kristian and Peter Peter. Players: Mads Mikkelson (One Eye), *Alexander Morton* (Barde), *Gary Lewis* (Kare), *Jamie Sives* (Gorm), *Stewart Porter* (Kenneth), *Maarten Stevenson* (Are), *Mathew Zajac* (Malkolm), *Gordon Brown* (Hagen), *Gary McCormack* (Hauk). *Produced by Johnny Andersen, Henrik Danstrup and Bo Ehrhardt. 93 mins.*

2011
DRIVE

Script: Hossein Amini (based on the novel by James Sallis). Photography: Morten Søborg. Production Design: Kim Lovetand Juleæk. Editing: Anne Østerud. Music: Povl Kristian and Peter Peter Players: Ryan Gosling (Driver), *Carey Mulligan* (Irene), *Bryan Cranston* (Shannon), *Albert Brooks* (Bernie Rose), *Ron Perlman* (Nino), *Oscar Isaac* (Standard), *Christina Hendricks* (Blanche). *Produced by Henrik Danstrup. 100 mins.*

DVD Focus

BFI

From a general strategy of releasing popular world cinema titles, BFI DVD has transformed into a platform for an exceptionally wide range of films that cover the length and breadth of British cinema. (Many of the titles now appear in a dual-format edition, with a Blu-ray disc and DVD.) In 2009, the label created another branch, BFI Flipside, featuring little-known or overlooked works from the 1960s and 1970s.

One of the great strengths of the label and which best reflects the BFI's commitment to documenting British life and culture is that the films are taken from the archive's incredible documentary library. What began as a chrono-logical overview of the 20th century has now segued into more specific collections, looking at the work of an industry or individual filmmaker.

Following on from 2010's fascinating *National Coal Board Collection: Portrait of a Miner* and the more polemic *Miner's Campaign Tapes*, comes **Tales From a Shipyard**. The second in the BFI's Working Life series, this two-disc collection brings together a wealth of material to present a portrait of life in Britain's shipyards. The 23 films span the period 1899–1974 and as such chart a history of the industry, from it's most productive period at the beginning of the 20th century, through to the early days of its demise. In doing so, the film's themes shift from tributes to the grandiosity of the structures built by British workers, through to a greater focus on the workers themselves. The collection includes the Oscar-winning *Seawards the Great Ships* (1960), directed by Hilary Harris and based on a treatment written by John Grierson. Also featured is Sean Connery's *The Bowler and the Bunnet* (1967), which details working practices at the Fairfields Shipyard on the Clyde. Connery recently re-edited the film, which is the version presented in this collection. In contrast to these more politicised films, the earlier silent films, featuring new scores composed and performed by Stephen Horne, are stunning documents of an era long gone. ***Special features:*** An excellent booklet, with details on each film and a fascinating essay by BFI curator Bryony Dixon and Dr Hugh Murphy; an extract from an interview with Sean Connery talking about labour relations in his film.

When it was given a limited release in late 2010, **A Day in the Life** was subject to rapturous praise from critics, celebrating the skill of documentary filmmaker John Krish. Its DVD release allows more audiences to watch the relatively small body of work by this remarkable director. The main feature is comprised of four shorts by Krish, made between 1953 and 1964, which defined him

The Elephant Will Never Forget

as one of Britain's most astute post-war filmmakers. The most famous of these films is *The Elephant Will Never Forget* (1953), a beautiful and elegiac send-off for London's tram system. Divided into two parts, the first highlights the role played by the trams as an artery, connecting people across the city while the second records the final day of their operation. The sense of loss felt through these final images, accompanied by a voiceover written by Krish, was at odds with the policy towards the tram system and led to the director being sacked by British Transport Films. Ironically, it is the film that came to define the organisation in later years. *They Took Us to the Sea* (1961) and *I Think They Call Him John* (1964) offer portraits from the two poles of the generational spectrum. The earlier film is an account of a group of children's journey to the seaside. Unlike earlier more regimented accounts of childhood, this is a starch-free, playful film which captures the joy of the children on their short vacation. *I Think They Call Him John*, by contrast, is a heartbreaking account of the indifference shown by society to the elderly. Detailing the daily life of a retired miner in a flat in St John's Wood, Krish conjures up a moving portrait of loneliness. Shot in wide-angle, which adds to the claustrophobic atmosphere, it is a powerful document whose minimalism only strengthens its sense of despair over society's neglect towards the old. Between these two films, Krish directed *Our School* (1962), an overview of life in a Secondary Modern School. If it is less emotive than the two films that bookend it, there is no denying the insight that this filmmaker offers into the lives of a young generation. ***Special features:*** A booklet featuring essays and details on each film; additional shorts *I Want to Go to School* (1959) and *Mr Marsh Comes to School* (1961); an interview with John Krish, recorded for this collection.

Few British documentary filmmakers are as acclaimed as Humphrey Jennings. He brought a lyricism and poetry to non-fiction film, at times elevating it to an art form. Some of

London Can Take It!

his films have previously appeared in other collections, but **The Complete Humphrey Jennings Vol. 1** is the first in a series of dedicated DVDs that bring together the filmmaker's entire body of work. This edition covers the period 1934–40, with 14 films looking at life in depression-era Britain and the outbreak of the Second World War. It includes his GPO work and the first of four films that detailed the heroism of people during the war. The most famous of these later films is *London Can Take It!* (1940), co-directed with Harry Watt and narrated by American journalist Quentin Reynolds. It details the battle to save the capital during the Blitz and highlights Jennings' lyrical style. Elsewhere, some of the early films are rudimentary, with Jennings yet to hone his particular style, but even these films display the patriotism that would be so prevalent in his most famous work. These records of rural life nevertheless offer a fascinating portrait of a bygone era.

Spare Time

Aside of the Wartime films, the standout entry in this collection is *Spare Time* (1939), a wonderful and insightful account of the leisure time experienced by workers as far afield as Pontypridd in Wales, Sheffield, Bolton and Manchester. Along with the other films in this collection, it whets the appetite for the next two volumes in this series. ***Special features:*** A booklet with essays and details on each film; the short *The Birth of the Robot* (1936), directed by Len Lye with Humphrey Jennings; alternative cuts of *The Farm*, *SS Ionian* and *London Can Take It!*

Great White Silence

A very different style of documentary, Herbert Ponting's **Great White Silence** (1924) records the fateful mission by Captain Scott and his team, to the South Pole in 1910–12. Ponting, a fellow of the Royal Geographical Society, had already a successful career as an ethnographic photographer when he was invited to be the official recorder of Robert Falcon Scott's mission. He chose to take a moving camera on the trip, although it was only on his return that the film became the primary record of the journey. The original plan was for Scott and Ponting to tour the world, showing the stunning photographs taken, supported by supplementary film clips, as a backdrop to Scott's lectures. However, following Scott and his team's failure to return, Ponting set about piecing together the hours of footage shot. The result is an astonishing record, not only of the team's life on the polar shelf, prior to their departure to the South Pole, but also of

the ingenuity of Ponting, who frequently put himself at risk to capture the most arresting footage. This beautifully restored version of the film features an atmospheric new score by Simon Fisher Turner. ***Special features:*** An illustrated booklet of essays; *90o South* (1933), Ponting's sound version of the film; newsreel footage and a Discovery Channel documentary about the restoration; a short film about Simon Fisher Turner's score.

A recently restored version of Jean Renoir's **French Cancan** brings back a resplendent palette to the French director's marvellous account of life in *fin de siècle* Paris. Jean Gabin is Danglard, a bar owner whose dwindling fortunes prompt him to open a venue that revives an unfashionable dance: the Cancan. The film then details the travails Danglard experiences, both in his professional and personal life, as he attempts to realise his dream. Loosely based on the life of Charles Zidler, who founded the Moulin Rouge, the film was Renoir's return to France after 13 years, and the first collaboration between the director and star since *La bête humaine* (1938). *French Cancan* is a joyous celebration of French culture in the late 19th century and littered with visual references to some of the country's most celebrated painters of the period. It is also a wonderful example of the director's lyrical style. Renoir's camera glides through the action, the director's keen eye picking up on the tiniest details, even down to a drunk on the street outside the club,

French Cancan

who ends the film with an appreciative bow. **Special features:** a beautifully illustrated booklet, with insightful essays on the film; a documentary on the making of the film and a short featurette on the restoration.

Deep End

No less in its inspiring use of colour is Jerzy Skolimowski's impressive **Deep End** (1970). John Moulder-Brown plays Mike, a young attendant at a local swimming pool. He is also known to offer 'special services' for some of the women who visit the pool. However, his principle focus is Susan (Jane Asher), his older co-worker, whom he fantasises over. His passion for her grows and, with Susan's occasional, playful encouragement, it becomes an obsession that threatens them both. Skolimowski's unique film was highly praised on its release, with Andrew Sarris comparing it to Godard, Truffaut and Polanski (with whom Skolimoski wrote the 1962 thriller *Knife in the Water*). Strange then that the film should have all but disappeared from British film history. This restored version goes some way in reviving the film's fortunes (its re-release in the cinemas was seen as a significant event). And because of its originality, it doesn't appear to have dated much. The baths could be from any time and Skolimowski maintains a tight grip on the exterior scenes, shying away from any trend, instead offering up a strange and alien London that reflects the mood of his story. Moulder-Brown and Asher are superb as the leads, whilst Diana Dors offers up one of the film's more surprising cameos, as a sex- and

football-obsessed patron who takes advantage of Mike's extra-curricular role. **Special features:** an illustrated booklet featuring an insightful essay by Yvonne Tasker; deleted scenes and the theatrical trailer; a short film, *Carless Love* (1976) directed by Francine Winham and starring Jane Asher; a new feature-length documentary about the film.

Masters of Cinema

Masters of Cinema began as a website in 2001 with its four co-founders spread around the world. In 2004 it joined forces with Eureka Entertainment Ltd, the leading UK distributor of silent and early films. Since then, the Masters of Cinema Series has gone from strength to strength. The label has been a fascinating case study in the promotion of Blu-ray over DVD. After initially introducing Blu-ray in 2008, the label decided in late 2009 to release certain titles only in that format. Sales were not strong and so dual-format editions were prepared. However, the label remains committed to Blu-ray, hoping that one day it will be able to release titles in that format only. They have even published the reasons for their support of the format, which can be downloaded from the label's website.

Following their earlier release of *Vengeance is Mine*, and continuing their championing of Japanese directors (which has seen the label release films by Mizoguchi, Teshigahara, Shinoda, Kinoshita, Naruse and Ichikawa), Masters of Cinema have turned their attention

The Ballad of Narayama

to further films by Shôhei Imamura. The best known of the three dual-edition releases is the director's exquisite 1983 Palme d'Or winner **The Ballad of Narayama**. Based on two stories by Shichirō Fukazawa, the film unfolds in a small rural village whose survival is predicated on population control and self-sufficiency. On reaching the age of 70, a villager must sacrifice themselves by travelling to Mount Narayama to die. Orin, a 69-year-old widow, accepts her fate and decides to spend her final year dealing with her family's problems and shortcomings, as well as those of her friends and neighbours. In its later stages, the film focuses more on the relationship between the woman and her son (Ken Ogata), leading up to the final, emotional journey up the mountain. **Special features:** an information-packed booklet, with essays, interviews, director's statements and production stills; theatrical trailers and behind-the-scenes footage; a 20-minute interview with Asian film specialist Tony Rayns.

Pigs and Battleships

Pigs and Battleships (1962) was Imamura's fifth feature and, in many ways, his breakthrough film. Still regarded as his most accessible work, it is a whistle-stop ride through the underbelly of the US Navy-occupied coastal town of Yokosuka, where a battle is raging between rival gangs over the local pork industry. A frenetically-paced crime drama is combined with a goofy romantic comedy about a low-level *yakuza* member and his pregnant girlfriend who wants him to go legit, the film helped define the Japanese New Wave (alongside Oshima's trilogy of 1960 films), particularly in its critique of Japanese authority. **Special features:** Imamura's debut feature *Stolen Desire* (1958); a booklet with essays and stills.

The Insect Woman

The women in Imamura's films are fascinating figures. The director stated that 'self-sacrificing women like the heroines of Naruse's *Floating Clouds* and Mizoguchi's *Life of Oharu* don't really exist'. As such, his heroines were earthier characters, as can be seen in **The Insect Woman** (1963). Tome is a peasant who moves to the city during the war, only to return home to help her family, where she gives birth to a girl, the result of her being raped by the son of her parent's landlord. After the war, she returns to the city and becomes a union organiser, before she is forced to take on various other roles that highlight the subservience of women. Opening with the shot of a beetle, Imamura details the minutiae of Tome's life, suggesting that she has no more power than the insect in Japanese society (the original Japanese title translates as *Entomological Chronicle of Japan*), whilst never making his heroine a victim. It is a powerful indictment of Japan's strictly regimented gender codes that avoids sentimentality, thanks to Sachiko Hidari's remarkable award-winning performance (Best Actress, Berlin Film Festival). **Special features:** Imamura's 1958 feature *Nishi-Ginza Station*; video conversation about *The Insect Woman* between Imamura and critic Tadao Satô; a booklet with an essay by Tony Rayns on both films featured in this edition.

A Man Vanishes (1967) is Imamura's play with form, as he documents the disappearance of a plastics salesman named Tadashi Oshima. From the outset, it is never quite clear what is real and what the director, along with his cast of professional and non-professional actors, have fabricated. Presaging the work of Abbas Kiarostami, particularly *Close-Up* (1990) and *Through the Olive Trees* (1994), the film, released on DVD only, is a startling and revealing analysis of the unreliability of the medium to document reality. It also explores the director's preoccupation with societal conformity and the possibility that Oshima's disappearance was linked to his failure to adhere to the standards that might have been expected of him. *Special features:* an informative booklet, with articles and interviews, featuring a review of the film by Nagisa Oshima; original theatrical trailer; a video interview with Tony Rayns; and interview conducted with the director by his son, filmmaker Daisuke Tengan.

Another Japanese feature released by Masters of Cinema last year, Masaki Kobayashi's **Harakiri** (1962) is a revisionist take on the

Harakiri

Jidai Geki genre, offering a brutal portrait of Japanese feudal society that, like the director's epic *The Human Condition* (1959–61) offers a withering attack on authoritarian power. When a *ronin* enters the court of a powerful lord to seek permission to commit ritual suicide on his property, he is suspected of seeking favour and an attempt to dissuade him is made by describing what happened the last time such permission was sought. Undeterred, the *ronin*'s commitment to his cause highlights the hypocrisy of the system. Like Mishima's *Patriotism* (1966), Kobayashi's film is a provocative account of honour and commitment, whose sparseness and simplicity belie a complex understanding of the machinations of Japan's complex political and feudal infrastructure. *Special features:* a booklet featuring an essay by Philip Kemp and a 1963 interview with Kobayashi; a 1993 Directors Guild of Japan interview with Masaki Kobayashi discussing the film with director Masahiro Shinoda; original theatrical trailer.

A number of titles were released exclusively on Blu-ray in limited editions. **Silent Running** (1971) is special effects whiz Douglas Trumbull's directorial debut and still one of the great environmentally oriented sci-fi films. Bruce Dern plays Freeman Lowell, a botanist aboard the *Valley Forge*, the spaceship carrying the last vestiges of Earth's flora, who is awaiting the call to return home and replenish the stark planet with the rich array of foliage. Instead, the crew receive orders to destroy the domes that house all the plants. Taking matters in to his own hands, Lowell sets forth on a journey, accompanied by three servile drones, into the deepest reaches of space, where the plants will live into eternity. With a soundtrack that features Joan Baez, the film's early 1970's Gaia-themed hippy elements still resonate, particularly in the emotionally engaging closing scenes. *Special features:* feature-length commentary by Trumbull and Dern; isolated music and effects track; a 'making of' documentary; two video pieces with Trumbull; a video interview with Dern; a booklet featuring artwork by Trumbull.

Silent Running

The label's release of **Touch of Evil** highlights how lustrous films can look in the Blu-ray format. Welles' 1959 classic, seen as closing the period of classic film noir, remains one of the director's best and most popular films. From it's acclaimed opening shot and subsequent investigation by Charlton Heston's detective into the machinations of a corrupt law enforcer (played by Welles) to the roll call of cameos and supporting performances, *Touch of Evil* is exemplary filmmaking. Moreover, if you already own the film, this edition is a must, not only because of the quality of the transfer (the disc features high-definition masters of five versions of the film), but also for the stunning extras.
Special features: four audio commentaries by producer Rick Schmidlin, Charlton Heston, critic F X Feeney, and Welles scholars James Naremore and Jonathan Rosenbaum; original

Touch of Evil

theatrical trailer and additional footage; two video pieces on the film and its restoration; a booklet featuring essays by Orson Welles, François Truffaut, André Bazin and Terry Comito, and a wealth of additional material.

Flicker Alley

Silent and pre-sound cinema is lovingly brought to life by Flicker Alley (the nickname of Cecil Court, in London, which was the centre of the British film industry during the silent film era). As Jeff Masino, who founded the company in 2002, stated, 'The company was born out of a passion for film history and a desire to bring filmmakers and films from out of the past to new audiences and renewed recognition. Known for projects that are the culmination of hundreds of hours of research, digital restoration, music composition and scoring, collectively, they reflect the expertise and shared passion of many talented collaborators.' It is impossible not to be seduced by the enthusiasm the label exudes for early cinema. Nowhere is this more apparent than in the sumptuous 5-disc collection of Georges Méliès' films. Now available in a more economically packaged edition, it highlights the dedication of Masino and his team in celebrating the brilliance of early cinema.

There were two outstanding releases from Flicker Alley in 2011. Danish-German director and noted cinematographer (for Carl Dreyer on a number of his early films) George Schnéevoigt's **Laila** (1929) is an epic love story that unfolds over decades, telling the story of a young girl (Mona Martenson) who is separated from her parents as a baby and raised by the Lap community out on the Arctic's frozen tundra. As she grows up, Laila is enmeshed in a tryst between her foster brother (Henry Gleditsch) and cousin (Harald Schwenzen). At the same time, she never feels entirely part of either world: the one she was born into and the other, in which she grew up. Aside of its narrative shortcomings, this adaptation of J. A. Frills' novel is a spectacular vision of an unforgiving landscape. Beautifully restored by

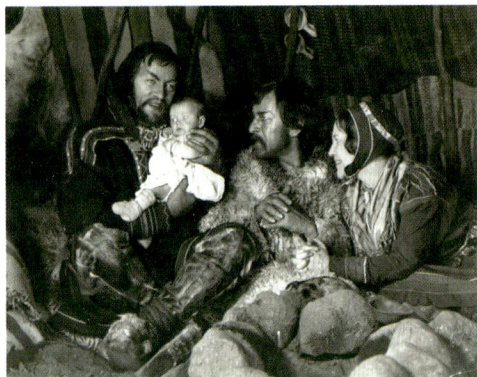

Laila

the Norwegian Film Institute, it features a new organ score by Robert Israel. **Special features:** the original diary manuscript of actor Tryggve Larssen written during the film's production; an illustrated essay by film historian Casper Tybjerg; rare photo galleries.

Landmarks of Early Soviet Film presents eight films – produced between 1924 and 1930 – in a four-disc edition. These films are presented with original Russian inter-titles and English subtitles (optional on four of the films), except for *Turksib* and *The Fall of the Romanov Dynasty*, which have full-screen English inter-titles. All the titles are new to DVD and as such, this is a remarkable collection. The titles are: Sergei M. Eisenstein's *Old and New* (1929); Dziga Vertov's *Stride, Soviet* (1926); Victor Turin's *Turksib* (1930); Esther Shub's *The Fall of the Romanov Dynasty* (1927); Boris Barnet's *The House on Trubnaya* (1928); Lev Kuleshov's *The Extraordinary Adventures of Mr. West in the Land of the Bolsheviks* (1924) and *By the Law* (1926), and Mikhail Kalatozov's *Salt for Svanetia* (1930). Of these, the final and rarely seen silent film by Eisenstein and Kuleshov's overtly propagandist piece are arguably the real treasures of this collection. *Mr. West* in particular is a treat. The first explicitly anti-American Soviet film, it employed techniques prevalent in American film of the time to highlight that culture's ignorance of life in the Soviet Union. However, the collection as a whole, featuring new scores by Robert Israel, Eric Beheim, Alexander Rannie and Zoran

Borisavljevic, is a must for anyone with more than a passing interest in cinema from this period. **Special features:** a booklet featuring essays by experts Maxim Pozdorovkin and Ana Olenina.

The Extraordinary Adventures of Mr. West in the Land of the Bolsheviks

Second Run
(Region 2)

An outstanding UK-based boutique label, Second Run has consistently surprised with its output. The label champions 'niche-market films' that 'anyone who seriously cares about cinema would want in their collection – but which, crucially, have never before been available anywhere in the world on DVD'. Extras are normally limited to interviews and a booklet essay, but the choice of films and the care and attention paid in ensuring the best quality transfer make the label essential for serious film lovers.

Father (1966) was the second feature by István Szabó. Set in the period between the end of the Second World War and the 1956

Father

uprising, it tells the story of a young boy who imagines his father – whom we see being buried in the film's opening scene – to be a hero of the war and grows up wanting to emulate him. However, when he reaches adulthood, his fantasies no longer sit so easily with him. Szabó's film, a beautifully directed work, seamlessly blends personal myth and social history, asking us to question our easy assimilation of history's grand narratives, begging us to avoid the myth and to seek the truth. **Special features:** a booklet featuring a typically insightful essay by Hungarian cinema expert John Cunningham.

Larks on a String

Another film from the same period, Jiří Menzel's wonderful **Larks on a String** (1969), like the director's earlier *Closely Observed Trains* (1966), was written by Bohumil Hrabal. Made during the Prague Spring, prior to the Soviet invasion, it was promptly banned by the newly installed regime and was not seen until its premiere at the Berlin Film Festival in 1990 (where it was awarded the Golden Bear). An absurdist comedy with strong political overtones and a wilful streak of biting satire, the film unfolds in a scrap metal yard where former members of the discredited bourgeoisie are meant to be working hard. Instead, they drink, play cards and pass comment on the state of society ('We'll

pour our peaceful steel down the imperialist warmongers' throats – hands off Korea!' comments one character, whilst in another scene, when crucifixes and typewriters are being dumped on a pile, someone comments, 'We'll also melt them down into a new kind of people.'). Best described by one critic as 'Orwelian burlesque', the film is prescient in its foretelling of how Communist rule would crumble and astute in its portrait of these rambunctious, wilful individuals. **Special features:** *Jiří Menzel: 7 Questions* – a recent reflection on the film shot by the director; a booklet featuring an essay by expert Peter Hames and an introduction by the film's cinematographer Jaromír Sofr.

Tumultuous political events also lie at the heart of Maria Saakyan's visually ravishing **The Lighthouse** (2006), one of Second Run's more frequent forays into contemporary film (other recent titles include Miguel Gomes' 2008 docu-drama *Our Beloved Month of August* and Pia Marais' uncompromising 2006 coming-of-age tale *The Unpolished*). *The Lighthouse* unfolds in the Caucusus region during the early 1990s, when Mayak (Anna Kapaleva) returns to her devastated village in order to convince her grandparents to move back with her to the safety of Moscow. However, the family's history is embedded in this area and although war has ripped apart the region, it has not been able to destroy its fabric. Set in the director's home town, the film's elliptical narrative avoids any conventional linearity in its approach to the

The Lighthouse

conflict that left much of Georgia, Azerbaijan and Armenia in ruins. Moreover, what concerns Saakyan is an engagement with place and identity more than any judgement on the war. As such, in terms of theme and its visual style, *The Lighthouse* stands in comparison with the work of Tarkovsky and Sokurov. **Special features:** Saakyan's short film *Farewell*; a booklet featuring an interview with Saakyan and two essays.

Artificial Eye
(Region 2)

Arguably the UK's most prominent first-run release label for mostly European releases, Artificial Eye has built-up an incredibly impressive back catalogue of titles from some of the world's greatest directors.

Solaris

The last year has seen the label bring out a number of collections. The most anticipated of these was **The Andrei Tarkovsky Collection**. The edition brings together the director's seven features, as well as the documentary *Meeting Andrei Tarkovsky* (2008), which was made to mark the 20th anniversary of the director's death. The film, directed by Dmitry Tarkovsky, features friends and colleagues who worked with Tarkovsky during his brief, but inspiring life. Unfortunately, none of the other extras that appeared on Artificial Eye's previous individual releases of the films are present. However, the quality of the films themselves

are much improved on the previous releases. Completists may wish to collect the exemplary versions of *Ivan's Childhood* (1962), *Andrei Rublev* (1966) and *Solaris* (1972) released by Criterion. But for anyone approaching Tarkovsky for the first time, or just wishing to own all the director's films, this is an exemplary and beautifully packaged collection.

The Abbas Kiarostami Collection offers an overview of the Iranian director's most recent work: the Palme d'Or winning *Taste of Cherry* (1997), *The Wind Will Carry Us* (1999), *Ten* (2002), *Certified Copy* (2010), and the documentaries *ABC Africa* (2001) and *One on Ten* (2004). The films each witness the director's style becoming increasingly sparse, before the change of direction with his most recent film – the first to feature a European cast. Together, the films are a document of the sophistication of this remarkable director's style, particularly *Ten*, a beguilingly simple film that offers an insight into contemporary Iran. One can now only hope that the director's earlier work, particularly his celebrated Koker Trilogy, will also become available.

Certified Copy

The most recent films of Paolo Sorrentino have been widely available, but **The Paolo Sorrentino Collection** not only brings *The Consequences of Love* (2004), *The Family Friend* (2006) and *Il Divo* (2008) together in one addition, it is finally possible to see the director's first feature *One Man Up* (2001). As with his subsequent films, Sorrentino's debut

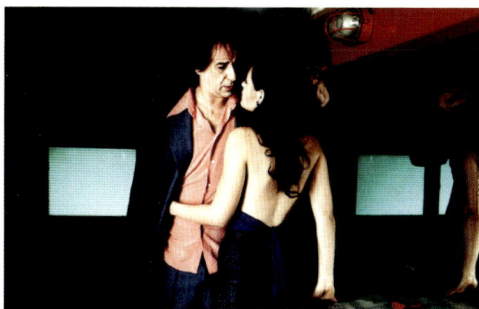

One Man Up

features Tony Servillo, this time playing one of two characters named Antonio Pisapia. He is a nighclub singer whose career is gradually dwindling. Andrea Renzi is the other Antonio, a footballer who suffers a serious injury and is relegated to watching his career go down the drain. Although the film veers uneasily between gritty drama and fantasy sequences, it is fascinating to see how Sorrentino's style developed between this and his remarkably assured sophomore feature, whose strange Mafia tale was one of the unexpected pleasures of the last decade.

Nicolas Philibert is one of French cinema's most acclaimed documentary filmmakers and **The Nicolas Philibert Collection** offers a tantalising variety of the director's films. The most famous film in this edition, and the film that made Philibert's name internationally, is *Être et Avoir* (2002), which details the director's time spent in the company of Georges Lopez, the sole teacher in a one-class primary school in rural France. Philibert's unobtrusive style captures a series of wonderful moments, whilst stressing the importance of Lopez in these children's lives. A very different subject, but no less revealing, is the director's most recent film *Nénette*. With his camera trained on the 40-year-old orang-utan in Paris's Jardin des Plantes, where she has resided since 1972, Philibert records the comments of visitors and staff members who each read different emotions and thoughts on Nénette's wonderfully expressive face. This zoological theme was first encountered in Philibert's work in 1994's *Animals*, which

details the renovation of the Zoology Gallery in the French capital's National Natural History Museum. A similar approach to the workings of a national institution can also be seen in *La Ville Louvre* (1990), which journeys through the back rooms and ante chambers of the vast art museum. Finally, and arguably most rewarding, is *Back to Normandy* (2007), which finds the director re-visiting the area where, in 1976, he assisted director René Allio on the making of *I, Pierre Riviere* (also available on Artificial Eye DVD), the re-enactment of a series of crimes that took place in the 19th century. Philibert not only encounters locals who appeared amongst the cast of the film, he documents the changes, social, economic and cultural, that have affected the communities since the film was made.

Nénette

Finally, Artificial Eye are releasing, over three editions, the films of Greece's most famous director. **The Theo Angelopoulos Collection Vols 1–3** includes all the director's features, from his powerful debut *The Reconstruction* (1970), through to his most recent feature *The Dust of Time* (2008). Featuring long, beautifully composed tracking shots, his films are a study in time, memory and the shifting landscapes upon which people live out their lives. They witness social upheaval, wars and the displacement of entire nations. However, within each work, no matter its scale, can be found intimate and moving dramas. Included are his most acclaimed works *The Travelling Players* (1975), *Ulysses' Gaze* (1995) and the Palme d'Or-winning *Eternity and a Day* (1998).

Eternity and a Day

As the *Village Voice*'s Michael Atkinson said of the film and Theo Angelopoulos's entire oevre, 'Time grows gargantuan, landscapes change, masses of people engage in epochal social phenomena. It's not a strategy dilettantes should entertain; Angelopoulos, one of Europe's most rigorous film artists, stands as the master of monumentalism.'

Axiom
(Region 2)

An excellent distributor, specialising in independent fare from around the world, Axiom has gradually built up an impressive library that spans the best films of Wim Wenders, including a superb box set of his documentaries, and works by John Sayles, Pablo Trapero, Peter Greenaway, Bernard Rose, Ramin Bahrani and Daniel Burman.

The standout release by Axiom was Lance Hammer's *Ballast* (2008). A true independent, the film is uncompromising in its vision of

Ballast

the American underbelly. It makes no grand statement about poverty or social exclusion – although the film has grown in significance and timeliness since its original domestic release, which was within weeks of Lehman's collapse and the start of the global economic crisis, in September 2008 – other than to portray the lives of one fractured family on the periphery of contemporary society, both geographically and financially. In style, it bears the hallmarks of Robert Bresson and the Dardenne brothers. However, it also continues the tradition of American films that have sought out life away from the hubbub of the cities and towns that have come to represent America on the screen. It is a remarkable achievement that deservedly saw the light of day outside the US.

Park Circus

Formerly known for simplifying rights owners' ability to offer their back catalogue for exhibition, Park Circus now also offer an eclectic collection of releases, ranging from classic features and silent films to a number of acclaimed documentaries. Moreover, the last year has seen them increase the number of restored classics released in UK cinemas, with a subsequent release on DVD and/or Blu-ray.

The label released two British features from the 1940s. Based on the immensely popular novel by Leonard Strong, David MacDonald's **The Brothers** is a full-blooded story of sexual intrigue, set on a remote Scottish island. Gainsborough favourite Patricia Roc plays Mary, who arrives on Skye only to find herself desired by both the Macrae siblings, John and Fergus, the sons of Hector, her guardian during her stay. When he dies, John insists that Mary marry him, but she actually loves Hector; so the stage is set for a battle between the brothers. The landscape is the star of the film, which MacDonald and cinematographer Stephen Dade capture brilliantly. However, Roc is somewhat miscast as Mary, making for an uneven drama. More impressive is Frederick Wilson's **Floodtide**, which features a young Gordon Jackson as the son of a Scottish

Floodtide

farmer desperate to leave the countryside and seek his fortune in the city. He gets his wish, finding work in the shipyards near Glasgow. However, his ambition soon gets the better of him and he risks alienation from his colleagues and his chance of a relationship with his boss's daughter. Corny at times, *Floodtide* is carried along by the conviction of all concerned, both in front of and behind the camera (the film is an interesting companion to the BFI collection on shipbuilding). If neither film is a major work in British film history, they at least offer two examples of films that were being made north of the English border at a time when Gainsborough and Ealing were stealing the country's cinematic thunder. ***Special features:*** both discs include an image gallery.

The Best Intentions

Bille August's Palme d'Or-winning **The Best Intentions** (1992) could be described, in Hollywood parlance, as the prequel to Ingmar Bergman's *Fanny and Alexander* (1982). Written by the great Swedish filmmaker, it is based on his parent's lives. He entrusted the script to August after seeing *Pelle the Conquerer* (1987)

(which also won the top prize at Cannes) and the younger director follows through with a magnificent rendering of the troubled relationship between a young married couple with wildly diverging views of life. Pernilla August (the director's wife, who was also awarded at Cannes) is exceptional as the bride who bears her husband's (Samuel Froler) misplaced pride and religious conviction, until she reaches breaking point. Set between 1909 and 1919 and unfolding over the course of three hours, *The Best Intentions* is more than a worthy companion piece to Bergman's own semi-fictional memoir. ***Special features:*** theatrical trailer.

Boudu Saved From Drowning

One of Jean Renoir's best loved films, **Boudu Saved From Drowning** (1932) made a welcome return to European screens last year, following the unveiling of the digitally restored print at the Cannes Film Festival. This lustrous, gorgeously photographed restoration is what appears on the Park Circus Blu-ray edition. More than the look of the film, however, is how Renoir's blistering social satire has lost none of its power. Michel Simon and Charles Granval excel as the tramp and his benefactor, but to single them out would be a disservice to everyone else involved in this marvellous film. It is flawless in its tale of hypocrisy and double standards, with Renoir taking René Fauchois' stage play and transforming it into pure cinema. ***Special features:*** 2010 theatrical trailer.

The Black Pirate

Before Albert Parker emigrated from the US to become an agent for stars such as James Mason, he directed a marvellous swashbuckler featuring a physically dexterous performance by Douglas Fairbanks. **The Black Pirate** (1926) is a classic tale of vengeance on the high seas. The Duke of Arnoldo (Fairbanks) vows to avenge his father's death after his ship is attacked by pirates. Taking on the guise of the Black Pirate, he infiltrates his enemy's ship, kills their captain and vows to rule the seas with them. On capturing the next ship they encounter, they find on board a women who claims to be a princess (Billie Dove). The Black Pirate convinces the men to hold her hostage, knowing that this may be the chance he has waited for to bring the crew to justice. Written by Fairbanks and shot using the primitive two-tone technicolor method that was first introduced in 1922, this is a rip-roaring ride that puts to shame any recent attempts at the genre. The energy mostly derives from its star's athletic performance, which never waivers. After his roles as Zorro and Robin Hood, this is perfect material for Fairbanks, who bounds through every scene. **Special features:** a fascinating commentary by film historian Rudy Behlmer.

Finally, following on from their creditable release of numerous Chaplin features, as well as The Chaplin Revue, Park Circus have gathered everything together into one handsome collection. The **Charlie Chaplin Collection** features all the filmmaker's major works: The Kid (1921), A Woman of Paris (1923), The Circus (1928), City Lights (1931), Modern Times (1936), The Great Dictator (1940), The Gold Rush (1942), Monsieur Verdoux (1947), Limelight (1952), A King in New York (1957), as well as The Chaplin Review (1959) and an additional disc featuring the shorts The Pilgrim (1923), Sunnyside (1919), A Day's Pleasure (1919), The Idle Class (1921) and Pay Day (1922). Now that the older MK2 collection is no longer available, this is by far the best collection around. It is a pity that Richard Schickel's exemplary documentary about Chaplin is not a part of any collection, or that the filmmaker's penultimate films, A King in New York (1957) is not included. As flawed as the film is, it remains a fascinating curio. However, completists are always likely to gripe at the lack of extra material, but there is more than enough here for the average Chaplin fan, with introductions to each of the films by David Robinson, outtakes, documentary featurettes and deleted scenes. Neatly packaged, this is an impressive collection and one of the highlight's of Park Circus' increasingly impressive output.

Modern Times

World Survey

6 continents | 83 countries | 100s of films...

Abu Dhabi Film Commission

Perfectly situation between East and West, with direct flights to Asia, Europe, the US and Australia, the United Arab Emirates' capital Abu Dhabi is easily accessible by filmmakers from around the globe, and also boasts some of the most spectacular filming locations in the world.

Liwa Desert 23° 3'19.04"N • 53°44'48.06"E

Abu Dhabi's Western region includes 60,000 square kilometres of desert featuring some of the tallest dunes outside the Sahara, as well as nature reserves, historic sites, a dazzling coastline and oasis. The city of Abu Dhabi offers ultra-modern buildings, like the Capital Gate, a skyscraper that is a steel-and-glass engineering marvel leaning 18-degrees to the West; Masdar City, the first zero-carbon, zero-waste city on the planet; and Ferrari World, the world's largest indoor theme park.

Capital Gate, Abu Dhabi National Exhibition Center 24°25'04.46"N • 54°26'11.74"E

Yas Marina Circuit 24°28'3.57"N • 54°36'21.55"E

Abu Dhabi has hosted international productions of every size, including Hollywood studio films such as *Syriana* and *The Kingdom*; multiple Discovery Channel and Al Jazeera Documentary series and the BBC series *Wild Arabia*; and a number of Bollywood blockbusters. Also, a great number of regional and international TV commercials and photo shoots for major brands such as General Motors, Range Rover, IPL Cricket League, Audi, Citroen Motors, Ferrari, FIA GT1 World Championship and HSBC.

Sheikh Zayed Grand Mosque 24°24'45.49"N • 54°28'29.34"E

All of these projects are facilitated by Abu Dhabi Film Commission, which is part of the Media Zone Authority – Abu Dhabi. The Film Commission was launched in 2009 and has a mandate to support the development of Abu Dhabi's growing film and television industry, and to promote the Emirate as a production

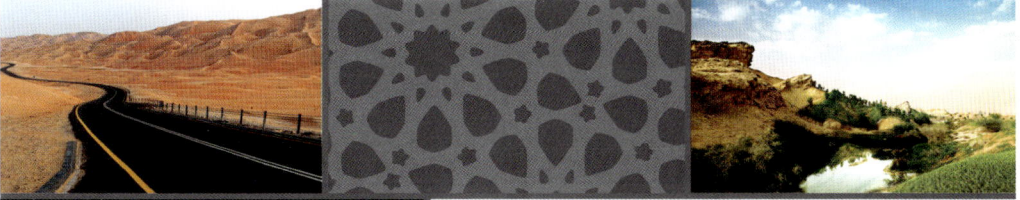

لجنة أبوظبي للأفلام
ABU DHABI FILM
COMMISSION

Support for location filming
Permits for filming in public locations
Initial scouting for potential locations

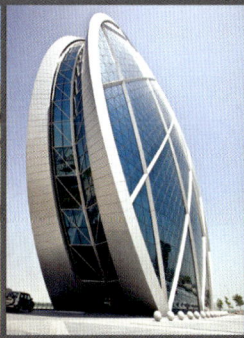

Scene enough...?
film.gov.ae

info@film.gov.ae | Tel. +971 (2) 401 2701

Zayed Sport City Stadium 24°24'57.26"N • 54°27'16.14"E

and filming location. In just three years, the Film Commission has backed over fifty UAE filmmakers, assisted with the production of over 600 shoots in the capital.

Abu Dhabi Film Commission also provided logistical support for the major broadcasters and media teams that visit the capital to cover major events such as the Formula 1 and the FIFA Club World Cup.

Filming at Aldar HQ Building 24°26'28.51"N • 54°34'32.07"E

The Film Commission offers support in finding unique locations, securing permits, equipment, experienced crews, studios and high-end postproduction facilities. The Film Commission also provides advice on script clearances and content approvals, script breakdowns, initial scouting for potential locations, and discounts and special deals. Its website (www.film.gov.ae) offers a comprehensive guide to filming in Abu Dhabi, including information on production companies, crew and equipment suppliers based in the UAE, and a complete database

of filming locations, as well as the latest news from the Abu Dhabi film industry.

twofour54 is the Middle East and North Africa (MENA) region's leading media and entertainment hub. twofour54 delivers advanced cohesive infrastructure supporting the creative community: twofour54 intaj (a state-of-the-art production complex) offers studios, digital and post production facilities, crews, broadcast and distribution facilities and the region's only 3D stereoscopic lab.

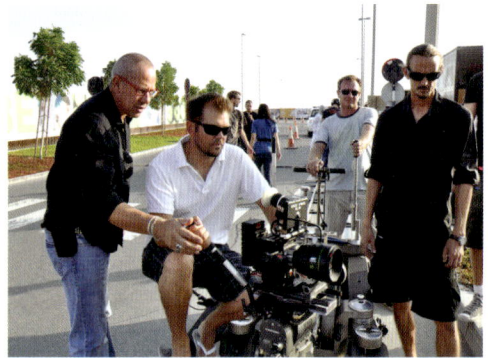

Film production in Abu Dhabi

twofour54 has attracted over 140 companies to date to its Abu Dhabi campus. These include several of the region's and the world's largest and most influential content creation companies, including Ubisoft, Sky News Arabia, Fox Intl Channels, CNN, BBC, Financial Times, Viacom, C Sky Pictures, Thomson Reuters, Cartoon Network, Blink Studios, Charisma and VERITAS Films.

twofour54 intaj production complex

ABU DHABI FILM
COMMISSION

Algeria Maryam Touzani

Times are undeniably difficult for Algerian cinema. An extremely low number of screens mean making a film profitable is, in essence, almost impossible. Distribution also suffers through the tough and lengthy bureaucratic procedures behind obtaining visas, plunging the sector even deeper into crisis. In the midst of this harsh reality, filmmakers still struggle to make their films, which manages to keep the industry alive and offering hope of better days. This past year, as has been the rule in recent times, has shown that the most distinguished productions are by Algerian directors living in the West, predominantly in France.

Renowned Franco-Algerian auteur Merzak Allouache scooped the Best Arab Narrative Film Award at the Doha Tribeca Film Festival with his latest feature, **Normal**, which follows a disillusioned Algerian youth in the wake of the 'Arab Spring' revolutions. Fouzi brings together a group of actors as the uprisings begin, showing them footage of a documentary he started shooting two years back, hoping to find an alternative ending by drawing on their reactions to current events. Allouache has directed a number of acclaimed films over the course of his thirty-year career; his first feature, *Omar Gatlato*, screened in Cannes' Directors' Fortnight sidebar in 1976. That film was not only credited with changing the course of Algerian cinema, but also recognised as a key film for the cinemas of the Maghreb.

Franco-Algerian actor-director Rabah Ameur-Zaimeche has landed back in the spotlight after winning the 2011 Jean Vigo award with his fourth feature, **Smuggler's Songs** (*Les Chants de Mandarin*). Scripted by the director himself, the film traces the misadventures of a group

Rabah Ameur-Zaimeche's **Smuggler's Songs**

of smugglers who, after the execution of their leader Louis Mandarin, a famous mid-18th century outlaw, set up black markets outside rural villages and write songs in his honour. The film is another solid work, following on from his previous features, *Wesh Wesh, What's Going On?* from 2002 and his two Cannes entries, *Back Home* and *Adhen*.

Another Franco-Algerian, Fatma Zohra Zamoum, returned with the much anticipated follow-up to her feature-length documentary debut *(Un)Lucky*, with a tale about childhood and love set in modern-day Algiers. **How Big Is Your Love** (*Kedach Ethabni*) recounts the story of Adel, whose parents send him to stay with his grandparents in Algiers for a weekend. As his stay is extended, he begins to feel that he has been there forever, with his grandparents attempting to reach out to him by involving him in their everyday lives.

After *The Yellow House*, Franco-Algerian director Amor Hakkar makes a welcome return with his latest feature, **A Few Days of Respite** (*Quelques Jours de Répit*). His latest drama is the story of a homosexual couple that has fled Iran, where their love has them condemned, in search of a safe haven in a small French village. Moshen, a former professor of French in the University of Teheran (played by Hakkar himself) and his younger companion Hassan, a photographer, meet Yolande, a lonely older woman who offers them help. The film has been selected for various international festivals, including Sundance.

Amor Hakkar's **A Few Days of Respite**

Regardless of the severe industry climate, new talents are emerging. No further proof is needed that the growing pool of short films. Farid Bentoumi's impressive **Burners** (*Brûleurs*), which was selected for many international festivals, tells the story of Amine, a young Algerian armed with an amateur camera who films his last moments in his home city before tracing his journey across the Mediterranean in search of a better life. In **Tomorrow, Algiers?** (*Demain, Alger?*), directed by Amin Sidi-Boumediène, three youngsters discuss their best friend's impending departure, as he silently packs his suitcase in the apartment above. Zakaria Saidani's **A Man, in Front of the Mirror** (*Un Homme, Face Miroir*) is the story of Zico, a university student surrounded by friends with whom he shares his time without being truly happy.

Farid Bentoumi's **Burners**

Amin Sidi-Boumediène's **Tomorrow, Algiers?**

The ministry of culture's newly-vested interest in the film industry offers some promise for the future. Resources have been mobilised by public institutions, notably to restore cinemas and improve domestic production. The creation of more multiplexes is also being planned. Émigré filmmakers are also playing a key role in maintaining the country's cinema and attracting international interest. But although recognition abroad is important, Algerian film needs a life within its own borders. As filmmakers and local officials try to come to a mutual understanding, the state's latest measures, if duly implemented in the coming year, should contribute positively to the future of Algerian film.

The year's best film

Normal (Merzak Allouache)
Smuggler's Songs (Rabah Ameur-Zaimeche)
A Few Days of Respite (Amor Hakkar)
How Big Is Your Love (Fatma Zohra Zamoum)

Directory

All Tel/Fax numbers begin (+213)
Cinémathèque Algérienne, 49 rue Larbi Ben M'Hidi, Algiers. Tel: (2) 737 548. Fax: (2) 738 246. www.cinematheque.art.dz

MARYAM TOUZANI is a freelance journalist based in Morocco and working internationally, specialising in the coverage of world cinema.

Argentina Alfredo Friedlander

2011 again established a record in cinema attendance (almost 45 million admissions) exceeding 2010 figures by 10 per cent. The number of films released domestically remained stable at 300 features, as did the number of local releases (100 films).

The 13th Buenos Aires International Film Festival (BAFICI) once again screened around 400 films in two competing sections. The international competition was won by Sylvain George's French production **Qu'ils reposent en révolte** while the national one was awarded to Nicolas Grosso's **Animal's Run** (*La carrera del animal*).

Gustavo Taretto's **Medianeras**

Milagros Mumenthaler's **Back to Stay**

The 26th International Film Festival of Mar del Plata, under the direction of veteran filmmaker José Martínez Suárez, had three different competing sections. Argentine director Milagros Mumenthaler personally received the international prize for her debut **Back to Stay** (*Abrir puertas y ventanas*). The prize for best film in the Latin American contest was awarded to Rosario García-Moreno's Peruvian feature **The Bad Intentions** (*Las malas intenciones*). Finally, the national competition was won by Nicanor Loreti's **Devil** (*Diablo*).

Argentine films were a strong presence at both Berlin and Cannes. The former saw the world premiere of **Medianeras**, Gustavo Taretto's feature debut. It is the story of Mariana and Martín, who live in opposite buildings in the same block and who constantly fail to meet. They then cross paths, but are unaware of each other's existence until an event changes the course of their lives. Cannes saw the unveiling of Pablo Giorgelli's **Las Acacias**, which picked up the Camera d'Or. It is a simple and sensitive story of a lonely truck driver who has driven for years between Asunción (Paraguay) and Buenos Aires. When he picks up a woman and her baby their three lives are destined to change.

Pablo Giorgelli's **Las Acacias**

Santiago Mitre's **The Student**

Arguably the best Argentine film of 2011, Santiago Mitre's **The Student** (*El estudiante*), tells the story of Roque (Esteban Lamothe), a young man who comes to Buenos Aires to attend college and soon realises that life there is not only about studying. He meets Paula (Romina Paula), an assistant professor at the faculty, who introduces him to political activism. Through political activism he finds true meaning to his life.

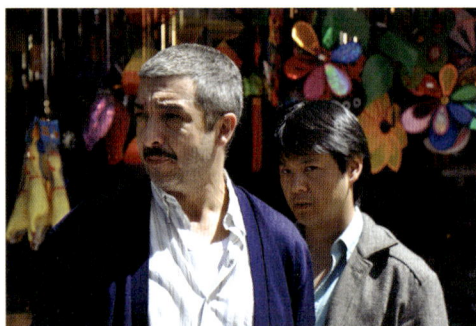

Sebastián Borensztein's **Chinese Take-Away**

The first ten films to top the year's box-office came form the United States, with each grossing around US$2 million. The best-placed Argentine movie (coming in eleventh) was Sebastián Borensztein's **Chinese Take-Away** (*Un cuento chino*). The film also picked up the top prize at Rome International Film Festival. Ricardo Darin plays Roberto, a loner whose friendship with a Chinese man opens up his world. The second most popular Argentine film was Marcos Carnevale's **Widows** (*Viudas*), with Graciela Borges and Valeria Bertucelli playing two women mourning for their husband and lover.

My First Wedding (*Mi primera boda*), a fairly successful local comedy directed by Ariel Winograd, starred Natalia Oreiro and Daniel Hendler as Leonora and Daniel, a Catholic and Jew, celebrating their wedding day. In a nervous state, Daniel loses the rings, which he then tries to hide from his fiancée. In the style of a classic farce, things soon blow out of all proportion. **Mount Bayo** (*Monte Bayo*), directed by Victoria Gilardi, is the story of Juana Keller, an 81-year-old matriarch who tries to commit suicide. As she lies in a coma, the lives of her daughters, son-in-law and grandchildren are acutely affected, drawing out the best and worst in each.

Fernando Spiner's **Aballay, the Man Without Fear** (*Aballay, el hombre sin miedo*) is the story of an unfriendly gaucho, resentful thief and murderer. While he violently murders a man, he sees the terrified look on the face of his victim's son. It is an image he can't erase, knowing that his act will result in vengeance. The film was selected by the Academy of Art and Cinematographic Sciences of Argentina to compete for Best Foreign Film at the 2012 Academy Awards.

Carlos Sorin's most recent film, **The Cat Vanishes** (*El gato desaparece*) opens with Beatriz (Beatriz Spelzini) taking her husband Luis (Luis Luque) out of the hospital he had been residing in for months, due to a nervous breakdown. Her feelings are unclear. Although she is happy to have him home, she worries that he may not be the man she once knew. It is a modest thriller in the style of – and an homage to – Alfred Hitchcock.

Carlos Sorin's **The Cat Vanishes**

Eva Perón was the subject of two films, albeit stylistically very different. María Seoane's **Eva From Argentina** (*Eva de la Argentina*) smartly combines animation and documentary, while Paula de Luque's **Juan and Eva** (*Juan y Eva*) opens with Eva meeting Juan Perón following the earthquake in San Juan city in January 1944. It is the story of a love affair, with Julieta Díaz and Osmar Nuñez convincing in the main roles.

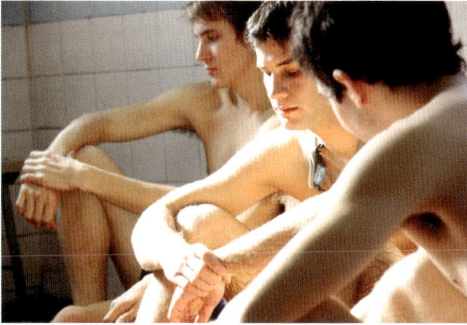

Marco Berger's **Absent**

Finally, several other interesting movies should be mentioned. Marco Berger's **Absent** (*Ausente*), Pablo Solarz's **Together Forever** (*Juntos para siempre*), Ana Katz's **The Marziano's Family** (*Los Marziano*), Leandro Ipiña's **Revolution** (*Revolución, el cruce de los Andes*) and Juan Minujin's **Cowboy** (*Vaquero*) all added colour to the country's cinematic output in 2011.

The year's best films
The Student (Santiago Mitre)
Las Acacias (Pablo Giorgelli)
Chinese Take-Away (Sebastián Borensztein)
Aballay, the Man Without Fear (Fernando Spiner)
The Cat Vanishes (Catlos Sorin)

ALFREDO FRIEDLANDER is a member of the Asociación de Cronistas Cinematográficos de Argentina. He writes regularly for leedor. com and presents films at the 56-year-old Cine Club Núcleo.

Directory
All Tel/Fax numbers begin (+54)
Critics Association of Argentina, Maipu 621 Planta Baja, 1006 Buenos Aires. Tel/Fax: 4322 6625. cinecronistas@yahoo.com.
Directors Association of Argentina (DAC), Lavalle 1444, 7° Y, 1048 Buenos Aires. Tel/Fax: 4372 9822. dac1@infovia.com.ar. www.dacdirectoresdecine. com.ar.
Directors of Photography Association, San Lorenzo 3845, Olivos, 1636 Buenos Aires. Tel/Fax: 4790 2633. adf@ba.net. www.adfcine.com.ar.
Exhibitors Federation of Argentina, Ayacucho 457, 1° 13, Buenos Aires. Tel/Fax: 4953 1234. empcinemato@infovia.com.ar.
Film University, Pasaje Guifra 330, 1064 Buenos Aires. Tel: 4300 1413. Fax: 4300 1581. fuc@ucine.edu.ar. www.ucine.edu.ar.
General Producers Association, Lavalle 1860, 1051 Buenos Aires. Tel/Fax: 4371 3430. argentinasonofilm@impsat1.com.ar.
National Cinema Organisation (INCAA), Lima 319, 1073 Buenos Aires. Tel: 6779 0900. Fax: 4383 0029. info@incaa.gov.ar.
Pablo Hicken Museum and Library, Defensa 1220, 1143 Buenos Aires. Tel: 4300 5967. www.museudelcinedb@yahoo.com.ar.
Producers Guild of Argentina (FAPCA), Godoy Cruz 1540, 1414 Buenos Aires. Tel: 4777 7200. Fax: 4778 0046. recepcion@patagonik.com.ar.
Sindicato de la Industria Cinematográfia de Argentina (SICA), Juncal 2029, 1116 Buenos Aires. Tel: 4806 0208. Fax: 4806 7544. sica@sicacine.com.ar. www.sicacine.com.ar.

Fernando Spiner's **Aballay, the Man Without Fear**

Armenia Susanna Harutyunyan

In 2012, Armenian Cinema will celebrate its 100th anniversary. Although there are a number of examples of earlier films shot by Armenians, the first Armenian 'film', a documentary by Vahan Zardaryan was presented to the public in 1912. Newspapers at the time listed the film's title as *Armenian Cinema*.

Nowadays, Armenian cinema produces two or three feature films, around eight shorts and fifteen documentaries annually. State funding of film production is channeled through the Armenian National Cinema Centre and 'Hayk' Documentary Film Studio.

In 2012, the state budget for the Armenian film industry remained as it had for the previous two years, at approximately US$1.2 million, with US$775,000 for narrative features and shorts, US$295,000 for animation and US$129,000 for documentary. This is clearly not enough to support the industry and so producers look to private funding and co-productions to supplement a film's budget.

Early in the year local audiences were treated to **Dawn Over Lake Van** (*Vanatzovun Arshaluyse*), directed by Artak Igityan and Vahan Stepanyan. It tells the story of an Armenian family that emigrates to the US.

Artak Igityan and Vahan Stepanyan's **Dawn Over Lake Van**

They assimilate in every way, but the memory of the Armenian genocide is too great to eclipse the culture they come from.

Natalia Belyauskene's **If Only Everyone**

Natalia Belyauskene's **If Only Everyone** (*Ete Bolore*) was written and produced by popular Armenian actor Mikayel Poghosyan. It looks at the post-war situation in Armenia, attempting to understand the nature of conflict and whether the hopes and dreams that they fight for are really worth the great cost expended in battle.

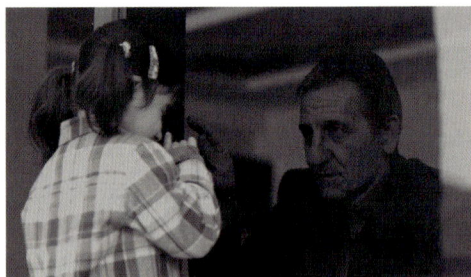

Edgar Baghdasaryan's **Forgiveness**

There are currently a number of local features in post-production. Edgar Baghdasaryan's **Forgiveness** (*Nerum*) features a protagonist who visits the town of his birth. Through the people he meets there, questions are raised over whether the man is able to erase the events of the past and if forgiveness after so many years is possible. In particular, whether he can repair the relationship with his son.

Narine Mkrtchyan and Arsen Azatyan's **The Glass Trinket** (*Apake Kaghazard*) tells the story of two young people in love, but for whom life takes an unsettling course. The boy is carrying out his military service, but discovers that his girlfriend is pregnant. Going AWOL to convince her to have an abortion, his mind is changed when he witnesses an incident on a train. However, such decisions may be outside of his control and his own actions have prompted the authorities to pursue him.

Narine Mkrtchyan and Arsen Azatyan's **The Glass Trinket**

Maria Sahakyan's **Alaverdi** (*Alaverdi*) is a psychological drama about a neglected teenager who struggles with her blossoming sexuality and suicidal tendencies, while searching for the father she has never met. The Armenian cinema year came to a close with the world premiere of Mikayel Vatinyan's feature debut **Joan and the Voices** (*Zhannan ev Dzajner*), which took place in October at Busan International Film Festival.

The impressive **Loading My Life** is the short debut and graduation film by Harutyun Shatyan, which was awarded the Golden Apricot Prize in the Armenian Panorama Competition at last year's Armenian Film Festival in Yerevan. It is about a student, a young family man, who is also ill, yet attempts to look at the bright side of life and find some happiness. A few days before completing his military service, the protagonist is diagnosed with diabetes and is discharged. With this

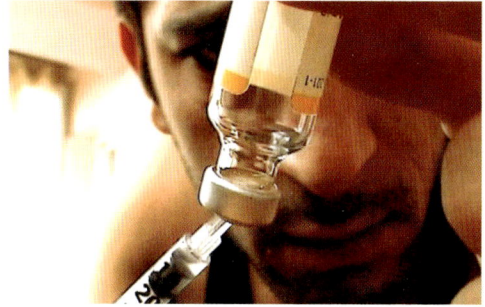

Harutyun Shatyan's **Loading My Life**

verdict his problems begin. The pressures of family life, added to which is the cost for his medical care, forces the man into a life of petty crime. The film looks at how our brightest and best can find themselves in a terrible situation due to unforeseen circumstances.

The year's best films
Joan and the Voices (Mikayel Vatinyan)
Loading My Life (Harutyun Shatyan)
If Only Everyone (Natalia Belyauskene)
Dawn Over Lake Van
(Artak Igityan and Vahan Stepanyan)

Directory
All Tel/Fax numbers begin (+374)
Armenian Association of Film Critics & Cinema Journalists, #3, Moskovyan Str., 0001 Yerevan. Tel/Fax: 10 52 10 47. aafccj@arminco.com. www. arm-cinema.am.
Armenian National Cinema Centre, 38, Pushkin Str., Yerevan. Tel/Fax: 10 51 82 30 (31). abovyans@ yahoo.com.
Golden Apricot Fund for Cinema Development, 3 Moskovyan Str., 0001, Yerevan. Tel/Fax: 10 52 10 42 (62). info@gaiff.am www.gaiff.am.

SUSANNA HARUTYUNYAN has been a film critic for the daily *Respublika Armenia* since 1991 and is the president of Armenia's Association of Film Critics and Cinema Journalists (the Armenian National Section of FIPRESCI) and the Artistic Director of Golden Apricot Yerevan International Film Festival.

Australia Peter Thompson

A popular hit, a piece of prestige filmmaking, a solid fact-based drama and a trio of cutting-edge indigenous (Aboriginal) films – these were highlights of Australian cinema in 2011. But the malaise of recent years continues and new technologies are reshaping the future in unpredictable ways.

Good-natured and crowd-pleasing, Kriv Stenders' **Red Dog** grossed more than AUS$21 million domestically – a rare feat for an Australian film. Set in the 1970s, in the almost exclusively male domain of a remote mining operation in Western Australia's Pilbara region, it's a throwback to a simpler, more easily-grasped world of stoicism in the face of a harsh environment and egalitarian conformism – known in Australia as 'mateship'. With a screenplay by Daniel Taplitz, from the novel by Louis de Bernieres, it's based on a true story-turned legend. The title character is a rusty-coloured kelpie/cattle dog, an Australian working breed. But this one comes and goes as he pleases, choosing his human companions rather than being chosen by them. Over time, he becomes a symbol of the invisible links holding the men – and the few women – of this fragile community together.

Kriv Stenders' **Red Dog**

Contrasted with moments of knockabout comedy, Red Dog's death and his subsequent elevation to sainthood is teary stuff.

Critically acclaimed and a welcome success, *Red Dog* is as much a sign of cultural confusion as an affirmation of shared values. It's not the first sentimental exploitation of man's best friend but the powerful chord it touches in many Australians indicates the appeal of old myths about the national character, similar to America's preoccupation with the Wild West and perhaps Britain's pride in the 'stiff upper lip'. Like it or not, the Australia of the 21st century is another country. Enthusiasm for *Red Dog* eclipsed discussion of its obvious flaws: clumsy storytelling, patchy performances and the perplexing inclusion of a tokenistic American lead character, played by Josh Lucas.

Fred Schepisi, now in his 72nd year, is one of the iconic figures of the Australian film revival of four decades ago. After the explosive impact of *The Chant of Jimmie Blacksmith* in 1978, he took off for L.A., blazing the trail that countless Australians still follow. He was more successful than most, with *Roxanne*, *The Russia House* and *Six Degrees of Separation* being some of the high points of his exiled years. He returned to make *Evil Angels* (released as *A Cry in the Dark* in the US) with Meryl Streep in 1988, but his attempts to launch other Australian films have been unsuccessful until now.

The Eye of the Storm is the first major feature to be adapted from the novels of Nobel Prize-winning author Patrick White (Jim Sharman directed *The Night, the Prowler* in 1978 based on a White novella and filmmakers including

Fred Schepisi's **The Eye of the Storm**

Joseph Losey have wrestled futilely with
Voss). White was and remains a towering
figure (he died in 1990) and his oeuvre has
become sacred ground, so any adaptation can
be expected to play it safe. Schepisi and his
screenwriter Judy Morris (*Babe: Pig in the City*,
Happy Feet) focus on the more tangible aspects
of White's story. Two middle-aged expatriate
children (Geoffrey Rush and Judy Davis) return
to the bedside of their dying mother (Charlotte
Rampling), Elizabeth Hunter, ostensibly to
secure a slice of the old girl's money. Elizabeth
is bunyip aristocracy, a member of the once-
dominant Anglo-Australian ruling class,
endowed with all its gimlet-eyed arrogance.
She does not intend to die gracefully.

The Eye of the Storm will be wheeled out
internationally as evidence that Australia
can still make classically crafted, high-toned
drama on the big screen – as it did thirty years
ago. Coincidentally, it belongs to the same
timeframe and nostalgic impulse as *Red Dog*,
recreating the 1970s, this time in Sydney, and
the leafy, upper-middle-class suburb where
White himself lived. The film's reception can
best be described as respectful with praise
for the performances of Rush, Davis and
especially Rampling, who plays both the young
and old Elizabeth.

Perhaps the film can't be expected to fully
explore the dichotomy in White's work: his
contempt for mainstream Australian life – he

called it The Great Australian Emptiness – and
his deep yearning for spiritual fulfilment, 'the
mystery and the poetry' beyond appearances.
He has been justifiably placed alongside Tolstoy,
Flaubert and Proust for the epic scale of his
work and his dense, poetic prose – territory
that apparently defies interpretation on screen.

The price paid for our post-colonial imperial
links is explored with greater moral and
emotional force in Jim Loach's **Oranges and
Sunshine**. Again, it's a look back at the recent
past: the true story of the forced deportation
from Britain of 150,000 poor children between
1947 and 1967. Some 10,000 were sent to
Australia where they were promised endless
sunshine and abundant fruit but found instead
deprivation and physical, even sexual, abuse.
Jim Loach (son of Ken), producer Camilla Bray
and writer Rona Monro spent several years
developing the screenplay from Margaret
Humphreys' memoir 'Empty Cradles' before
deciding that it was the story of Humphreys
herself that would be the spine of the film.
Hugo Weaving and David Wenham play
the principle characters Jack and Len, who
galvanize Humphreys (Emily Watson) into
uncovering their traumatic stories and the full
extent of the tragedy. All three performances
are stunningly powerful.

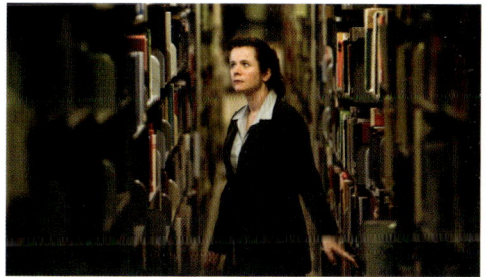

Jim Loach's **Oranges and Sunshine**

Oranges and Sunshine is an authentic British-
Australian co-production, both on a creative
and financial level. Shot mostly in Australia
with local cast and crew, it is co-produced
by Emile Sherman and Ian Canning, partners
in See-Saw Films, which also produced *The
King's Speech*. Sherman has figured strongly

in the Australian context over the last decade, with credits such as *Rabbit-Proof Fence*, *Candy* and *Disgrace*. At least four more of his productions are slotted to appear over the next year including Steve McQueen's erotic drama **Shame**, Tony Krawitz's **Dead Europe** (based on the novel by Christos Tsiolkas) and Ian Iqbal Rashid's romantic comedy **American English**.

Indeed, the contemporary history of Australian film could be substantially told by referring only to the actors, production personnel and technicians working internationally: the likes of Russell Crowe, Guy Pearce, Cate Blanchett, Sam Worthington, Simon Baker, Nicole Kidman, Anthony LaPaglia, Naomi Watts, Hugh Jackman, Mia Wasikowska, Peter Weir, Jane Campion, Baz Luhrmann, George Miller, John Seale, Dean Semler, Andrew Lesnie and more. Not yet 40, Emile Sherman has been as globally significant as any of them and yet he remains firmly rooted on Australian soil. If one is searching for signs of a hopeful future, he's one of them.

In 2007, John Howard's conservative government introduced legislation that has come to be known as the 'intervention' in response to claims of social breakdown and rampant child sexual abuse in remote Aboriginal communities. Extra police and troops were sent in, individual freedoms curtailed and lands seized. The measures have been debated ever since, particularly within Aboriginal communities themselves. The issues are extremely complex and can't be summed up in a few words, but they are reflected in a trio of powerful recent films.

Ivan Sen's **Toomelah** looks at one community in crisis through the eyes of ten-year-old Daniel (Daniel Connors), a tough kid from a broken family who wants nothing better than to emulate the local drug dealer Linden (Christopher Edwards). Daniel's is one of those uncanny child performances – we see his world with a clarity born of naivety and compelling inner strength. But it's not pretty. The denizens of Toomelah, an isolated old mission station, live in poisonous limbo and

when a new drug dealer moves into Linden's territory, things get very ugly.

Ivan Sen is one of Australia's most prolific indigenous filmmakers. His feature-directing debut *Beneath Clouds* (2002) gained international attention for its understated dramatic style and lyrical imagery. *Toomelah* is much more stripped back, photographed by Sen himself with a handheld camera, documentary-style. But there's plenty going on at different levels and there's a palpable reality to the people and their interactions although all are non-actors.

Ivan Sen's **Toomelah**

Indigenous stories were long regarded as 'box-office poison' and films like *Toomelah* are still avoided. Phillip Noyce's *Rabbit-Proof Fence* from 2002 went a long way towards changing attitudes and the David Gulpilil-inspired *Ten Canoes* (2006) and, more recently, *Bran Nue Dae* (Rachel Perkins, 2009), are charming and funny. But it's the uncompromising spirit of the Sen film and others like it that sets Australia's indigenous cinema apart.

Beck Cole's **Here I Am** is ruthless in its depiction of indigenous social dysfunction. Karen (Shai Pittman) is released from prison determined to be reunited with her young daughter. But her mother Lois (prominent academic and social activist Marcia Langton) has other ideas. Any sentimental notions of Aboriginal family loyalty, often invoked as the saving grace of disadvantaged communities, are swept aside.

Beck Cole's **Here I Am**

Brendan Fletcher's **Mad Bastards** may be more accessible, but it covers similar ground. TJ (Dean Daley-Jones) is a hard man trapped in a cycle of alcohol and violence, but one drunken brawl too many sets him on a pilgrimage to connect with his 13-year-old son Bullet (Lucas Yeeda), who lives in the remote northwest corner of Australia known as The Kimberley (now the site of furious mining speculation). TJ comes up against the local cop, indigenous man Texas (Greg Tait) and their bare-knuckle fight in a parched desert landscape is brutal.

Brendan Fletcher is white, but *Mad Bastards* is the result of deep collaboration with his principal actors. The same can be said of *Rabbit-Proof Fence* (Noyce) and *Ten Canoes*, which was co-directed by Rolf de Heer (with Peter Djiggir), but where De Heer essentially played a mentoring role. Nevertheless, the issue of non-Aboriginal filmmakers tackling indigenous subjects is vexed, with many seeing it as yet another form of exploitation. That's unfortunate, but it also demonstrates how far sensibilities have travelled from even two decades ago.

Brendan Fletcher's **Mad Bastards**

More significant is the energy and sense of urgency of indigenous films. Aboriginal Australians represent less than three per cent of the population but they occupy a much greater slice of the nation's consciousness and therefore its identity. *Toomelah*, *Here I Am* and *Mad Bastards* may be grim and confronting but they also look forward to a more cohesive, constructive future.

As suggested above, many significant Australian filmmakers are not working at home. The lure of global rewards are irresistible, it seems, and local success a stepping-stone to the doorways of agents and producers in the US. One consequence is the proliferation of genre-based films. Blame Tarantino – amongst a host of others – who waxed lyrical about Australian genre pictures of the 1970s in *Not Quite Hollywood* (2008). The Kennedy-Miller *Mad Max* trilogy was a game changer and, more recently, the James Wan and Leigh Whannell *Saw* franchise has been a box-office goldmine.

Michael Henry's **Blame**

Current disciples of the trend are Adam Blaiklock with his psychological thriller **Caught Inside**, about a surfing safari gone wrong – with echoes of Noyce's *Dead Calm* (1989) and last year's *Triangle* (Christopher Smith) – and Michael Henry with his thriller **Blame**, about a group of young friends who wreak justice on a supposed sexual predator, only too late to discover their mistake. Veteran Simon Wincer revisits the horse-racing territory he exploited successfully two decades ago in *Phar Lap*, this time with **The Cup** and the drama behind

Jonathan Teplitsky's **Burning Man**

the horse that won the 2002 Melbourne Cup. Credited with perhaps more originality is Jonathan Teplitsky (*Better Than Sex*, *Gettin' Square*) who delves into grief and anger in **Burning Man**, about an English chef (Matthew Goode) who, after the death of his young wife, tries to put his life back together with a generous selection of other women.

Also resisting formula is Daniel Nettheim with **The Hunter**. It appears to be about the search for a surviving example of the Tasmanian Tiger, a species of carnivorous marsupial believed extinct for several decades. But the hunter, played by Willem Dafoe, is on a mission from a mysterious European biotech company. Dafoe brings much-needed authority due to the overpowering atmosphere of the dark and lonely Tasmanian wilderness. There's an interwoven plot about the conflict between loggers and environmentalists, and good performances from Sam Neill and Frances O'Connor.

Daniel Nettheim's **The Hunter**

The Hunter is based on a novel by Julia Leigh, who makes her directing debut with her self-scripted 'erotic fairytale', **Sleeping Beauty**. Quickly accepted into Official Competition at Cannes under the guiding hand of producer Jane Campion, Leigh's dream run faltered, with reviews ranging from guarded to hostile. It's not the first time someone has been elevated to the role of director in Australia without any experience whatsoever behind the camera. It happened to another gifted novelist, Richard Flanagan, in 1998 with his *The Sound of One Hand Clapping*. Like too many others who stumble at the starting gates, Flanagan hasn't directed again. But for all its weaknesses, *Sleeping Beauty* has some genuine virtues, including ravishing imagery and the presence of the remarkable Rachael Blake (*Lantana*, *Tom White*) and veterans Chris Haywood (*Strikebound*, *Shine*) and Peter Carroll.

Julia Leigh's **Sleeping Beauty**

It's said that if no one is happy with government policy, it must be about right. If so, Australian cinema is travelling well. But the truth may be less reassuring – mostly what you hear is the gnashing of teeth. And what you get from the Government and its agencies is, sadly, mostly spin.

Taxpayer-funded bureaucracies have mushroomed and the 40 per cent Producer Offset is still in place – it will have a huge impact on the bottom line of Baz Luhrmann's **The Great Gatsby**, starring Leonardo DiCaprio and Carey Mulligan, as it did for his *Australia* – the sum was never disclosed, but possibly as much as AUS$80million. Alex Proyas's

Paradise Lost with Bradley Cooper and Camilla Belle will also benefit. George Miller's **Happy Feet Two** is another: this massively complex CGI epic just could not have been made without tax breaks. No matter how you look at it, public funding and regulation remain essential ingredients of Australian cinema and home entertainment. Television companies are obliged to invest in Australian content and several major recent miniseries are a sign of increased strength in that area.

But cultural policy and especially film production is still bedevilled by the superstition that art (and entertainment, if you insist on separating them) can somehow pay its/their way through marketplace mechanisms, instead of being seen extensions of education – a means by which a community builds self-awareness and resilience. Of course, public acceptance and enthusiasm for movies is important, so box-office results are a useful indicator, but they are not the whole story and, like all statistics, can be fatally skewed.

It's hard to see past the smoke and mirrors. I contend that Australian film production falls far short of where it should be in terms both of quality and quantity. Like a piglet coated with lard, the secret of how best to nurture creative growth still eludes our grasp. But if the future is less than rosy, there are shafts of sunlight between the clouds. There's talent, experience and determination all around – witness the work of Emilc Sherman.

And it has to be seen in the context of the technological revolution taking place within film production, but also for exhibition and audience behaviour. There are so many unpredictable possible outcomes. George Miller believes that interactive entertainment offers undreamed-of possibilities and he's committing huge resources to it. But, again, government action will be crucial. Miller wants the 40 per cent Producer Offset extended to video games before other countries including Canada (which already has a 40 per cent rebate) beat us to the punch.

Jim Loach's **Oranges and Sunshine**

The year's best films
Oranges and Sunshine (Jim Loach)
Mad Bastards (Brendan Fletcher)
Toomelah (Ivan Sen)

Directory
All Tel/Fax numbers begin (+61)
Australian Directors Guild (ADG), PO Box 211, Rozelle NSW 2039. Tel: (2) 9555 7045. Fax: (2) 9555 7086. www.adg.org.au.
Australian Entertainment Industry Association (AEIA), 8th Floor, West Tower, 608 St Kilda Road, Melbourne, VIC 3004. Tel: (3) 9521 1900. Fax: (3) 9521 2285. aeia@aeia.org.au.
Film Australia, 101 Eton Rd, Lindfield NSW 2070. Tel: (2) 9413 8777. Fax: (2) 9416 9401. www.filmaust.com.au.
The National Screen and Sound Archive, GPO Box 2002, Canberra ACT 2601. Tel: (2) 6248 2000. Fax: (2) 6248 2222. enquiries@screensound.gov.au. Stock: 3,800 Western Australian titles.
Screen Australia, Level 4, 150 William St, Woolloomooloo NSW 2011. Tel: (2) 8113 5800. Fax: (2) 9357 3737. www.screenaustralia.gov.au.
Screen Producers Association of Australia (SPAA), 34 Fitzroy Street, Surry Hills NSW 2010. Tel: (2) 9360 8988. Fax: (2) 9360 8977. spaa@spaa.org.au www.spaa.org.au

PETER THOMPSON is an award-winning filmmaker and writer. He has also been reviewing and presenting movies on Australian television for thirty years.

Austria Gunnar Landsgesell

As an actor Karl Markovics (the lead in *The Counterfeiters*) is eminently experienced. He has now moved behind the camera with his feature debut **Breathing** (*Atmen*). The 49-year-old surprised many with this years most vivid Austrian film.

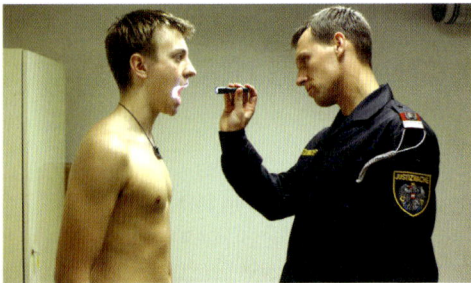

Karl Markovics' **Breathing**

The film is a portrait of a 19-year-old-boy convicted of homicide. Eager to leave the juvenile detention centre, he opts to find a job while on day parole, attempting to gain a foothold at the municipal undertakers. Gradually, Markovics makes us understand this restrained young man and the cold, cynical world he is a product of. What marks the film out is its avoidance of bleakness, producing instead a gripping drama. Markovics shows a thorough understanding of the language of cinema (aided by Martin Gschlacht's cinematography) and has immediately marked himself out as one of Austria's finest filmmakers.

Like *Breathing*, the dismal drama **Michael**, the feature debut of casting director Markus Schleinzer, was invited to Cannes. The film draws on recent stories of child kidnapping and abuse, but *Michael* focuses on the perpetrator and not the victim. The result is a bland work that is less provocative than expected and indecisive in terms of its narrative and overall message.

So 2011 was the year of the newcomers in Austrian cinema. Marie Kreutzer, one of the country's most promising talents, also presented her feature debut, **The Fatherless** (*Die Vaterlosen*), at the Berlinale. A psychodrama narrated through flashbacks, Kreutzer assembles four estranged siblings who meet for the first time in years following the death of their father. Raised in a hippie-like commune, their reunion prompts them to return to certain unresolved episodes from the past.

Kreutzer takes a courageous step in embarking on an ensemble piece for her first film. Moreover, her tapestry of familial relations is a complex one in which the audience must strive to understand all its facets. *The Fatherless* is both challenging and rewarding viewing for engaged audiences.

Barbara Eder's **Inside America**

Barbara Eder's debut **Inside America** is an extraordinary cinematic experience. Shot in a Texas high school and employing a semi-documentary style, it details life for the students – a far remove from the existential enquiries of much Austrian cienma.

Only *Breathing* performed successfully at the local box office. But all these films played well at international festivals, bolstering the profile of Austrian film generally.

As most of these films are never likely to do well at the box office, the industry relies on the success of more genre-based fare, such as horror and comedy, to boost the coffers. Horror met with 3D for the first time in Austrian cinema with Markus Welter's **One Way Trip**, yet another version of youth-camp-slasher-horror film that takes place deep in some woods.

Once again, it is the output of non-fiction film that makes up an essential part of Austria's filmmaking scene. Some well-known filmmakers offered fascinating accounts of the world around us. Nikolaus Geyrhalters' **Abendland**, is a nightly trip through Europe and the activities after most people have gone to sleep. It is a collection of beautiful composed images of Europe after dark.

What will 2012 hold for Austrian filmmaking? It is expected to be a very strong year. Michael Haneke is set to present a more intimate film, **Amour**, a love story in old age. In **Paradise** (*Paradies*) Ulrich Seidl tells three inter-connected stories about sexuality in Kenya, Catholicism and a weight-loss camp. And Barbara Albert (*Northern Skies*) returns after a long time away from cinema with **The Other World**, detailing a young woman's enquiry into her grandparent's involvement in National Socialism.

The year's best films
Breathing (Karl Markovics)
Inside America (Barbara Eder)
Abendland (Nikolaus Geyrhalter)

GUNNAR LANDSGESELL is a freelance writer for *Blickpunkt: Film*, *Format*, *the gap*, *kolik*, *ray filmmagazin*. He is also Co-Editor of *Spike Lee* (Bertz Verlag Berlin, 2005).

Nikolaus Geyrhalter's **Abendland**

Directory
All Tel/Fax numbers begin (+43)
Austrian Film Museum, Augustinerstr 1, A-1010 Vienna, Tel: (1) 533 7054-0. Fax: (1) 533 7054-25. office@filmmuseum.at. www.filmmuseum.at.
Filmarchiv Austria, Obere Augartenstr 1, A-1020 Vienna. Tel: (1) 216 1300. Fax: (1) 216 1300-100. augarten@filmarchiv.at. www.filmarchiv.at.
Association of Austrian Film Directors, c/o checkpointmedia Multimediaproduktionen AG, Seilerstätte 30, A-1010 Vienna. Tel/Fax: (1) 513 0000-0. Fax: (1) 513 0000-11. www.austrian-directors.com.
Association of Austrian Film Producers, Speisingerstrasse 121, A-1230 Vienna. Tel/Fax: (1) 888 9622. aafp@austrian-film.com. www.austrian-film.com.
Association of the Audiovisual & Film Industry, Wiedner Hauptstrasse 53, PO Box 327, A-1045 Vienna. Tel: (1) 5010 53010. Fax: (1) 5010 5276. film@fafo.at. www.fafo.at.
Austrian Film Commission, Stiftgasse 6, A-1070 Vienna. Tel: (1) 526 33 23-0. Fax: (1) 526 6801. office@afc.at. www.afc.at.
Austrian Film Institute (OFI), Spittelberggasse 3, A-1070 Vienna. Tel: (1) 526 9730-400. Fax: (1) 526 9730-440. office@filminstitut.at. www.filminstitut.at.
Location Austria, Opernring 3, A-1010 Vienna. Tel: (1) 588 5836. Fax: (1) 586 8659. office@location-austria.at. www.location-austria.at.
Vienna Film Fund, Stiftgasse 6, A-1070 Vienna. Tel: 526 5088. Fax: 526 5020. office@filmfonds-wien.at. www.filmfonds-wien.at.

Belgium Erik Martens

Steven Spielberg's *The Adventures of Tintin: The Secret of the Unicorn* is not a Belgian film, but thousands of Belgians seemed eager to adopt it as such. They gave the film a 'warm welcome home' at its world premiere in Brussels, in October. The cartoons of Tintin are a key element in the Belgian collective consciousness, alongside René Magritte's bowler hats, Marcel Broothaers' mussels, French fries, and of course, the inevitable Belgian beer and chocolates.

Jean-Pierre and Luc Dardenne's **The Kid with a Bike**

On a second, slightly less mythological level, are Belgian filmmakers Jean-Pierre and Luc Dardenne, who completed their latest feature. There is always a sense of occasion with their films. Over the last two decades, every three years the Dardennes make a film that always wins prizes at Cannes. 2011 could have seen them win their third Palme d'Or. Instead, **The Kid with a Bike** (*Le gamin au vélo*) walked away with the Grand Prix (shared with Nuri Bilge Ceylan's *Once Upon a Time in Anatolia*).

The Kid with a Bike is an interesting new step in the brother's career. Whereas in previous films the grim social backcloth of the drama drew a lot attention to itself, the Dardennes set their latest story within a much lighter context.

Belgian star Cécile De France plays light-hearted hairdresser Samatha, who decides, without really understanding why, to take care of Cyril, a teenager who has been deserted by his father. But trouble seems to follow the boy, making Samantha's life much more difficult. The film was rapturously received by local critics, more unanimously so than the brother's previous film, *The Silence of Lorna*.

After the 'Famous Belgians' there are a number of films made by reasonably established filmmakers, whose output is still relatively modest. Filmmakers such as Bouli Lanners, who directed **The Giants**, and Dominique Abel, Fiona Gordon and Bruno Romy, who made **The Fairy** (*La fée*).

The Kid with a Bike, *The Giants* and *The Fairy* were all selected for Cannes. Bouli Lanners' first entry at the competition (in the 'Directors' Fortnight') confirms his talent for creating mysterious landscapes and gloomy characters. Black humour goes hand-in-hand with the sad and the sinister. The film's main characters are three teenagers who, once again, are left to fend for themselves by their parents. They decide to stick together in order to survive in a hostile environment. The universe that Lanners draws us into is fascinating, but this time both

Bouli Lanners' **The Giants**

plot and characters lack the precision of his previous two films.

The Fairy is something completely different. It's main character is a fairy, but a very down-to-earth variation, one who takes care of the needy. The fairy is played by Fiona Gordon, with Dominique Abel as her charge, a night porter at a hotel. The two become literally intertwined and experience the strangest events. As with the directors' previous films (*Rumba* and *The Iceberg*), it's all about pantomime, slapstick and playful choreography, much like their influences, Jacques Tati and Buster Keaton.

Dominique Abel, Fiona Gordon and Bruno Romy's **The Fairy**

Gust Van Den Berghe was the fourth Belgian in Cannes. In 2010 he was selected with *Little Baby Jesus of Flandr*, an interesting student short that was turned into a feature. **Blue Bird** is based on Maurice Maeterlinck's symbolist stage play, which Van Den Berghe relocates to a small African village. A child makes a magical trip, involving a bird, his deceased grandparents, children with white caps 'that are waiting to be born' and spirits that live in the forest. The narrative is not always cogent, but the direct style of the performances and the strong visual style makes for an attractive film, particularly the use of blue and the cinemascope format.

A similar observation could be made of the equally experimental **Portable Life** by Dutch photographer-turned-filmmaker Fleur Boonman. In it, a young woman, played by Ella-June Henrard travels around the world. The journey may also a spiritual one, but

Fleur Boonman's **Portable Life**

psychology and narration take a back seat to a photographer's experience of these sumptuous, often exotic, locations.

Of the new filmmakers, Nicolas Provost made the biggest impression. **The Invader** (*L'invahisseur*) tells the straightforward story of an illegal immigrant who washes up, barely alive, on a nudist beach. For the rest of the film, Amadou, impressively played by Issaka Sawadogo, attempts to find his way around Brussels. He does what he can to find his way in the city's underbelly, working as a cheap, illegal labourer on a construction site. With its lush images and accompanying soundtrack, drawing on the director's experience in experimental video, the film clearly highlights the double standards of modern society, between the haves and have-nots.

Nicolas Provost's **The Invader**

Issaka Sawadogo also appears in Kaat Beel's feature debut **Swooni**, once again playing a character called Amadou. Here too the character ends up in Brussels, this time accompanied by his son Joyeux. However, they are separated by an incident involving the police. Theirs is just one story in a tapestry of contemporary life that also features a Belgian couple dealing with their marital problems and a dying mother trying to make peace with her daughter. It is atmospherically shot by Frank Van Den Eeden, who also shot *The Invader*, although the film would have profited from more control of its emotional engagement.

Belgium's Dutch-speaking cinema, which is more geared towards popular fare, produced two comedies that reached a broader public than was intended. Guy Goosens' **Frits & Freddy** is a grotesque comedy about two eccentrics who become crooks. They stage a kidnapping but soon find themselves in trouble. The film was privately financed, with no support from the Flemish Film Fund. It is also interesting to note that the film's dialogue uses the Antwerp dialect, which is not standard Dutch. This appears to have become a trend with recent Dutch-speaking productions.

Geoffrey Enthoven's **Hasta la vista** featured a number of social issues, but remained a broad comedy about three physically disabled young-sters who hire a bus and a driver for a holiday to Spain, where they hope to have sex for the first time. Like *Frits & Freddy*, this is hardly the most subtle or sophisticated form of comedy.

As a whole, local cinema has performed well over the last year. Even with financial, economic and political crises rocking this small country, more films are being made. Thanks to the tax shelter scheme more money is drawn into the industry and audience attendance for domestic product is increasing year-on-year. One of the stranger particularities is that this sizeable – and growing – audience is mainly Dutch-speaking (Flemish). So last year's box-office success, Michael Roskam's *Bullhead*, sold more tickets than the whole of French-speaking Belgian cinema combined.

ERIK MARTENS is editor of DVD releases at the Royal Belgian Film Archive and a freelance film critic for different media.

The year's best films

The Kid with a Bike (Jean-Pierre & Luc Dardenne)
The Invader (Nicolas Provost)
The Fairy (Dominique Abel, Fiona Gordon and Bruno Romy)
Blue Bird (Gust Van Den Berghe)
The Giants (Bouli Lanners)

Gust Van Den Berghe's **Blue Bird**

Directory

All Tel/Fax numbers begin (32)
Royal Belgian Film Archive, 3 rue Ravenstein, 1000 Brussels. Tel: (2) 551 19 00. Fax: (2) 551 19. info@cinematek.be. www.cinematek.be
Communauté Française de Belgique. Le Centre du Cinéma et de l'Audiovisuel, Boulevard Léopold II 44, 1080 Bruxelles. Tel: (2) 413 35 01. Fax: (2) 413 20 68. www.cfwb.be/av
Wallonie Bruxelles Images (WBI), Place Flagey 18, 1050 Bruxelles. Tel: (2) 223 23 04. Fax: (2) 218 34 24. info@wbimages.be. www.wbimages.be
Wallimage, Rue du Onze Novembre 6, 7000 Mons. Tel: (6) 540 40 33. Fax: (6) 540 40 39. info@wallimage.be. www.wallimage.be.
Ministry of the Flemish Community. Media & Film, Arenbergstraat 9, 1000 Brussels. Tel: (2) 553 45 50. Fax: (2) 553 45 79. film@vlaanderen.be. www.flanders.be
Flemish Audiovisual Fund (VAF), Bischoffsheimlaan 38, 1000 Brussel. Tel: (2) 226 06 30. Fax: (2) 219 19 36. info@vaf.be. www.vaf.be
Flanders Image, Bischoffsheimlaan 38, 1000 Brussels. Tel: (2) 226 06 30. Fax: (2) 219 19 36. flandersimage@vaf.be. www.flandersimage.com

Bolivia José Sánchez-H.

Hollywood productions dominated Bolivian cinemas once again in 2011. Local digital productions increased in quantity but not necessarily quality. Bolivian audiences remain less than enthusiastic about them, preferring mainstream fare from North America.

During the first six months of 2011, around ten films by young directors were released in cinemas and to an unresponsive public. Martin Boulocq's **The Old People** (*Los viejos*) is based on Rodrigo Hasbún's 'Carretera'. Shot in the state of Tarija with a screenplay written by Boulocq and Hasbún, the film tells the story of Toño, who returns home from exile to the uncles who raised him. The son of parents who disappeared during the country's military dictatorship, he is confronted with the reality that his adoptive father is old and seriously ill, and his high school sweetheart is now a single mother. This astute drama, which works well as a metaphor for the country's relationship with its past, is a successful collaboration between Boulocq and director Juan Carlos Valdivia, who produced it.

Martin Boulocq's **The Old People**

The most anticipated films of 2011 were directed by Jorge Sanjinés and Marcos Loayza. At the time of writing, neither film has yet to

Jorge Sanjinés' **Insurgent Bolivia**

be released. Last year marked 45 years since Sanjinés made his first feature, *That's The Way It Is*, which won the Great Young Directors Award at the Cannes Film Festival. Considered Bolivia's most influential director, Sanjinés returns after seven years with **Insurgent Bolivia** (*Bolivia Insurgente*). A period film based on extraordinary indigenous figures who have been ignored by mainstream Bolivian history, Sanjinés apparently blends history and fiction with a script that features numerous protagonists, opening with the rebellion against Spanish rule in 1781 by an indigenous leader known as Tupac Katari. *Insurgent Bolivia* was shot in the states of Beni, Cochabamba, Oruro, Santa Cruz, and Tarija, and moves between that early uprising and more recent events in 2010.

Marcos Loayza's **Sleeping Beauties** (*Las bellas durmientes*) is a comedy about a policeman named Quispe who is asked to investigate a horrendous crime that took place in Santa Cruz. In his investigation, he uncovers information he wishes he didn't know about his colleagues and himself. Quispe is played by Luigi Antezana, who stars alongside twenty models, including Santa Cruz's carnival queen, Andrea Aliaga, and Miss Bolivia 2011, Yessica Mouton.

Marcos Loayza's **Sleeping Beauties**

New productions are appearing on the horizon, despite harsh economic conditions. The current trend appears to be collaborations between filmmakers, which may reap both creative and economic dividends. Co-productions also remain a viable way of funding, as is the continued financial support of such international organisations as Ibermedia.

Directory

All Tel/Fax numbers begin (+591)
Cinemateca Boliviana, Calle Oscar Soria, Prolongación Federico Zuazo s/n, Casilla 9933, La Paz. Tel: (2) 211 8759. informaciones@cinematecaboliviana.org, www.cinematecaboliviana.org
Consejo Nacional de Cine (CONACINE), Calle Montevideo, Edificio Requimia, Piso 8, La Paz. Tel: (2) 244 4759. contacto@conacine.net. www.conacine.net.

JOSÉ SÁNCHEZ-H. is a filmmaker and co-author of *The Art and Politics of Bolivian Cinema* (1999). He teaches in the dept. of Film and Electronic Art at California State University, Long Beach.

لجنة أبوظبي للأفلام
ABU DHABI FILM
COMMISSION

Bosnia & Herzegovina Rada Sesić

Is it possible to make use of the horrible devastation of war to improve on the current situation of cinema production at home? It was a question that Bosnia & Herzegovina's Association of Filmmakers recently considered in a guide to potential film locations for international co-productions. Next to images of unspoiled mountain landscapes and coastal vistas were actual war locations, replete with devastated buildings and the detritus of battles that took place in the recent past. Despite the current economic crisis, it is an example of how the country's film industry is becoming more organised and realising the assets, both geographical and creative that it can boast of.

Not that everything works perfectly. Due to certain domestic political quarrels and misunderstandings, the country missed out on fully realising the potential of hosting the large crew of Angelina Jolie's directorial debut *In the land of Honey and Blood*. She had originally chosen to shoot in Bosnia, but ended up filming in Hungary. Thankfully, many Bosnian actors were cast in key roles in the film, including Sarajevo's Zana Marjanovic in the lead role. Both Jolie and Brad Pitt made a surprise appearance at the Sarajevo Film Festival, where the actress-turned-director was the recipient of the Heart of Sarajevo award.

War stories still dominate the country's output. Namik Kabil's **Inside** (*Unutra*) tells the story of a man who survived his own killing in the Srebrenica massacre. He is burdened by the unbearable sense of guilt of his surviving an atrocity in which so many did not. With its sober and minimalist look and direct, confrontational narrative, it follows the central character as he encounters six different

Namik Kabil's **Inside**

Serbian women and is forced to face the sense of hatred he feels for an entire nation, only to realise that not everyone is the same. This realisation causes him to break down, yet is a sign of hope in basic human values. 'It is as sane as we are, living in present Bosnia', commented the filmmaker whose previous film *Nightguards* premiered at the Venice Film Festival in 2008.

Of the many strategies to make a film without financing is to shoot completely on one's own, using only a mobile phone camera. It was an approach adopted by filmmaker Nedzad Begovic in the intriguing documentary **A Cell Phone Movie**. This charming, witty and playful film won the Heart of Sarajevo for best regional documentary at the Sarajevo Film

Nedzad Begovic's **A Cell Phone Movie**

Festival. Shooting over a period of three years, Begovic used the advantages of the medium in a fast, direct, intimate manner; the result is an entertaining film that taps into current issues.

Young female director Nejra Latic Hulusic completed her short documentary **Her Cinema Love**, which was co-directed with Dutch colleague David-Jan Bronsgeest. The grief of a mother whose son died from sniper fire is movingly presented through this portrait of Sena. She operates a legendary cinema that doubled up as a shelter during the war. Today, one of the volunteers who helps out at the cinema café is a Serb who, during the war, was a sniper on the street where Sena lived. An incredible story, it attracted a great deal of controversy upon its release, resulting in its withdrawal from cinemas in Sarajevo, although it played to great acclaim elsewhere.

Nejra Latic Hulusic and David-Jan Bronsgeest's **Her Cinema Love**

Among several new documentaries, Vesna Ljubic's **A Bosnian Rhapsody ... on the Edge of Science** (*Bosanska rapsodija ... na rubu znanosti*) earned much praise and was chosen to screen at IDFA. It starts with unveiling several traditional herbalist recipes known in Bosnian history among all ethnic groups, guiding us through the urge of people to get healed by any available method and heading towards identifying the contemporary illnesses of the whole society. Ljubic, the first female director of feature films in Bosnia, nourishes a very unique style which perfectly blends cinematic poetry, authentic factuality and subtle irony.

Room for contemplation and self-reflection is nicely given within the investigative journalistic documentary **Hero of our Times** (*Heroj naseg doba*) by Seki Radoncic. The film tells the incredible story of a Montenegrin former police officer who received national and international medals for saving human lives during the war, but is now recognized by surviving witnesses as one of the perpetrators of atrocities carried out against Bosnian Muslims during the war.

One of films that is appreciated in the whole region is the entertaining though serious documentary that follows the history of the music group Plavi Orkestar (Blue Orchestra) in the film **Orchestra** (*Orkestar*) by Pjer Zalica. With appearances of notable former Yugoslavian politicians combined with cultural icons, especially musicians, this captivating story, on which the crew worked for three years, gives an intriguing inside view into the spirit of the West Balkan region over the last 25 years.

Award-winning director Jasmila Zbanic is preparing her new fiction feature **Love Island** (*Otok ljubavi*) that will come out in 2013, but is also producing an intriguing docu-fiction directed by producer of her previous films, Damir Ibrahimovic. **A Russian** (*Rus*) is the story of a man who changed three names, three political systems, three wives and three religions. He is a member of the Russian mafia, son of a famous Bosnian film director, but also a boy looking for love. Combining elements of documentary and fiction, this intriguing structure opens up the dramatic experience of a real-life character through the directed encounter with well-known Croatian actor Leon Lucev, who is here positioned as a sort of psychotherapist.

After the success with *Snow*, Aida Begic is making a new film under production of Golden Bear-winning Turkish director Semih Kaplanoglu. **Bait** (*Mamac*) will recount the stories of people who were born during the 1990s siege of Sarajevo and are now in their early 20s. Rahima and Nedim are brother and sister who lost their parents in the war. They want to be successful in life. This warm human drama explores the director's vision of the possible 'Bosnian dream'.

Although most cinemas have been shut down in the last two decades – while some fifteen film festivals have popped up to serve four million inhabitants – the capital city has now got a modern art-house cinema run by students. The Kriterion cinema that has been erected in collaboration with the well-known Amsterdam student cinema with the same name is the new Mecca for local followers of documentaries and non-mainstream fiction.

The year's best films
A Cell Phone Movie (Nedzad Begovic)
Inside (Namik Kabil)
Her Cinema Love (Nejra Latic Hulusic and David-Jan Bronsgeest)
A Bosnian Rhapsody ... on the Edge of Science (Vesna Ljubic)
A Russian (Damir Ibrahimovic)

Directory
All Tel/Fax numbers begin (+387).
Academy for Performing Arts, Obala, Sarajevo. Tel/Fax: 665 304.
Association of Filmmakers, Strosmajerova 1, Sarajevo. Tel: 667 452.
Cinemateque of Bosnia & Herzegovina, Alipasina 19, Sarajevo. Tel/Fax: 668 678. kinoteka@bih.net.ba.

RADA SESIĆ is a filmmaker, critic, curator and festival programmer based in the Netherlands. She is programme advisor of IFFR and one of the selectors for IDFA, and heads the documentary competition at the Sarajevo Film Festival. She also makes documentaries and short films, and guest lectures at the Dutch Film Academy and mentors at international workshops for documentary films.

Brazil Helen Beltrame

S ome fifteen years after the *Retomada* – considered the rebirth of Brazilian cinema – the country's production seems to be back on its feet. From less than five films produced in 1994, Brazil reached a total of thirty features produced in 2001, and fast approached the 100 mark in 2011, after two consecutive years of 81 films being released.

One cannot deny that the improvement in Brazilian cinema's output numbers is linked to the increasing interest of the international community in the country itself. With the economic boost credited to its factory worker-turned-President Lula and Guerrilla fighter successor Dilma Roussef, and on the verge of hosting two major sports events in the next few years – FIFA's World Cup in 2014 and Olympic Games in 2016 – Brazil has been in the spotlight and all national industries, including film, have benefited from it.

Marco Dutra and Juliana Rojas' **Hard Labour**

However, the effervescence of Brazilian cinema can certainly be credited to its own improvement in quality as much as quantity. Over the last year, it remained a dominant force at international festivals: Karim Ainouz's

Tiago Mata Machado's **The Residents**

The Silver Cliff (*O Abismo Prateado*) and Marco Dutra and Juliana Rojas' **Hard Labour** (*Trabalhar Cansa*) were screened at Cannes, Clarissa Campolina and Helvécio Marins Jr.'s **Girimunho** and Júlia Murat's **Histórias que só existem quando lembradas** at Venice; Eduardo Nunes' **Southwest** (*Sudoeste*) at Rotterdam, and both Tiago Mata Machado's **The Residents** (*Os Residentes*) and José Padilha's **Elite Squad: The Enemy Within** (*Tropa de Elite 2*) at Berlin.

Brazilian documentary was honored with a special proramme at this year's IDFA (International Documentary Film Festival Amsterdam) and Eduardo Coutinho's **Songs** (*Canções*) was screened in competition. Brazil has also been present at most of the international festivals for short films, another rising branch of production in the country.

Brazil also appears to have a shot at the Academy Awards for the first time since 2002 (*City of God*) with *Elite Squad: The Enemy Within*, which claimed the biggest box office in Brazilian history and also won significant foreign attention – not a frequent combination for a domestic production.

As with so many other countries, Brazilian films face the frequent chasm between international validation given to art-house releases and audience recognition at the box office, which is geared more towards mainstream fare. Most of the country's 'export movies' found difficulty in finding distribution at home and remain, in most cases, unseen by large swathes of the domestic audience, restricted instead to art-house cinemas.

Brazil has continued with the tradition of popular TV-related features. Up to the end of November, seven national productions had reached the one million ticket sales benchmark, an increase of 40 per cent over 2010. The list is comprised of titles almost completely unknown to international markets and audiences: **Cilada.com**, derived from an homonymous TV sitcom; **De pernas para o ar**, starring TV comedian Ingrid Guimarães; **Bruna Surfistinha**, based on a middle-class prostitute's diary; **Assalto ao Banco Central**, about the Central Bank robbery in 2005; **O homem do Futuro**, produced by Conspiração Filmes; **O Palhaço**, featuring TV star Selton Mello, and **Qualquer Gato Vira-Lata**, a light comedy featuring several TV soap opera stars. Except for *Bruna Surfistinha*, all the films were co-produced by Globo Filmes, a branch of the powerful media company Rede Globo.

In terms of distribution, the Brazilian productions are clearly being helped by the government 'quotas' resolution passed in 2005, which determine that every cinema in Brazil screens, depending on its size, between two and eleven Brazilian feature films for a certain minimum period throughout the year. Before leaving office in 2010, former President Lula increased those numbers to between three and fourteen, which came into force at the beginning of 2011.

However, Brazilian cinema-goers, like most other countries, are subject to the vicissitudes of Hollywood. As a result, the top ten highest box-office titles each year will rarely include a national production.

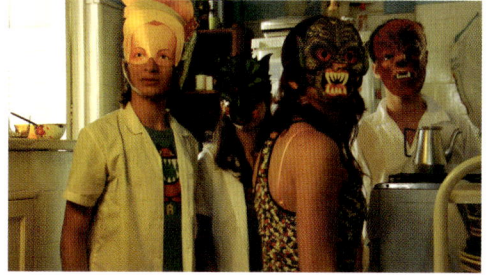

Felipe Bragança and Marina Meliande's **A Alegria**

The year's best films
Riscado (Gustavo Pizzi)
Southwest (Eduardo Nunes)
A Alegria (Felipe Bragança and Marina Meliande)
Estamos Juntos (Toni Venturi)
Hard Labour (Marco Dutra and Juliana Rojas)

Directory
All Tel/Fax numbers begin (+55)
ANCINE (National Agency for Cinema), Praça Pio X, 54, 10th Floor, 22091-040 Rio de Janeiro. Tel: (21) 3849 1339. www.ancine.gov.br.
Brazilian Cinema Congress (CBC), (Federation of Cinema Unions/Associations), Rua Cerro Cora 550, Sala 19, 05061-100 São Paulo. Tel/Fax: (11) 3021 8505. congressocinema@hotmail.com. www.congressocinema.com.br.
Cinemateca Brasileira, Largo Senador Raul Cardoso, Vila Clementino 207, 04021-070 São Paulo. Tel: (11) 5084 2318. Fax: (11) 5575 9264. info@cinemateca.com.br. www.cinemateca.com.br.
Grupo Novo de Cinema, (Distributor), Rua Capitao Salomao 42, 22271-040 Rio de Janeiro. Tel: (21) 2539 1538. braziliancinema@braziliancinema.com. www.gnctv.com.br.
Ministry of Culture, Films & Festivals Dept, Esplanada dos Ministerios, Bloco B, 3rd Floor, 70068-900 Brasilia. www.cultura.gov.br.

HELEN BELTRAME has worked as a producer of the modern theatre company Sutil Companhia de Teatro and as editor of the Rio International Film Festival dailies. In 2009 she joined Zazen Produções and was directly involved in the structuring of Brazilian's first independent distribution company Nossa Distribuidora.

Bulgaria Pavlina Jeleva

The financial instability of Bulgarian cinema that dominated 2010 continued throughout 2011. At the end of 2010, the tension within film circles reached breaking point and filmmakers, frustrated, took to the streets. They protested against the lack of transparency in the attempt to change the Film Industry Act, aiming to remove the legal guarantee of financial support for at least seven features each year. On December 22, 2010 filmmakers agreed on the establishment of a Film Fund with authorities. Furthermore, there was the promise of commitment to the preparation of a national strategy regarding the development of the Bulgarian film industry.

FERA (Federation of European Film Directors) president István Szábo supported the cause by writing to the Bulgarian Prime Minister, Boyko Borisov, calling on him to honour the Film Act and to 'secure the modest minimum of seven features'. Furthermore, he warned that 'the recent fine renaissance of Bulgarian cinema could be easily wiped out'.

Throughout 2011, the National Film Centre tried to partially cover the €10million obligation to various film productions. The suspension of the selection sessions from the beginning of 2010 continued untill December 2011 when, under conditions of severe financial restraint, the only session of the year was held.

Against this background, the box-office takings of a few titles were relatively good. Three directorial debuts reignited interest in domestic product. Ilian Djevelekov's **Love.net**, a seductive romantic comedy dedicated to IT obsessions, Viktor Chouchkov Jr.'s **Tilt**, a film that dealt with generational differences, and Ivan Vladimirov and Valery Yordanov's

Sneakers, in which six young people 'sneak away' to a lonely beach on the Black Sea coast, all impressed audiences.

However, the biggest surprise of the year was the eccentric comedy **Operation Shmenti Capelli**, written by and starring popular actor Vladislav Karamfilov-Vargala and directed by Ivan Mitov. Based on a popular idiomatic expression characterising people who like to shuffle and bamboozle others with superficial commitments, Karamfilov played two roles: the Big Guy, a brutal criminal linked to the secret service, and the Little Guy, an unemployed teacher crushed by the system. Audiences adored the amusing metaphor on economic and political power and sympathised with Karamfilov-Vargala's heroic effort of raising €500,000 by re-mortgaging his property in order to fund the film.

Ivan Mitov's **Operation Shmenti Capelli**

Audiences also responded kindly to Dimitar Kotsev-Shosho's **Lora From Morning Till Evening**, which was made with only €5,000 and shot on a Canon 7D. With the same 'low budget' Yassen Grigorov directed **Little-Big**, which drew on the various styles of Bulgaria's contemporary music scene. Atanas Hristoskov's debut and Bulgaria's first hip-hop film **NO.1** detailed the conflict between two schools located within the same building, which transforms into a turf war. The film, shot on high definition, won the Golden Rose award at the Varna Film Festival in October.

Kamen Kalev's second film **The Island**, in which French and Danish actors Laetitia Casta and Thure Lindhardt appear in a love story set on a mysterious Black Sea island, provoked some bewilderment due the irrational blend of romance and the grotesque. Konstantin Bojanov's debut, **Ave**, was described as the 'most sincere film' after Kalev's adored debut *Eastern Plays*. The love story between two hitchhikers, young Ave who creates false identities for herself and the alienated art student Kamen, attracted sizable critical acclaim.

Konstantin Bojanov's **Ave**

Although the revival of Bulgarian cinema is now internationally recognized, the future of the industry is still uncertain. Neither the protests nor the commitment of the government led to the actual implementation of the Film Industry Act and the establishment of a Film Fund. The Ministry of Culture budget for film in 2011 was barely more than €5million and the scheduled €6million for 2012 remains insufficient.

Dimitar Kotsev-Shosho's **Lora From Morning Till Evening**

Ilian Djevelekov's **Love.net**

The year's best films
Ave (Konstantin Bojanov)
Operation Shmenti Capelli (Ivan Mitov)
Love.net (Ilian Djevelekov)
NO.1 (Atanas Hristoskov)
Lora From Morning Till Evening (Dimitar Kotsev-Shosho)

Directory
All Tel/Fax numbers begin (+359)
Ministry of Culture, 17 Stamboliiski St, 1000 Sofia. Tel: (2) 980 6191. Fax: (2) 981 8559. www.culture.government.bg.
National Film Centre, 2A Dondukov Blvd, 1000 Sofia. Tel: (2) 987 4096. Fax: (2) 987 3626 www.nfc.bg.
Bulgarian National Television, 29 San Stefano St, 1000 Sofia. Tel: (2) 985 591. Fax: (2) 987 1871. www.bnt.bg .
National Academy of Theatre & Film Arts, 108A Rakovski Street, 1000 Sofia. Tel: (2) 9231 231/233
Bulgarian National Film Library, 36 Gurko St, 1000 Sofia. Tel: (2) 987 0296. Fax: (2) 987 6004 bnf.bg/en/film_library/ or www.ceebd.co.uk/ceeed/un/bg/bg023.htm
Bulgarian Film Producers Association, Tel: (2) 8860 5350. Fax: (2) 963 0661. geopoly@gmail.com.
Union of Bulgarian Film Makers, 67 Dondukov Blvd, 1504 Sofia. Tel: (2) 946 1068. Fax: (2) 946 1069 www.filmmakersbg.org.

PAVLINA JELEVA is a film critic and journalist, regularly contributing to many Bulgarian newspapers and magazines. Having been national representative on the boards of Eurimages and FIPRESCI, she is now artistic and foreign-relations director of her own film company.

Canada Tom McSorley

Canadian cinema continued its international tendencies in 2011, both behind and in front of the camera. Big and medium-sized budget international co-productions, like last year's *Barney's Version*, are seen to improve chances for box-office success and well as international festival exposure and foreign sales.

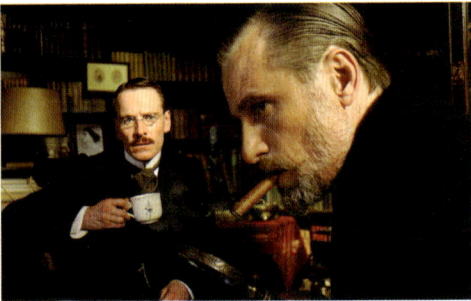

David Cronenberg's **A Dangerous Method**

The most high profile of these productions is David Cronenberg's **A Dangerous Method**, which premiered at Venice, and stars Viggo Mortensen and Michael Fassbender as Sigmund Freud and Carl Jung, respectively, working through their complex dramas of psychology and sexuality in Vienna. Montreal filmmaker Jean-Marc Vallée's latest, **Café de Flore**, with Vanessa Paradis, is set in both present-day Montreal and in Paris during the turbulent late 1960s. Elsewhere, Endre Hules' Canadian-Hungarian-Slovenian co-production, **The Maiden Danced to Death**, alternates its action between Canada and Hungary, as a Montreal-based Hungarian expatriate dance promoter tries to get a Budapest dance troupe ready for an international tour. In arguably the highest profile international co-production of the year, Indian-born Toronto filmmaker Deepa Mehta is currently completing her screen adaptation of Indian-born British writer Salman Rushdie's **Midnight's Children**.

Weaving together these strands of Canada's increasingly multi-ethnic society, the search for commercial success, and international casting is Robert Lieberman's predictable cross-cultural rom-com confection, **Breakaway**. When a group of eager but athletically-challenged Sikh-Canadians decide to form their own ice hockey team and compete against the powerful and infamous Hammerheads, chaos ensues on and off the ice. Cast with pop stars such as Akshay Kumar, Drake and Russell Peters, *Breakaway* also features American actor Rob Lowe as the beleagured coach of the upstart team. Energetic and occasionally witty, *Breakaway* did not score at the box office.

In another region of the internationalist tendency in Canadian filmmaking this year, *Trailer Park Boys* creator Mike Clattenburg's **Afghan Luke** ponders Canada's presence in Afghanistan in an offbeat drama of a freelance journalist who uncovers some very unsavoury behaviour by soldiers stationed there. It is a film that delves into Canada's role in international geopolitics, and raises troubling, relevant questions about the Canada's oft-invoked self-image as international good guys.

Endre Hules' **The Maiden Danced to Death**

Donald Shebib's **Down the Road Again**

In English-speaking Canadian cinema, it was a year of returning veteran filmmakers. In addition to Cronenberg probably the most veteran of them all, legendary Canadian director Donald Shebib, resurfaced with **Down the Road Again**, an uneven but moving sequel – made four decades later -- to his seminal English-Canadian feature from 1970, *Goin' Down the Road*, about two Atlantic Canadians who travel to Toronto to seek their fortune.

Guy Maddin's **Keyhole**

Fittingly, a filmmaker whose work reveals the considerable influence of Shebib, Bruce McDonald, also returned with **Hard Core Logo II**, a sequel to his tale of a punk rock band's raucous, ill-fated reunion tour, *Hard Core Logo* from 1996. Guy Maddin's noirish, claustrophobic melodramatic odyssey, **Keyhole** (starring Jason Patric and Isabella Rossellini) involves a gangster named Ulysses who returns home and works his way through the murk of past and present to get to his wife, who awaits in her bedroom upstairs.

While seemingly more premeditated than Maddin's organically oneiric previous works, *Keyhole* remains compelling viewing.

Given her already lengthy and impressive career as an actress, Sarah Polley is, in some sense, a veteran, although her latest directorial effort, **Take This Waltz**, is only her second feature, following her remarkable debut in 2006, *Away From Her*. Starring Michelle Williams and Seth Rogen as Margot and Lou, this is the story of a couple whose marriage is tested when Margot becomes intensely attracted to their neighbour, Daniel (Luke Kirby).

Sarah Polley's **Take This Waltz**

Another talented actress turned filmmaker is Ingrid Veninger, whose second solo directorial effort, **i am a good person/i am a bad person**, is an observant study of a mother/daughter relationship as they travel through Europe together and apart. Vancouver's prolific Carl Bessai continued his 'family trilogy' with **Sisters & Brothers**, an amusing and insightful look at four sets of siblings. Michael Dowse (*Fubar, Fubar II*) returned with **Goon**, an insightful and often hilarious comedy about Canada's national sport, revolving around a behemoth hockey player, Doug Glatt (Seann William Scott), recruited to fight and fight only.

Leonard Farlinger's wry **I'm Yours** features Rossif Sutherland and Karin Vanasse as Robert and Daphne, who meet at a party in New York and decide to drive to Canada. Along the way, more than a few borders are crossed. Notably absent from the roster of veteran Canadian filmmakers in 2011 is Atom Egoyan. While working on his next feature project, Egoyan was appointed a Distinguished Scholar at his *alma mater*, the University of Toronto, and is working on directing a theatrical production to be mounted in 2012.

Philippe Falardeau's **Monsieur Lazhar**

Cinema in Quebec continued to impress in 2011, following on the international success of Denis Villeneuve's *Incendies* in 2010. Philippe Falardeau's **Monsieur Lazhar** (Canada's official submission to the Oscars for Best Foreign Language Film) is a tender and surprising drama about an Algerian immigrant in Quebec who, in his role as a substitute teacher, befriends two children who are trying to cope with traumatic events in their lives. Stephane Lafleur's **Familiar Grounds** (*En terrains connus*) is a tale of suburban anomie revolving around a brother and sister who try to deal with the death of their mother and their cantankerous father.

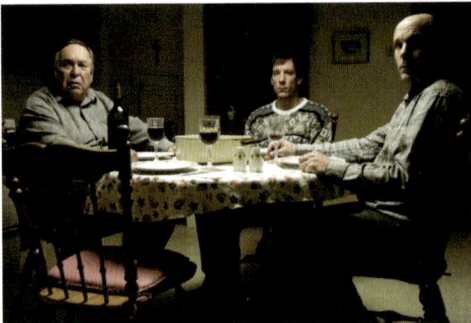

Stephane Lafleur's **Familiar Grounds**

One of the most engaging and commercially successful films of the year was Ken Scott's **Starbuck**. The film stars Patrick Huard (see also *Bon Cop, Bad Cop*) as Daniel Wozniak, a middle-aged man working in the family butcher shop and trying to pay off his serious debts and keep his life together. To make matters worse, Daniel is visited by a lawyer who tells him that his sperm donations of two decades earlier have resulted in 533 children, about 150 of whom want to meet their biological father. From this fertile premise, *Starbuck* then unfolds its amusing meditation on the meaning of parenthood, community, and, in Daniel's prodigious case, fatherhood.

Ken Scott's **Starbuck**

Canada's esteemed documentary tradition delivered such works as Léa Pool's **Pink Ribbons**, a sensitive and politically charged film about breast cancer. Harold Crooks and Mathieu Roy's **Surviving Progress** offers a trenchant and perceptive exploration of the very idea of 'progress' itself in our civilization. Also excellent is Montreal filmmaker Tony Asimakopoulos's utterly absorbing personal portrait-cum-diary about his Greek-Canadian origins, his family, and struggles with drug addiction, **Fortunate Son**.

In addition to the returns of several veteran Canadian filmmakers, this year yielded a number of very impressive debut features from new talents: Anne Emond's **Nuit #1**, for example, is a Breillat-inspired, intimately nuanced drama about a one-night sexual and existential stand between two twenty-

Anne Emond's **Nuit#1**

something Montrealers who meet in a dance club; Guy Edoin's **Wetlands** (*Marécages*) is a haunting, poetic drama of a rural Quebec family's dairy farm in economic collapse; **Romeo Onze**, by Ivan Grbovic, is an understated, deeply moving story of a young Lebanese-Canadian man's search for romance online as well as escape from his tyrannical father; Yonah Lewis and Calvin Thomas co-wrote and co-directed their deft 'no-budget' coming of age story, **Amy George**, about Jesse (Garbiel del Castillo Mullaly), a teenager who wants to be more than friends with his neighbour, Amy (Emily Henry). These four films, in addition to Nathan Morlando's visually arresting debut feature about a fabled Canadian gangster, **Edwin Boyd**, signal a very bright future indeed for Canadian cinema.

Guy Edoin's **Wetlands**

The year's best films
Starbuck (Ken Scott)
Wetlands (Guy Edoin)
Take This Waltz (Sarah Polley)
Keyhole (Guy Maddin)
Monsieur Lazhar (Philippe Falardeau)

Directory
All Tel/Fax numbers begin with (+1)
Academy of Canadian Cinema & Television, 172 King St E, Toronto, Ontario, M5A 1J3. Tel: (416) 366 2227. Fax: (416) 366 8454. www.academy.ca.
Canadian Motion Picture Distributors Association (CMPDA), 22 St Clair Ave E, Suite 1603, Toronto, Ontario, M4T 2S4. Tel: (416) 961 1888. Fax: (416) 968 1016.
Canadian Film & Television Production Association, 151 Slater Street, Suite 605, Ottawa, Ontario, K1P 5H3. Tel: (613) 233 1444. Fax: (613) 233 0073. ottawa@cftpa.ca.
La Cinémathèque Québécoise, 335 Blvd de Maisonneuve E, Montreal, Quebec, H2X 1K1.Tel: (514) 842 9763. Fax: (514) 842 1816. info@cinematheque.qc.ca. www.cinematheque.qc.ca.
Directors Guild of Canada, 1 Eglinton Ave E, Suite 604, Toronto, Ontario, M4P 3A1. Tel: (416) 482 6640. Fax: (416) 486 6639. www.dgc.ca.
Motion Picture Theatre Associations of Canada, 146 Bloor Street W, 2nd Floor, Toronto, Ontario, M5S 1P3. Tel: (416) 969 7057. Fax: (416) 969 9852. www.mptac.ca.
National Archives of Canada, Visual & Sound Archives, 344 Wellington St, Ottawa, Ontario, K1A 0N3. Tel: (613) 995 5138. Fax: (613) 995 6274. www.archive.ca.
National Film Board of Canada, PO Box 6100, Station Centre-Ville, Montreal, Quebec, H3C 3H5. Tel: (514) 283 9246. Fax: (514) 283 8971. www.nfb.ca.
Telefilm Canada, 360 St Jacques Street W, Suite 700, Montreal, Quebec, H2Y 4A9. Tel: (514) 283 6363. Fax: (514) 283 8212. www.telefilm.gc.ca.

TOM McSORLEY is Executive Director of the Canadian Film Institute in Ottawa, a Sessional Lecturer in Film Studies at Carleton University, film critic for CBC Radio One, and a Contributing Editor to *POV Magazine*.

لجنة أبوظبي للأفلام
ABU DHABI FILM
COMMISSION

Chile Hugo Diaz Gutiérrez

Sadly, 2011 witnessed the depature of Raúl Ruiz, one of Chile's greatest filmmakers who died at the age of 70.

It was also a turbulent year. A student social movement not only resulted in the Sebastian Piñera administration reaching its lowest level of approval amongst the population, it raised the issue of quality free education. Amidst of this tension, cultural bodies and filmmakers were open in their support the students' cause.

José Luis Torres' **Summer**

Sebastian Lelio's **The Year of the Tiger**

Two films based on the 2010 earthquake were released in quick succession, with filmmakers both exploiting the disaster and looking at it from a social level. **03:34, Earthquake in Chile** (*03:34, Terremoto en Chile*) by Juan Pablo Ternicier, presents a descriptive, albeit shallow, interpretation of the tragic event, employing three interconnected narratives and aimed squarely at the commercial market. By contrast, Sebastian Lelio's **The Year of the Tiger** (*El año del tigre*) is a powerful drama about a middle-aged convict, Manuel, struggling to find his family in the aftermath. The film develops strong characters and simple, yet solid, storytelling. An Independent Jury Award, and praise by *Variety* and the *Hollywood Reporter* at the Locarno Film Festival, saw the film go on to participate at

festivals in Toronto and Mar del Plata. At home, it was selected for Valdivia and later and would also screen at the 4th Cine//B Film Festival.

José Luis Torres Leiva presented a slow-paced poetic vision of the world in **Summer** (*Verano*). The film looks at the relationships amongst people during one hot summer day at a thermal resort in southern Chile. Venice Film Festival selected it for the Orizzonti section.

Nostalgia For Light (*Nostalgia de la luz*), a unique documentary written and directed by Patricio Guzmán, created in co-production with Germany and Spain, suggests the world is a much smaller place than we think, where everything is interconnected. He draws parallels between the astronomers who make

Patricio Guzmán's **Nostalgia For Light**

![Abu Dhabi Film Commission logo]

the most of the Chilean desert heights and the relatives of those whose lives were taken by the Pinochet regime and who are likely buried in the same location as the scientists work; one group look towards the sky, while the other furrow through the earth, both experiencing hope and despair. Beautifully shot, the film was premiered in Cannes in 2010 and received the European Film Award for Best Documentary.

The Best Chilean Film Award, handed out at the Santiago Film Festival, went to Oscar Godoy's **Ulysses** (*Ulises*). It tells the story of Julio, a Peruvian teacher who has to survive class hostility and xenophobia in Santiago de Chile. A raw but honest film, it explores the Ulysses Syndrome when immigrants suffer the stress of being separated from loved ones, in allusion to the mythological hero.

Oscar Godoy's **Ulysses**

After seven years, Andrés Wood directed another Chilean submission for the Foreign Language Academy Awards. **Violeta Went to Heaven** (*Violeta se fue a los cielos*) is a biopic of Violeta Parra, one of the most influential folk artists in Latin America. Superbly played by Francisca Gavilán, the musical biopic captured audiences with its emotional and stylish narrative. It was the top-grossing domestic film of 2011.

Despite current political instability, Chilean cinema is growing. Each year, the range of themes and styles becomes more ambitious, with the industry finding the right balance between art and commerce.

Andrés Wood's **Violeta Went to Heaven**

The year's best films
Violeta Went to Heaven (Andrés Wood)
The Year of the Tiger (Sebastián Lelio)
Ulysses (Oscar Godoy)
Nostalgia for the Light (Patricio Guzmán)
Summer (José Luis Torres Leiva)

Directory
All Tel/Fax numbers begin (+56)
Consejo Nacional de la Cultura y las Artes, Fondo de Fomento Audiovisual, Plaza Sotomayor 233, Valparaíso. Tel: (32) 232 66 12. claudia.gutierrez@consejodelacultura.cl. www.consejodelacultura.cl
Corporación de Fomento de la Producción (CORFO), Moneda 921, Santiago. Tel: (2) 631 85 97. Fax: (2) 671 77 35. lordonez@corfo.cl. www.corfo.cl.
Ministerio de Relaciones Exteriores, Dirección de Asuntos Culturales, Teatinos 180, Santiago. Tel: (2) 679 44 07. Fax: (2) 699 07 83. acillero@minrel.gov.cl. www.minrel.cl

HUGO DIAZ GUTIÉRREZ is a journalist, screenwriter, film critic, and former editor of the Catalogue of the Valdivia International film Festival and FIDOCS.

China Luna Lin

On the surface, China's film industry continues to grow in 2011, continuing the two-year boom that began in 2009. Box-office revenue reached US$1.9billion up to the end of November, a 40 per cent increase on the previous year. The number of multiplexes also increased. However, after two years of explosive growth, the industry, and particularly outside interests who threw themselves into the business, are seeing the bitter light of day. Most local productions experienced fierce competition in the market and ended up losing money or seeing little profit. Cinema developers also found it more difficult to recoup their investment. More importantly, the audience has become increasingly disappointed with quality of the films on offer.

At the end of 2010 and beginning of 2011, Jiang Wen's western-styled action drama **Let the Bullets Fly** (*Rang Zi Dan Fei*) impressed Chinese audiences with the story of an intriguing battle of wits between bandits, government officials and local gangsters during the 1920s. Ge You's enthralling performance and the mild political satire have pushed the film's box office to an astonishing US$105million, making it the most successful Chinese film to date. Jiang Wen, also known for

Peter Chan Ho-sun's **Wu Xia**

the Cannes-winning World War II satire drama *Devils on the Doorstep*, imbued his first action film with high commercial values, but also offered something distinctive and new to an audience who are used to fancy choreography and wire work. The film's Spaghetti Western-style and its ornate period features also offered a refreshing experience.

Contrary to the success of *Let the Bullets Fly*, 2011 was a year of setbacks for many other action/martial arts films. Peter Chan Ho-sun's **Wu Xia**, starring Donnie Yen, Takeshi Kaneshiro and Tang Wei, is set in 1917 and tells the story of a martial arts fighter who wishes to retreat to a remote village and a peaceful life. However, he becomes inadvertently involved in a duel between a sheriff and his old clan. The film's

Jiang Wen's **Let the Bullets Fly**

Siu-Tung Ching's **The Sorcerer and the White Snake**

attempt to break the tradition of martial arts films with new devices and plot mechanisms was not appreciated by audiences, who stayed away from the film. Other martial arts period dramas such as **The Sorcerer and the White Snake** (*Bai She Chuan Shuo*), starring Jet Li and Eva Huang, about an ancient legend in which a young scholar falls for a beautiful women without knowing she is the thousand year-old white snake in human form; and **Mural** (*Hua Bi*), starring Sun Li in another fantasy feature, also performed poorly.

According to local distributors, about 90 per cent of the domestic production released in China in 2011 lost money. This decline is worse than it had been in 2010, which saw 80 per cent of all the films released failing to recoup their original investment. It is a serious situation that shows little sign of improving.

China's State Administration of Radio, Film and Television (SARFT) estimates that by the end of 2011, film production volume will be around 500 films, which is around the same as

Teng Huatao's **Love is Not Blind**

last year. The total box-office revenue of 2011 is likely to reach US$2billion. In the exhibition sector, industry players say that there will probably be in the region of 2,500 new screens opening by the end of the year, making the total number in excess of 8,000.

However, compared with the box-office growth in 2011, it is not that difficult to see that the per-screen average takings has dramatically decreased. Essentially, not as many people are going to see the films. Zhao Jun, CEO of Guangdong Province Film Corporation, stated that the per-screen average dropped more than 40 per cent in 2011. And most of the cinema managers report that their revenue dropped between 10 and 40 pre cent. This, according to Zhao, reflects the consequences of the hasty development of the cinema business, both in terms of production and exhibition.

Gu Changwei's **Love For Life**

While 2010 saw many romantic comedies failing both commercially and critically, the last year witnessed something of an improvement. Gu Changwei's **Love For Life** (*Zui Ai*), starring Zhang Ziyi and Aaron Kwok, is an unconventional love story set in a so-called AIDS village. Zhang and Kwok play a couple diagnosed as being HIV-positive. The film deals with their battle, both against the disease and for each other, against seemingly insurmountable odds.

Love is Not Blind (*Shi Lian San Shi San Tian*), directed by Teng Huatao, is the dark horse of

2011. This cute contemporary drama set in Beijing chronicles the 33 days following a young woman's break-up with her boyfriend and the beginning of a new romance. Two new actors, Wen Zhang and Bai Baihe, created a refreshing on-screen chemistry in this Chinese version of *Bridget Jones' Diary*. The film was made on a relatively small budget of US$1.5million, but took in more than US$50million locally. It is proof that big budgets and explosions are not necessary to draw in crowds. The film's marketing strategy, using Weibo (Chinese Twitter) and various social networks, is regarded as a perfect model case for film marketing. It has also made stars of its two leads.

Zhang Meng's **The Piano in a Factory**

If *Love is Not Blind* saw new talent shooting up the ranks of the industry, others saw their star rise a little more gradually. Zhang Meng's **The Piano in a Factory** (*Gang De Qin*), starring Qin Hailu and Wang Qianyuan, is a contemporary story set in cold northeastern China and is about a loving father who attempts to build a piano from scratch in order to win the heart, and custody, of his daughter. Zhang's sincere and humorous take on the simple dream of a group of ordinary people saw the film pick up a number of nominations at the Golden Horse Awards, with actor Wang Qianyuan winning the Best Actor award at Tokyo International Film Festival. However, the film saw little box-office traction from local audiences.

Du Jiayi's **Kora** (*Zhuan Shan*), which starred Chang Shu-hao and was a contemporary road

Teng Yong-hsing's **Return Ticket**

movie about a young man's bicycle journey to Tibet, also received little interest from audiences.

Return Ticket (*Dao Fuyang Liubai Li*) focuses on something of a rare topic in contemporary Chinese cinema. It deals with the life of a cleaning lady who leaves her village for Shanghai in order to make a living. She joins up with other cleaners who, when they realise that they cannot return home for the Chinese New Year, decide to rent an illegal bus. Sophomore filmmaker Teng Yong-hsing's poetic style blends well with the film's sharp take on people living at the lower end of city life. It won the Best Original Screenplay and Best Supporting Actress prizes at the Golden Horse Awards. Sadly, the film is still struggling to secure a theatrical release in China.

Zhang Yimou's **The Flowers of War** (*Jinlin Shisan Chai*) set during Japan's invasion of Nanjing, prior to the outbreak of World War II, is an ambitious film that combines thrilling battle

Du Jiayi's **Kora**

scenes, soul-stirring drama and convincing performances by Christian Bale and Chinese newcomer Ni Ni. Zhang succeeds in avoiding the clichés and mythology that surround the Nanking Massacre, instead creating a moving story about humanity. In one of the film's most memorable moments we see, from a small girl's point of view, a group of prostitutes sacrificing their lives in order to save a group of choir girls from the brutality of Japanese soldiers.

In fact, before winning box-office and critical acclaim, Zhang's film had already won a battle against China's film exhibitors. *The Flowers of War* producer, Zhang Weiping, requested a 2 per cent rise in the box-office revenue share, from 43 to 45 per cent, but was rejected by the majority of China's theatre owners. The dispute was later settled and the exhibitors yielded to Zhang's request, agreeing to a 45 per cent share of the box-office revenue for the distributor, with the exhibitors taking 55 per cent. After the dispute, SARFT suddenly announced a new policy, suggesting that exhibitors take less than 50 per cent of all box-office revenue. This has been generally seen as an important victory for filmmakers against cinema owners.

Zhang Yimou's **The Flowers of War**

Jiang Wen's **Let the Bullets Fly**

The year's best films
Let the Bullets Fly (Jiang Wen)
Love For Life (Gu Changwei)
Love is Not Blind (Teng Huatao)
The Flowers of War (Zhang Yimou)
The Piano in a Factory (Zhang Meng)

Directory
All Tel/Fax numbers begin (+86)
Beijing Film Academy, 4 Xitucheng Rd, Haidian District, Beijing 100088. Tel: (10) 8204 8899. http:www.bfa.edu.cn.
Beijing Film Studio, 77 Beisanhuan Central Rd, Haidan District, Beijing 100088. Tel: (10) 6200 3191. Fax: (10) 6201 2059.
China Film Archive, 3 Wenhuiyuan Rd., Xiao Xiao Xitian, Haidian District, Beijing 100088. Tel: (10) 6225 4422. chinafilm@cbn.com.cn.
China National Film Museum, 9, Nanying Rd., Beijing 100015. Tel: (10) 64319548. cnfm2007@yahoo.com.cn

LUNA LIN is a Beijing-based journalist and consultant who contributes to the Beijing *City Weekend magazine* and consults several Beijing-based film companies.

Colombia Pedro Adrián Zuluaga

Colombian cinema seems to have undergone an identity crisis in 2011. The response to this situation has been a polarisation between mainstream entertainment and more art-house fare. These poles were best represented by Carlos César Arbeláez's **The Colours of the Mountain** (*Los colores de la montaña*) and Alejandro Landes's **Porfirio**.

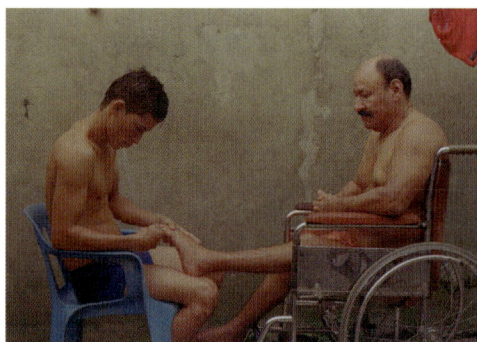

Alejandro Landes's **Porfirio**

Carlos César Arbeláez's **The Colours of the Mountain**

The former achieved great success in the domestic market and played well at a number of festivals, in addition to being selected as the Colombian entry for the Best Foreign Film Award at the 2012 Oscars. The film offered a realistic account of the plight of children having to leave their homes because of an armed conflict; it was shot on location and features remarkable performances by its cast. Audiences responded well to the completely new viewpoint from which the conflict was shown.

Porfirio screened at the 'Directors' Fortnight' in Cannes and will be the gala opening of the revamped Festival de Cine de Cartagena in February 2012. It tells the real-life story of a handicapped man who hijacks an airplane to attract the attention of the Colombian government. The film's protagonist is the perpetrator of the actual hijacking, but the film's style ensures that it remains at one remove from reality. The aesthetic choices made by Landes resulted in the film's appeal to a narrower audience.

Another risky and innovative film is **All Your Dead Ones** (*Todos tus muertos*) by Carlos Moreno, which opened in Sundance, winning the Best Cinematography award. It tells the story of a massacre that occured on the country's election day, but as with *Porfirio*, it avoids any direct or graphic representation of the event. *All Your Dead Ones* employs black, absurdist humour to comment on the indifference of the establishment in the face of violence.

Carlos Moreno's **All Your Dead Ones**

Another film that employed a more intimate approach to social, political or violent events was Gabriel Rojas's **Karen Cries on a Bus** (*Karen llora en un bus*). The film, which premiered at Berlin, follows the exploits of a woman who attempts to liberate herself from chauvinistic oppression and is clearly inspired by Nora, the central character of Ibsen's 'A Doll's House'.

Colombian Postcards (*Postales colombianas*) by Ricardo Coral and **Silence in Paradise** (*Silencio en el paraíso*) by Colbert García both opened during the second half of the year and offer a much more immediate and less elaborate drama. Both are constructed around episodes related to the illegal hearings and extrajudicial executions that the right-wing government of Álvaro Uribe Vélez carried out from 2002 to 2010. The first is narrated as a series of comedy sketches, while the second flirts with melodrama.

Jaime Osorio's **El Paramo**

El Paramo (*El páramo*) by Jaime Osorio and **Greetings to the Devil** (*Saluda al diablo de mi parte*) by Juan Orozco, are the countriy's main genre entries. However, they still draw on the harsher issues facing Colombian society. Osorio's horror film depicts a platoon of soldiers who gradually lose their minds during battle. Adopting the thriller mode, Orozco follows one man as he avenges those who kidnapped him.

If there is a trend that dominated 2011, it was the industry's uncertainty over what it is that audiences crave. At the same time, funding remains an issue. While Congress processed a law to promote foreign investment for films shot in Colombia, there are internal battles for control of this disparate and far from fully organised industry.

The year's best films
Porfirio (Alejandro Landes)
The Colours of the Mountain (Carlos César Arbeláez)
El Paramo (Jaime Osorio)
All Your Dead Ones (Carlos Moreno)
Greetings to the Devil (Juan Orozco)

Directory
All Tel/Fax numbers begin (+57)
Colombian Association of Documentary Film Directors, Calle 34, No 6-59, Bogotá. Tel: (1) 2459961. alados@aladoscolombia.com / www.aladoscolombia.com
Colombian Film Archives, Carrera 13, No 13-24, Piso 9, Bogotá. Tel: (1) 2815241. Fax: (1) 3421485. info@patrimoniofilmico.org.co / www.patrimoniofilmico.org.co
Colombian Film Commission, Calle 35, No 4-89, Bogotá. Tel: (1) 2870103. Fax: (1) 2884828. info@filmingcolombia.com / www.filmingcolombia.com
Film Promotion Fund, Calle 35, No 4-89, Bogotá. Tel: (1) 2870103. Fax: (1) 2884828. claudiatriana@proimagenescolombia / www.proimagenescolombia.com
Ministry of Culture, Film Division, Calle 35, No 4-89, Bogotá. Tel: (1) 2882995. Fax: (1) 2855690. cine@mincultura.gov.co / www.mincultura.gov.co
Kinetoscopio Magazine, Carrera 45, No 53-24, Medellín. Tel: (4) 5134444. Fax: (4) 5132666. kinetoscopio@kinetoscopio.com / www.kinetoscopio.com
Cinemateca Distrital, Carrera 7, No 22-79, Bogotá. Tel: (1) 2837798. Fax: (1) 3343451. direccioncinemateca@fgaa.gov.co / www.cinematecadistrital.gov.co

PEDRO ADRIÁN ZULUAGA is a journalist and film critic who has contributed to Colombian and international magazines and newspapers.

Croatia Tomislav Kurelec

The last year saw only five films funded by the Croatian Audiovisual Centre. However, there were also five independently-funded films, which makes the most number of releases since 2009. Faced with severe economic crisis at home, Croatian filmmakers have became more inventive in finding alternative funding, often through co-productions with other countries and supported by EU organisations. This explains the participation of so many other countries in the production of Croatian films (in total, nine of the films were produced with foreign involvement). The cooperation has imbued the Croatian film industry with new ideas and contributed to the stalling of any ongoing project due to a lack of funds.

2011 was less successful in terms of quality, with only Tomislav Radić's **Kotlovina** offering any real substance. The film is named after one of Croatia's typical dishes, a meat mix where each ingredient retains is own specific flavour, but at the same time the aroma created makes for a unique specialty. Radić also blends the protagonists in his film in the same manner. They are members of a large family, along with neighbours and friends, who gather at a country house and who want to celebrate their Croatian traditions, including Kotlovina, to a relative who fled socialist Yugoslavia with her mother many years before. Radić skilfully builds each character, playing with the popular stereotypes of the Croatian mentality, as well as the country's political demographic, to explore both traditional and modern trends and attitudes in Croatian society. Directing the film like a true virtuoso and employing a documentary style, Radić uses the family gathering to evoke a microcosm of Croatian society.

Stanislav Tomić, the author of some forty documentary films, worked with a low budget for his first feature, **Josef**, which deals with Croatian soldiers in the Austro-Hungarian army during World War I who found themselves on the battlefields of Russia. The film is spectacular and offers an interesting yet bizarre tale about identity tags that a soldier inherits from his deceased brother-in-arms, which later save the life of a Russian officer. Tomić successfully depicts the horrors of war and an individual's loss of identity during battle. His film is also full of fascinating details, such as the name inscribed on the identity tag – Josip (the Croatian for Josef) Broz – which was the name of the Yugoslav president Tito, alluding to suspicions regarding his Croatian nationality, as he spoke his mother tongue with a noticeable Russian accent.

Stanislav Tomić's **Josef**

Aldo Tardozzi's debut deals with more contemporary themes – youth, the night life and clubbing in Zagreb – in his fascinating thriller **Blurs** (*Fleke*). The director recreates an authentic ambience and atmosphere in a film that shows the length two girls go to in order to survive a horrendous night.

Perhaps more intriguing is experimental film director Dan Oki's **Darkness** (*Mrak*).

Dan Oki's **Darkness**

His second feature-legth film, shot in black and white, is an off-beat crime drama about a serial killer and his family and friends, which successfully combines the aesthetic influence of the French New Wave with the Mediterranean mentality and the atmosphere of Split, Croatia's largest city on the Adriatic coast.

Also worth noting is a current trend towards children's films. This season saw two extremely good film productions. Daniel Kušan's **Koko and the Ghosts** (*Koko i duhovi*) is based on his father Ivan Kušan's novel about a group of boys who help to capture a thief pretending to be a ghost, in order to scare people away from hunting for buried treasure. The film received the Pula Film Festival Audience Award.

Tomislav Žaja's **The Little Gypsy Witch** (*Duh babe Ilonke*) is an inventive combination of the realistic and fantastic, which tells the tale of an atypical Gypsy girl and her family, who leave a settlement to live in an apartment in Zagreb

Daniel Kušan's **Koko and the Ghosts**

and are faced with being ostracised by their own community.

Despite the economic difficulties, Croatian film production is on the rise. And although the audience figures have once again decreased, the interest in local films – particularly comedies – has given filmmakers fresh impetus to focus their energies. And if last year was not one of Croatia's best, there exists the talent to ensure the industry keeps working.

The year's best films
Kotlovina (Tomislav Radić)
Josef (Stanislav Tomić)
Darkness (Dan Oki)
Blurs (Aldo Tardozzi)
Koko and the Gosts (Daniel Kušan)

Tomislav Radić's **Kotlovina**

Directory
All Tel/Fax numbers begin with (+385)
Hrvatski filmski savez (Croatian Film Clubs' Association), Tuškanac 1, 10000 Zagreb. Tel / Fax: (1) 484 8764. vera@hfs.hr
HAVC – Hrvatski audiovizualni centar (Croatian Audiovisual Centre), Zvonimirova 20, 10000 Zagreb. Tel: (1) 465 5439 Fax: (1) 465 5442 info@havc.hr.

TOMISLAV KURELEC has been a film critic since 1965, mostly on radio and television. He has directed five short films and many television items. From 2007 to 2009 he was the artistic director of the Days of the Croatian Cinema festival in Zagreb.

Cuba Jorge Yglesias

A tendency to deal with sordid aspects of Cuban society has characterised a number of film releases over the last year. One of them, Juan Carlos Cremata's **Chamaco**, is a tough story of gay juvenile prostitution, as well as institutional and personal corruption. Reprtedly filmed with a budget of only US$100, it has an underground quality which is in stark contrast to its theatrical mise-en-scène. Night time in Havana has never been so tragic and oppressive.

Ian Padrón's **Habanastation**

Gerardo Chijona's **Ticket to Paradise**

Gerardo Chijona's **Ticket to Paradise** (*Boleto al paraíso*) had a great impact on its audience, thanks to the representation of what its director calls a 'lethal mixture of inexperience, ignorance, innocence and abusive families'. The film is based on the true story of some youths who, in 1993, chose to be infected with AIDS in order to enter a sanatorium where they seek refuge. By contrast, Ian Padrón's **Habanastation** is a variation on the 'Prince and the Pauper' theme – an urban fable about two boys who studied in the same school, one of whom was son of a well-known musician and lived in a huge mansion, while the other lived in a shanty town. By chance, the 'rich'

boy has to spend some hours in the kingdom of his 'poor' schoolmate. In style the film might be the closest Cuban cinema has come to Bollywood.

Filmed in just fourteen days, Enrique Álvarez´s **Marina** tells the story of a young girl who returns to her native city, Gibara, to discover that her father has died, his house no longer belongs to her, and the life of people that she once knew has changed. Only when she meets a young fisherman and his grandfather does she begin to re-orientate herself to her circumstances. A contemplative work, slow-paced and with little dialogue, it is an unusual chamber piece.

Enrique Álvarez's **Marina**

Alejandro Brugués' **Juan of the Dead**

An unexpected surprise arrived with **Juan of the Dead** (*Juan de los Muertos*), a zombie comedy written and directed by Alejandro Brugués. Paying homage to many works of the genre, it tells the story of a group of misfits who decide to make a profit out of fighting the zombie invasion of their homeland. The combination of cartoonish humour and political allusions offers a pointed commentary on contemporary Cuban life.

Jorge de León's **Bad Girl**

The last year also produced some fine documentaries. **Bad Girl** (*La niña mala*) is a shrewd work by Jorge de León. A black and white triptych about a teenage girl who lives in a mountainous region in east Cuba, it begins with scenes of her daily life in a humble hut, followed by the sermon of a preacher against vice and covetousness and ends with images of a party that saw the girl's sexuality flourish.

Marcel Beltran's **Open String** (*Cuerda viva*) documents the lives of Anolan, a viola player who lives with her mother in Havana and Gerardo, a Sierra Maestra peasant. Though seemingly very different, they share a strong commitment to their work and the fear of not achieving their goals. Damián Sainz's **Jeffrey:**

The Project (*Jeffrey, el proyecto*) was another fascinating portrait, about a body builder who migrates to the US wanting to follow in the steps of his idol, Arnold Schwarzenegger.

Together, these films show Cuban cinema to be fully active and full of passion and ideas.

The year's best films
Chamaco (Juan Carlos Cremata)
Juan of the Dead (Alejandro Brugués)
Bad Girl (Jorge de León)

Juan Carlos Cremata's **Chamaco**

Directory
All Tel/Fax numbers begin (+53)
Cuban Institute of Art and Cinema Industry (ICAIC), Calle 23, No 1155, Entre 8 & 10, Vedado, Havana. Tel: (7) 8383650. Fax: 8333281. internacional@icaic.cu. www.cubacine.cu.
Escuela Internacional de Cine y TV, Carretera Vereda Nueva, Km 4½, San Antonio de Los Baños. Tel: (47) 383152. Fax: 382366. eictv@eictv.org.cu. www.eictv.org.
Festival Internacional del Nuevo Cine Latinoamericano, Calle 2, No. 411, Entre 17 & 19, Vedado, Havana, Cuba CP 10400 festival@festival.icaic.cu, habanafest@festival.icaic.cu (World Registration). www.habanafilmfestival.com

---

JORGE YGLESIAS is a poet and film critic, and Professor of Film History and Chair of Humanites at the International School of Film and Television of San Antonio de los Baños, Cuba.

Cyprus Ninos-Feneck Mikelidis

Although the establishment of a cultural organisation, promised three years ago by the ministry of Culture and Education, has yet to be implemented, the Cultural Services of the Ministry have been quite busy, financing various projects and festivals (Cyprus Film Days, Short Film Festival etc).

For the promotion of Cyprus as a place for filming by foreign production companies, the Cultural Services have been keeping a stand at Thessaloniki Film and Drama Festivals, as well as at Cannes. Together with the Advisory Film Committee and the Union of Film Directors, they are looking into incentives for the promotion of co-productions with other countries.

Over the course of the last year, the Ministerial Committee for Films approved the financing of six short film projects, one feature documentary, three scriptwriting projects for low-budget features and three for higher-budget films. In the meantime, five short films, one documentary and ten feature films are currently in production.

A number of Cypriot films have been shown at various festivals – three short films in the Drama Short Film Festival and Yiannis Economides' **Knifer**, which opened the Panorama of European Cinema Film Festival.

Elias Dimitriou's **Fisn'n'Chips**

It went on to pick up seven prizes at the Greek Film Academy Awards, including Best Film, Best Direction and Best Screenplay.

Newcomer Elias Dimitriou's **Fish'n'Chips** is a light, fresh and warming comedy that participated at festivals in Montreal and Montpelier. It tells the story of an immigrant Greek Cypriot, working at a fish and chip shop in London, who decides to return to Cyprus to start a similar business there, only to find out that things are not as easy as he imagined.

Elias Dimitriou's **Fisn'n'Chips**

Three feature films are currently nearing completion: Andreas Pantzis's **The Joy and Sorrow of the Body** (*I hara ke I thlipsi tou somatos*), Aliki Danezi-Knudsen's **Chinatown: The Three Shelters** and Christina Hadjizachariou's **Loveless Zorica**.

Directory

Ministry of Education and Culture of Cyprus, Cultural Services/Cinema Section, Kimonos Street, Nicosia, 1434. Tel: (+357 2) 2800 0982.

NINOS-FENECK MIKELIDIS is an historian of Greek cinema and film critic for the Athens daily newspaper *Eleftherotypia*. He is also the founder and director of the Panorama of European Cinema film festival in Athens.

لجنة أبوظبي للأفلام
ABU DHABI FILM
COMMISSION

INTERNATIONAL FILM GUIDE CYPRUS | 99

FILMING in CYPRUS

Locations, Incentives, Resources

There's always a new world to discover.

Cyprus lies at the crossroads of three continents, where East
meets West, where deep blue seas, sandy beaches,
captivating forests, breathtaking mountains, unique
archaeological sites, monasteries, churches and enchanting
locations await for you to discover them.

Probably your next filming destination.

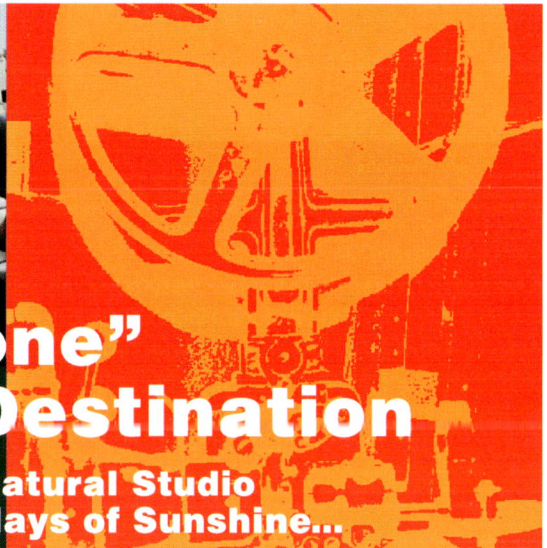

The "all in one"
Filming Destination
One Island. One natural Studio
with almost 360 days of Sunshine...

Ministry of Education and Culture of Cyprus
Cultural Department (Cinema Advisory Committee)
Kimonos and Thoukididou, 1434 Nicosia, Cyprus
Tel.: 0035722800982 Fax.: 0035722809506
Email: echristo@cytanet.com.cy   http:www.moec.gov.cy

Czech Republic Jana Záhorková

zech cinema in 2011 saw the release of 25 features and 19 documentaries, and the loss of a towering figure of European culture and politics.

For the first time in years, Hollywood returned to Prague. Despite the reduction in film incentives, Tom Cruise brought his team to the country, placing Czech locations at the top of the international box-office chart with the succesful *Mission Impossible: Ghost Protocol.*

Miroslav Ondruš's **Vendetta**

Over the last year, there was a noticable increase in genre films made by Czech directors, a contrast to the social dramas that had dominated the national cinema over previous years. The thriller was represented by a young generation of filmmakers. Miroslav Ondruš debuted with **Vendetta** (*Vendeta*), the story of a doctor who hungers for revenge after his teeanage daughter was raped and murdered by her schoolmates. Ondruš built tension through the strong performances of Ondřej Vetchý and Oldřich Kaiser.

Tomáš Řehořek's **Czech Made Man** balances thrilling drama with bitter comedy. It tells the story of a businessman who profits from people's stupidity. Řehořek, who debuted a

Zdeněk Jiráský's **Flower Buds**

year ago with a docu-dramatic investigation of the Pervitin community in Prague in the late 1980s, here once again shows his skill as a director. However, the film that may likely garner plaudits come the awards season is Zdeněk Jiráský's drama **Flower Buds** (*Poupata*).

Petr Nikolaev, who replaced an ailing Alice Nellis on **Lidice**, delved into complex human relationships with the story of a man who unintentionally kills his son in a fight, and because of his incarceration would eventually be the only remaining survivor of Lidice village which was burned to the ground by Nazis. The film starred Karel Roden, who would also appear in **The Therapy** (*Terapie*), an

Petr Nikolaev's **Lidice**

international HBO production. It is the first time that Czech television has been involved in such as ambitiuos venture.

Director Jiří Vejdělek turned in another comedy with **Men in Hope** (*Muži v naději*), while F. A. Brabec directed the country's first 3D feature, **In the Duvet** (*V peřině*). Unfortunately, critics were dismissive of his naïve family musical.

A potential international hit, **Alois Nebel**, is a visually striking animated feature directed by Tomás Lunák, based on the artwork of Jaroslav Rudiš. Employing the rotoscope technique, the adaptation of Rudiš's comic trilogy was unveiled at Venice and is a possible contender for the 2012 Oscars. The only question is whether it will be nominated as a feature or animated film.

Matěj Mináč's **Nicky's Family** (*Nidkycho rodina*) is about the 669 – mostly Jewish – children saved by Nicolas Winton, who brought them to the UK, saving them from death in concentration camps. The film picked up awards at Karlovy Vary, Jerusalem and Montreal. Sir Nicolas Winton, now 101 years of age, attended the film's premiere in Prague.

The year also saw former Czech president, political writer and playwright Václav Havel debut, at the age of 74, as a film director. **Havel's Leaving** (*Odcházení*) divided audiences with its absurd story, based on one of Havel's plays. Although his ambition remained as strong as ever, his inexperience as a filmmaker was evident. Sadly, prior to Christmas, he passed away. His loss was measured by the international community, as well as the local populace, who attended a memorial service in his honour.

Next year will see **The Last of Aporver** (*Poslední z Aporveru*), a 3D fantasy that Tomáš Krejší has been working on for over ten years. It is an homage to the great Czech filmmaker and animator Karel Zeman. The same director is also preparing the first post-revolution adaptaion of Karel Čapek's **Battle with Salamanders** (*Válka s mloky*).

Tomáš Luňák's **Alois Nebel**

The year's best films
Alois Nebel (Tomáš Luňák)
Lidice (Petr Nikolaev)
Perfect Days (Alice Nellis)
Poupata (Zdeněk Jiráský)
Vendeta (Miroslav Ondruš)

Directory
All Tel/Fax numbers begin (+420)
Association of Czech Filmmakers (FITES), Pod Nuselskymi Schody 3, 120 00 Prague 2. Tel: (2) 691 0310. Fax: (2) 691 1375.
Association of Producers, Národní 28, 110 00 Prague 1. Tel: (2) 2110 5321. Fax: (2) 2110 5303. www.apa.iol.cz.
Czech Film & Television Academy, Na Îertvách 40, 180 00 Prague 8. Tel: (2) 8482 1356. Fax: (2) 8482 1341.
Czech Film Centre, Národní 28, 110 00 Prague 1. Tel: (2) 2110 5302. Fax: (2) 2110 5303. www.filmcenter.cz.
FAMU, Film & Television Faculty, Academy of Performing Arts, Smetanovo 2, 116 65 Prague 1. Tel: (2) 2422 9176. Fax: (2) 2423 0285. kamora@f.amu.cz. Dean: Karel Kochman.
Ministry of Culture, Audiovisual Dept, Milady Horákové 139, 160 00 Prague 6. Tel: (2) 5708 5310. Fax: (2) 2431 8155.
National Film Archive, Malesická 12, 130 00 Prague 3. Tel: (2) 7177 0509. Fax: (2) 7177 0501. nfa@nfa.cz. www.nfa.cz.

JANA ZÁHORKOVÁ is a Czech journalist. She is the editor of the culture section of news portal *iDNES.cz* and also writes for *MF DNES* newspapers.

Denmark Christian Monggaard

I t's difficult not feeling a bit like Alice travelling through Wonderland when you look at Danish cinema over the course of the last year – it is nothing if not paradoxical.

Apparently, everything is going very well. Early in 2011, Susanne Bier won an Oscar for *In a Better World*, Lars von Trier created headlines at his press conference in Cannes, while Kirsten Dunst won an award for her performance in the Danish director's apocalyptic **Melancholia**. Also in Cannes, Trier's younger colleague, Nicolas Winding Refn, won the director award for his first American production, *Drive*. And then, in December, the Danes scooped up no fewer than five awards at the European Film Awards in Berlin. Susanne Bier won for directing, *Melancholia* won three prizes, including Best European Film, and the Danish actor Mads Mikkelsen was presented with an award for European Achievement in World Cinema.

Lars von Trier's **Melancholia**

There are Danish directors travelling abroad – to Britain and America – to direct films, and Danish actors acting in everything, from David Fincher's *The Girl with the Dragon Tattoo* to Steven Spielberg's *War Horse*. And if that wasn't enough, in December the Danish Film Institute released numbers showing that Danish films had sold more than 3.4 million tickets in Denmark in 2011, which raised the domestic market share to 28 per cent, the third best year in the last decade and the best since the record set in 2008. Why are we still complaining then?

Birgitte Stærmose's **Room 304**

Danish production companies are still struggling. Just five of the 24 feature films produced last year account for 60 per cent of all the tickets sold. The remaining 19 films more or less under-performed, with five titles (**Beast**, **Room 304**, **Skyscraper**, **Miss Julie**, **Love is in the Air**) selling less than 3,000 tickets each, while a sixth (**ID:A**) just managed to scrape past 10,000 tickets.

Although all but one of the Danish films released were produced with substantial government support, those numbers tell the story of an industry fighting to stay alive. Companies are scaling back and laying-off staff. Even Zentropa, Lars von Trier and Peter Aalbæk Jensen's maverick company, at the forefront of Danish cinema for the last twenty years, is now having serious financial problems.

On top of all this comes uncertainty of what the future might have in store for the film industry in terms of distribution and sales. The internet has changed everything and the film industry, particularly the exhibition sector, is desperately trying to find a model that will still make money as more films are released simultaneously in cinemas and on VoD and DVD/Blu-ray platforms.

That day is not far off and the film industry's different players are arguing over how to test the different possibilities, including shortening or even dispensing with the hold back-period between the cinema and VoD/DVD releases. Everybody is nervous and nobody wants to take too much of a chance.

2011 has also been a lacklustre year artistically. Although a few high points have reaffirmed one's belief in Danish cinema, most of these films come from one specific sphere – the family drama.

Lars von Trier's *Melancholia* is a fascinating and beautiful drama about two sisters, depression and the end of the world. Again, Trier defies our expectations and begins the film with the very destruction of Earth. He then backs up, detailing the events at a large family gathering, in the days leading up to the apocalypse. The Prelude of Wagner's *Tristan und Isolde* underscores the drama of two very different sisters, played by Dunst and Charlotte Gainsbourgh, who gradually realise their fate. The film only sold 60,000 tickets in Denmark, but performed well internationally.

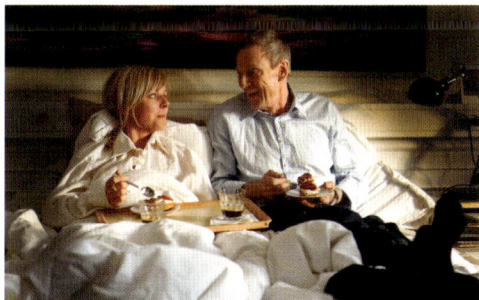

Pernille Fischer Christensen's **A Family**

Martin Zandvliet's **A Funny Man**

A Funny Man (*Dirch*), Martin Zandvliet's follow up to his critically acclaimed debut *Applause* from 2009, was the bestselling Danish film of the year, with 483,000 tickets sold. It told the entertaining yet tragic story of one of Denmark's most beloved comedians and actors, Dirch Passer. Dirch was indeed a funny man, but he also wanted to be taken seriously as an actor, which audiences wouldn't, or couldn't, tolerate, which caused him great pain and eventually broke him. Nikolaj Lie Kaas delivers a strong performance as Dirch, who has worked closely with the actor's father, the comedian and actor Preben Kaas.

Esben Toft Jacobsen's **The Great Bear**

Other highlights of 2011 include Esben Toft Jacobsen's **The Great Bear** (*Den kæmpestore bjørn*), a beautiful animated fairy-tale about two quarrelling siblings and a gigantic, but very sweet bear. Pernille Fischer Christensen's **A Family** (*En familie*) is a harrowing drama about a dying father (Jesper Christensen) and his beloved daughter (Lene Maria Christensen). Lotte Svendsen's entertaining

Lotte Svendsen's **Max Embarassing 2**

Max Embarrassing 2 (*Max Pinlig 2*) about
teenager Max (Samuel Heller Seiffert) and his
mother (Mette Horn), who is, frankly, rather
embarrassing. Heidi Maria Faisst's brilliant
Rebounce (*Frit fald*) tells the tale of a confused
teenage girl (Frederikke Dahl Hansen) and her
relationship with her irresponsible mother
(Anne Sofie Espersen), who doesn't know
how to be a mother. Finally, Kresten Vestbjerg
Andersen, Thorbjørn Christoffersen and Philip
Einstein Lipski's funny and foulmouthed
animated feature **Ronal the Barbarian** (*Ronal
Barbaren*), is an irreverent riff on both *The Lord
of the Rings* and *Conan the Barbarian*.

Vestbjerg Andersen, Christoffersen and Einstein Lipski's **Ronal the Barbarian**

The year's remaining commercial hits were
mostly broad comedies, including Rasmus
Heide's **All for One** (*Alle for én*), Ole Christian
Madsen's **SuperClásico**, Niels Nørløv's **The
Reunion** (*Klassefesten*), or so-called family
films, such as Peter Dodd's animated **Freddy
Frogface** (*Orla Frøsnapper*) and Claus Bjerre's
Father of Four – Back to Nature (*Far til fire –
tilbage til naturen*). *SuperClásico* was the best
of the bunch, selling 185,000 tickets and telling
the rambunctious story of a boring Danish man

(Anders W. Berthelsen), who visits a colourful
and vibrant Buenos Aires to win back his wife
(Paprika Steen) who is living with an Argentine
footballer.

Ole Christian Madsen's **SuperClásico**

The big disappointment of 2011 was the failure
of the youth-oriented film, with Simon Staho's
musical *Love is in the Air* (*Magi i luften*), Hans
Fabian Wullenweber's **Bora Bora** and Rune
Schjøtt's *Skyscraper* (*Skyskraber*) all falling
short artistically. It also caused quite a stir that
Staho's film received nine million Danish kroner
(€1.2million) in government support while
selling a paltry 2,983 tickets, but still managed
to secure state funding for his next feature.

Christoffer Boe tried to shake things up
with the Cronenberg- and Żuławski-inspired
relationship-drama *Beast*, which deservedly
didn't find an audience, while Christian E.
Christiansen failed to marry a character-
based drama with *Bourne*-style action in the
overwrought thriller *ID:A*.

Christian E. Christiansen's **ID:A**

Eva Mulvad's **The Good Life**

Few Danish documentaries made an impact at the local cinemas, although a few good films were made. Eva Mulvad's **The Good Life** (*Det gode liv*) echoed the Maysles Brothers' classic *Grey Gardens* in its touching story of a mother and daughter who have fallen on very bad times. Anne Regitze Wivel's **Svend** portrayed the director's late husband, the idealistic Danish politician and former minister Svend Auken. And in Mads Brüggers **The Ambassador** (*Ambassadøren*), the director buys himself diplomatic status and travels to central Africa to become rich and expose the corruption and depravation of the region. It's certainly not a dull film and, as always with Mads Brügger, his methods were hotly debated at screenings and in the media.

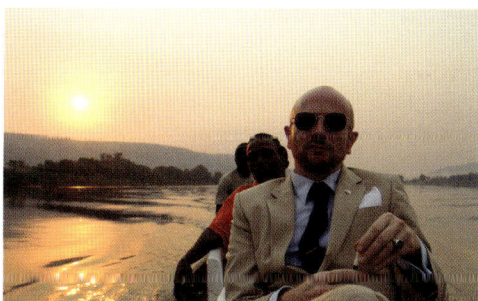

Mads Brüggers' **The Ambassador**

CHRISTIAN MONGGAARD is the film editor and film critic at the daily Danish newspaper *Information*. He has written/contributed to several books on films, freelances for different magazines and regularly serves on FIPRESCI juries at film festivals around the world.

The year's best films
A Funny Man (Martin Zandvliet)
Rebounce (Heidi Maria Faisst)
A Family (Pernille Fischer Christensen)
Melancholia (Lars von Trier)
The Good Life (Eva Mulvad)

Heidi Maria Faisst's **Rebounce**

Directory
All Tel/Fax numbers begin (+45)

Danish Film Institute/Archive & Cinemateque (DFI), Gothersgade 55, DK-1123 Copenhagen K. Tel: 3374 3400. Fax: 3374 3401. dfi@dfi.dk. www.dfi.dk. Also publishes the film magazine, Film.

Danish Actors' Association (DSF), Sankt Knuds Vej 26, DK-1903 Frederiksberg C. Tel: 3324 2200. Fax: 3324 8159. dsf@skuespillerforbundet.dk. www.skuespillerforbundet.dk.

Danish Film Directors (DF), Vermundsgade 19, 2nd Floor, DK-2100 Copenhagen Ø. Tel: 3583 8005. Fax: 3583 8006. mail@filmdir.dk. www.filmdir.dk.

Danish Film Distributors' Association (FAFID), Sundkrogsgade 9, DK-2100 Copenhagen Ø. Tel: 3363 9681. Fax: 3363 9660. www.fafid.dk.

Danish Film Studios, Blomstervaenget 52, DK-2800 Lyngby. Tel: 4587 2700. Fax: 4587 2705. ddf@filmstudie.dk. www.filmstudie.dk.

Danish Producers' Association, Bernhard Bangs Allé 25, DK-2000 Frederiksberg. Tel: 3386 2880. Fax: 3386 2888. info@pro-f.dk. www.producent-foreningen.dk.

National Film School of Denmark, Theodor Christensen's Plads 1, DK-1437 Copenhagen K. Tel: 3268 6400. Fax: 3268 6410. info@filmskolen.dk. www.filmskolen.dk.

Ecuador Gabriela Alemán

Documentary film played a major role in Ecuadorian cinema in 2011. Fernanda Restrepo's **With My Heart in Yambo** (*Con mi corazón en Yambo*) not only broke box-office records locally, it became a key factor in re-opening a judicial case that involved the disappearance of the Restrepo brothers in the late 1980s. The documentary, told from the point of view of the director of the film who is also the sister of the disappeared men, explores the power of memory, both individual and collective. In the process of detailing the kidnapping, torture and disappearance of her brothers in 1988, she reconstructs Ecuador's recent past and the authoritarian government of León Febres Cordero. Restrepo's achievement will likely be prized as one of the country's best films for years to come.

Fernanda Restrepo's **With My Heart in Yambo**

2011 was also the first year the National Film Counsel (Consejo Nacional de Cine) partially financed all Ecuadorian films distributed domestically. However, even with state support, it still takes an average of five years to see a film go from script to screen. This may change with the increased profile of local films and the elevated profile of directors such as Yanara

Carla Valencia's **Grandfathers**

Guayasamín, Carla Valencia, Sebastián Cordero and Tania Hermida. Each of these filmmakers saw their films competing at international festivals. Guayasamín's animated short **Behind the Mirror**, about the 19th century painter Joaquín Pinto, competed in the Havana Film Festival; Carla Valencia's **Grandfathers** won the Best Documentary award at Biarritz; Cordero's fourth film, **Fisherman**, competed at San Sébastian, and Hermida's long-awaited second feature, **In the Name of the Girl** (*En el nombre de la hija*), screened at the Havana and Rome film festivals.

Tito Jara's **Behind You**

Even though documentary output dominated in terms of quality, the biggest-grossing film of the year was Tito Jara's **Behind You** (*A tus espalda*), a drama that looked at class differences in modern-day Quito. Hermida's *In*

Hermida's **In the Name of the Girl**

the Name of the Girl, which portrayed the life of a nine-year-old girl living in 1970s Ecuador, also performed well. Cordero's *Fisherman*, which focused on the temptations faced by a poor man who could make money through the drug trade, opened in late December and looked set to perform well over the Christmas period.

Of the documentaries, Bernard Josse and Etienne Moine's **Growing Up** (*Grandir*) is a moving documentary about child/adult relations in the Ecuadorian region of Pifo. Gabriela Calvache's **The Silent Walls** (*Labranza oculta*), explores a different way of approaching the history of Ecuador's capital – the protagonists are the bricklayers restoring a 17th century house. Cristina Carrillo's **Curly Haired** (*La Churon*), explores religious devotion and migration, while Miguel Alvear's **Beyond the Mall** (*Más allá del mall*) employs a Chinese box structure – a fake documentary resembling a fiction film that is actually a documentary in its attempt to question the very notion of filmmaking in Ecuador. It is a true delight, funny, reflexive and critical, and the must see film of the year.

Bernard Josse and Etienne Moine's **Growing Up**

A number of films are due out in 2012. They include new works by Javier Andrade, Sandino and Wilson Burbano, Alfredo León and Iván Mora. The Burbano's are likely to be the first in cinemas, having almost completed post-production.

The year's best films
Beyond the Mall (Miguel Alvear)
With My Heart in Yambo (Fernanda Restrepo)
Grandfathers (Carla Valencia)
Growing Up (Bernard Josse and Etienne Moine)
Joaquín Pinto, Defying Oblivion (Yanara Guayasamín)

Miguel Alvear's **Beyond the Mall**

Directory
All Tel/Fax numbers begin (+593)
INCINE, Vizcaya E13-39 & Valladolid, Tel. 290 4724, info@incine.edu.ec, www.incine.edu.ec
Cine Memoria Corporation, Veintimilla E8-125, Quito, Tel. 290 2250, info@cinememoria.org, www.cinememoria.org
Consejo Nacional de Cine (CNC), www.cncinecuador.blogspot.com

GABRIELA ALEMÁN is a freelance reporter and the author of six fiction books. Her latest, *Album de familia*, has been optioned for a film. She teaches at USFQ and UASB in Ecuador and is currently working on an anthology of Latin American horror movies.

Egypt Sherif Awad

The year began with revolution in Egypt, which affected all areas of film production and distribution, not to mention audience's cinema-going habits.

The mid-January period, normally a popular time for cinemas, was completely wiped-out with most theatres closed, particularly those in downtown Cairo and Alexandria. Eventually, Egyptian producers had to pull their new releases, after just a few weeks of playtime, when their publicity campaigns failed to attract audiences, who remained in Tahrir Square or followed the news on TV. With cinemas cancelling their midnight shows due to nationwide curfews, the regional box-office loss exceeded US$5million.

Karim Abdel-Aziz in **We Will Be Right Back**

Early releases that received some exposure at the box office included Ahmed Ezz's vehicle **365 Days of Happiness** (*365 Youm Saada*) and Karim Abdel-Aziz in **We Will be Right Back** (*Fasel Wa Naood*). The former is a romantic comedy in which Ezz plays a wealthy womaniser who eventually falls in love with a beautiful young woman only to discover she has just one year to live. Directed by Said El-Marok, known for his work on Lebanese music videos, his debut is similarly glitzy, but the film's lavish settings sat at odds with the country's current state. *We Will be Right Back* found Karim

Abdel-Aziz in his usual cocktail of action and comedy, in which he plays a lower-class, widowed taxi driver looking for his kidnapped young son. The film's two screenwriters, on the basis of what they delivered, seem to have suffered from writer's block. The result is overly indebted to Sylvester Stallone's *Over the Top* and Christopher Nolan's *Memento*.

The names of many stars who openly opposed or criticised the revolution were eventually gathered in a so-called 'Black List' that demanded the boycotting of their works. Among these victims was comedian Talaat Zakereya, whose summer release **The Elephant in the Handkerchief** (*El-Feel Fel Mandeel*) bombed at the box office as a direct result of a campaign across social media that urged filmgoers to keep away from screens showing the film.

Emad Abou-Ghazy, the newly appointed Minister of Culture, decided to cancel all film festivals and art events in Egypt until the end of 2011, apparently for security reasons. However, within a few months, he re-thought his decision and allowed the 27th Alexandria Film Festival for Mediterranean Countries to go ahead, awarding it the usual annual grant of US$200,000. It became the first festival and art event to take place in the aftermath of the revolution.

A number of new film associations have been formed in order to set up their own festivals in 2012. Luxor, Sharm Al-Sheikh and Cairo – in a new format – are among the festivals scheduled for the new year.

A large number of short films and documentaries were shot about the revolution, many by young and upcoming filmmakers,

ABU DHABI FILM
COMMISSION

Neveen Shalaby's **I and the Agenda**

employing every piece of technology – from cellphones to digital cameras. As a result, the festival in Alexandria created a special programme for these films. It included Neveen Shalaby's documentary **I and the Agenda**, which questioned the conspiracy theories behind foreign intervention in the Arab Spring. Established filmmakers also went to the Cannes festival with **18 Days**, a collection of short films screened as part of the tribute to Egyptian revolution.

18 Days

A number of figures in the Egyptian film industry saw their profiles raised over the last year. *Screen International* profiled actress Arwa, who appears in **None But That, Like Today** and rising filmmaker Ayten Ameen, director of the segment *The Bad* in the documentary **Tahrir 2011: The Good, the Bad and the Politician**, which premiered in Venice. *Variety Arabia* focused on Amr Waked as one of five Most Promising Arab Filmmakers in a special event during the Abu Dhabi Film Festival.

Films such as **Tahrir 2011, 18 Days** and Amr Salama's sophomore feature **Asma'a** were co-funded by Gulf film festivals, where they received their exclusive Arab premieres. However, they are still awaiting an Egyptian release. *Asma'a* is inspired by a true story and shot on 16mm. Its eponymous heroine is a young woman, played by Heind Sabry, who hides from her father and teenage daughter the news that he is HIV-positive.

Amr Salama's **Asma'a**

Most of the released films during the three main seasons of summer and the two feasts of Eid Fitr and Eid Adha showed that producers preferred to finance comedies rather than big-budget action films. A comedy like **Tick Tick Boom** starring Mohamed Saad, who also wrote the screenplay, woefully took advantage of the themes of the January 25 revolution for small gains at the regional box office. Saad plays Tekka, a character similar to his idiotic Lemby creation, who becomes embroiled in the chaotic aftermath of the revolution, when criminals broke out of jails and police stations. Because the audience was fed up with Saad's unfunny mannerisms,

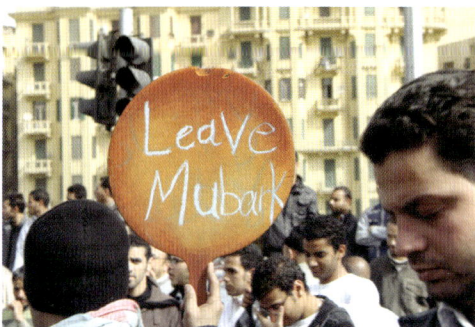

Tahrir 2011: The Good, the Bad and the Politician

the film performed worse than expected, coming in second to **Pyramids Avenue** (*Sharei El-Haram*), a musical comedy which takes place in and around the nightclubs of this famous tourist attraction. It stars singer Saad El-Soghayar and bellydancer Dina. Eid Adha also saw Ahmed Mekky return with an unconventional comedy called **Sima Aly Baba**, which is the name of a famous cinema in downtown Cairo that used to play second-run films *à la* grindhouse cinemas. The comedy had two segments: the first is a spoof of *Star Wars*, with Mekky transferred to another galaxy, while the second takes place in a farm with Mekky playing a bully returning home to his old flame. Like all of Mekky's comedies, *Sima Aly Baba* doesn't know its audience, with the many barely-hidden sexual innuendos often appearing tasteless. Other comedies continued to rip-off their American originals; **Me or Him** (*Yana Ya Howa*) reworked Jim Carrey's *Me, Myself and Irene* while **X-Large** remodelled Eddie Murphy's *The Nutty Professor* for its popular star Ahmed Helmy.

18 Days

With the release of twenty feature films in 2011, compared to thirty in 2010, Egyptian film production faces many challenges, both in terms of quality and quantity. However, the future very much rests of the political outcome of the next year or so.

The year's best films

18 Days (Sherif Arafa, Mariam Abou-Ouf and many others)
Tahrir 2011: The Good, The Bad and The Politician (Tamer Ezzat, Ayten Amin and Amr Salama)
Asma'a (Amr Salama)
I and the Agenda (Neveen Shalaby)

Directory

All Tel/Fax numbers begin (+20)
Chamber of Film Industry, 1195 Kornish El Nil, Industries Union Bldg, Cairo. Tel: 578 5111. Fax: 575 1583.
Egyptian Radio & TV Union, Kornish El Nil, Maspero St, Cairo. Tel: 576 0014. Fax: 579 9316.
National Egyptian Film Archive, c/o Egyptian Film Centre, City of Arts, Al Ahram Rd, Guiza. Tel: 585 4801. Fax: 585 4701. President: Dr Mohamed Kamel El Kalyobi.
National Film Centre, Al-Ahram Ave, Giza. Tel: 585 4801. Fax: 585 4701.

SHERIF AWAD is an Egypt-based film and art critic who also curates cinema and art across Europe. Besides his many contributions to Arab and European publications, he produces TV shows in the pan-Arab area.

ABU DHABI FILM
COMMISSION

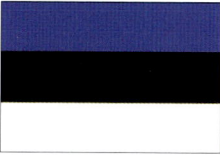

Estonia Jaan Ruus

Despite the economic recession, eight full-length features, including one animation, were made in Estonia in 2011. Moreover, it was this very animation film, **Lotte and the Moonstone Secret** (*Lotte ja kuukivi salads*), which collected 40 per cent of the annual box-office revenue of Estonian-produced films, ending up in sixth place in the total rankings of the year's top earners. Directors Heiki Ernits and Janno Põldma continue the story of the tomboy dog-girl character who debuted in a 2000 TV series, this time in a sweet and heartfelt road movie fairy-tale. Lotte has also become a very popular local merchandising brand, often outstripping the revues of imported, internationally renowned characters' spin offs.

International festivals responded well to **Graveyard Keeper's Daughter** (*Surnuaiavahi tütar*), Katrin Laur's cautionary anti-alcohol tale of the relationship between a mother and her eight-year-old daughter. It was awarded the Best Film of the Estonian programme of Tallinn's Black Nights Film Festival, the jury's statement singling out the 'director's respect for the life struggles of her protagonists'. Caring for a people – or, rather, the lack of it – has been a regular theme in recent Estonian

media. This may very well be the reason why such a warm reception was given to *Lotte and the Moonstone Secret*'s directors' statement regarding the absence of violence in their film. It was also a theme of discussion regarding Rainer Sarnet's expressive, theatrical take on Dostoyevsky's **The Idiot** (*Idioot*). The visually polished film (it was shot by Mart Taniel) is nevertheless a somewhat eclectic take on the novel, although the compassionate and soul-searching Count Moshkin (Risto Kübar) easily found sympathy among a recession-era audience.

Sulev Keedus's **Letters to Angel**

Two striking films employed a poetic approach to their subject matter, although their appeal remained local. Playwright Mart Kivastik offers hope in an old man's twilight years

with **A Friend of Mine** (*Üks minu sõber*), the writer's directorial debut. While in the richly metaphorical **Letters to Angel** (*Kirjad Inglile*), Sulev Keedus, who has found endless inspiration in the films of Andrei Tarkovsky, paints a desolate picture of a small Estonian town as seen through the eyes of an Estonian returning from Afghanistan and who has converted to Islam. By contrast, the tediously crude comedy **Farts of Fury** (*Kormoranid ehk Nahkpükse ei pesta*) followed a group of ageing rockers as they attempted a comeback.

Andres Maimik and Kaidi Kaasik's **Kuku, I Will Survive**

Feature documentaries offered a more rewarding experience. Kristina Norman's **A Monument to Please Everyone** (*Et meeldiks kõigile*) is a tragicomic profile of the two architect-engineers who designed the new national symbol, the War of Independence Victory Column. As it follows them on their journey to Canossa, the film profiles the various eccentric characters they encounter along the way. Andres Maimik and Kaidi Kaasik's tough documentary **Kuku, I Will Survive** (*Kuku: mina jään elli*), depicts the never-ending fight with alcoholism by the renowned film actor Arvo Kukumägi. Arko Okk explores the possibilities of 3D through the recollections of the popular late President Lennart Meri in **Monologues 3D** (*Monoloogid 3D*), while internationally renowned photographer Raphael Gianelli-Meriano interviews a socially conscious Estonian poet and essayist in **The Kaplinski System** (*Kaplinski süsteem*) and the Estonian-Finnish-Swedish-Cuban documentary **El Medico: The Cubaton Story** (*Cubaton*) looks at the conflict between a folk music enthusiast and the music industry. However,

the year's most important film **The New World** (*Uus maailm*), which took radio journalist Jaan Tootsen five years to make, is a chronicle of the hope and dreams of activists in a small community who attempt to live a bohemian lifestyle. By turns funny and sad, Tootsen's film is a moving sociological document that led to much debate in the media and went on to win the Neitsi Maali (Maali the Virgin) award, which is awarded to the year's best Estonian film by the the Estonian Association of Film Journalists.

Local animated shorts continue to prosper at international festivals. Last year's surreal puppetry film **Sky Song** (*Taevalaul*), by Mati Kütt, toured 36 festivals, while Ülo Pikkov's **Body Memory** (*Keha mälu*), depicting the existential fight of 'cord men', visited as many as 51 festivals in the three months following its premiere.

Ülo Pikkov's **Body Memory**

State grants for the film industry have remained at the same level despite the recession, although producers are feeling the rising cost of production. The Estonian Film Foundation has prioritised the financing of comedy and children's films, and intends to employ expert advice from distribution and marketing specialists in order to attract larger audiences.

The general cinema attendance has increased slightly, rising to two million in 2010, the first time it has achieved this figure since the country's independence, over two decades ago. The number of international releases exhibited locally has increased dramatically, reaching 191 in 2011. On top of that are the 22 Estonian features and documentaries.

Box-office revenues are also growing, having reached €7.8million in 2010. The top ten films highlight the popularity of animated features – the top six films are all animated.

Although the price of the average cinema ticket fell to €3.7 in 2010, by the turn of 2011/2012 the price had risen to €6.5 for evening and weekend screenings in multiplex cinemas. There are twelve permanently operating cinemas in the country.

Another memorable cinematic event was the site-specific coastal screening of **60 Seconds of Solitude in Year of Zero** (*60 sekundit üksindust aastal Null*), part of the closing ceremony of Capital of Culture year in Tallinn, which featured minute-long films from all over the world collected by Veiko Õunpuu and Taavi Eelma.

In April 2012, Estonian cinema will celebrate its 100th anniversary, when Tartu's cinema 'Imperial' screened a demonstration of footage showing biplanes flying over the town. It was filmed by the country's first cameraman Johannes Pääsuke. A whole year of festivities is planned, with the country's president acting as patron. To celebrate the anniversary, the Estonian Association of Film Journalists, along with film academics, selected the ten best Estonian films of the last century. They are: *Autumn Ball* (Veiko Õunpuu, 2006); *The Madness* (Kaljo Kiisk, 1968); *The Springtime* (Arvo Kruusement, 1969); *The Last Relic* (Grigori Kromanov, 1969); *Georgica* (Sulev Keedus, 1998); *The Ideal Landscape* (Peeter Simm, 1980); *Nipernaadi* (Kaljo Kiisk, 1983); *The Hotel of the Dead Alpinist* (Grigori Kromanov, 1979); *Keep Smiling, Baby!* (Leida Laius and Arvo Iho, 1985); *The Temptation of St Tony* (Veiko Õunpuu, 2010).

JAAN RUUS works as a film critic for the leading Estonian weekly, *Eesti Ekspress*. He is the founder of the Estonian FIPRESCI and the Artistic Director of Tallinn Black Nights Film Festival's competition programme.

Jaan Tootsen's **The New World**

The year's best films

The New World (Jaan Tootsen)
Letters to Angel (Sulev Keedus)
Kuku, I Will Survive
(Andres Maimik and Kaidi Kaasik)
A Monument to Please Everyone
(Kristina Norman)
The Memory of Body (Ülo Pikkov)

Directory

All Tel/Fax numbers begin (+372)
Estonian Film Foundation, Uus 3, 10111 Tallinn. Tel: (6) 276 060. Fax: (6) 276 061. film@efsa.ee. www.efsa.ee.
Estonian Association of Film Journalists, Narva mnt 11 E, 10151 Tallinn. Tel: 5533 894. Fax: (6) 698 154. margit.tonson@ekspress.ee
Estonian Filmmakers Union, Uus 3, 10111 Tallinn. Tel: (6) 464 164. Fax: (6) 464 068. kinoliit@kinoliit.ee. www.kinoliit.ee.
Association of Estonian Film Producers, Lootuse pst 62, 11616 Tallinn. Tel: 5646 7769. produtsendid@produtsendid.ee
Union of Estonian Cameramen, Faehlmanni 12, 15029 Tallinn. Tel: 5662 3069. Fax: (6) 568 401. bogavideo@hot.ee.
Association of Professional Actors of Estonia, Uus 5, 10111 Tallinn. Tel: (6) 464 512. Fax: (6) 464 516. enliit@enliit.ee. www.enliit.ee.
Estonian National Archive's Film Archive, Ristiku 84, 10318 Tallinn. Tel: (6) 938 613. Fax: (6) 938 611. filmiarhiiv@ra.ee. www.filmi.arhiiv.ee.
Media Desk Estonia c/o Estonian Film Foundation, Uus 3, 10111 Tallinn. Tel: (6) 276 065. Fax: (6) 276 061. mediadesk@efsa.ee. www.mediadesk.efsa.ee.
Tallinn University's Baltic Film and Media School, Sütiste tee 21, 13419 Tallinn. Tel: (6) 268 124. Fax: (6) 268 108. info.bf@tlu.ee.

Finland Antti Selkokari

In a whirlwind year for Finnish film production, there were 31 film premieres, of which 24 were features and seven were feature-length documentaries. The output was exceptionally high compared with previous years, when the number of productions varied between eight and twelve. This upward curve is explained by the rise of production subsidies channeled through the Finnish Film Foundation. As a result, Finnish films enjoy a total market share of just under 20 per cent. The overall number of admissions for domestic films is expected to be 1.3 million, a decline over previous years, surprising many in the industry.

The most popular domestic release of the year was Swedish director-on-loan Anders Engström's **The Kiss of Evil** (*Vares – pahan suudelma*), which premiered in January and went on to attract a large cross-over audience, racking up 200,000 admissions. A detective thriller based on a local bestselling pulp novel by Reijo Mäki, it featured private eye Jussi Vares handling cases, with a steady supply of damsels and drinks always close to hand. The film's production company, Solar Films, is focusing on the international cinema and TV market with a collection of six films based on Mäki's novels. The films will be directed by Engström and Lauri Törhönen.

Statistically, the most impressive release of the year was Aki Kaurismäki's **Le Havre**, attracting 150,000 admissions. There is little doubt that the positive publicity the film attracted following its screening at Cannes helped. Kaurismäki's story of a young illegal immigrant befriended by a man who shines shoes in the eponymous French port once again highlighted his skill as a filmmaker whose stories resonate universally.

Aki Kaurismäki's **Le Havre**

A documentary of note was **Battle for the City** (*Taistelu Turusta*) by the veteran documentary filmmaker Jouko Aaltonen. He collated impressive footage of the urban landscape in Turku, the former Finnish capital, where a group of businessmen, politicians and architects have combined their mutual interest in redesigning the area, resulting in the loss of historic buildings in favour of a business-oriented utopia. Aaltonen mixes contemporary footage with archive recordings in order to tell the sad story of how progress developed in so many Finnish towns.

Ville Jankeri was one of the year's most impressive new directors. **Sixpack** (*Pussikaljaelokuva*) chronicled events surrounding three young men adrift in their neighbourhood, Kallio. The former proletarian quarters are now occupied by eccentrics who prevent the trio from leaving. It is based on the first novel by Finnish literary phenomenon Mikko Rimminen.

The quantity of films did not translate into better quality across the board. This may account for the decrease in audience attendance. The most depressing proof of this were a number of travesties that focused on or around the subject of celebrity. Elias Koskimies's **Dirty Bomb** (*Likainen pommi*) is a foul-mouthed black comedy in which a music company is desperately searching for a teenager they can transform into a pop sensation. Tuomas Summanen's **Risto** features a celebrity actor who is paralysed in an accident, but when he witnesses how much he can make from his disability, he conceals the fact that he has made a full recovery. Both features fell very short in their attempt to satirise the media. Ultimately, they appeared as little more than extended episodes of a TV sitcom.

Hannes Vartiainen and Pekka Veikkolainen's **The Death of an Insect**

One of the most beautiful and well-traveled films of the year was an experimental short, **The Death of an Insect** (*Erään hyönteisen kuolema*), by Hannes Vartiainen and Pekka Veikkolainen. The eight-minute film combines animation techniques from stop-motion to the 3D modelling of scanned insects and is intoxicating in its sweep. A pleasure to both the eyes and ears – the impressive visuals, in which an insect melds into a DNA spiral and other such wondrous images, is accompanied by Joonatan Portaankorva's jazzy score – it has been an international festival favourite since it made its domestic debut in late 2010.

If the art of film was not always evident throughout the year, the year in Finnish film ended on a high note with the return of Taru Mäkelä and **The Storage** (*Varasto*), her first film in twelve years. It follows a cunning sales girl in a paint shop and how she entraps one of the warehouse workers. The film successfully

Taru Mäkelä's **The Storage**

combines romantic comedy with the current fears over unemployment. Based on a novel by the Finnish cult writer Arto Salminen, it reflects his morbid sense of humour, which has gained him a reputation as a particularly acrid social commentator.

The year's best films

Le Havre (Aki Kaurismäki)
The Storage (Taru Mäkelä)
Battle for the City (Jouko Aaltonen)
The Death of an Insect (Hannes Vartiainen and Pekka Veikkolainen)
Sixpack (Ville Jankeri)

Jouko Aaltonen's **Battle for the City**

Directory

All Tel/Fax numbers begin (+358)
Finnish Film Foundation, Kanavakatu 12, FIN-00160. Tel: (9) 622 0300. Fax: (9) 622 0305. ses@ses.fi. www.ses.fi

---

ANTTI SELKOKARI is a film critic and journalist, who lives in Helsinki.

France Michel Ciment

According to statistics French cinema does not appear to have had it this good since at least 1966. 2010 registered over 206 millions spectators (up 2.9 per cent) and French films took 35.7 per cent of the domestic market (73.7 million tickets sold). The final results of 2011, though not yet compiled, look set to be even better.

Eric Toledano and Olivier Nakache's **Intouchables**

The 263 French films released in 2010 would represent 39 per cent of gross income, among which 18 attracted audiences in excess of one million. The winner of the 2011 box office, **Intouchables** (attracting over 14.5 million spectators), is likely to come in third in the list of the most successful domestic releases of all time, after *Bienvenue chez les Ch'tis* (20.4 million) and *La Grande Vadrouille* (17.3 million). And with 5,500 screens (the largest in Europe), 40 per cent equipped with a digital projection thanks to the help of the National Centre of Cinema (CNC), which has also supported 3D, exhibition has never been so prosperous.

From an artistic point of view, the investment in middle-sized budgets has increased, striking a healthy balance between big productions and small films, which is encouraging. The domination of American films is less prominent than in other countries, although Hollywood still leads the way – particularly among younger audiences – with an audience share of 98 million in 2010 (47.5 per cent of the market). Other European films have shown a spectacular increase with 31 million tickets sold – 15 per cnet of the market. However, this is likely due to the success of *Harry Potter and the Deathly Hallows* and *Inception*, which can hardly be characterized as non-Hollywood product. Conversely, the non-European, non-American films have shown a strong decline, attracting only 3.49 million people, highlighting the meagre state of cultural diversity. The year's top-ten box-office successes bears witness to the domination of Anglo-Saxon fare, with all but two titles coming out of Hollywood studios.

Among the 51 films that registered sales of more than a million tickets, eleven were made in 3D. However, this new technical phenomenon – accompanied by increased ticket prices – does not seem to be quite so enamoured by audiences. A poll showed that of the people tested two-thirds voiced a strong diffidence, while the two biggest successes of the year were shot in the normal format. They were also both comedies, the genre most favoured by the public. The 131 comedies released represented 22 per cent of the films screened and garnered 24.6 per cent of all tickets sold.

The number of documentaries released, 76 in all, broke previous records, representing 13.2 per cent of the films shown, but only 2.6 per cent of the box office. This contrasts strikingly with the small number of animation films (at 24, just 4.2 per cent of the total number of releases), which garnered 16.5 per cent of the

ABU DHABI FILM
COMMISSION

box office – by far the best ratio of all the film categories. There was disappointment with the slight decline at the box office for art-house films, making up just 26.4 per cent of the box office. The year also confirmed an equal share between the monthly receipts, each one totalling at least ten million, while the summer – following the American example – dominated.

French film production also broke records with 261 features (up 31), 143 of which were entirely financed by French companies, 60 with a majority of French funds and 58 with a minority co-production credit. There were not as many feature debuts (63 – 31 per cent of the total – against 42.3per cent in 2009) and less second films (33 – 16.3 per cent – against 20 per cent). This is not a bad sign, considering the number of mediocre fledgling directors. As usual TV channels and especially the private sector (Canal+, TPS Star, Ciné-Cinéma) contributed massively to this production, as well as the Avance sur recettes, which helped the financing of 58 films (among which were 19 feature debuts); 175 different companies produced 203 films, with Les Films d'ici leading with seven films, while big companies such as Pathé and Gaumont producing less than five. This may explain the extreme diversity of the production, as well as some daring experiments.

Distribution showed stability, with 575 films released (down 0.2 per cent). American cinema represented 25 per cent with a healthy increase of European films (up by 23), mostly from Spain, Italy and Germany. There were 121 films screened in digital, another sharp increase (from 23 in 2009 and 57 in 2008). The exhibition sector also proved to be very stable, with 5,500 screens grouped in 2,050 venues. Four new multiplexes opened, taking the total to 178, representing 58.5 per cent of the audience share.

The most spectacular crisis was the bankruptcy of Quinta industries. The Tunisian producer Tarak Ben Ammar, who claimed ten years ago to have saved the French

laboratories LTC and Duran, went broke at the very moment his latest film **Black Gold**, a poor man's *Lawrence of Arabia* directed by Jean-Jacques Annaud, became a commercial and artistic failure. Not only did 115 people lose their jobs, but the completion of a number of films was at stake, along with a film library that numbered in the thousands.

Michel Hazanivicius's **The Artist**

The Cannes Film Festival once again proved to be the best showcase for French films and foreign films with French backing. The most striking example was **The Artist**, selected at the last moment for the competition, which saw Jean Dujardin pick up the Best Actor prize and would go on to garner the most nominations for the 2012 Golden Globes. This pastiche of the age of silent movies, about the fall of a famous comedian and the rise of his potential sweetheart, was brilliantly executed by Michel Hazanivicius, already a master of parodies with *OSS 117*.

Polisse, a docu-drama about a police squad confronted with various criminals in a popular Parisian district, won the Jury Prize for its director Maïwenn, who displayed her usual talent in directing her actors with energy. Both films proved immensely successful at the box office, bridging the gap between auteur cinema and the general audience.

Another competition highlight, but less popular with audiences, was 80-year-old Alain Cavalier's **Pater**. The director plays himself as the president of the Republic, in a dialogue

Maïwenn's **Polisse**

with his prime minister (Vincent Lindon). It is a delightful divertimento, where scenes of chatting and preparing a meal are interspersed with malicious political comments. A less successful entry was idiosyncratic director Bertrand Bonello's **House of Tolerance** (*L'Apollonide*), a static pictorial evocation of a bordello at the end of the 19th century.

Bruno Dumont's **Outside Satan**

The official sidebar section, 'Un Certain Regard', screened three films worthy of the competition and should be ranked as some of the best releases of the year. **Outside Satan** (*Hors Satan*), by Bruno Dumont, shows the director at his peak in exploiting the natural beauty of the northern French landscape, a major character in the story of a magus who both heals and kills people. Pierre Schoeller's second film, **L'Exercice de l'État**, is one of the few truly excellent French political films, which analyses the doubts and shortcomings of a minister and his relationship with his cabinet head, played with conviction by Olivier Gourmet and Michel Blanc. **The Snows of**

Kilimanjaro (*Les Neiges du Kilimandjaro*) is a new opus by Robert Guediguian, which deals with two groups of working-class and lower-middle-class people in Marseilles. These characters, played by the director's wife Ariane Ascaride, Jean-Pierre Darroussin and Gérard Meillan, realise that their life-long left-wing commitment has left them disillusioned, especially when they are robbed of their savings by burglars who belong to the same class. However, Guediguian's moral tale ends with confidence in man's capacity for generosity.

Pierre Schoeller's **L'Exercice de l'État**

An increasing number of directors dealt with social issues in France. Aki Kaurismaki was in competition at Cannes with **Le Havre** (FIPRESCI award and Delluc prize for best French film of the year), a melancholy fable about racism, unemployment and the economic crisis, with a touch of Carné's *Quai des Brumes*, which was shot in the same city. In **Early One Morning** (*De bon matin*), Jean-Jacques Moutout, who has always shown an interest in corporate societies and their pressures on the individual, portrays an employee (played by Jean-Pierre Darroussin) who kills two of his colleagues before committing suicide. The film is an investigation into the reasons of his act.

Cedric Kahn, one of the best directors of his generation, unveiled **A Better Life** (*Une vie meilleure*), about an attempt by a young man (Guillaume Canet) to start a new life by buying a restaurant in the country after he meets the woman of his dreams, but who becomes the prey of his creditors. The theme of debt is also present in *Welcome* director Philippe Lioret's **Toutes nos envies**, an adaptation by of Emmanuel Carrère's *D'autres vies que la mienne*. In linking a character fighting the sub-prime mortgage meltdown and another struggling against a cancer, Lioret might weaken his narrative, but this suggestion nevertheless highlights the seriousness posed by both.

This concern for social issues was also featured in a number of films 'inspired by real events'. This trend, which often lacks imagination, is normally a field reserved for American dramas and is probably due to the influence of TV and media headlines in general. **Rebellion** (*L'Ordre et la Morale*), about the murder of dozens of natives in New Caledonia by the French police, with the support of both the socialist president François Mitterrand and the conservative Prime Minister Jacques Chirac, allowed Mathieu Kassovitz to make his first good film in a decade. It offers a courageous political stance and is impressive for standing by its convictions. Two cases of judicial errors were featured in actor Roschdy Zem's second feature **Omar Killed Me** (*Omar m'a tuer*), which deals with the wrongful imprisonment of a gardener, Omar Raddad, for the murder of his landlady; and Vincent Gareng's **Guilty** (*Présumé coupable*), which traces the ordeal of a man (an extraordinary Philippe Torreton) unjustly accused of sexually abusing children. The latter film finds its strength in concentrating on its protagonist

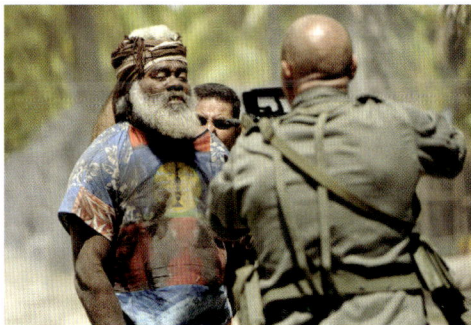

Mathieu Kassovitz's **Rebellion**

and not trying to deal with the whole dossier of the famous 'affaire d'Outreau'.

Two other films failed in reconstructing historical events. Luc Besson's lacklustre **The Lady** reduces the political struggle of Aung San Suu Kyi (a creditable Michelle Yeoh) to a melodramatic story between the Noble Peace prizewinner and her husband. Even more perfunctory was Xavier Durringer's **Conquest** (*La Conquête*), a tepid reenactment of Nicolas Sarkozy's campaign to become president.

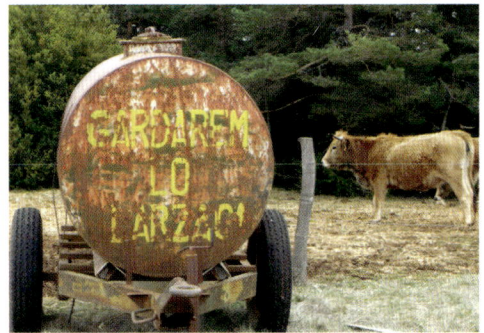

Christian Rouaud's **Tous au Larzac**

A slew of documentaries also confirmed an interest in social issues. Among the best was **Tous au Larzac** by Christian Rouaud, recalling the action (1971–81) by a group of peasants in the centre of France who fought against a law that expelled them from their farms in order for a military camp to be built. Regis Sauder's **Children of the Princess of Cleves** (*Nous, Princesses de Clèves*) is an indirect riposte to Sarkozy, who once declared that this classical French novel was not worthy of its place in the education syllabus. Fifteen teenagers from a modest background discuss the pertinence of the book and how it relates to their own experiences. Equally impressive was **Mafrouza**, a twelve-hour investigation by Emmanuelle Demaris into the slum district of Alexandria, which is built on a Greco-Roman necropolis.

A number of animation artists entered the fantasy realm with their latest features. Joann Sfar, after his biopic of Gainsbourg, adapted his comic strip **The Rabbi's Cat** (*Le Chat du*

Joann Sfar's **The Rabbi's Cat**

rabbin), a tale that evokes the peregrinations of a cat as far as Africa, where he meets Tintin. Inspired by tales from the West Indies, Mexico and Tibet, Michel Ocelot, working in 3D for the first time, employs Chinese shadows in **Les Contes de la nuit** to prove once again his elegance and his wit in the field of animation. Marjane Satrapi's and Vincent Paronnaud's **Chicken With Plums** (*Poulet aux prunes*) also came from her comic strip, but featured live actors remembering family life during the Shah's reign in Iran. A virtuoso exercise, the film baffled some with its elliptical narrative.

Pascal Rabaté's **Holidays in the Sun** (*Ni à vendre Ni à louer*) is a series of vignettes shot in the spirit of Tati, where various characters spend their holidays at a seaside resort, rarely meeting each other but experiencing incongruous incidents. But one of the best films of the year was **Le Tableau** by Jean-François Laguionie, a master of French animation who, in the spirit of Paul Grimault, invents a poetic world where characters, in a painting left unfinished, start to search for the vanished artist and, through the canals of Venice and the deep recesses of a forest, experience a series of encounters. The beauty of the palette enhances the political and aesthetic narrative, which seduced both parents and children alike.

Marjane Satrapi and Vincent Paronnaud's **Chicken With Plums**

Comedies may be numerous in French cinema, but few achieve any artistic status. Olivier Nakache and Éric Tolédano's *Intouchables* is one of the biggest money-makers of all time and proved to be better cinematographically than *Bienvenue chez les Ch'tis*. This Capra-esque utopia of the friendship between a tetraplegic billionaire and a black man from the suburbs proved irresistible for an audience experiencing social and economic problems. The success was due mostly to the performances of François Cluzet and Omar Sy, as well as a number of comic scenarios created by the screenwriters. Another utopian comedy and likewise very popular, was Philippe le Guay's **The Women on the 6th Floor** (*Les Femmes du 6e*), about a rich bourgeois man, played by Fabrice Luchini, who falls in love with his maid living on its sixth floor and whom he is willing to follow to her native Spain.

Jean-François Laguionie's **Le Tableau**

Female directors, besides Maïwenn, also marked the year. **Tomboy**, the second feature of Céline Sciamma, is a delicate study of a young girl who, outside her family circle, pretends to be a boy. This study of gender ambiguities was admirably served by the sensitive performance of Zoe Heran. The sleeper hit of Cannes' 'Critics Week' was another second feature, this time by Valérie Donzelli, entitled **La guerre est déclarée**. It is a Lellouchian drama about two parents dealing with a child who has a brain tumor. Reminiscent of the *nouvelle vague* (employing voice-over, popular music, handheld camera etc), the film has much gusto and energy. In her third feature, **Goodbye First Love** (*Un* amour de jeunesse), Mia Hansen-Løve portrays the troubled heart of her heroine, torn between the youth of a lover and the maturity of a Norwegian architect. She undoubtedly has a delicacy of touch, but it occasionally verges on the conventional.

Claude Miller's **Voyez comme ils dansent**

Finally, Philippe Garrel in **Un été brûlant** offered a pale imitation of his usual themes of romantic love and poetic spleen, while Claude Miller in **Voyez comme ils dansent** proved again that he is one of the major talents of French cinema. It looks at how James Thiérrée's (Charlie Chaplin's grandson and an exceptional acrobat and stand-up comedian) character is viewed by two women (played by Marina Hands and Maria Sansa), at different times in his life.

The year's best films

L'Exercice de l'État (Pierre Schoeller)
Outside Satan (Bruno Dumont)
Voyez comme ils dansent (Claude Miller)
Le Tableau (Jean-François Laguionie)
The Snows of Kilimanjaro (Robert Guediguian)

MICHEL CIMENT is president of FIPRESCI, a member of the editorial board of *Positif*, a radio producer and author of more than a dozen books on cinema.

Directory

All Tel/Fax numbers begin (+33)

Archives du Film, 7 bis rue Alexandre Turpault, 78395 Bois d'Arcy. Tel: (1) 3014 8000. Fax: (1) 3460 5225.

Cahiers du Cinema, 9 passage de la Boule Blanche, 75012 Paris. Tel: (1) 5344 7575. Fax: (1) 4343 9504. cducinema@lemonde.fr

Centre National de la Cinématographie, 12 rue de Lubeck, 75016 Paris. Tel: (1) 4434 3440. Fax: (1) 4755 0491. webmaster@cnc.fr. www.cnc.fr.

Cinémathèque de Toulouse, BP 824, 31080 Toulouse Cedex 6. Tel: (5) 6230 3010. Fax: (5) 6230 3012. contact@lacinemathequedetoulouse.com. www.lacinemathequedetoulouse.com.

Cinémathèque Française, 4 rue de Longchamp, 75116 Paris. Tel: (1) 5365 7474. Fax: (1) 5365 7465. contact@cinemathequefrancaise.com. www.cinematequefrancaise.com.

Ile de France Film Commision, 11 rue du Colisée, 75008 Paris. Tel: (1) 5688 1280. Fax: (1) 5688 1219. idf-film@idf-film.com. www.iledefrance-film.com.

Institut Lumière, 25 rue du Premier-Film, BP 8051, 69352 Lyon Cedex 8. Tel: (4) 7878 1895. Fax: (4) 7878 3656. contact@institut-lumiere.org. www.institut-lumiere.org.

Positif, 3 rue Lhomond, 75005 Paris. Tel: (1) 4432 0590. Fax: (1) 4432 0591. www.johnmichelleplace.com.

Unifrance, 4 Villa Bosquet, 75007 Paris. Tel: (1) 4753 9580. Fax: (1) 4705 9655. info@unifrance.org. www.unifrance.org.

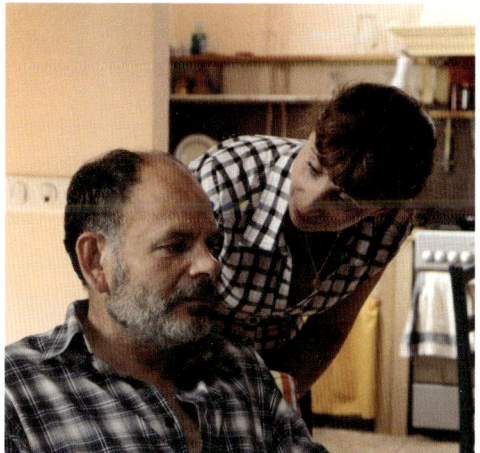

Robert Guediguian's **The Snows of Kilimanjaro**

Georgia Nino Ekvtimishvili

Georgia is the next post-Soviet country after Russia and the Baltic states to become a member of Eurimages in 2011. The annual state cinema subsidy is barely enough for two medium-budget films, so finances were this time divided between dozens of projects, giving them starting money that at least allowed them the freedom to seek further funding through new partnerships. This strategy also allowed for a new cinema magazine *Film Print* (its predecessor disappeared after the post-war financial crisis) and a new award, the Best Script, which is part of a literature competition. Going forward, the main priorities of state funding in 2012 will be the support of script development and European co-production.

Keti Machavariani's **Salt White**

Keti Machavariani's feature debut **Salt White** (*Marilivit tetri*) is a drama about a lonely waitress, working in a summer resort, who is raising money for a café in her hometown. A homeless teenage girl enters her life, who has been dreaming of the coast. She also encounters a policeman who hopes to help her achieve her dream. The film competed at Karlovy Vary, Montreal and Montpellier, and won a Special Prize for Outstanding Actor and the Best Debut Award at Cottbus.

Tamar Shavgulidze's **Born in Georgia**

Another feature debut, Tamar Shavgulidze's post-war drama **Born in Georgia** (*Dabadebulebi Sakartveloshi*) looks at the impact of the conflict on four youths. They are disappointed with a reality they are unable to change, as the war made them weak and their future vague. The conflict is both a mental and physical – as a result of landmines – presence in society, which the film skilfully highlights. The Russian/Georgia conflict is also detailed in **5 Days of War** (*Agvistos khuti dge*), Renny Harlin's American-Georgian action film. Overly propagandist, the tells tells the story of a successful mission by American war correspondents who successfully reported on the conflict, from the heart of the action.

Renny Harlin's **5 Days of War**

Based on a true story, Gikorgi Maskharashvili's criminal drama **The Watchmaker** (*Mesaate*) takes issue with an unfair legal system, the lack of professionalism in the media and the general cruelty of a vengeful society. Making a documentary about someone suspected of serial murders, two journalists discover that the suspect is not guilty, but the accused remains doomed.

Tornike Bziava's Georgian-French short **Nest** (*Bude*) is a very human story about the relationship between an old man and his son. Their still, modest life details how responsibilities shift as one generation grows old and the other comes of age.

Salome Jashi's **Bakhmaro**

Salome Jashi's Georgian-German documentary **Bakhmaro** (*Bakhmaro*) is about the residents of a house in a small Georgian town. The three-story building is full of life, pregnant with the sense of change in society, yet remains a symbol of post-Soviet Georgia. The film received a nomination for Best Documentary at the Asia-Pacific Screen Awards and received an Honorary Mention at the Leipzig International Festival for Documentary and Animated Film, as well as the Best Central and Eastern European Documentary Film award at Jihlava International Documentary Film Festival.

In Konstantine Esadze's documentary **Not White, Black** (*Tetri ara, shavi*), the main character attempts to buy a used car in Germany, in order to bring it back to Georgia and sell it. Zaza Rusadze's and Rusudan

Chkonia's feature debuts **A Fold in My Blanket** (*Chemi sabnis naketsi*) and **Keep Smiling** (*Gaigimet*) will be released in 2012. Rusadze's film is about a young man and his quest to escape from the conformity of society, while *Keep Smiling* is story of ten women competing in a beauty contest for mothers.

The year's best films
Salt White (Keti Machavariani)
Nest (Tornike Bziava)
Bakhmaro (Salome Jashi)
Not White, Black (Konstantine Esadze)

Directory
All Tel/Fax numbers begin (+995)
Batumi International Arthouse Film Festival, 6000 Batumi, Heidar Abashidze st. 14. Tel./fax: (22) 272 479. info@biaff.org. www.biaff.org
Film Studio – Remka, 36 Kostava st., 0179 Tbilisi, Tel: (32) 990 542. Fax: (32) 933 871. remka@remkafilm.ge. www.remkafilm.ge.
Georgian National Film Center, 0105 Tbilisi, Georgia # 4 Z. Gamsakhurdia Sanapiro, 4th Floor. Tel/Fax: (32) 999 200; (32) 999 102, info@gnfc.ge
Independent Filmmakers' Association – South Caucasus" (IFA-SC), Head Office – Georgia, Niko Nikoladze Street 1, Apt. 12, 0108 Tbilisi. Tel: (32) 93 12 50 Fax: (32) 50 60 68. ifasc@ifasc.org.ge.
Ministry of Culture, Monuments Protection and Sport, 4, marjvena sanapiro, 0105 Tbilisi, Georgia, Tel: (32) 987 430, info@mc.gov.ge
Sakdoc Film – 2007, 121 Zemo Vedzisi St., 0160 Tbilisi. Tel: (93) 24 32 72/(93) 32 39 29. info@sakdoc.ge. www.sakdoc.ge.
Sanguko Films, 7 Tamarashvili St., 0162 Tbilisi Tel: (32) 22 40 61. info@sanguko.ge. www.sanguko.ge.
Shota Rustaveli Theater and Film Georgian State University, 0108 Tbilisi, 19 Rustaveli, Tel: (32) 99 94 11; Fax: (32) 98 30 79. www.tafu.edu.ge
Tbilisi International Film Festival, 0112 Tbilisi, Agmashenebeli ave. 164. Tel: 47 51 82. Fax: 35 67 60. office@tbilisifilmfestival.ge. www.tbilisifilmfestival.ge

NINO EKVTIMISHVILI is a freelance journalist who specializes in cinema and art in Georgia.

لجنة أبوظبي للأفلام
ABU DHABI FILM
COMMISSION

Germany Andrea Dittgen

Apart from Til Schweiger's continuing success with yet another lukewarm comedy, the related issues of 3D and digitisation of cinemas shaped German cinema in 2011. While American audiences have become more discerning, Germans have clearly embraced the format despite the higher ticket prices, with 20 per cent of all tickets sold going to 3D films, while on the production side, 3D has become the domain of documentaries and kids entertainment.

The finest example of a 3D film made in Germany was Wim Wenders' **Pina**, an homage to the great German choreographer Pina Bausch. Composed without a story line, Wenders shows her contemporary pieces of performance art carried out by her favourite and closest dancers on stage and, for the first time, also outdoors. The result is a landmark in German film history: effects of remarkable depth in an artificial movie, which still manages to come across as natural. With its 500,000 admissions in Germany alone, the documentary made the top ten of domestic productions for the year.

Werner Herzog's **Cave of Forgotten Dreams**

For **Cave of Forgotten Dreams** (*Die Höhle der vergessenen Träume*) Werner Herzog also chose 3D to create a unique and exclusive journey through the Chauvet caves in Southern France, capturing the oldest pictures of mankind on the narrow sided rocks. It was rewarded with more than 200,000 admissions in the film's first week.

Christian Ditter's **Vicky and the Treasure of the Gods**

The children's film **Vicky and the Treasure of the Gods** (*Wickie auf großer Fahrt*) by Christian Ditter, the sequel to 2009's *Vicky the Viking*, also went 3D – and even though its effects were far from the technical mastery Wenders and Herzog exhibited, the cute new adventure of the little red-haired Viking boy attracted more than a million viewers.

Four other 3D productions made the cut: **Berliner Philharmoniker: A Musical Journey in 3D** by Michael Beyer, which documented the famous orchestra's trip to Shanghai with eight 3D/HD cameras; the animated **Laura's Star and the Dream Monsters** (*Lauras Stern und die Traummonster*), which catered to the youngest film goers; the abysmal independent horror thriller **Iron Doors** by Stephan Manuel (a man wakes up, locked in a bank vault, with no way to escape) and the co-production **The**

Three Musketeers, filmed all over Germany by Paul W. S. Anderson (1.2 million admissions). Digitisation in Germany is not at the same high level it is in France – even the multiplexes have yet to completely transfer to digital – therefore the German Federal Film Board launched a special programme, first for art-house theatres and smalltown cinemas only, to finance the new technology with €15million, to be followed by €4.5million for multiplexes.

Tim Fehlbaum's **Hell**

The rise of genre films, which began in 2010, led to promising horror films such as Tim Fehlbaum's **Hell**, with Hannah Herzsprung, which surprised the audience with its extraordinarily stylish look. The sun in this post-apocalyptic film is so bright and hot that survival of the fittest becomes the norm, which leads to cannibalism. Acclaimed director Roland Suso Richter set his children's film **Jungle Child** (*Dschungelkind*), based on the book of the same title, in the woods of Papua New Guinea and created an exotic drama about a little German girl caught between warring clans. Other children's films included the sequel

Andreas Dresen's **Stopped on Track**

Lilly the Witch – The Journey to Mandolan (*Hexe Lilly – Die Reise nach Mandolan*) by Harald Sicheritz, which was a cross between reality and 2001 Arabian nights, and attracted 650,000 admissions. The animated **Princess Lillifee and the Little Unicorn** (*Prinzessin Lillifee und das kleine Einhorn*) by Hubert Weiland and Ansgar Niebuhr, in which a young girl joins forces with a helpless little unicorn, also attracted 600,000 viewers. In a way, the third comedy in a row by notorious German actor/director Til Schweiger, **Kokowääh**, is a children's film too, thanks to the presence of his daughter, who dominates the story. It ended its run with 4.3 million admissions.

Yasemin Samdereli's **Almanya – Welcome to Germany**

The German-Turkish comedy **Almanya – Welcome to Germany** (*Almanya – Willkommen in Deutschland*), which tackled the story of Turkish immigrants in Germany with a welcome mix of intelligent humour and subtlety, became another box-office hit, racking up 1.2 million admissions. Other notable entries were Chris Kraus's beautifully photographed period drama, **Poll**, set on the brink of World War I in an Estonia populated by Russians and Germans alike; Andres Veiel's well-intentioned but muddled **If Not Us, Who?** (*Wer wenn nicht wir*), about the earliest beginnings of the Red Army Faction; and Andreas Dresens's **Stopped on Track** (*Halt auf freier Strecke*), a harrowingly realistic cancer-drama.

Late in the year, Roland Emmerich, the German king of disaster movies, tried something new with a medium-budget project filmed back home in Germany.

Roland Emmerich's **Anonymous**

Anonymous attempts to re-write the history of Shakespeare and his output, which the film argues may have been written by another.

In 2011, the market share of domestic productions maintained the level of 20 per cent, while the box office for the first six month went up to 61.5 million admissions (up two per cent on 2010, which was already a good year). Sales reached €453million, second only to 2002's figures.

After the death of Bernd Eichinger, the leading German producer of the last thirty years, it wasn't long before another producer stepped up to the mark. Stefan Arndt raised €100million to shoot the literary adaption **Cloud Atlas** (*Der Wolkenatlas*), the biggest German production ever, with Tom Tykwer and Andy and Lana Wachowski co-directing. The film, starring Tom Hanks, Susan Sarandon and Halle Berry, will hopefully hit cinemas around the world in 2012.

The year's best films
Pina (Wim Wenders)
Stopped on Track (Andreas Dresen)
Hell (Tim Fehlbaum)
Cave of Forgotten Dreams (Werner Herzog)
Almanya – Welcome to Germany (Yasemin Samdereli)

Directory
All Tel/Fax numbers begin (+49)
Deutsches Filminstitut-DIF, Schaumainkai 41, 60596 Frankfurt am Main. Tel: (69) 961 2200. Fax: (69) 620 060. info@deutsches-filminstitut.de. www. deutsches-filminstitut.de.

Deutsches Filmmuseum Frankfurt am Main, Schaumainkai 41, 60596 Frankfurt am Main. Tel: (69) 2123 8830. Fax: (69) 2123 7881. info@deutsches-filmmuseum.de. www.deutsches-filmmuseum.de.
Federal Film Board (FFA), Grosse Praesidentenstr 9, 10178 Berlin. Tel: (30) 275 770. Fax: (30) 2757 7111. www.ffa.de.
Filmmuseum Berlin-Deutsche Kinemathek, Potsdamer Str 2, 10785 Berlin. Tel: (49 30) 300 9030. Fax: 3009 0313. info@filmmuseum-berlin.de. www.filmmuseum-berlin.de.
German Films Service & Marketing GmbH, Herzog-Wilhelm-Strasse 16, 80331 Munich, Tel: (89) 599 787-0. Fax: (89) 599 78730. info@german-films.de. www.german-films.de.
Münchner Stadtmuseum/Filmmuseum, St Jakobsplatz 1, 80331 Munich. Tel: (89) 2332 2348. Fax: (89) 2332 3931. filmmuseum@muenchen.de. www.stadtmuseum-online.de/filmmu.htm.
New German Film Producers Association, Agnesstr 14, 80798 Munich. Tel: (89) 271 7430. Fax: (89) 271 9728. ag-spielfilm@t-online.de.
Umbrella Organisation of the Film Industry, Kreuzberger Ring 56, 65205 Wiesbaden. Tel: (611) 778 9114. Fax: (611) 778 9169. statistik@spio-fsk.de.

Wim Wenders' **Pina**

ANDREA DITTGEN is a film critic and editor of the daily newspaper *Die Rheinpfalz*, and contributor to the magazine *Filmdienst*. She also is a member of the board of the German Film Critics Association and head of department of membership of the International Federation of Film Critics.

Greece Ninos-Fenek Mikelidis

The continuing economic crisis has taken a heavy toll on Greek film. Notwithstanding the passing of the a Greek law on cinema, the Greek Film Centre, under its new seven-member Board of Directors (headed by filmmaker Grigoris Karantinakis) has, for the past two years, not been funded by the Ministry of Culture. The result has been fewer films. And those directors or producers who had been officially granted – at least on paper – some subsidies stil had to shoot their films on a privately-funded shoestring. In contrast to this, ERT, the state television network, recently renewed it script committee, which was in hibernation for two years. They will distribute the 1.5 per cent revenue on film production and are now pressing ahead with choosing scripts for funding with the €9million budget that has accumulated during the period they were dormant. ERT has also decided to use a large percentage of its budget solely to produce scripts by new writers.

Profits, compared with previous years, were at their lowest level, with Nicos Koutelidakis's most commercial film **The Christmas Tango** attracting less than 150,000 admissions, which is better than a more artistic film like Yorgos

Nicos Koutelidakis's **The Christmas Tango**

Lanthimos's **Alps**, which attracted an audience of just 3,000. Compare that to his previous film, *Dogtooth*, which racked up 30,000. Feature film production was down to twenty for the year, with some still awaiting domestic distribution.

Yorgos Lanthimos's **Alps**

One of the most interesting films of the year was **Children's Town** (*I polis ton pedion*), a low-budget production by newcomer Yiorgos Gigapeppas. It won the FIPRESCI and Greek Critics' Association prizes at the Thessaloniki film festival. The film shows how pregnancy, combined with the recent economic crisis, affects the lives of four couples, among them a woman who chooses abortion whilst another, a poor immigrant, manages to give birth at home, assisted by a Greek neighbour. Gigapeppas adopts a low-key, realistic style for these parallel stories, whilst drawing out engaging performances from his actors.

In his nourish thriller **Unjust World** (*Adikos kosmos*), which picked up the Best Director prize at San Sébastian, Philippos Tsitos presents a 'slice of Greek life' through the work of a police investigator who desperately tries to be just in an unjust world. The investigator's decisions over whether to confirm the accusations against small-time crooks, criminals and other members of the underworld, or let them free, depend on his amateur psychology during interrogation. Tsitos also uses a low-key approach, reminiscent of Mike Leigh's films, to present a detailed and clear picture of the various situations the characters become embroiled in, always placing their actions in the context of their social background.

Yiorgos Lanthimo's *Alps* screened at Venice and is an uneven, in parts unconvincing, black comedy about a group of people who have created a strange, illegal group – the 'Alps' – who decide to imitate dead people in order for their loved ones to deal with their grief.

Menelaos Karamangiolis's **J.A.C.E.** is an ambitious, visually striking, but overlong film about a young illegal immigrant growing up in Greece, and his passage from the benevolent guardianship of a gentle Jewish shop-owner to a criminal ring that trades in human trafficking. The episodic, 153-minute film, covers a range of issues, from abduction, child traficking, prostitution, incest, the selling of vital organs, police corruption and vengeance, with a style that shifts throughout.

Zacharias Mavroidis's **The Guide**

The multi-faceted, often crazy image of contemporary Athens and its architecture is satirised in Zacharias Mavroidis's comedy **The Guide** (*O Xenagos*). Its protagonist is a young country boy guiding visiting foreign architects

Yiorgos Yeorgopoulos' **Tungsten**

around the city. Another portrait of Athens can be found in Yiorgos Yeorgopoulos's **Tungsten**, which features a bus ticket-collector, a couple on the verge of separation and two teenagers roaming the streets of Athens with a gun. This exciting black-and-white feature debut tackles the role violence plays in city life and how it shapes our lives.

A schematic script, unconvincing performances and somewhat stilted direction undermine Constantine Giannaris's **Man at Sea**, which deals with the problems of immigration through the tragedy that follows a mutiny by sailors on board a tanker. It is sparked by the captain's decision to save the illegal immigrants on board a sinking ship.

Peppermint director Costas Kapakas's **Magic Hour** is an uneven, occasionally amusing road movie about two men who roam Greece with a casket that contains anything but a dead person. In **Paradise** (*Paradisos*), Panayiotis Fafoutis employs an Atlman-esque approach to narrative structure to tell the story of four couples during the

Layia Yourgou's **Red Sky**

Patras carnival. Sadly, the film is littered with too many clichés to be anything more than interesting. In the uneven **Red Sky** (*Kokkinos ouranos*), Layia Yourgou focuses on a love triangle between two men and a German woman on a distant, barren strip in Crete. And Antonioni's *L'avventura* comes to mind in newcomer Aris Balafoukas's **Brethlessness** (*Apnea*), which concerns a young swimmer reminiscing about a lost love.

Loukia Rikaki's **Drawings: Sotiria** (*Shedio Sotiria*) is a moving documentary based on an exhibition of paintings by students of the national Fine Arts School. They are inspired by life at the first – but now closed – public sanatorium, Sotiria. Special mention should also be made of the short film **The New-Born** (*To pistoma*), directed by newcomer Yiorgos Fourtounis, which picked up the Best Film prize at Drama Short Film Festival. Shot in black and white, with its unforgettable images drawing comparison with the work of Béla Tarr's, it tells the story of a bandit who returns to his village to find his wife with a new-born baby. He kills her lover and forces her to bury her child alive.

However grim the economic situation, both established and new Greek directors are pressing ahead with plans for new films, whilst others have already finished theirs. Among directors with films in post-production are: Nicos Panayiotopoulos with **Blood Bonds** (*Desma ematos*); Dimitris Athanitis with **Three Days of Happiness** (*Tris meres eftychias*); Elizabeth Chronopoulou with **Hannibal at the Gates** (*Annivas pro ton pylon*); Yiannis Fangras with **Forget-Me-Not**; Bambis Makridis with **L** and Vassilis Mazomenos with **Exile**. Meanwhile Theo Angelopoulos has begun shooting his new opus, **The Other Sea** (*I alli thalassa*), as has Yiannis Smaragdis with **God Loves Caviar** (*O theos agapa to haviari*).

Philippos Tsitos' **Unjust World**

The year's best films
The City of Children (Yiorgos Gigapeppas)
Unjust World (Philippos Tsitos)
The New-Born (Yiorgos Fourtounis)

Directory
All Tel/Fax numbers begin (+30)
Association of Independent Producers of Audiovisual Works (SAPOE), 30 Aegialias, 151 25 Maroussi. Tel: (210) 683 3212. Fax: (210) 683 3606. sapoe-gr@otenet.gr.
Greek Film Centre, President: George Papalios, 7, Dionysiou Aeropagitou, 117 42 Athens. Tel: (210) 367 8500. Fax: (210) 364 8269. info@gfc.gr. www.gfc.gr.
Greek Film, Theatre & Television Directors Guild, 11 Tossitsa, 106 83 Athens. Tel: (210) 822 8936. Fax: (210) 821 1390. ees@ath.forthnet.gr.
Hellenic Ministry of Culture, 20 Bouboulinas, 106 82 Athens. Tel: (210) 820 1100. w3admin@culture.gr. http://culture.gr.
Hellenic Film Academy, 12 Athinas Street, 182 33, Athens. press@fogfilms.org.
Union of Greek Film Directors and Producers, 33 Methonis, 106 83 Athens. Tel: (210) 825 3065. Fax: (210) 825 3065.
Union of Greek Film, TV & Audiovisual Sector Technicians (ETEKT-OT), 25 Valtetsiou, 106 80 Athens. Tel: (210) 360 2379/361 5675. Fax: (210) 361 6442. etekt-ot@ath.forthnet.gr.

NINOS-FENECK MIKELIDIS is an historian of Greek Cinema and film critic for the Athens daily newspaper *Eleftherotypia*. He is also the founder and director of the Panorama of European Cinema film festival in Athens.

Hong Kong Tim Youngs

The China factor remained the talk of Hong Kong's film business in 2011. The year saw the city's filmmakers continue to work largely along two lines: delivering productions that could appeal to the sprawling mainland China market, and smaller works to satisfy the hometown crowd.

Johnnie To's **Don't Go Breaking My Heart**

To see the contrasts of the two directions in play, viewers need look no further than two films from top director Johnnie To. Early in the year, moviegoers across China saw charm personified in **Don't Go Breaking My Heart** (*Daan sum naam nui*), a mass-market love-triangle set in Hong Kong and Suzhou. The first in a new string of pop pictures from To and regular collaborator Wai Ka-fai, this sleek movie readily entertained, but lacked the stronger edge audiences had come to expect from the director. To's **Life Without Principle** (*Duet ming gam*) later in the year, however, offered more daring themes in a freewheeling, observational drama about money-mad Hong Kong. As the film's dryly comic banking, property-market and gangland scenes played out against the euro-zone crisis, local audiences found much of relevance to them.

Johnnie To's **Life Without Principle**

Playing safe for the mainland still makes business sense. Ever since Hong Kong and the mainland's Closer Economic Partnership Arrangement in 2003 helped the city's filmmakers reach screens throughout China via co-productions, cross-boundary collaboration has been common. Censorship hassles and a divide in audience tastes remain, but takings in the mainland's multiplexes can vastly outweigh those in Hong Kong, and the accompanying increased budgets can be handy too.

Take Peter Chan's **Wu Xia**, which elegantly blended a detective story with martial arts action. Drawing on lush mainland locales, boasting top stars and studded with fabulous fight sequences, *Wu Xia* is a perfect high-concept popcorn film. High-end fantasy

Peter Chan's **Wu Xia**

also worked for a number of Hong Kong filmmakers. Gordon Chan served up **Mural** (*Wah bik*), an adventure set in a parallel world and equipped with classy art direction and effects. And Wilson Yip delivered **A Chinese Ghost Story** (*Sin nui yau wan*), remaking the 1986 classic with flashy effects and a delightful sense of nostalgia.

Tony Chan and Wing Shya's **Love in Space**

Among the films with a contemporary setting, **Love in Space** (*Chuen kau yit luen*), a gentle pop romancer from Tony Chan and Wing Shya, was the standout. It rekindled the multi-narrative formula of the co-directors' previous *Hot Summer Days* and once again they lent their proceedings – this time Australia, mainland China and sequences in orbit around the Earth – a Hollywood-style sheen. Felix Chong and Alan Mak's **Overheard 2** (*Sit ting fung wan 2*) aimed for more grounded thrills, as it followed a stock market theme and depictions of business-world big shots.

Felix Chong and Alan Mak's **Overheard 2**

2011's centenary of the Xinhai Revolution, a major event in Chinese history, sparked several

epics. Most impressive was Herman Yau's **The Woman Knight of Mirror Lake** (*Ging hung nui hap chau gan*). The tale of a famous heroine boasted fun, action, gender-equality and a politically interesting plotline about young revolutionaries. Among other centennial works was Jackie Chan and Zhang Li's **1911** (*San hoi gaap ming*), sadly playing like a clumsy retelling of textbook entries.

The year's co-production oddity was **Mysterious Island** (*Gu dou ging wan*), cheapo horror nonsense from Chung Kai-cheong. Delivering fright scenes despite censorship constraints (ghosts are banned in mainland films) and starring a popular mainland TV starlet, the picture scored big across the boundary but was largely ignored locally. Another anomaly was Jeff Lau's **East Meets West** (*Dung sing sai jau 2011*), a polished superhero comedy-romance with a crazed Hong Kong style that also opened strongly in the mainland.

Chung Kai-cheong's **Mysterious Island**

While the appeal of co-productions looms large, some Hong Kong filmmakers are happy forgoing a mainland theatrical release. Christopher Sun's **3D Sex and Zen: Extreme Ecstasy** (*3D yuk po tyun ji gik lok bo gaam*) scored worldwide publicity with its adults-only novelty of classic-literature-based sleaze and modern film technique. At home in Hong Kong, the film even attacted visiting mainlanders.

Youth films remain a key area for local themes. Wilson Chin's **Lan Kwai Fong** (*Hei ngoi yeh po*) wooed the nightclub set with racy

Patrick Kong's **Love Is Not the Only Answer**

themes and the chance to see loose morals go unpunished on the silver screen – another no-no in mainland co-productions. In **Let's Go!** (*Bou wai jin deui ji cheut dung la! Pung yau!*), from director Wong Ching-po, viewers could witness a bizarre, sometimes ultra-violent blend of housing-estate nostalgia and an anime-influenced superhero story. Wong Jing and Patrick Kong's scrappy ghouls 'n' girls comedy **Hong Kong Ghost Stories** (*Mang gwai ngoi ching gu si*) was loaded with local hot topics and gossip gags. And Kong's solo work **Love Is Not the Only Answer** (*Yan yeuk lei fun hau*) from earlier in 2011 continued a series of small relationship pictures that have gone down well with young cinemagoers.

Hong Kong's indie filmmakers are also tackling concerns close to home. Jessey Tsang's **Big Blue Lake** (*Dai laam wu*) looked at life in the director's home village, combining narrative fiction with interviews. And **1+1**,

Christopher Sun's **3D Sex and Zen: Extreme Ecstasy**

an accomplished short from Mo Lai, told of people being displaced by a railway project. *1+1* received a theatrical release after a win in the city's Fresh Wave International Short Film Festival, an annual showcase of young filmmakers' work that is growing in stature.

Ching Siu-tung's **The Sorcerer and the White Snake**

While Hong Kong certainly didn't lack variety in 2011, inconsistent film quality remained an issue. Filmmakers still need to win back steady support from a sceptical home crowd, as well as keeping mainlanders and audiences further afield in the loop. Paying no favours to the industry were high-profile underperformers like Frankie Chan's **Legendary Amazons** (*Yeung mun nui jeung*), a period epic shackled with a dismal script and disappointing battlefield action. Even veteran filmmaker Ching Siu-tung's family-friendly fantasy feature **The Sorcerer and the White Snake** (*Bak seh chuen shuet*) was disappointing, thanks to an onslaught of poor CGI at its climax. The summer saw a parade of low-quality mid-size works, largely made for the youth market, which slinked in and out of cinemas with little notice – particularly unfortunate given the excitement and quality in the mid-budget segment a year ago. Also worrying was the shortage of outstanding new local talent in front of the camera; skilled mainland actors appearing in pricier co-productions outshined local performers.

Fortunately, valuable PR for Hong Kong cinema came late in 2011 when Ann Hui's intimate

Ann Hui's **A Simple Life**

biopic **A Simple Life** (*Tou je*) won major prizes overseas, starting with the Best Actress award at the Venice Film Festival. The film was held from mainstream Hong Kong release for months as buzz-building awards accumulated, boosting anticipation but making the film a 2012 release for many. *A Simple Life*'s delayed showings placed it high on film buffs' must-see lists toward the end of 2011.

Other attractive upcoming films are Tsui Hark's year-end 3D swordplay spectacular **Flying Swords of Dragon Gate** (*Lung mun fei gaap*); Dante Lam's epidemic thriller **The Viral Factor** (*Yik jin*); Johnnie To's high-altitude love story **Romancing in Thin Air** (*Gou hoi but ji luen II*); Soi Cheang's car-racing thriller **Motorway** (*Che sau*); Pang Ho-cheung's romantic comedy **Love in the Buff** (*Chun-giu yu Chi-ming*); and, more than two years after its off-again, on-again shoot began, Wong Kar-wai's martial-arts biopic **The Grandmaster** (*Yat doi jung si*).

The year's best films
Wu Xia (Peter Chan)
Life Without Principle (Johnnie To)
The Woman Knight of Mirror Lake (Herman Yau)
Don't Go Breaking My Heart (Johnnie To)
Love in Space (Tony Chan and Wing Shya)

TIM YOUNGS is a Hong Kong-based writer and programme consultant for Italy's Udine Far East Film Festival.

Directory
All Tel/Fax numbers begin (+852)
Hong Kong Film Archive, 50 Lei King Rd, Sai Wan Ho. Tel: 2739 2139. Fax: 2311 5229. www.filmarchive.gov.hk.
Film Services Office, 40/F, Revenue Tower, 5 Gloucester Road, Wan Chai. Tel: 2594 5745. Fax: 2824 0595. www.fso-tela.gov.hk.
Federation of Hong Kong Filmmakers, 2/F, 35 Ho Man Tin St, Ho Man Tin, Kowloon. Tel: 2194 6955. Fax: 2194 6255. www.hkfilmmakers.com.
Hong Kong Film Directors' Guild, 2/F, 35 Ho Man Tin St, Ho Man Tin, Kowloon. Tel: 2760 0331. Fax: 2713 2373. www.hkfdg.com.
Hong Kong International Film Festival Society, 21/F, Millennium City 3, 370 Kwun Tong Rd, Kwun Tong. Tel: 2970 3300. Fax 2970 3011. www.hkiff.org.hk
Hong Kong, Kowloon and New Territories Motion Picture Industry Association (MPIA), Unit 1201, New Kowloon Plaza, 38 Tai Kok Tsui Rd, Kowloon. Tel: 2311 2692. Fax: 2311 1178. www.mpia.org.hk
Hong Kong Film Awards Association, Room 1601–1602, Austin Tower, 22–26 Austin Ave, Tsim Sha Tsui, Kowloon. Tel: 2367 7892. Fax: 2723 9597. www.hkfaa.com.

Wong Kar-wai's **The Grandmaster**

Hungary John Cunningham

A s hinted at in last year's review, the Hungarian film industry has been through some serious problems in the last twelve months or so. The Hungarian Parliament, where Viktor Orbán's right wing FIDESZ party holds a 68 per cent majority, has drastically cut funding for the Hungarian Motion Picture Foundation, some sources stating that the cuts are as much as 80 per cent. This has resulted in many film projects being cancelled or, at best put on hold.

The worst hit were those productions already underway when the news was announced and it is rumoured that as many as forty productions, at various stages of development, have stalled and are unlikely to resume. Some producers and backers have been left with large debts, which they are unable to repay. One of the casualties of this process was the annual Hungarian Film Week, usually held in late January/early February, which was postponed.

Andy Vajna, the former Hollywood-based producer of *Rambo* and *The Terminator*, has been appointed as a government commissioner to take charge of overseeing the film industry, a move which has not been greeted with universal enthusiasm within the Hungarian film industry. As an indication of the feelings generated by these moves, in February a group of Hungarian filmmakers signed a declaration condemning the new policy, part of which stated that, 'The Hungarian government has decided to replace a democratic self-governing structure ensuring pluralism with a one-person decision-making system'. Signatories included, Miklós Jancsó, Béla Tarr, Ildikó Enyedi and Márta Mészáros and they were supported by non-Hungarian luminaries such as Gus Van Sant and Tilda Swinton.

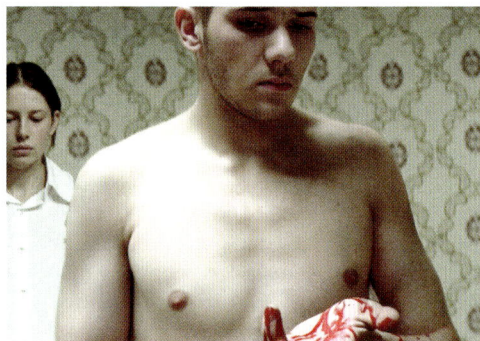

Kornél Mundruczó's **Tender Son – The Frankenstein Project**

When the 42nd Hungarian Film Week finally took place in May it was a much pared-down affair with relatively few films on offer and of these only a handful were worthy of comment. It was significant that two of the main films screened, Kornél Mundruczó's **Tender Son – The Frankenstein Project** (*Szelid teremetés – a Frankenstein terv*) and Ágnes Kocsis's **Adrienn Pál** (*Pál Adrienn*), had been released the previous year. The former walked off with the Best Director award while the latter won Best Film. Of the remaining films, the most notable were **East Side Stories**, an omnibus film comprised of four excellent shorts by Csaba Bollók, Ferenc Török, Mark Bodszár and Szabolcs Hajdu, all of which, in one way or another, comment on the some of the social

Agnes Kocsis' **Adrienn Pál**

Gábor Dettre's **Antigone**

changes in Hungary in recent years. Gábor Dettre's minimalist but powerful adaptation of **Antigone** impressed many, while György Szomjas offered a delightful music documentary **Eastern Wind: The Film** (*Keleti szél: a film*). Another documentary of note was Gábor Zsigmond Papp's **The Enemy is Amongst Us** (*Az ellenség köztünk van*), which looked at the fates of three Hungarians who, in very differing ways, all become involved in some kind of spying activity.

Other than these films the 42nd Film Week was a rather sad affair. It looks as if the Film Week will now be permanently dropped, with talk of it being replaced by an International Film Festival. Whether or not this is viable, given the crowded film festival calendar in Europe, remains to be seen.

Since the Film Week, there have been other developments. In September a 'list' was published of filmmakers who will receive some financial support. Topping the list, rather predictably perhaps, was István Szabó, as well as funding for a bio-pic of Ferenc (Franz) Liszt. Szabó's film **The Door** (*Az ajtó*), an adaptation of Magda Szabó's book of the same name and starring Helen Mirren, has been in post-production for some time, but according to sound designer Christian Conrad 'it should be in cinemas worldwide later this year or early next'.

Béla Tarr's long anticipated **The Turin Horse** (*Turini ló*) has been released to great critical acclaim. It was also chosen to represent Hungary at the Academy Awards in the Best Foreign film category. However, given the kind

of film it is, its chances of it winning seem slight to say the least. In numerous interviews the director is sticking to his guns about this being his last film.

Béla Tarr's **The Turin Horse**

A few films were released after the Film Week. Péter Bergendy's **The Examination** (*A vizsga*) is set in 1957 and includes amongst its cast popular actor Péter Scherer. It has some parallels to the German film *The Lives of Others* and asks the perennial question about any country's secret service – who keeps an eye on the spies? Adaptations of the work of Sándor Márai are becoming more popular. The latest work to transfer to the big screen is **Adventure** (*Kaland*), a tale of love and deceit set in 1940, directed by József Sipos and starring German Gerd Böckmann and local actor Sándor Csányi. Another release, György Molnár's **In/Out Tawaret** (*Ki/be Tawaret*), details the odd-ball life of a female poet.

Péter Bergendy's **The Examination**

Although Hungary is not generally known as a destination for refugees, its geographical position means that, either temporarily or permanently, it acts as home for many people from around the world. This little known aspect of Hungarian life is on display in Oszkár Viktor Nagy's documentary **Between Two Worlds** (*Két vilag közt*), which follows the fortunes of four refugees as they attempt to carve a new life for themselves.

What the future holds for Hungarian filmmaking remains unclear and there are many unanswered questions, for example what will happen to the animation and documentary sectors? Some directors have already spoken about making minimal-budget films as their response to the lack of funding and even organising an alternative film festival. Others have moved abroad and it is possible that the Film Directors Guild may simply go into limbo until 2014 (the year of the next election). At the moment much remains at the level of speculation.

József Sipos' **Adventure**

The year's best films
The Turin Horse (Béla Tarr)
East Side Stories (Csaba Bollók, Ferenc Török, Hajdu Szabolcs, Mark Bodszár)
Antigone (Gábor Dettre)
The Examination (Péter Gegrendy)
Adventure (József Sipos)
Eastern Wind: The Film (György Somjas)

Directory
All Tel/Fax numbers begin (+36)
Association of Hungarian Filmmakers, Városligeti fasor 38. Budapest, Hungary-1068, filmszov@t-online.hu

Mark Bodszár's **East Side Stories**

Association of Hungarian Producers, Eszter utca 7/B. Budapest, Hungary-1022, mail@mpsz.org.hu, www.mpsz.org.hu
Hungarian Directors Guild, Ráday utca 31/K., Budapest, Hungary-1092, mrc@filmjus.hu, www.mmrc.hu
Hungarian Film Alliance (Magyar Filmunió), 38 Városligeti fasor, Budapest, Hungary - 1068. Tel: (1) 351 7760, 351-7761 Fax: (1) 352 6734. filmunio@filunion.hu
Hungarian Independent Producers Associations, Róna utca 174. Budapest, Hungary-1145, eurofilm@t-online.hu
Hungarian National Film Archive, Budakeszi út 51/E. Budapest, Hungary-1021, www.filmintezet.hu
Hungarian Society of Cinematographers (H.S.C.), Róna utca 174. Budapest, Hungary-1145, hsc@hscmot.hu, www.hscmot.hu
MEDIA Desk Hungary, Városligeti fasor 38. Budapest, Hungary-1068, info@mediadesk.hu, www.mediadesk.hu
Motion Picture Public Foundation of Hungary Városligeti fasor 38. Budapest, Hungary-1068 mmka@mmka.hu, www.mmka.hu
National Film Office, Wesselényi utca 16. Budapest, Hungary-1075, info@filmoffice.hu, www.nationalfilmoffice.hu

JOHN CUNNINGHAM is Senior Lecturer in the Department of Stage and Screen at Sheffield Hallam University, UK. He is the author of *Hungarian Cinema: From Coffee House to Multiplex* (Wallflower Press, 2004) and is Principal Editor of the journal *Studies in Eastern European Cinema*.

لجنة أبوظبي للأفلام
ABU DHABI FILM
COMMISSION

Iceland Eddie Cockrell

I n the wake of Iceland's financial meltdown and the volcanic eruptions that once again brought the country to the world's attention for all the wrong reasons, it would be difficult to point to another national cinema that has been more resilient in the face of economic uncertainty.

Gaukur Úlfarsson's **Gnarr**

The year's films, consistent with the country's recent output, were strong in theme, execution and local reception. Though a late 2010 release, director Gaukur Úlfarsson's **Gnarr** is a genially cheeky feature-length documentary, charting the unlikely rise of comedian Jón Gnarr to mayor of Reykjavik. The film distinguished itself at New York's Tribeca and Toronto's HotDocs film festivals.

2011 began with writer-director Marteinn St. Thórsson's challenging and ambitious **Stormland** (*Rokland*). Perhaps best encapsulated as a determined cross between Eliseo Subiela's *Dark Side of the Heart* and Barbet Schroeder's *Barfly*, the film follows the shambling Böddi (Ólafur Darri Ólafsson), a bitter romantic determined to tame the world. The film was invited to screen at the 2011 Hamburg festival.

March brought two local features. Screenwriter-lead actor Thorsteinn Gudmundsson's **Our Own Oslo** tells of the combustible relationship between a straight-laced engineer and the scatter-brained single mother he takes up with following an impulsive one-night stand in the Norwegian capital. Prolific writer-director Olaf de Fleur's **Polite People** is the fish-out-of-water story of a conniving businessman who takes on more than he can handle when he becomes involved in small-town politics and peccadilloes.

Confidently performed and impeccably photographed in Iceland's northern wilderness, writer-director Hafsteinn Gunnar Sigurdsson's **Either Way** is a slyly funny two hander about a couple of mismatched highway maintenance

Hafsteinn Gunnar Sigurdsson's **Either Way**

men in the 1980s, whose hostility turns to genuine affection as they help each other out of off-screen romantic jams.

Only a week later came the inevitable third installment in the immensely popular *Sveppi* series. **The Magic Wardrobe** finds the gaggle of man-children led by the curious and resourceful Sveppi (TV personality-turned-franchise-founder Sverrir Thor Sverrisson) freeing one of their number from the title dresser.

Rúnar Rúnarsson's **Volcano**

The very end of September saw the much-anticipated release of writer-director Rúnar Rúnarsson's immensely assured and deeply affecting feature debut and Cannes Film Festival entry **Volcano**. Veteran actor Theodór Júlíusson is magnificent as a recently retired school custodian whose gruff ways are tempered considerably when his wife suffers a severe, coma-inducing stroke. Rúnarsson's Bergmanesque approach to his protagonist's tortured existence and elusive redemption announces him as a filmmaker of insight and gravitas.

Deserved winner of awards at festivals in Chicago, Reykjavik and Transylvania, *Volcano* is Iceland's official submission to the Best Foreign Language Film category of the 84th Academy Awards in 2012.

Also in late September came the independently produced family film **L7: Hrafnar, Sóleyjar og Myrra** from directors Eyrún Ósk Jónsdóttir and Helgi Sverrisson, in which a 13-year-old girl keeps her recently-deceased father's memory alive by joining the local theatre company he so loved.

October saw the simultaneous release of two very different films: the long-in-gestation animated epic **Legends of Valhalla: Thor** and de Fleur's third film of the year, the hard-boiled crime drama **City State** (his second is **Adequate Beings**, a documentary about the economic struggles of a small Icelandic town). Neither feature was made available for review, and will thus be covered in next year's edition.

Back on firm footing after a delay in the 2009 edition, the Edda Film and TV awards bestowed their Film of the Year award on director Árni Ólafur Ásgeirsson's **Undercurrent** (*Brim*) in a gala ceremony in late February. Nominated in 12 categories, the intense drama set largely on a fishing boat won a total of six awards.

Árni Ólafur Ásgeirsson's **Undercurrent**

Dagur Kári's English-language drama **The Good Heart**, written about in the 2010 edition of the IFG but not released in Iceland until the following year, won five of the 11 categories in which it was nominated, including director and screenplay. *Stormland* earned awards for Ólafur Darri Ólafsson as Actor of the Year and Elma Lísa Gunnarsdóttir as Actress in a Supporting Role.

Demonstrating once again the Icelandic film industry's reverence for its recent past, the Icelandic Film and TV Academy's Honorary Prize went to veteran director Hrafn Gunnlaugsson. His *Viking Trilogy*, fondly referred to by some as 'cod westerns' and encompassing the features *When the Raven Flies* (1984), *In the Shadow of the Raven* (1987) and *Embla* (1991), helped put Icelandic cinema on the map for an entire generation of film buffs and genre aficionados.

On the business side of things, the domestic box office remained durable in the face of adversity. The nine Icelandic features released up to November 2011 were one off the pace of 2010, with the possibility of Baltasar Kormákur's **The Deep** opening at Christmas. The total box office for Icelandic films screened in those months was US$1.07million – roughly nine per cent of the US$11.17million recorded by the domestic box in this time, and just a little less than the US$11.13million from 2010.

Admissions themselves were down 4.5 per cent, from 1,346,389 in 2010 to 1,285,644 in 2011 – a remarkably small dip considering the ongoing struggle for disposable income and the increasing attractiveness of alternative forms of media and entertainment.

During a typically candid question-and-answer session during the resurgent Reykjavik International Film Festival in late September, Hungarian master Béla Tarr, recipient of the Lifetime Achievement Awards, could have been describing the dedication and resilience of the Icelandic film industry itself when he advised young filmmakers to 'be yourself, find your style, your way… Don't forget what you really want to say. There is no recipe, the recipe is you.' Seen through the prism of that metaphor, Icelandic cinema is holding steady on a slow simmer.

Marteinn St. Thórsson's **Stormland**

The year's best films
Volcano (Rúnar Rúnarsson)
Either Way (Hafsteinn Gunnar Sigurdsson)

Directory
All Tel/Fax numbers begin (+354)
Association of Film-Rights Holder in Iceland, Laugavegur 182, 105 Reykjavík. Fax: 588 3800. smais@smais.is. www.smais.is.
Film Directors Guild of Iceland, Hverfisgata 54, 101 Reykjavík. Fax: 562 7171. ragnarb@hive.is. http://skl-filmdirectors.net.
Film in Iceland Agency, Borgartún 35, 105 Reykjavík. Tel: 561 5200. Fax: 511 4040. info@filminiceland.com. www.filminiceland.com.
Icelandic Film Centre, Hverfisgata 54, 101 Reykjavík. Tel: 562 3580. Fax: 562 7171. info@ icelandicfilmcentre.is. www.icelandicfilmcentre.is.
Icelandic Film Makers Association, Hverfisgata 54, PO Box 1652, 121 Reykjavík. formadur@filmmakers.is. www.filmmakers.is.
Icelandic Film & Television Academy/EDDA Awards, Hverfisgata 54, 101 Reykjavík. Tel: 562 3580. Fax: 562 7171. hilmar@eddan.is. http://eddan.is.
National Film Archive of Iceland, Hvaleyrarbraut 13, 220 Hafnarfjordur. Tel: 565 5993. Fax: 565 5994. kvikmyndasafn@kvikmyndasafn.is.
SÍK - Association of Icelandic Film Producers, Hverfisgata 54, PO Box 5367, 125 Reykjavík. sik@ producers.is. www.producers.is.
Statistics Iceland, Borgartún 21a, 150 Reykjavík. Tel: 528 1000. Fax: 528 1099. information@statice.is. www.statice.is/statistics/culture/cinemas.

EDDIE COCKRELL is a film critic and consulting programmer whose reviews and movie writing have appeared in *Variety*, *The Washington Post*, *The Sydney Morning Herald* and *The Australian*.

India Uma Da Cunha

As 2011 came to a close, India's cinema scene showed ample signs of a sea change – for the better. 2010 was a poor year, with a box office numbed by lacklustre blockbusters. However, it was also one of discovery, in which the more modest films made by new filmmakers found a following.

2010 saw a sprinkling of films with unusual stories that were linked in some way to contemporary life: our expectations and frustrations. Aamir Khan Productions backed two realistic films that had people talking, both in India and internationally. One was Anusha Rizvi's *Peepli Live* (about two impoverished farmers in danger of losing their land to the government, whom the media transform into unwilling martyrs) and Kiran Rao's *Dhobi Ghat* (on the layers of life and meaning in teeming Mumbai city). Dibakar Banerjee's *Love, Sex and Dhoka* offered three stirring stories that depicted deceit in today's world, while Vikramaditya Motwane's *Udaan* (detailing an adolescent's flight from oppressive parental control) was the first Indian film in seven years to screen at Cannes.

Other films by new directors that attracted attention were Abhishek Sharma's *Tere Bin Laden* (a spoof on America's war against terrorism) and Raj Nidimoru's *Shor in the City* (a crime drama that unfolds in the heart of Mumbai). Even the year's runaway success, *Dabangg*, featuring the unfailing Salman Khan, was by a new director, Abhinav Kashyap. The film presents a convoluted thriller on sibling rivalry, aggravated by individual interests.

Another popular, commercially-oriented debut that felt very different to the industry's usual fare, Abhishek Chaubey's *Ishqiya*, features

Abhinay Deo's **Delhi Belly**

two robbers whose hidden booty finds them at the mercy of a wily widow. There was also UTV's surprise hit, *Delhi Belly*, a zany comedy about diamonds and diarrhoea, which built up a cult following amongst India's youth. These harbingers of changing audience tastes paved the way in 2011 for how corporations and financiers perceived potential projects.

The big studios, particularly the likes of UTV, Viacom 18 and Balaji Motion Pictures, saw that audiences now demanded more savvy content with a personal context and appeal. They also realised that lower budgets and bypassing exorbitantly-priced stars meant higher returns on a lower investment. The studios contracted younger, more internationally-attuned and

Raj Nidimoru's **Shor in the City**

free-thinking minds to make films for them. of these, Anurag Kashyap lead the way. His production, **Michael**, directed by another first-time filmmaker, Ribhu Dasgupta, premiered at the Toronto International Film Festival. The US rights were picked up by Fortissimo. The film follows an honest police officer who, on losing his job, unfairly becomes a target of vengeance.

The Venice Film Festival featured two confident art-house features. Gurvinder Singh's **Alms for the Blind Horse** (*Anhey Ghore Da Daan*), produced by India's National Film Development Corporation, is a fascinating portrait of village people being uprooted from their ancestral homes by ruthless estate agents, while Amit Dutta's **The Golden Bird** (*Sonchidi*) is a 52-minute film about two travellers in search of a mythic aircraft.

Gurvinder Singh's **Alms for the Blind Horse**

Vikram Malhotra, the COO of Viacom 18, announced an impressive 2012 line-up: Sujoy Ghosh's **Kahani**, followed by Vishal Mahadkar's debut, **Blood Money** (co-produced by Mahesh Bhatt's Vishesh Films), Anurag Kashyap's two-part **Gangs of Wasseypur**, Ram Gopal Verma's **Department**, David Dhawan's **Chashme Buddoor** and Sushir Mishra's latest untitled feature. The combination of established studio names with a new breed of feisty directors conveys how commercial interests are reaching out to the independent filmmaking.

Realising that contemporary stories which involve audiences both emotionally and intellectually have become increasingly

Mangesh Hadawale's **Watch India Circus**

popular, a flurry of independent producers have set out on their own. Several actors have followed the lead taken by top stars, such as Shahrukh Khan, Aamir Khan, Amitabh Bachchan, Ajay Devgn, Kamal Hassan and others of their ilk, who run their own production companies. One is Vivek Oberoi, whose first film, **Watch Indian Circus** (*Dekh Indian Circus*), directed by Mangesh Hadawale (his second film after his lauded 2009 debut *Tingya*), is a village tale that cleverly interpolates the tricks and trade of the election process with the needs of the common people. The film picked up the Audience Award at the 2011 Busan International Film Festival. Other actors transforming themselves into producers include Preity Zinta, Dia Mirza, Aftab Shivdasani and Abhay Deol.

India's new cinematic spirit appears to be crossing continents, evident in the vibrant 2011 Film Bazaar held by the National Film Development Corporation in Goa, towards end November. Here, high calibre distributors, sales agents and producers from abroad clearly showed their belief and confidence in the newly revitalised Indian cinema. As many as 25 scripts, written by Indians or on subjects that deal with India, found foreign co-producers coming aboard with guidance and funding. These India-centric films will be fine-tuned to meet international needs, thereby gaining a head start before they hit festivals and larger markets.

2011 also saw American films inching their way into the domestic market, winning over India's previously die-hard addicts of local fare. Over the first six months of the year, 110 American films were imported into the country (next came Hong Kong with six and Germany with five). In the same period, 106 films were made in Hindi. Films in the English language are being dubbed into Indian dialects and quite often dominating their Indian counterparts. Interestingly, **Mission Impossible: Ghost Protocol** was released in India six days before its US opening (a significant draw must have been the film's climactic sequences, set in Mumbai), while Sony Pictures released **The Adventures of Tintin** locally a full six weeks before its Stateside opening. Both films enjoyed a remarkable box-office run.

India produces the largest number of films in the world, 800 to 1000 films a year, while accounting for only one per cent of global film industry revenues. According to the 2011 FCCI (Foundation for Critical Choices for India) report, the Indian film industry revenue share is expected to grow to US$3billion by 2015. The mainstream Hindi film industry also dominates other entertainment platforms, such as music, live entertainment and television, where popular films and film-based programmes attract the highest ratings. Only cricket is a close rival.

With recent Hindi blockbusters failing to attract viewers, producers are taking successes made elsewhere and adapting them into Hindi films. Three of the most successful films of 2011 are Hindi remakes of South Indian blockbusters, each one maintaining the original title. The remake of a Malayalam hit, Siddique's **Bodyguard**, starring Salman Khan, is about a bodyguard whose over-zealous measures of protection snowballs into various predicaments. It became Bollywood's second-highest grossing film of all time, topped only by Aamir Khan's 2009 hit *3 Idiots*. **Ready**, also starring Salman Khan, was Bollywood's second-highest grossing film of the year. It is a remake of a Telugu blockbuster and set in Thailand, and focuses on a wealthy bachelor

Siddique's **Bodyguard**

smitten by an orphan girl whose avaricious uncles get in their way. **Singham**, starring Ajay Devgn, a remake of a 2010 Tamil blockbuster, is a rousing action film about an honest cop caught in a political nexus of corruption.

Several Indian films secured a worldwide commercial release and achieved significant success. The most notable were Anubhav Sinha's **Ra.One** starring Shahrukh Khan, Zoya Akhtar's Spanish-set road movie **Zindagi Na Milegi Dobara** and *Bodyguard*. Pointing to yet another increasing trend, the first two films performed far better amongst the Indian diaspora than at home. It is another factor that distributors now need to take into account.

Anubhav Sinha's **Ra.One**

Never before has there been such a heady camaraderie between film professionals from abroad and their Indian counterparts. A spate of entertainment celebrities visited India, the latest being Tom Cruise, promoting the local release of *Mission Impossible: Ghost Protocol*, accompanied by co-star Anil Kapoor.

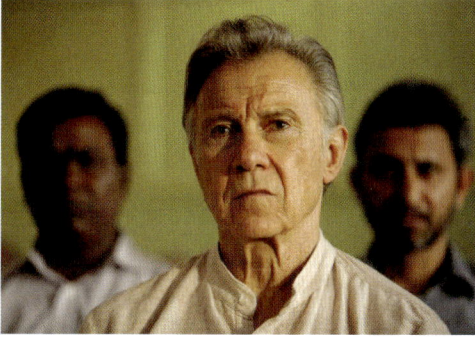

Kranti Kanade's **Gandhi of the Month**

'It is a filmmaker's dream to come to India and shoot', said Ang Lee, echoing the thoughts of several international filmmakers presenting films shot in India or that relate to India. Many of these will be premiered in 2012. They include Deepa Mehta's magnum opus, **Winds of Change**, based on Salman Rushdie's celebrated *Midnight's Children*. Lee's **Life of Pi** is based on Yann Martel's novel, in which 12-year-old Pi is set adrift following the sinking of a boat in the Pacific ocean, on a lifeboat accompanied by a zebra, hyena, orang-utan and a 450-pound Bengal tiger. Roland Joffe's **Singularity**, starring Bipasha Basu, narrates the romantic story of a female royal bodyguard and a British soldier, set apart by two time zones. Mira Nair's **The Reluctant Fundamentalist**, based on the 2007 Mohsin Hamid novel, is a thriller about a young Pakistani man chasing corporate success on Wall Street. Kranti Kanade's debut feature **Gandhi of the Month**, stars Harvey Keital as a secular expatriate American schoolmaster in India who struggles against a tide of anti-Christian sentiment that threatens his students, his school and his life. And Baz Luhrmann's **The Great Gatsby**, starring Leonardo DiCaprio and Carey Mulligan will also feature Indian screen icon Amitabh Bachchan.

India's regional cinema still surfaces from tiny pockets around the country, despite the dominance of the flashy star-studded Hindi scene. In its favour was the film industry's selection as the country's Oscar submission the Malayalam film **Abu, Son of Adam** (*Adaminte Makan Abu*), directed by Salim

Ahmed. It is a low-budget, heartfelt drama dealing with basic human values and which looks into the deeper meanings of religion. Another Tamil film, **Azhagarsamy's Horse** (*Azhagarsamyin Kutharai*), premiered at the Toronto Film Festival and has since been doing the festival rounds. Kerala and Bengal remain in the forefront of literary adaptations with a strong realistic slant. Himanshu S. Khatua's Orissan drama **The Inheritance** (*Mitira Bandhana*) is a disturbing portrayal of how a small traditional town changes when modernisation gives it a facelift.

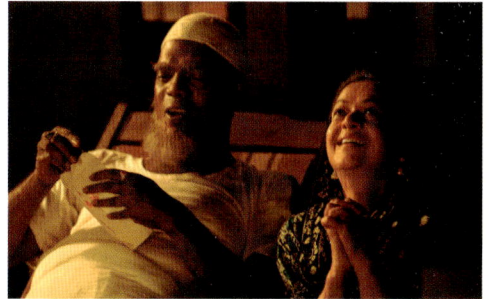

Salim Ahmed's **Abu, Son of Adam**

More films are being made in English by Indian filmmakers, based either in India or abroad. **Delhi in a Day**, the debut of Paris-based Prashant Nair, which picked up the Best Feature award at the second Indian Film Festival in Houston, is a refreshing take on the double lives in a stately Indian home, balancing a wealthy family's indulgent lifestyle with the domestics in the kitchen who wait on them.

Prashant Nair's **Delhi in a Day**

Finally, the most memorable contribution to film in 2011 has to be gutsy actress Vidya Balan, who put on eleven kilos to bring back rounded curves and full figure to the Indian screen. In

Milan Luthra's **The Dirty Picture**

her daring film **The Dirty Picture**, Balan cast aside her demure Indian persona to take on the raunchy role of a screen siren (based on the late real-life actress, Silk Smita from Kerala), parading her bursting-at-the seams fleshiness in skimpy, revealing costumes. The film, a huge hit, made her the rage.

The year also saw the loss of formidable giants of Indian cinema such as Shammi Kapoor and Dev Anand, director Jagmohan Mundhra and composer Bhupen Hazarika.

The year's best films
Lucky (Avie Luthra)
The Dirty Picture (Milan Luthra)
Mitira Banddhana (Himanshu S. Khatua)
Dekh Indian Circus (Mangesh Hadawale)
Cotton for My Shroud (Nandan Saxena and Kavita Bahl)

Directory
All Tel/Fax numbers begin (+91)
Film & Television Institute of India, Law College Rd, Pune 411 004. Tel: (20) 543 1817/3016/0017. www.ftiindia.com.
Film Federation of India, B/3 Everest Bldg, Tardeo, Bombay 400 034. Tel/Fax: (22) 2351 5531. Fax: 2352 2062. supransen.filmfed@hotmail.com. www.filmfed.org.
Film Producers Guild of India, G 1, Morya House, Veera Industrial Estate, OShiwara Link Road, Andheri (W), Mumbai 400 053. Tel: (22) 6691 0662/2673 3065. Fax: (22) 6691 0661. guild@filmtvguildindia.org. www.filmtvguildindia.org.

National Film Archive of India, P.O. Box No. 810, Law College Rd, Pune 411 004. Tel: (20) 2565 2259. Fax: (20) 2567 0027. nfaipune@gmail.com. www.nfaipune.gov.in.
National Film Development Corporation Ltd, Discovery of India Bldg, Nehru Centre, 6th Floor, Dr Annie Besant Rd, Worli, Bombay 400 018. Tel: (22) 2496 5643/2435 5069/2494 9856. Fax: 2496 5646. nfdc@nfdcindia.com. www.nfdcindia.com.
Central Board of Film Certification, Bharat Bhavan, 91 E Walkeshwar Road, Mumbai 400 006. Tel: (22) 2362 5770 Fax: (22) 2369 0083. rocbfcmum@rediffmail.com

UMA DA CUNHA is a Mumbai-based film critic, and edits the quarterly periodical *Film India Worldwide*. She also works as a freelance researcher and journalist, and is a programmer for various international festivals, specialising in Indian cinema.

Iran Amir Esfandiari & Kamyar Mohsenin

t all started at the Berlinale, when Asghar Farhadi's **A Separation** (*Jodayee-e Nader as Simin*) won three main awards: Best Ensemble Actors, Best Ensemble Actresses and Best Film. At the same time, the film grabbed five awards, including Best Director, at the National Competition in Iran and was equally praised by jury and audiences at Fajr Film Festival, the country's main cinematic event. However, Farhadi's return to Berlin after his triumph with *About Elly* was sensational.

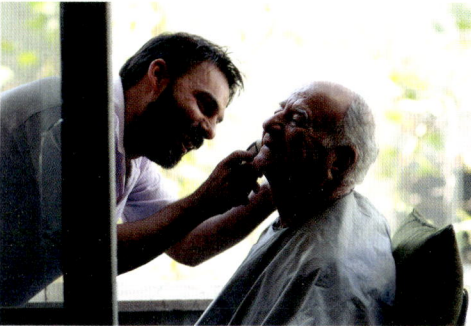

Asghar Farhadi's **A Separation**

In Iran Farhadi was partly criticised for pre-senting a group of characters who preferred to hide behind their lies and also omitting the scene of the accident upon which the narrative twists. That said, the story of internecine familial drama attracted the audiences when it was released in March, during the Iranian New Year Holidays. Opening with a static medium shot of the couple in front of an unseen judge, the film depicts the director's preoccupations with a world twisted by mendacity and ill judgment. Interestingly, *A Separation* faced numerous controversies during its production and distribution. There was interruption from the evaluation board during shooting, protests at its premiere in Berlin over the court verdict

against two Iranian filmmakers (Jafar Panahi and Mohammad Rasoulof, whose new films were screened at Cannes in May), much online chatter about the film prior to its domestic release and even discussion following its submission as the Iranian entry to the 2012 Academy Awards.

A Separation grossed US$1.5million in Tehran, making it one of the highest earners of the year. Masoud Dehnamaki's **The Outcasts 3** (*Ekhraji-ha Seh*), a disputable parody of Iran's presidential election, also performed well, grossing US$1.7million.

Surprisingly, at the beginning of summer, Rambod Javan's highly acclaimed comedy **No Entry for Men** (*Voroud-e Agahayan Mamnoue*), focusing on the story of the only male teacher in a girl's school in Iran, became a sensational hit, selling more than US$1.78million tickets in Tehran. As a popular-actor-turned-director, Javan was impressive in corralling his actors and delivering a series of finely tuned comic moments that recalled the work of Ernst Lubitsch. Other comedies fared less well at the box office, with audiences generally interested in very different fare.

Rambod Javan's **No Entry for Men**

The country, with its population of 75 million and just 450 theatres between them, still remains under utilised as a market for films.

In February, 90 new Iranian feature films were submitted to the 29th edition of the Fajr International Film Festival, with applicants representing many generations of filmmakers. As founders of New Iranian Cinema in 1969, Dariush Mehrjui and Masoud Kimiaie returned with new films. Mehrjui's **The Beloved Sky** (*Aseman-e Mahboub*), which detailed the spiritual journey of a medicine man, picked up the Best Director award in the international section, while Kimiaie's **The Crime** (*Jorm*) won Best Film in the national competition. It pleased his fans, but also attracted criticism – a situation the director has had to face since making his breakthrough feature, *Qaiser*, in 1969.

Dariush Mehrjui's **The Beloved Sky**

The surprising presence of younger directors stunned international viewers. Negar Azarbaijani's **The Facing Mirrors** (*Ayne-ha-ye Rouberou*) brought two girls, one a transsexual, the other devoutly religious, together in a tightly driven drama. It picked up the International Jury's Special Prize. The film became a subject of curiosity for many viewers.

Some of the younger directors' films were characterised by their unique portrayal of individual's lives. A group of alienated men in their perilous work on the electric transmission towers in remote areas of the country was the subject of Mohammad Ebrahim Moayyeri's **Lifeline** (*Galougah*), which will be released

domestically and internationally in 2012, as well as Amir Saghafi's debut, **Death is My Business** (*Marg kasb o kar-e man ast*), which has drawn comparisons with Yilmaz Guney's *Yol*.

Reza Mir-Karimi's **A Cube of Sugar**

A number of other films impressed the public. Alireza Davoudnezhad's **Salve** (*Marham*), a breathtaking look at the gulf between the old and younger generations in Iran, was presented through the parallel stories of an unsavoury young man and his relationship with his grumpy, wealthy grandmother, and a drug-addicted girl and her loving, caring grandmother. Davoudnezhad employed a dynamic handheld style to document the action. Reza Mir-Karimi's **A Cube of Sugar** (*Ye Habbeh Ghand*) is an escapist, playfully observational account of a wedding banquet that is stalled by the death of an old uncle. It received mixed reviews, especially for its narrative and characterisation, but its inventive camera style and subtle production design impressed. Maziar Miri's frantic **Felicity-Land** (*Sa'adat Abad*), dwelling on three middle-class couples who meet for

Maziar Miri's **Felicity-Land**

Bahram Tavakkoli's **Here Without Me**

a dinner party and gradually reveal their tragic secrets to each other, was an impressively intimate drama. Bahram Tavakkoli's **Here Without Me** (*Inja bedoun-e man*), a daring adaptation from Tennessee Williams' *The Glass Menagerie*, featured bravura performances, particularly Fateme Motamed Arya, who received the Best Actress award at Montreal. Vahid Mousaian's **Golchehreh** told a moving story of the love of cinema during the Taliban's control of Kabul, while Ahmad Reza Motamedi's **Alzheimer**, which won the Special Jury Prize at Taormina, depicted a woman who doesn't believe her husband is dead following an accident and draws on metaphysical and philosophical themes.

Mohammad Reza Bozorgnia's **The Maritime Silk Road**

Elsewhere, there were films that were fully supported but failed meet expectations. Even Mohammad Reza Bozorgnia's **The Maritime Silk Road** (*Rah-e Abi-e Abrisham*), a big-budget historical spectacle was not successful at the box office, albeit due to different reasons, while abroad, Jafar Panahi and Mojtaba Mir-Tahmasb's **This is not a film** (*In yek film nist*) and Mohammad Rasoulof's **Good Bye** (*Be omid-e didar*) were greatly publicised for reasons unconnected to cinema.

The year's best films

A Separation (Asghar Farhadi)
Salve (Alireza Davoudnezhad)
Here Without Me (Bahram Tavakkoli)
No Entry for Men (Rambod Javan)
Alzheimer (Ahmad Reza Motamedi)

Alireza Davoudnezhad's **Salve**

Directory

All Tel/Fax numbers begin (+98)
Farabi Cinema Foundation – International Affairs, Tel: (21) 22741254. Fax: (21) 22734953. fcf1@dpi.net.ir.
IRIB Media Trade, Tel: (21) 22548032. Fax: (21) 22551914. info@iribmediatrade.com.
Documentary and Experimental Film Center, Tel: (21) 88511241. Fax: (21) 88511242. int@defc.ir.
Iranian Young Cinema Society, Tel: (21) 88773114. Fax: (21) 88779073. intl@iycs.ir.
Visual Media Institute. Tel: (21) 88673281. Fax: (21) 88673280. info@visualmediains.com.

AMIR ESFANDIARI is Head of International Affairs of Farabi Cinema Foundation, and has served as a member of selection committees and juries at different film festivals. As a board member of Asia-Pacific Film Festival (currently) and CIFEJ (formerly), he has also written and presented various papers on promotion and marketing of quality films.

KAMYAR MOHSENIN has worked as a film critic and TV host in film programmes over fifteen years. He is also in charge of Research and Studies in International Affairs at the Farabi Cinema Foundation.

Israel Dan Fainaru

elebrating the first decade of the Cinema Law, which changed the whole perspective of film production in the country, Israeli cinema once again had no reason to complain in 2011. It was present at every major film event, more often than not invited into the most prestigious sections. It picked up several important awards and even had a major box-office hit at home. All this to prove it has not lost its grip, either on domestic audiences or internationally.

It started in February with **Lipstikka** (*Odem*), a controversial competition entry at Berlin, which rubbed a considerable part of the audience the wrong way. The second feature directed by Jonathan Segalle, better known as a film and TV actor, its script went through a long and painful gestation period before settling into the story of two Palestinian women meeting in London years after having left their homeland. Despite dedicated performances by Clara Khouri and Nathalie Attya, the picture disturbed the Palestinians by introducing an objectionably promiscuous Arab teenager; annoyed Israelis because she was coerced into having sex with an Israeli soldier; and disappointed everyone else with a cop-out ending that diffused the message the film had attempted to deliver.

Much better received, but in a parallel Berlin section, the Panorama, Michal Aviad's **Invisible** (*Lo Ro'im Alaich*) once again combined sexual politics and the Middle East conflict. Two women, both raped by the same man, meet many years later and try to help each other with their trauma. Based on a true story, the film is didactic and clinical in its treatment. Ronit Elkabetz gives a highly-strung performance as one of the victims,

a married woman with a strong left-wing political agenda. The film has since travelled extensively to festivals all over the world and was awarded the Best Israeli Film prize at the Haifa Film Festival. However, it has yet to be released domestically.

Josef Cedar's **Footnote**

Josef Cedar picked a Best Script award in Cannes for **Footnote** (*Hea'rat Shulayim*), though the response of the media was far from unanimous in its praise. Warmly received by the English-speaking press, it was sharply criticised, particularly by French critics, who seemed to be immune to its charm. It details the relationship between two Talmudic scholars – a father and son. The parent is conservative, surly and frustrated, while his offspring is much trendier and popular. Not only do they clash over their beliefs, but almost everything else in life. It is a smoothly written and deftly directed piece, which ended the year as the biggest-grossing Israeli film at the domestic box office. It also picked up most of the Ophir awards (Israel's version of the Oscars) and is on its way to represent the country in the Foreign Language section at next year's Academy Awards.

Yossi Madmoni's **Restoration**

Yossi Madmoni took **Restoration** (*Boker Tov Adon Fidelman*) to Karlovy Vary after collecting an earlier award in Sundance. Although the film never strays outside the boundaries of a conventional narrative, it still walked away the prize for Best Film at the Czech festival. It is an intimate portrait of a grumpy old furniture restorer, dedicated to his craft, whose life is turned upside down when his partner, in charge of the mundane financial aspects of the business, suddenly dies, leaving behind a mountain of unpaid debts. Thanks to a masterful performance by Sasson Gabai, the film went on to win the top award at Jerusalem, a decision hotly disputed by the supporters of another contender, Nadav Lapid's **The Policeman** (*HaShoter*).

The plot of Lapid's film is divided into three separate sections. First we are introduced to a macho anti-terrorist police unit, before following a bunch of bourgeois kids spouting tired slogans against social injustice and preparing their own revolution against the corrupt bureaucracy running the country, before reaching its climax, when the cops and rebels clash violently at a high society wedding. Visually enticing – it was flashily shot by Shai Goldman, Israel's top cinematographer – but lacking any detailed characterisation and indulging in a rather shallow and simplified political metaphor of Israel today, it has caught the attention of quite a few international festivals. The film received a Special Jury Prize at Locarno and has gathered quite a following among Israel's younger film critics.

Eran Kolirin's **The Exchange** (*Hithalfut*), his unexpected follow-up to the enormously successful *The Band's Visit*, caught audiences at Venice by surprise. They were prepared for another crowd-pleasing evening, but instead were subjected to a whimsical, existentialist reflection on the individual bubble each of us live in and of one man's attempt to break out of it. An assistant lecturer, happily married to an architect graduate, decides there is more to life than the narrow, stultifying routine of his existence. As he explores the unpredictable aspects of every simple action, he gradually severs all ties with his life, stepping into a world that is both more wondrous and less predictable than anything he had known before. Admired by some for his courage and taken to task by others for his mystifying approach, Kolirin may offer a less than satisfactory conclusion to his film, but it is without a doubt one of the more challenging domestic releases of the last year.

Adding to this year's achievements, there were a couple of remarkable documentaries unveiled at the Jerusalem Film Festival, which must certainly be bound for international exposure. Arnon Goldfinger's thoughtful **The Flat** (*HaDira*) probes into the profound cultural ties of the German Jews with their country of origin, ties that even the Holocaust cannot undo. Meanwhile, Raanan Alexandrowicz's **The Law in These Parts** (*Shilton HaKhok*) offers a searing portrait of how concepts of elementary law are twisted and perverted in the West Bank by some of the country's most respected jurists, all of them bent on defending Israeli interests.

Raanan Alexandrowicz's **The Law in These Parts**

Most countries would probably be more than happy with such a crop. In Israel, the enthusiasm has remained muted. The feeling is that none of these films, whatever their response at home or abroad, managed to fulfil the expectation and fear of stagnation that, after several upbeat years, is easy to detect. There is more discontent brewing on the horizon. A number of young filmmakers, displeased with the policies of the domestic film funds, which they find too conventional, are trying to launch their own 'independent' movement. That is, they start shooting using their own limited resources, without the blessing of any fund and then, when they run out of money, apply to the funds for modest help to complete their project. Several ventures of this kind are now ready to hit the market and are looking for interested exhibitors (not an easy task by any means), but none have, as yet, made a lasting impression outside their own personal circle of supporters.

At the other end of the spectrum, exhibitors, who would rather see them involved in less personal and more commercial features, are putting more pressure on the funds. If this happened, the results would likely resemble last year's lame extravaganza *This is Sodom* (an *Asterix*-style historical spoof featuring popular TV comics) and this year's clumsy **Little Simico's Great Fantasy** (*Hanfatasia HaGdola Shel Simico HaKatan*), a throwback to the late, non-lamented 'bourekas' comedies, whose ethnic characterisations were insulting for anyone who cared enough to take them seriously. That both were made with state money augurs trouble for the future.

DAN FAINARU is co-editor of Israel's only film magazine, *Cinematheque*, former director of the now defunct Israeli Film Institute and a regular reviewer for *Screen International*.

Arnon Goldfinger's **The Flat**

The year's best films

The Flat (Arnon Goldfinger)
The Exchange (Eran Kolirin)
Footnote (Josef Cedar)
The Law in These Parts (Raanan Alexandrowicz)
Restoration (Yossi Madmoni)

Directory

All Tel/Fax numbers begin (+972)
Israel Film Archive, Jerusalem Film Centre, Derech Hebron, PO Box 8561, Jerusalem 91083. Tel: (2) 565 4333. Fax: (2) 565 4335. jer-cin@jer-cin.org.il. www.jer-cin.org.il.
Israel Film Fund, 12 Yehudith Blvd, Tel Aviv 67016. Tel: (2) 562 8180. Fax: (2) 562 5992. info@filmfund.org.il. www.filmfund.org.il.
Israeli Film Council, 14 Hamasger St, PO Box 57577, Tel Aviv 61575. Tel: (3) 636 7288. Fax: (3) 639 0098. etic@most.gov.il.
Tel Aviv Cinema Project, 29, Idelson St, Tel Aviv 65241. Tel. (2) 525 5020. info@cinemaproject.co.il. www.cinemaproject.org.il.
The New Fund for Cinema and Television, 112, Hayarkon St, Tel Aviv. Tel. (3) 522 0909. info@nfct.org.il. www.nfct.org.il

Eran Kolirin's **The Exchange**

لجنة أبوظبي للأفلام
ABU DHABI FILM
COMMISSION

Italy Lorenzo Codelli

Silvio Berlusconi's crumbling regime has endowed us with two symmetrical 'prodigies': a major economic and political crisis, and a flood of film comedies. His own muscular production and distribution empire, Medusa, is leading this lucrative trend, which is far from new, but has never previously attained such magnitude. Among the hundred or so Italian features released in 2011, around half were comedies – mostly cheaply concocted vehicles for TV clowns, rashly assembled adaptations of fashionable sitcoms, or sequels to previous moribund ideas.

Gennaro Nunziante's **Such a Beautiful Day**

Checco Zalone, a bald, equine entertainer from Bari, whose pseudonym means 'Such-a-coarse-fellow' and was launched by Berlusconi's low-brow networks, saw his second film **Such a Beautiful Day** (*Che bella giornata*, directed by his local pal Gennaro Nunziante) speed past Roberto Benigni's *Life Is Beautiful* and *Titanic* as the country's highest earning film. It attracted a staggering €43.4million. Zalone plays out his broad verbal gags through his dim-witted and out-of-touch alter-ego. In a similar vain, Neapolitan jester Alessandro Siani struggled to exploit the late, genial Massimo Troisi's absurdist humour in **The Worst Week of My Life** (*La peggior settimana della mia vita*, by Alessandro Genovesi).

Among other comedians attempting to expand their fan base through film are Claudio Bisio, Vincenzo Salemme, Massimo Boldi, Paolo Ruffini and the team of Francesco Mandelli and Fabrizio Biggio. Luciana Littizzetto, the crudest joker of the bunch, set the tone for a collection of comediennes, that include Paola Cortellesi, Nancy Brilli, Anna Foglietta, Lucia Ocone and Isabella Ragonese.

Some comedy performers have attempted to elevate the level of humour, aiming for satire. For instance, Giambattista Avellino's **Some Say No** (*C'è chi dice no*) wittily mocks the national career system, which is based on family and class connections. Francesco Patierno's biting **Things from Another World** (*Cose dell'altro mondo*) attacks the spread of racism against immigrants, showing a rich northern town from where, one stormy night, all foreigners suddenly disappear. Massimiliano Bruno's **Nobody Can Judge Me** (*Nessuno mi può giudicare*) shows how jobless girls survive by becoming sex escorts, while Antonio Albanese transferred his small screen incarnation as a corrupt politician to the large screen with **Whatsoeverly** (*Qualunquemente*, by Giulio Manfredonia). Unfortunately, like

Giambattista Avellino's **Some Say No**

some of his less ambitious colleagues, he forgets that monologues and repartées work less well in the cinema. **Boris the Movie** (*Boris il film*), by the trio of Giacomo Ciarrapico, Mattia Torre and Luca Vendruscolo, updates the Sky TV sitcom *Boris* in order to deride the Italian film industry. A ferocious, frequently funny attack on the amateurism of people who rule a once-glorious business, old sharks such as Aurelio De Laurentiis and his Christmas farces get their comeuppance.

Newcomers also have more career prospects if they choose the current 'easy to please' path. Renowned screenwriters Francesco Bruni and Ivan Cotroneo sadly followed this route with their directorial debuts. **Scialla!** and **Kryptonite in the Bag** (*La kryptonite nella borsa*) were both formulaic comedies. The same could also be said of another new director, Gianni Pacinotti, with his weak sci-fi parody **The Last Terrestrian** (*L'ultimo terrestre*).

Gianni Pacinotti's **The Last Terrestrian**

Will this mushrooming trend last or will it burn out? It is a far cry from the 'commedia all'italiana' trend of the 1960s and 1970s. These days, there is not an Ugo Tognazzi, Alberto Sordi, Marcello Mastroianni or Nino Manfredi amongst the ranks of the inferior comedians. These 'inheritors' are also urged to function simply as multiplex' fillers, for one or two weekends, rather than as stars imbued with charisma and skills as actors.

Many serious filmmakers are beginning to lose hope of seeing their projects reach the

Paolo Sorrentino's **This Must Be the Place**

screen. Following a long silence, Gianni Amelio had to emigrate to France to direct **The First Man** (*Le premier homme*), an adaptation of an Albert Camus story. International festivals like Cannes, Berlin, Toronto and Venice still help Italian auteurs in terms of recognition, even if their domestic audiences are slight. The commercial success of Paolo Sorrentino's **This Must Be the Place** is a lucky exception to that rule. Young audiences identified with the aged, stoned rock star, marvellously played by Sean Penn. This long-haired has-been is searching for a Nazi who killed his father. A journey through the US and its ghostlands, and one inside the protagonist's empty soul, are brought to the screen with dazzling style, thanks to Sorrentino's direction and Luca Bigazzi's camerawork. And they are aided in no small part by David Byrne's music. Sorrentino also published his first novel, *Everybody's Right* (*Hanno tutti ragione*), confirming his multi-hyphenate talent.

Habemus Papam, Nanni Moretti's first work since *The Caiman*, is a bittersweet fairy-tale set during the election of a Pope. Michel

Nanni Moretti's **Habemus Papam**

Piccoli plays a French cardinal who has doubts at being elected Pontiff. Moretti plays a frustrated, atheist psychoanalyst who has been brought in to help convince him to accept the position. Opening as a lampoon of Vatican pompousness, *Habemus Papam* ascends to a sceptical depiction of *any* form of human leadership: moral, religious or political.

Gianni Di Gregorio's **The Salt of Life**

In **The Salt of Life** (*Gianni e le donne*), Gianni Di Gregorio's sequel to his brilliant *Mid-August Lunch*, he once again plays his cinematic alter-ego, a sixty-something Roman *bon vivant*, who clashes with modern times. This time his problems are with modern women; so approachable and unpredictable, particularly in comparison with his profligate nonagenarian mother (Valeria De Franciscis). Inspired by Jacques Tati, Blake Edwards and Aldo Fabrizi, Di Gregorio's light touch and elegant mood elicit rare pleasures.

Pupi Avati has frequently revisited his large family's legendary past, and many of his films are realisations of his late mother's tales. In **The Big Heart of the Girls** (*Il cuore grande delle ragazze*), the saga becomes grotesque. During the Fascist era, in a village peopled by ugly, pungent freaks and sex maniacs, a young Casanova (singer Cesare Cremonini playing Avati's grandfather) falls in love with a neurotic blonde (Micaela Ramazzotti). But on the night of their marriage, he elopes with a hotel maid. The bizarre romance ends well many years later, but in the meantime Avati has constructed a mirror for our times. The

repulsion of characters and the betrayal they commit, lacking any whiff of nostalgia that permeated his previous work, is a hard, but riveting tonic.

Andrea Segre, an acclaimed documentary maker from Venice, directed his first feature film, **Li and the Poet** (*Io sono Li*). Luca Bigazzi's rainy chiaroscuros and expressionist fogs confer a breathtaking look on the Venetian lagoon. A Chinese barmaid (Zhao Tao) has a 'brief encounter' with a desperate Yugoslav fisherman (Rade Serbedzija). The film is one of several – of varying quality – which look at the immigrant experience. In Ermanno Olmi's **The Cardboard Village** (*Il villaggio di cartone*), his protagonists come from a very different world. Immigrants enter a church, looking for refuge from the cops. There they meet a priest (Michael Lonsdale), himself a symbol of an archaic, idealistic Catholicism. Olmi's biblical parable encourages us to accept our African guests, but also to encourage them to remain what they are, and hopefully to return to their continent, making it flourish like Paradise, since ours appears to be beyond salvation. The philosophical dialogue is reminiscent of Pier Paolo Pasolini.

Ermanno Olmi's **The Cardboard Village**

Applauded at Cannes' 'Directors' Fortnight', **Heavenly Body** (*Corpo celeste*) by Alice Rohrwacher (sister of award-winning actress Alba Rohrwacher) is a coming-of-age story set around a small church in Calabria. A young girl faces a crisis of conscious as she approaches her confirmation. Conscious echoes of other representations of 'religious repressions', from Fellini's to Bergman's, do not mar this ambitious debut.

Submitted to the Academy Awards, Emanuele Crialese's **Terraferma** offers a further look at the immigrant experience. This time from a tiny Sicilian island a few miles off the North African coast. A family of fishermen give refuge to some illegal immigrants, but later decide to report them to the authorities. Crialese aims at blending social criticism with satire. But an excess of picturesque imagery, along with overly mannered performances, tarnish a well-intentioned effort.

Emanuele Crialese's **Terraferma**

Cristina Comencini adapts her latest bestselling novel in **When the Night** (*Quando la notte*). It is a snow-set melodrama about a mother who might be beating her baby and who is pursued by a gruff mountain guide. Despite wooden performances by Claudia Pandolfi and Filippo Timi, Comencini still draws some thrills from her story.

The Jewel (*Il gioiellino*), Andrea Molaioli's second opus following his 2006 mega-hit *The Girl by the Lake*, is a bold exposé based on the Parmalat industry's scandalous crash. Remo Girone and Toni Servillo perfectly embody the CEO and the main accountant of a dairy company, which for a long time was on the brink of collapse, aided by amoral politicians and unscrupulous bankers. This unflinching, if occasionally arid, dissection of corporate malfeasance offers a fascinating microcosm of our troubled times.

Andrea Segre's **Li and the Poet**

The year's best films

This Must Be the Place (Paolo Sorrentino)
Habemus Papam (Nanni Moretti)
The Salt of Life (Gianni Di Gregorio)
The Big Heart of the Girls (Pupi Avati)
Li and the Poet (Andrea Segre)

Directory

All Tel/Fax numbers begin (+39)
Filmitalia-Cinecittà, Via Tuscolana 1055, 00173 Rome. Tel. (06) 722 861. Fax: (06) 7228 6324. www.filmitalia.org/mission.asp?lang=ing
Cineteca del Comune, Via Riva di Reno, 40122 Bologna. Tel: (051) 204 820. www.cinetecadibologna.it.
Cineteca del Friuli, Via Bini 50, Palazzo Gurisatti, 33013 Gemona del Friuli, Udine. Tel: (04) 3298 0458. Fax: (04) 3297 0542. cdf@cinetecadelfriuli. org. http://cinetecadelfriuli.org.
Cineteca Nazionale, Via Tuscolana 1524, 00173 Rome. Tel: (06) 722 941. www.snc.it.
Fondazione Cineteca Italiana, Villa Reale, Via Palestro 16, 20121 Milan. Tel: (02) 799 224. Fax: (02) 798 289. info@cinetecamilano.it. www.cinetecamilano.it.
Fondazione Federico Fellini, Via Oberdan 1, 47900 Rimini. Tel (0541) 50085. Fax: (0541) 57378. fondazione@federicofellini.it. www.federicofellini.it/.
Museo Nazionale del Cinema, Via Montebello 15, 10124 Turin. Tel: (011) 812 2814. www.museonazionaledelcinema.org.

LORENZO CODELLI is on the board of Cineteca del Friuli, a Cannes Film Festival adviser and a regular contributor to *Positif* and other cinema-related publications.

Japan Katsuta Tomomi

The Japanese film industry was severely affected by the earthquake and tsunami that hit the Tohoku area, in the northern part of the Japanese main island of Honshu, on 11 March. Matters were then compounded by the Fukushima nuclear plant crisis. Cinemas in this area, like so many other buildings, were literally swept away by the tsunami, while the power shortage reduced the numbers of screenings in cinemas all over Japan. Many distributors pulled films or cancelled theatrical releases of any films that might recall the disaster, such as Clint Eastwood's *Hereafter* and Feng Xiangang's *Aftershock*. A number of productions were also cancelled. The box-office gross for 2011 is estimated to drop by 20 per cent from the previous year.

However, the box-office decline was not only caused by the disaster. The role adopted by the large TV companies over the last 15 years, accruing almost half the annual receipts with their blockbusters, many of which are adaptations of popular manga stories, novels and small-screen dramas, has resulted in the gradual decline in art-house films. These mainstream behemoths also profited by elaborate ad campaigns and promotions. However, audiences appear to have tired of these films, resulting in a noticeable decrease in attendance figures. Last year, a number of high-profile blockbusters met with

Hirayama Hideyuki's **Oba: The Last Samurai**

disappointing results. A live-action version of the late 1970s TV space-opera anime **Space Battleship YAMATO** earned a decent US$52million, but that paled compared to the figures normally associated with its star Kimura Takuya, Japan's most lucrative actor. Other under-achievers included **GANTS**, a sci-fi action sequel and **Andalusia: Revenge of the Goddess** (*Andarusia: Megami no Fukushu*), a crime thriller shot in Spain with another previously impervious box-office draw, Oda Yuji.

Shindo Kaneto's **Postcard**

Amongst what is seen as a low-key year for Japanese film, a few titles still managed to stand out. Shindo Kaneto's **Postcard** (*Ichimai no Hagaki*) is a satire about a war widow which unfolds both during and following the aftermath of World War II. Shindo, who is now 99-years-old and was a survivor of that conflict, expressed his anger against the war with his trademark visual style and sharp sense of humour. Another war film, Hirayama Hideyuki's **Oba: The Last Samurai** (*Fokkusu to Yobareta Otoko*), depicted the struggle to survive by Captain Oba and his troops in the jungle in Saipan, which was occupied by Allied Forces following the defeat of Japan. Cleverly avoiding more controversial issues such as patriotism or the cruelty of the Japanese army, the film focuses on the nobility and dignity of men trapped in a hopeless situation. Both films added something new to traditional genre fare, avoiding superficial heroics or sentimentality.

Tomita Katsuya's **Saudade**

Indie filmmakers have found a new social issue as their material: illegal immigrants. In his black comedy **Hospitalite** (*Kantai*), first-time director Fukada Koji successfully highlights the strain of xenophobia that runs deep in the Japanese psyche, with the tale of one hardworking family's collapse through the intervention in their lives of an illegal immigrant. In **Saudade**, Tomita Katsuya showed the depressing reality of working-class youths in a rural town, whose antipathy towards immigrants becomes increasingly dangerous. Both films were produced on low budgets, but were acclaimed by critics and audiences alike, and were prominent on the festival circuit.

Two buddy movies offered traditional, well-made, fare. **Tada's Do-it-All House** (*Mahoro ekimae Tada Benriken*), an offbeat comedy-drama by Omori Tatsushi, features a handyman

Omori Tatsushi's **Tada's Do-it-All House**

and his childhood friend who are trying to find happiness in the world whilst dealing with an assortment of characters, from prostitutes, a neglected young boy who is involved in drugs and hardened gangsters. **The Detective is in the Bar** (*Tantei wa Bar ni iru*) is a clever pastiche of film noir, which follows a private detective and his reluctant assistant who are involved in a murder case. All the tropes of the genre are present – the femme fatale, a brutal crime syndicate, guns and fist fights – but the skillful mix of comedy and thriller makes for engaging entertainment.

Comedy is once again becoming an increasingly popular genre in Japan. Mitani Kouki has taken a lead in reviving it. His fifth feature, **Once in a Blue Moon** (*Suteki na Kanashibari*), is a hilarious screwball comedy featuring a ghost who goes to court as a witness for a defendant accused of murder. Mitani's breathless film is replete with witty dialogue and amusing visual gags. Another critical and commercial success, it went on to earn around US$50million at the box office.

Love Strikes! (*Moteki*) also generated huge laughs. A film version of a popular TV drama by director Oone Hitoshi, it depicts a geek who suddenly finds women attracted to him. Reflecting the Japanese trend of passiveness amongst young men towards women, it showcased the delusion of a frustrated youth within a dazzling genre-bending narrative.

Ishii Yuya, one of the most cutting-edge filmmakers of his generation, directed **Mitsuko Delivers** (*Hara ga Kore nannde*). Another off-beat comedy, it tells the story of a young woman who is single and pregnant, with no job, no money or home, but extremely easy-going and with limitless generosity. The heroine's selfless devotion to others in trouble brings a fresh attitude to audiences suffocated by the economic situation.

Aoyama Shinji's **Tokyo Park** (*Tokyo Koen*) investigated the possibility of human contact in a modern world of solitude and mutual distrust

Koreeda Hirokazu's **I Wish**

with his story of people regularly gather in one park. Koreeda Hirokazu displayed hope for the future in **I Wish** (*Kiseki*), an adventure about two brothers who are separated. Both films may not have found the directors at their best, but they nevertheless reflect their unique view of society and the world around them.

Sakamoto Junji's **Someday**

Sakamoto Junji's **Someday** (*Oshikamura Soudouki*) deals with a man in his late sixties who has been living in a mountainous village alone after his wife left him 18 years earlier, running away with his best friend. Both return to the village and he discovers that his ex-wife is suffering from Alzheimer's disease. He is faced with the moral question of whether he can forgive and take care of her. Most of all, he must work out whether he still loves her. The man's agonising is interspersed with the villagers' excitement over a forthcoming Kabuki festival. Sakamoto skilfully demonstrates life's balance between richness and sorrow. Sadly, the film's lead actor, Harada Yoshio, died shortly after the film opened.

The disaster in March may have damaged much, but out of it has sprung a well of creativity. In 2012, the fruits of many people's suffering will be witnessed in Sono Shion's **Himizu**, a drama about isolated teenagers, which saw Sometani Shota and Nikaido Fumi win the Marcello Mastroianni award at Venice. By changing the script following the earthquake and shooting in the disaster area, Sono powerfully explores moral questions such as the nature of sin and the capacity for forgiveness, or possibility restart one's life.

Yamada Yoji may also complete **Tokyo Family**, his version of Ozu Yasujiro's *Tokyo Story*, on which shooting was postponed just after the earthquake, in order to change the script so that it takes in the recent, tragic events.

The year's best films

Someday (Sakamoto Junji)
I Wish (Koreeda Hirokazu)
Saudade (Tomita Katsuya)
Love Strikes! (Oone Hitoshi)
Tada's Do-it-All House (Omori Tatsushi)

Directory

All Tel/Fax numbers begin (+81)
Kawakita Memorial Film Institute, Kawakita Memorial Bldg, 18 Ichiban-cho, Chiyoda-ku, Tokyo 102-0082. Tel: 3265 3281. Fax: 3265 3276. info@kawakita-film.or.jp. www.kawakita-film.or.jp.
Motion Picture Producers Association of Japan, Tokyu Ginza Bldg 3F, 2-15-2 Ginza, Chuo-ku, Tokyo 104-0061. Tel: 3547 1800. Fax: 3547 0909. eiren@mc.neweb.ne.jp.
National Film Center, 3-7-6 Kyobashi, Chuo-ku, Tokyo 104-0031. Tel: 5777 8600. www.momat.go.jp.

KATSUTA TOMOMI is a journalist and main film critic for the *Mainichi* newspapers. He has published a book about the actress Kagawa Kyoko who performed in the films of Kurosawa, Mizoguchi, Naruse and Ozu.

Kazakhstan Gulnara Gabikeyev

I t is clear that there is change afoot within the filmmaking community in Kazakhstan. The directors who followed what has now been termed as the 'Kazakh New Wave', the generation of filmmakers between 35 and 45 years old, have been remarkably active. Of these, Nariman Turebayev's **Sunny Days** gained the highest profile, thanks to its screening at the Locarno Film Festival. It is a story of both emotional and physical loss: over several days, a young man loses his girlfriend, his best friend, water and electricity in his house, as well as the means to communicate with the world, before finally disappearing himself.

Nariman Turebayev's **Sunny Days**

Theatre director Gulsina Myrgaliyeva stepped behind the camera for the first time with **Kausar**, which also played at numerous festivals, including Busan and Mumbai. It was shot on the lunar-like landscape of Mangistau, in western Kazakhstan and offers a portrait of the reserved beauty of nature in this world, as well as the people who live in it. A young girl is expecting a child, but because it was conceived through violence, she does not want it. However, whilst in hospital, she sees how other women suffer through their inability to conceive and begins to think twice about the course of action she has to take.

Erlan Nurmukhambetov and Sano Sindziu's **The First Rains of Spring**

Erlan Nurmukhambetov and Sano Sindziu's Japanese-Kazakh production **The First Rains of Spring** picked up the Grand Prix at the Eurasia Film Festival. It details the reincarnation of an old lady from Altai to a young Russian girl, whilst a parallel story shows a man and his wife traveling across country to lay that same woman, their grandmother, to rest. It is a charming and visually lyrical film that perfectly captures aspects of the Kazakh psyche.

Another New Wave filmmaker, Gaziz Nasyrov directed **Gakku**, which is set in the 1990s, where students rent out their dormitory lodgings at an hourly rate in order to make money, with inevitable consequences. In **Realtor**, Adilkhan Erzhanov tells the story of

Adilkhan Erzhanov's **Realtor**

an enterprising young businessman who is selling Kazakh land to Japanese realtors. Only the place he is selling is the burial land of his ancestors. When he attempts to move the sepulchral stone, he falls into the past, when the fight for the land was violent and bloody.

The most anticipated films of 2012 are by established Kazakh directors. Darezhan Omyrbayev's **Student** is a modern version of Dostoyevsky's *Crime and Punishment*. Akan Satayev's historical drama **Mynbala** (*Thousand Teenagers*) is a story of one thousand orphans who fought the Dzhungars after their parents had already perished in the battle to protect their homeland. The final film, Ermek Tursunov's **The Old Man Walks in Steppe** is the most eagerly awaited. The director's previous film, *Kelin*, made it to the Academy Award shortlist for Best Foreign Language Film in 2010. His new project is an adaptation of Ernest Hemingway's 'The Old Man and the Sea'. However, instead of the sea there is the Kazakh steppe and in the place of fish and sharks, there are sheep and wolves. Each of these films are an attempt at understanding our role here – our place in this world.

Gaziz Nasyrov's **Gakku**

The year's best films
The First Rains of Spring
(Sano Shinju and Erlan Nurmukhambetov)
Kausar (Gulsina Mirgalieva)
Gakku (Gaziz Nasyrov)
Realtor (Adilkhan Erzhanov)
Sunny Days (Nariman Turebayev)

GULNARA ABIKEYEVA is a prominent Kazakh film critic and an author of five books about the cinema of Central Asia. She is artistic director of Eurasia Film Festival that is held annually in Almaty, Kazakhstan.

Akan Satayev's **Mynbala**

لجنة أبوظبي للأفلام
ABU DHABI FILM
COMMISSION

Lithuania Auksė Kancerevičiūtė

Lithuanian cinema is currently struggles for its financial legacy. The new version of the film law is still being debated in parliament, which could finally establish a National Film Centre and provide guaranteed financial support for the local film industry.

In 2011 only one locally-produced feature film was released. Domestic funding remained the same as 2010, with approximately €1 million from the government. The Lithuanian Ministry of Culture supported the production of three features: **Santa**, by Marius Ivaškevičius (just over €260,000), **Lošėjas**, by Ignas Jonynas (€1.1 million) and **Dovydo akmuo**, by Šarūnas Bartas (€200,000). A documentary budget came in just shy of €250,000.

Yet the year also offered much encouragement for the industry. Lithuanian filmmakers and producers are increasingly pursuing the potential of co-productions with foreign investors and institutions. For the first time, the Lithuanian film industry was featured in the European Film Market at the Berlinale. The stand was organised by the Ministry of Culture, the public company Eksportuojanti Lietuva and MEDIA Desk Lietuva (the International Cultural Programme Centre).

Donatas Ulvydas' **Tadas Blinda. Beginning**

More than twenty enterprises and organisations have made themselves available to represent Lithuania, including Kino vilkai, which is a collection of eight enterprises based in Vilnius, Tremora Era Film, Monoklis, organisers of festivals such as the Vilnius International Film Festival 'Cinema Spring' and Kaunas International Film Festival, as well as representatives from Skalvija and Pasaka cinemas.

Donatas Ulvydas' **Tadas Blinda. Beginning** (*Tadas Blinda. Pradžia*), an historical action drama about a Lithuanian folk hero, broke all records at the local box office. Tadas Blinda (1846–77) fiirst appeared on the screen forty years ago and has often been compared to Robin Hood. According to film producer Žilvinas Naujokas, the film not only depicts the adventures of the eponymous hero, but also the struggle of ordinary people against their oppressors, blending action, romance and humour. It has so far racked up 278,000 admissions since its national premiere on 20 September.

Mantas Kvedaravičius made a powerful debut with the documentary **Barzakh**, produced by Finnish director Aki Kaurismäki. The Lithuanian-Finnish co-production played at DocPoints – Helsinki Documentary Film Festival, as well as the Panorama Dokumente programme at the Berlinale, where it was awarded the Amnesty International award and Ecumenical Jury prize. The film investigates cases of torture and disappearance in the North Caucasus. It was made over three years in Chechenya, offering a detailed chronicle of suffering, which avoids sentimentality. The film also received the FIPRESCI prize at Tallinn Film Festival, the Grand Prix in the International Programme of the BelDocs Documentary

Film Festival, the Silver Crane Award for Best Lithuanian Documentary and the Best Baltic Documentary Film award at Vilnius Documentary Film Festival.

Mindaugas Survila's **The Field of Magic** (*Stebuklų laukas*, 2011) a docu-poem about people living in the Buda forest near the defunct Kariotiškės dump, was enthusiastically received by local audiences in Lithuania. Survila also produced the film, which she worked on for four years, over time capturing the increasingly disparate community of 'unknown' people, highlighting the lack of humanity in contemporary society.

Mindaugas Survila's The Field of Magic

Audrius Stonys, the famous Lithuanian documentary filmmaker, who skilfully uses metaphor to draw out meaning in his work, directed **Ramin** (*Raminas*), about the lost love of the 75-year-old Georgian wrestler Ramin Lomsadze, who once won seven matches in 55 seconds. It details the old man's final, toughest fight – with loneliness. It opened the Vilnius Documentary Film Festival and participated at Festival dei Popoli in Florence.

Lithuanian National Radio and Television, the country's public broadcaster, produced the documentary **How We Played the Revolution** (*Kaip mes žaidėme revoliuciją*), which was directed by Giedrė Žickytė. A story about the people who fought for the independence of their country, was co-produced with Gilles Perez and Treize Au Sud (France). From a group of architects who, in 1984, jokingly formed a band, the film details the rise of the social movement that

Mantas Kvedaravičius's Barzakh

grew into the Rock Marches and became the Singing Revolution, which helped forge the countries future.

The year's best films
Barzakh (Mantas Kvedaravičius)
The Field of Magic (Mindaugas Survila)
Tadas Blinda. Beginning (Donatas Ulvydas)
How We Played the Revolution (Giedrė Žickytė)
Ramin (Audrius Stonys)

Directory
All Tel/Fax numbers begin (+370)
Independent Producers Association of Lithuania
Kraziu st. 21, LT-01108 Vilnius. Tel: 682 96 128, 682 96 128. indy.prod.associationLT@gmail.com
The Ministry of Culture of Republic of Lithuania
Basanavičiaus g. 5 | LT-01118 Vilnius. Tel: (85) 219 3443 Fax: (85) 262 3120 | www.lrkm.lt
Lithuanian Filmmakers Union, Vasario 16-osios 13 / Šermukšnių 1, LT-01107 Vilnius. Tel: 5 212 0759 Fax: 5 212 0759. lks@kinosajunga.lt; info@kinosajunga.lt www.kinosajunga.lt
Lithuanian Film Studio, Laisvės pr. 3, LT - 04215 Vilnius. Tel: 5 276 3444, 5 276 3444 Fax: 5 276 4254. info@lfs.lt www.lfs.lt
Lithuanian Central State Archives, O. Milasiaus 21, Vilnius -10102. Tel/Fax: 52/47-78-29, 52/76-53-18. lcva@takas.lt
www.lfc.lt (information about Lithuanian films online) info@lfc.lt

---

AUKSĖ KANCEREVIČIŪTĖ is a film critic and journalist, who writes for the Lithuanian film magazine *Kinas*. She is a coordinator of the 'German Film Days' in Lithuania and lecturer at Skalvija Film Academy.

Mexico Carlos Bonfil

When discussing Mexican cinema, local film festivals have become a reliable barometer in measuring the quality and impact of new releases, the achievements or shortcomings of their screenwriters, and identifying promising new talent. Festivals also confirm or invalidate press judgments throughout the year, as the films open at local cinemas, either at mainstream or art-house venues. Above everything else, what is clear from looking at the films that travel the festival circuit is that documentary, much more than narrative filmmaking, is the most vigorous form of expression in contemporary Mexican cinema.

Tatiana Huezo's **The Tiniest Place**

Political issues are at the core of the best crop of recent documentaries. Tatiana Huezo's **The Tiniest Place** (*El lugar más pequeño*) records the brutality of the Salvadoran civil war. Between 1979 and 1992, 80,000 people died, with an unknown number missing. The conflict devastated entire towns, if not the entire nation. One of those devastated places was the small town of Cinquera, considered by the government, the national guard and the paramilitary as an epicentre of subversion – a guerrilla's refuge. Some families displaced by state terror return years later to the barren town, now overrun by snakes and the ghosts of the missing. They walk atop of the remains of

family members and acquaintances, scattered and buried under mounds that are the only signs of the mass graves beneath. They come back to recover their memories and to rebuild a new town because, as one of them says, 'the land is like another family member'.

The same spirit triggers the memories of the characters in **The Open Sky** (*El cielo abierto*), a moving evocation of the complex personality of Monsignor Oscar Romero, who occupies a senior position in the Church and who, upon hearing about the planned execution of a dissident priest by the authorities in El Salvador, abandons his religiously conservative stance in order to embrace the peasants' cause. He then becomes, as the saying goes, 'the voice of the voiceless': the red archbishop, the new bastion of that liberation theology reviled by the higher Catholic hierarchy, which conspires with businessmen, land owners and the spokesmen of the dictatorship who spread the hatred slogan 'Be a patriot, kill a priest'. Blending interviews with peasants and remarkable archive material, Gonzalez returns to key moments of Romero's pastoral work, whilst recalling the invectiveness of the controlled media and brutal repression of the state.

One of the most successful documentaries of recent years is Roberto Hernandez and Geoffrey Smith's highly controversial **Presumed Guilty** (*Presunto Culpable*), a harrowing indictment of legal abuses inflicted by the Mexican police and judicial system on a daily basis. It tells the real story of José Antonio Zuñiga, who was unjustly imprisoned for two years for a crime he did not commit. Two lawyers took on the case and videotaped the whole legal procedure, including the verbal confrontation between the accused

Roberto Hernandez and Geoffrey Smith's **Presumed Guilty**

and a young witness who appeared to be little more than a police stooge, which exposed the unfairness of the system. The film prompted outrage from the public. Attempts to legally suppress the film only made it more popular.

Another case of abuse, of a very different nature, is highlighted in Alejandra Sanchez's documentary **Agnus Dei, God's Lamb** (*Agnus Dei, cordero de Dios*), where a man recalls the sexual abuse he endured as a minor at the hands of a priest. Although the prelate is clearly identified and his whereabouts revealed, the case has still gone unpunished. The victim speaks of his determination to seek justice and this film, like *Presumed Guilty*, details the problems the country faces in dealing with individual's rights.

Alejandra Sanchez's **Agnus Dei, God's Lamb**

Narrative films, by contrast, have mostly shrunk away from engaging with social or political issues. They focus more on intimate stories that detail conflicts in family and domestic life. Comedy, particularly Hollywood-style romantic comedies, remain popular with audiences.

Sadly, the films that do find wide distribution in Mexico are almost always lacking in originality and are designed for immediate consumption with little thought to longevity.

There were a few attempts at breaking this rule of narrative conformity. Huatey Viveros's **My Universe in Lower Case** (*Mi universo en minúsculas*) details the search by a Catalonian woman for her father, whom she hasn't seen since she was a child, in Mexico City. All she has to go on is an old photograph and the vague details of a street he may have lived on. The film works as an overview of life in the teeming metropolis, through foreign eyes.

Gerardo Naranjo's **Miss Bala**

Gerardo Naranjo's **Miss Bala** is a pessimistic 'rites of passage' tale. A young Mexican woman, who aspires to be the local beauty queen, aspiring for the title of Queen of Beauty in her homeland, finds herself trapped in a web of drug-related gang violence and political corruption. It is a vigorous indictment of the complicity of political power with the economic interests of the same drug cartels it claims to fight. It also looks at how the central character succumbs to her situation, only to be betrayed by all concerned. With little graphic violence and the subtle suggestion of a society in a state of moral disarray, Naranjo offers a powerful and bitter tale of a whole country engaged in an unwinnable battle against crime and widespread corruption.

Newcomer Michel Lipkes's **Malaventura** views the world through the eyes of an apparently defeated and disillusioned old man. Experimental in structure, there is no traditional narrative in the film, whose tone is dry, with the singular expression on the man's face conveying the pain of living in a hostile environment. Although it makes for uneasy viewing, the film has a visual richness and a radical style that is uncommon in current Mexican cinema.

Arturo Ripstein returned after five years with the controversial **The Reason of the Heart** (*Las razones del corazón*). An adaptation of Gustave Flaubert's *Madame Bovary*, restricting the narrative to the final part of the novel and transposing the action to a poor area of Mexico City. With its claustrophobic atmosphere, lusciously photographed in black and white, the characters indulge in acts of moral abjection, showing the extremes to which passion may lead. As Emilia degrades herself in her adulterous love affair with a saxophone player, her husband reaches depths of moral decay and self-lacerating humiliation, which transform the film into an ordeal and a dubious aesthetic achievement. Radical moral pessimism has been a constant in Ripstein's work. Disliked by many viewers, yet praised by critics both locally and abroad, his recent films have produced a sense of unease and distaste among large audiences.

The biggest surprise of the year came from Argentinean filmmaker Paula Markovitch, who has been living and working in Mexico for the last seventeen years. She was the

screenwriter on Fernando Eimbcke's popular *Duck's Season*. Her feature debut, **The Prize** (*El premio*), profits from its minimal approach that never negates the lyricism of its story, the rule of a military dictatorship as seen through the eyes of a six-year-old girl. She is tasked with submitting homework that valorises the state. Winning the school prize for her work, she becomes estranged from her mother, who was a victim of that very same government. This powerful film was one of the few signs of hope for the future of narrative cinema in Mexico.

The year's best films
Miss Bala (Gerardo Naranjo)
The Prize (Paula Markovitch)
Presumed Guilty
(Roberto Hernandez and Geoffrey Smith)
The Tiniest Place (Tatiana Huezo)
Agnus Dei, God's Lamb (Alejandra Sanchez)

Directory
All Tel/Fax numbers begin (+52)
Cineteca Nacional, Avenida México-Coyoacán 389, Col Xoco, México DF. Tel: 1253 9314. www.cinetecanacional.net.
Association of Mexican Film Producers & Distributors, Avenida División del Norte 2462, Piso 8, Colonia Portales, México DF. Tel: 5688 0705. Fax: 5688 7251.
Cinema Production Workers Syndicate (STPC), Plateros 109 Col San José Insurgentes, México DF. Tel: 5680 6292. cctpc@terra.com.mx.
Dirección General de Radio, Televisión y Cinematografía (RTC), Roma 41, Col Juárez, México DF. Tel: 5140 8010. ecardenas@segob.gob.mx.
Instituto Mexicano de Cinematografía (IMCINE), Insurgentes Sur 674 Col del Valle, CP 03100, México DF. Tel: 5448 5300. mercaint@institutomexicanodecinematografía.gob.mx.

Paula Markovitch's **The Prize**

CARLOS BONFIL is a film critic for *La Jornada*, a leading Mexican newspaper. He is also the author of *Through the Mirror: Mexican Cinema and its Audiences* (1994).

Morocco Maryam Touzani

Morocco gradually continues its ascent within the international film community, setting the standard for neighbouring countries. The past year has yet seen another increase in feature production, now around twenty, in addition to significant festival presence abroad. And although short-term setbacks of cinema closures remains a concern, a genuine interest from both the state and public in general could reverse this trend. The 52 annual festivals and cinematic events that take place across the country is proof of this.

Roschdy Zem's **Omar Killed Me**

Abdelhaï Laraki's **Love in the Medina**

Abdelhaï Laraki's **Love in the Medina** (*Les Ailes de l'Amour*) is set in the medina of Casablanca. Young Thami loves his job as a butcher, while braving the wrath of his father, a conservative man who descends from a long line of religious judges. In handling the meat, Thami discovers another, less acceptable, passion – women. And in Zineb he soon finds love.

Director Roschdy Zem's **Omar Killed Me** (*Omar M'a Tuer*) is Morocco's official submission for the 2012 Academy Awards. A Franco-Moroccan co-production, it tells the story of Omar Raddad, who was jailed in the early 1990s for the brutal murder of a wealthy French woman, for whom he was employed as a gardener. However, three years after sentencing, a writer convinced of his innocence launches his own investigation. The film explores the prejudices uncovered in this battle against injustice.

Filmmaker Faouzi Bensaidi continues his exploration of genre, moving into film noir territory with the taut **Death for Sale** (*Mort à Vendre*). The story unfolds in Tetouan, a city wedged between the mountains of northern Morocco. Malik, Alla and Soufiane, who make a living as pickpockets, decide to upgrade their game and rob the town's biggest jewellery store.

Faouzi Bensaidi's **Death for Sale**

Driss Mrini's **Larbi**

Driss Mrini's directorial debut dates back to 1983, with *Bamou*. He returned last year with **Larbi**, a fascinating film inspired by the life of the outstanding footballer Haj Larbi Benbarek, who was nicknamed 'The Black Pearl.'

Leïla Kilani career so far includes the two acclaimed documentaries *Tangiers: The Burners' Dream* and *Our Forbidden Places*. Her feature debut, **On the Edge** (*Sur la Planche*), premiered at Cannes. It is the story of four young Moroccan girls in Tangier who pursue a dream they will never attain. Another first-time director, Hisham Lasri, produced a remarkable feature with the unconventional **The End**. The film tells the story of M'key, a parking attendant who falls in love with Rita, a young woman caught up in her brothers' gang life. Ingenious narration, stylish cinematography and a strong sense of the world in which the story unfolds contribute the films originality.

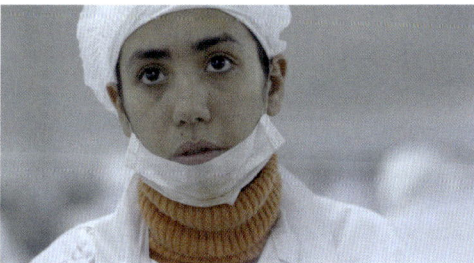

Leïla Kilani's **On the Edge**

After *Islamour*, director Saad Chraibi returned to one of his favourite subjects – the plight of women – with **Women in Mirrors** (*Femmes en Mirroirs*), in which a famous young

photographer living in Paris is called back to her home country after almost a decade, in order to aid her ailing mother.

Nabil Ayouch's **My Land**

Nabil Ayouch who has firmly established his position as one of Morocco's most significant directors, made the documentary **My Land**. Born in France to a Muslim Moroccan father and a Jewish mother of Tunisian descent, he gives voice to old Palestinian refugees who fled to Lebanon in 1948, never returning to their land. These testimonies are witnessed by young Israelis that now live on that same land, which they feel deeply attached to. Memory and the politics of ownership converge in this powerful and deeply personal work.

Hicham Lasri's **The End**

The year's best films
My Land (Nabil Ayouch)
Omar Killed Me (Roschdy Zem)
On the Edge (Leïla Kilani)
The End (Hicham Lasri)

MARYAM TOUZANI is a freelance journalist based in Morocco and working internationally, specialising in cinema.

Netherlands Leo Bankersen

It felt like a paradox. On the one hand, Dutch film was enjoying a very successful year, particularly in terms of its box-office figures. Forty-two feature films and documentaries were released over the course of the year. Although this was slightly less than 2010, audience attendance reached a new record. However, the most talked about topic was the sombre prospect of a severe reduction of government support for film and other arts, taking effect from 2012. In her opening speech at the Netherlands Film Festival (September 21–30) director Willemien van Aalst compared the government policy with a destructive tornado that will dramatically change the cultural landscape of the Netherlands.

Will Koopman's **Viper's Nest**

Yet, at the very same festival, a representative of Pathé felt confident enough to predict total attendance in Dutch cinemas to reach a record high of 30 million in 2011. Even more satisfying was the 20 per cent market share of Dutch film. True enough, much of this success was owed to the 1.9 million tickets sold for Will Koopman's **Viper's Nest** (*Gooische vrouwen*), a comedy based on a popular television series often described as the Dutch version of *Sex and the City*.

Other titles also performed very well. A surprise hit (released in December 2010)

Maria Peters' **Sonny Boy**

was Steffen Haars' and Flip van der Kuil's anarchistic pulp comedy **New Kids Turbo**, also based on a television series. Many critics hated it, but with over one million tickets sold – a number not often achieved by a Dutch film – who cares? The predictable sequel, **New Kids Nitro**, which featured more explosions, followed. Aiming at more conventional tastes was Maria Peters' moving drama **Sonny Boy**. Based on historical events, it tells the story of an impossible interracial relationship during in World War II. The film was put forward as the Dutch Academy Awards contender.

Among the strong end-of-year releases destined to keep Dutch market share high is Maarten Treurniet's **The Heineken**

Maarten Treurniet's **The Heineken Kidnapping**

Kidnapping (*De Heineken ontvoering*), a partially fictionalised account of the notorious kidnapping of Dutch beer magnate Alfred Heineken in 1983. This well-received thriller features Rutger Hauer in an impressive performance. The versatile Hauer also appeared in Paula van der Oest's **Black Butterflies**, about South-African poet Ingrid Jonker (Carice van Houten). At the Netherlands Film Festival this gripping biopic was awarded with the Golden Calf for Best Film, with Van Houten taking the Best Actress prize.

The November release of Reinout Oerlemans' **Nova Zembla** was also destined to attract a sizable audience. An adventure film based on a famous 16th-century polar expedition, it is the first Dutch feature in 3D.

One of the most engaging examples of this year's selection of kids and family films – a genre Dutch filmmakers have mastered well – is **Taking Chances** (*Patatje oorlog*). Nicole van Kilsdonk tells the story of a girl concerned about her father, a doctor in a war zone, infusing it with creativity and wit. It picked up the Best Dutch Film award at the Cinekid Festival. Now celebrating its 25th anniversary, Cinekid is widely regarded as one of the most prominent festivals for children's films worldwide. However, that opinion is not necessarily shared by the policy makers of the right-wing Dutch government.

Urszula Antoniak's **Code Blue**

There were also some fine new examples of the Dutch 'new wave', as it is sometimes called abroad. Urszula Antoniak's **Code Blue**, about a nurse secretly helping people to die, was selected for Cannes' 'Director's Fortnight' programme. Though reviews were mixed, this

uncompromising take on intimacy, death and loneliness offers a sense of a major issue at stake.

Another unconventional take on intimacy and sex can be found in **Brownian Movement**, which was selected for the Berlin Forum. At the Netherlands Film Festival, Nanouk Leopold picked up the Golden Calf for Best Director and Best Screenwriter for this one.

Nanouk Leopold's **Brownian Movement**

The road movie **Rabat**, by newcomers Jim Taihuttu and Victor Ponten, was something of a surprise. Unwilling to wade through the process of applying for funding by conventional means, they employed a shoestring budget to film the story of three young Moroccan-Dutch men travelling to the land of their parents. It is a film made with passion and verve, which saw Nasrdin Dchar receive the Golden Calf for Best Actor.

An even more promising debut is Marco van Geffen's low-key psychological thriller **Among Us** (*Onder ons*) about a Polish au pair living an isolated life on a neat Dutch housing estate. This first episode of a planned trilogy on Dutch suburban life, it premiered at Locarno.

Marco van Geffen's **Among Us**

Leonard Retel Helmrich's **Position Among the Stars**

From the rich harvest of documentaries only a few can be mentioned here. **Position Among the Stars** (*Stand van de sterren*), the final episode of Leonard Retel Helmrich's trilogy on Indonesian life, was released this year. This impressive and lively example of cinéma vérité was already chosen as the best film at the International Documentary Filmfestival Amsterdam in 2010 and was put forward by HBO as an Academy Award contender.

Tom Fassaert's **An Angel in Doel**

The Berlinale (Forum section) selected Tom Fassaert's **An Angel in Doel** (*De engel van Doel*), about the last inhabitants of a soon-to-be demolished Belgian village. Shot in stunning black and white, the intimate observations gradually become a moving contemplation about life, death and change.

The Golden Calf for best documentary went to **Not Without You** (*Niet zonder jou*) by Petra Lataster-Czisch and Peter Lataster, which

follows an elderly couple (Lataster's parents) in the last year of their life together.

The International Film Festival Rotterdam celebrated its 40th edition with screenings and cinema-related activities unfolding across 40 extra locations. Together with the related Hubert Bals Fund and the Cinemart, it continues to be an important supporter of independent cinema worldwide. The three winners of the Tiger Competition were **The Journals of Musan** (Park Jung-Bum, South Korea), **Finisterrae** (Sergio Caballero, Spain) and **Eternity** (Sivaroj Kongsakul, Thailand). Finding Dutch distributors for these Tigers, however, is becoming increasingly difficult.

When festival director Ally Derks opened the other major film festival in the Netherlands, the International Documentary Film Festival Amsterdam, she looked back at an 'incredible year'. She not only mentioned the meltdown of economies and climates but also a new revolutionary spirit, from the Arab Spring to Occupy Wall Street, and noted that 'the need for documentary is greater then ever'.

This 24th IDFA edition (November 16–27), whose attendance rose to 200,000, opened with the rather spectacular Danish undercover documentary **The Ambassador**, by Mads Brügger, who was brave enough to dive headfirst in the shady African world of false diplomatic passports, diamonds and corrupt politicians. By contrast, the closing ceremony saw the main prize awarded to the very unpolitical **Planet of Snail**, by South Korean Seung-Jun Yi. It is an intimate and poetic impression of the life of someone who is deaf and blind. The Best Dutch Documentary award went to Jessica Gorter for **900 Days**, highlighting how different the real stories of those who survived the siege of Leningrad (1941–44) are very from propagandistic myth.

Will Dutch cinema be able to prolong its vitality in 2012? A new hit in the making is **Family is All** (*Alles is familie*), not really a sequel but a follow-up to the immensely enjoyable

2007 hit *Love is All*. A much smaller film that is already attracting attention is **170 Hz**, the first feature by Joost van Ginkel, which was selected for the Busan Film Festival and will be released domestically in 2012. This tragic love story, fuelled with high-octane passion, features dialogue in sign language and bold, expressionistic visuals.

The year's best films
Code Blue (Urszula Antoniak)
Position Among the Stars
(Leonard Retel Helmrich)
An Angel in Doel (Tom Fassaert)
Among Us (Marco van Geffen)
Taking Chances (Nicole van Kilsdonk)

Directory
All Tel/Fax numbers begin (+31)
Association of Dutch Film Critics (KNF), PO Box 10650, 1001 ER Amsterdam. Tel: (6) 2153 4555. info@filmjournalisten.nl. www.filmjournalisten.nl.
Cobo Fund, PO Box 26444, Postvak M54, 1202 JJ Hilversum. Tel: (35) 677 5348. Fax: (35) 677 1955. cobo@cobofonds.nl. portal.omroep.nl/cobofonds/. Contact: Jeanine Hage.
Dutch Federation for Cinematography (NFC), PO Box 143, 1180 AC Amstelveen. Tel: (20) 426 6100. Fax: (20) 426 6110. info@nvbbureau.nl. www. nfcstatistiek.nl/index2.html. Contact: Wilco Wolfers.
EYE Film Institute Netherlands, Sandra den Hamer, Vondelpark 3, PO Box 74782, 1070 BT Amsterdam. Tel: (20) 589 1400. Fax: (20) 683 3401. info@eyefilm.nl. www.eyefilm.nl.
Filmmuseum, Sandra den Hamer, Vondelpark 3, PO Box 74782, 1070 BT Amsterdam. Tel: (20) 589 1400. Fax: (20) 683 3401. info@filmmuseum.nl. www.filmmuseum.nl.
Holland Film, Claudia Landsberger, Jan Luykenstraat 2, 1071 CM Amsterdam. Tel. (20) 570 7575. Fax (20) 570 7570. hf@hollandfilm.nl. www.hollandfilm.nl.
International Documentary Film Festival Amsterdam, Frederiksplein 52, 1017 XN Amsterdam. Tel: (020) 627 3329. Fax: (020) 638 5388. info@idfa.nl. www.idfa.nl.
International Film Festival Rotterdam, PO Box 21696, 3001 AR Rotterdam. Tel: (10) 890 9090. Fax: (10) 890 9091. tiger@filmfestivalrotterdam.com. www.filmfestivalrotterdam.com.

Nicole van Kilsdonk's **Taking Chances**

Ministry of Education, Culture and Science, Arts Dept, PO Box 16375, 2500 BJ Den Haag. Tel: (70) 412 3456. Fax: (70) 412 3450. www.rijksoverheid. nl/ministeries/ocw.
Netherlands Film and Television Academy (NFTA), Markenplein 1, 1011 MV Amsterdam. Tel: (20) 527 7333. Fax: (20) 527 7344. info@filmacademie.nl. www.filmacademie.nl. Contact: Sytze van der Laan.
Netherlands Film Festival, Willemien van Aalst, PO Box 1581, 3500 BN Utrecht. Tel: (30) 230 3800. Fax: (30) 230 3801. info@filmfestival.nl. www.filmfestival.nl.
Netherlands Film Fund, Jan Luykenstraat 2, 1071 CM Amsterdam. Tel: (20) 570 7676. Fax: (20) 570 7689. info@filmfonds.nl. www. filmfund.nl. Contact: Doreen Boonekamp.
Netherlands Institute for Animation Film (NIAf), PO Box 9358, 5000 HJ Tilburg. Tel: (13) 532 4070. Fax: (13) 580 0057. niaf@niaf.nl. www.niaf.nl. Contact: Ton Crone.
Netherlands Institute for Sound and Vision, Sumatralaan 45, 1217 GP Hilversum. Tel: (35) 677 5555. Fax: (35) 677 3307.
Rotterdam Media Fund, Lloydstraat 9F, 3025 EA Rotterdam. Tel: (10) 436 0747. Fax: (10) 436 0553. info@rmf.rotterdam.nl. www.rff.rotterdam.nl. Contact: Jacques van Heijningen.

LEO BANKERSEN is a freelance film critic, contributing regularly to *de Filmkrant*, the largest independent film magazine in the Netherlands.

New Zealand Peter Calder

The most striking New Zealand film of 2011 had not so much as a frame shot south of the equator. It was made in Manhattan on a consumer handicam and the 'cast' comprised a mysterious Ukrainian beauty named Masha (who, when we first meet her, is carrying a slice of cake on a plate), and anyone the filmmaker encountered on the street.

Florian Habicht's **Love Story**

Love Story, which was paid the compliment of being selected as the opening night attraction at the New Zealand International Film Festival, wasn't supposed to be made at all. Its maker, German-born Kiwi Florian Habicht, whose previous films include off-beat Kiwiana documentaries *Kaikohe Demolition* and *Land of the Long White Cloud*, was the inaugural recipient of a philanthropic scholarship, which sends New Zealand artists to New York for as long as they can make US$62,000 last. There is no expectation to produce any work, but Habicht's industrial-strength whimsy, in which he asked New Yorkers to decide which direction the story should next take, was a delight – a feather-light rumination on the filmmaking process and the nature of connectedness. And his decision to call Masha, who had not seen the film, from the stage after the world premiere screening, was an inspired piece of showmanship and the perfect finishing touch.

The standout feature of the year was also rooted in real life. Roseanne Liang's previous documentary *Banana in a Nutshell* was a modest and heartfelt portrait of the difficulty she faced as the daughter of Chinese immigrants who had fallen in love with a pakeha (European New Zealander). The documentary caught the eye of veteran producer John Barnett (*Whale Rider*, *Sione's Wedding*) who persuaded Liang there was a feature in it and the result, **My Wedding and Other Secrets**, was a funny and touching rom-com that reflected the country's multicultural make-up.

Far less amusing, but deeply impressive, was **Operation 8: Deep in the Forest**, an unabashedly partisan and polemical documentary that anatomised the 2007 police raids of sixty houses around the country, in relation to an alleged paramilitary training camp. The events, which introduced the word 'terrorist' into the domestic political discourse for the first time, caused deep consternation among civil rights groups – not least because all but a few firearms charges were dropped. Wellington activist filmmakers Errol Wright and Abi King-Jones' balanced, if hardly dispassionate, film made a valuable contribution to debate.

Errol Wright and Abi King-Jones' **Operation 8: Deep in the Forest**

Gerard Smyth's **When a City Falls**

The catastrophic earthquakes that ravaged Christchurch in September 2010 and February 2011 generated so many thousands of hours of television footage that a film might have seemed superfluous. But in **When a City Falls** community filmmaker Gerard Smyth added much to the record with an effectively discursive view of the quakes and their aftermath, which emphasised the human dimension, rather than taking the incident-driven approach that news crews adopted. The film's first half is saturated in a piercing irony, since it documents the first earthquake – in which no one died – and shows people celebrating their lucky escape. The February shake, which claimed 181 lives, was the fourth worst in our history.

If the rest of the national output was less accomplished, there was certainly work that spoke to New Zealanders' sense of themselves. Notable was **Billy T: Te Movie** (the 'te' is Maori for 'the'), which celebrated the life of much-loved Maori comedian Billy T. James, who died tragically young some twenty years ago. James – or Billy, as everyone knew him – was a household name, but the film's view of him was disappointingly devoid of nuance. Much has been made of how Billy's Maori carica-tures made 'us laugh at ourselves', but he was widely reviled by radicalised Maori and it is at least arguable that he pandered to crude stereo-types without deflating them – or the rednecks who subscribed to them – one little bit. The film, by veteran actor-director Ian Mine (*Came a Hot Friday*) skated around all this in favour of reverential reminiscence and archive clips.

The serious stinker of the year was the UK-NZ co-production **Tracker**, a plodding and convoluted bounty-hunter western in which Ray Winstone played a Boer War vet pursuing Temuera Morrison (*Once Were Warriors*) across a mountainous wild frontier. The scenery was marvellous, but such imagery is ten-a-penny in this neck of the woods.

Ian Sharp's **Tracker**

More successful was Paul Murphy's **Love Birds**, which paired local comedy export Rhys Darby (*Flight of the Conchords*; *Yes Man*; *The Boat That Rocked*) with the chirpy, goofy English actress Sally Hawkins (Mike Leigh's *Happy Go Lucky*) in an endearingly sugar-coated entertainment. Darby played a broken-hearted chap whose moping is interrupted by the arrival on his roof of an equally depressed duck, which leads him to pretty ornithologist Holly. The sophomore effort of the writer-director team behind the local sleeper hit *Second Hand Wedding* didn't fire as well as it probably deserved.

Paul Murphy's **Love Birds**

Special mention has to go to Tusi Tamasese's feature debut **The Orator**, in cinematic terms the year's most accomplished film. The first truly Samoan feature film – shot entirely in the Samoan language and written and directed by a Samoan – the New Zealand Film Commission and the Samoan Government financed the project. It is a powerful and impressive achievement – a sort of Pasifika *High Noon*.

The impelling irony of *The Orator* is that the film's hero is a dwarf who must, er, rise to the challenge and prove that the bonds of love can sometimes trump those of blood. It's hard to think of a film more rooted in its setting – its cultural context is indistinguishable from its meaning and the sublime cinematography of Kiwi doyen Leon Narbey made it both luscious and gripping.

Tusi Tamasese's **The Orator**

The centre-right Government, re-elected in November, lowered the eligibility threshold for a production subsidy scheme, largely to ensure we remained as attractive as Australia as a location, but it is likely to enable more New Zealand feature films to be brought into production over the next two years. That development, together with the new micro-budget Escalator scheme, designed to finance modest first-time features, bodes well for the immediate future of an industry that has not been as decimated as one might have expected by the global economic downturn.

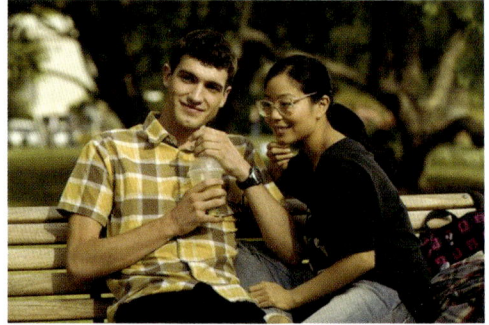
Roseanne Liang's **My Wedding and Other Secrets**

The year's best films

My Wedding and Other Secrets (Roseanne Liang)
The Orator (Tusi Tamasese)
Love Story (Florian Habicht)
Operation 8: Deep in the Forest (Errol Wright, Abi King-Jones)
When a City Falls (Gerard Smyth)

Directory

All Tel/Fax numbers begin (+64)
Film New Zealand, PO Box 24142, Wellington. Tel: (4) 385 0766. Fax: (4) 384 5840. info@filmnz.org.nz. www.filmnz.com.
New Zealand Film Archive, PO Box 11449, Wellington. Tel: (4) 384 7647. Fax: (4) 382 9595. nzfa@actrix.gen.nz. www.filmarchive.org.nz.
New Zealand Film Commission, PO Box 11546, Wellington. Tel: (4) 382 7680. Fax: (4) 384 9719. marketing@nzfilm.co.nz.
Ministry of Economic Development, 33 Bowen St, PO Box 1473, Wellington. Tel: (4) 472 0030. Fax: (4) 473 4638. www.med.govt.nz.
Office of Film & Literature Classification, PO Box 1999, Wellington. Tel: (64) 471 6770. Fax: (4) 471 6781. information@censorship.govt.nz.
Screen Production & Development Association (SPADA), PO Box 9567, Wellington. Tel: (4) 939 6934. Fax: (4) 939 6935. info@spada.co.nz.

PETER CALDER is the chief film critic for the *New Zealand Herald*, the country's major newspaper.

Nigeria Steve Ayorinde

The concept of the New Nigerian Cinema finally saw the light of day, with the better part of 2011 spent celebrating a number of professionals in Nollywood who value quality over quantity.

Teco Benson's **Two Brides and a Baby**

More than a thousand films still passed through the National Film and Video Censors Board, but amongst these were a collection that were universally praised. There films were supported by a sizable budget, were given higher-profile marketing campaigns and also played well at festivals. And along with the praise lavished on these films, there were filmmakers celebrated for their work in the industry. Six directors were honoured with Nigeria's highest national award for their contribution to the motion picture industry.

It was not a good year for comedy. One of the most celebrated comic actors, Babatunde Omidina (Baba Suwe), was arrested, allegedly for drug trafficking. He was detained for 24 days, with authorities hoping that any drugs he may have consumed, with the intention of transporting, would be expelled. In the end he was released and a court awarded him about US$16,000 in compensation. Knowing that

Nollywood derives much inspiration from real-life incidents, comedy fans expect Omidina, the star of **Baba Londoner** and arguably the most prolific actor in Yoruba-language cinema, to adapt the story for release some time next year.

Romance dominated the big screen over the last year, from Tade Ogidan's **Family on Fire**, a cross-country tale that took five years to produce, to Teco Benson's **Two Brides and a Baby**, a contemporary urban tale about one married couple's problems. Even Funke Akindele's much-anticipated **Return of Jenifa** over-romanticised a surreal, funny drama about a village girl who moves to the city and transforms into a diva.

Funke Akindele's **Return of Jenifa**

Arguably the cinematic highlight of the year, Kunle Afolayan's **Phone Swap**, is a smart romantic comedy that had all the elements to make it a box-office hit. It is a well-directed and engaging film from a director who earlier in the year had delivered **Breeze**. Also produced by the actor-director's Golden Effects Company, it was financed by the Securities and Exchange Commission (SEC), a federal government agency, and intended to rekindle people's interest in stockbroking.

Mildred Okwo's **The Meeting**, a romantic thriller largely shot in Abuja, the government-dominated capital city, ranks among the year's best in terms of its charm and the impressive performance by Rita Dominic, who also co-produced.

However, the message that resonated throughout the industry was that Nollywood will continue to witness a thousand cheap quality films that are meant for use in homes or at video clubs, but the few that were celebrated by the industry are steering the course of the industry's future. That was the message that the African Movie Academy Awards (AMAA), now in its seventh year in existence, stated. Fidelis Duker's Abuja International Film Festival, which is attempting to forge a new Nigerian cinema, is also a vocal advocate of these new trends in Nollywood.

Daniel Okoduwa's **Gossip Nation**

Daniel Okoduwa's **Gossip Nation**, a thriller set within metropolitan Lagos, will be released in cinemas in 2012. As will Lancelot Imasuen's epic romantic drama **Adesuwa**. Next year also sees the merger of the Censors Board and Nigerian Film Corporation. If this move works, Nollywood may be guaranteed of a shift in gear towards an increased number of quality-oriented productions.

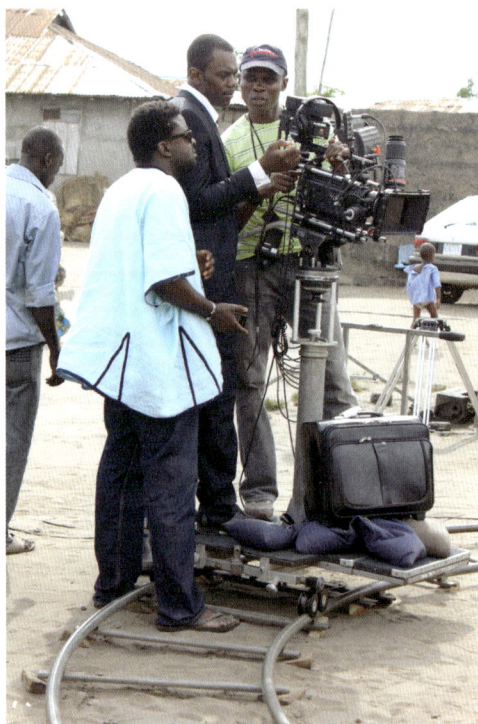
Kunle Afolayan filming his latest feature **Phone Swap**

The Year's Best Films
Phone Swap (Kunle Afolayan)
The Meeting (Mildred okwo)
Imala (Andy Amenechi)
Two Brides and a Baby (Teco Benson)
The Return of Jenifa (Funke Akindele)

STEVE AYORINDE is a film critic and Editor-in-Chief of *National Mirror* newspaper. He is a member of FIPRESCI and sits on the Jury of African Movie Academy Awards (AMAA). He is the author of *Masterpieces: A Critic's Timeless Report* and *Abokede*, a cultural biography.

Norway Trond Olav Svendsen

In 2011 the Norwegian film industry celebrated its first century of narrative cinema. One hundred years ago, the cinema owner Halfdan Nobel Roede produced the first batch of Norwegian melodramas. Since then there has been a steady output, with the first half-century reaching a pinnacle in the 1950s, which saw the production of ten films per year. A volume published to coincide with the anniversary contains some revealing statistics. The total number of Norwegian films produced is nearing 900, with the last 15 years accounting for a third of these. No period can compare to the present and, with perfect timing, last year saw the industry hit an all-time high of thirty releases. Along with this exceptional production rate came the highest domestic grosses and one of the biggest market shares ever.

Morten Tyldum's **Head Hunters**

This large batch was, of course, a mixed bag. It ran the gamut of realism, melodrama, children's film, action, crime, horror and documentary. As usual, crime was the box-office winner. Norwegians love crime fiction and some of the country's best writers have now developed a considerable following abroad. The market, whether for books or films, shows no sign of diminishing. After seven films adapted from Bergen-based

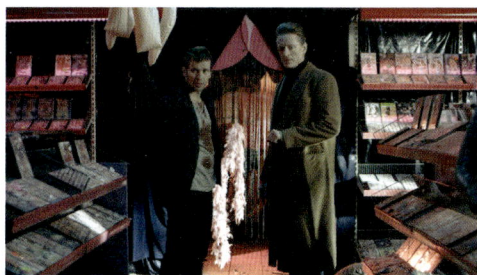

Magnus Martens' **Jackpot**

Gunnar Staalesen stories, the crime wave is now being led by Jo Nesbø. Even Martin Scorsese has reportedly expressed an interest in his novels. Meanwhile, Morten Tyldum's **Head Hunters** (*Hodejegerne*), starring Aksel Hennie and Danish actor Nikolaj Coster-Waldau, became a huge domestic hit. It is an effectively told tale of greed and art, which develops into something labyrinthine and increasingly sinister. Magnus Martens followed suit in late Autumn with another Nesbø-written story, the bloody and macabre action comedy **Jackpot** (*Arme riddere*). This time round audiences were less convinced.

Between those releases, Pål Sletaune continued his exploration of anxiety and paranoia with the sharp psychological thriller **Babycall**, based on his own script and featuring the Swedish actress Noomi Rapace (*The Girl with the Dragon Tattoo*). It deals with a single mother hiding from a violent husband and trying to protect her young son from unknown forces. The film was made with a sure hand, but ultimately it proved to be more clever than profound.

A handful of films generated a great deal of interest both at home and abroad. Arild Andresen's **The Liverpool Goalie** (*Keeper'n*

Arild Andresen's **The Liverpool Goalie**

til Liverpool) was voted best children's film at the Berlin Festival. Sundance gave Anne Sewitsky's **Happy, Happy** (*Sykt lykkelig*) a rousing reception. While Joachim Trier's second feature **Oslo, August 31st** (*Oslo, 31. August*) was very well received in Cannes.

Happy, Happy is Sewitsky's directorial debut. She graduated from the Norwegian film school in 2006 and has an award-winning short and television work to her credit. Written by Ragnhild Tronvoll, the film tells the story of two couples in a small community in rural Norway, one living there permanently and the other moving temporarily from the big city in order to repair their marriage. But soon adultery and betrayal is afoot. The characters are all convincing, with Agnes Kittelsen outstanding as Kaja. Joachim Rafaelsen is impressive, but his character, particularly the suggestion of latent homosexuality, could have been developed more. Interestingly, considering the cruelty of the characters, the film never fails to keep its positive view of the world or the subtle use of comedy. Sewitsky went on to make a fine film for children, **Totally True Love**

Anne Sewitsky's **Totally True Love**

(*Jørgen + Anne = sant*), which received its world premiere at Berlin.

For many, *Oslo August 31st* was the film of the year. It received a strong festival run, at Cannes and Haugesund, before its Norwegian premiere. It is a remarkably strong follow-up to Trier's 2006 feature debut, *Reprise*. The film opens with Anders on day release from a clinic where he has been treated for heroin addiction. Anders Danielsen Lie is excellent in the lead role, his performance perfectly balanced between intelligence and vulnerability. However, the most striking aspect of the film is the assurance with which Trier tells his story. As we witness Anders reuniting with friends, Trier offers up a subtle portrait of a generation, one that seems slightly lost in the world. His mis-en-scene employs Oslo as a character. The Norwegian capital, full of parks and situated immediately on brink of the wilderness, forms a perfect backdrop upon which we witness Anders' predicament unfold.

Joachim Trier's **Oslo, August 31st**

Jens Lien's **Sons of Norway** (*Sønner av Norge*) was, in some ways, the most lively and entertaining film of the year. It is a comedy set in the late 1970s about the kind of super-tolerant parenting that presumably was a general feature of the period, and about the advent of punk music. Based on an autobiographical novel by Nikolaj Frobenius, it deals with the life of a 14-year-old boy in an Oslo suburb after his mother suddenly dies. Young Åsmund Høeg is compelling and believable in the lead role, as is Sven Nordin as his tolerant and somewhat unorthodox father. Lien explores the contrast between the

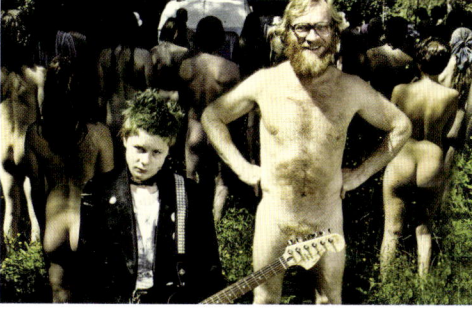

Jens Lien's **Sons of Norway**

warmth of the characters and the alienating qualities of the advancing modern age, but perhaps too preoccupied with the details of period. However, he remains a sharp observer and possesses a grasp of cinematic language that permeates even the smallest details. He also has an ace up his sleeve: John Lydon (Johnny Rotten of Sex Pistols fame) makes a short cameo appearance.

Some will say that Per-Olav Sørensen's debut **People in the Sun** (*Mennesker i solen*) displays more ambition that quality. However, it did offer a markedly different kind of story and style. Based on a play by Swedish comedian Jonas Gardell and with Dane Ghita Nørby in one of the leading roles, it is a comedy aimed squarely at a local market. Told in the form of a fable, portraying a group of people vacationing somewhere in Sweden as signs of doomsday appear. They are superficial and unsympathetic in their daily life, and their reactions when the world starts to fall apart are predictable. the party must go on. Gradually, however, their plight worsens. Sørensen finds it hard to sustain his concept to the end, but succeeds in creating a rather lively satire with some funny moments.

The large production slate in Norway is supported by a number of different initiatives implemented by the government. It has been created for use by commercial and more artistic fare. Following a record year like 2011 will always be difficult and the production rate will likely not repeat itself, perhaps reducing to 25 films. However, with so many filmmakers

appearing on the scene over the last 15 years, the conditions are there for them to continue to inspire and entertain.

The year's best films
Oslo, August 31st (Joachim Trier)
Happy, Happy (Anne Sewitsky)
Head Hunters (Morten Tyldum)

Anne Sewitsky's **Happy, Happy**

Directory
All Tel/Fax numbers begin (+47)
Henie-Onstad Art Centre, Sonja Henie vei 31, 1311 Høvikodden. Tel: 6780 4880. post@hok.no.
Norwegian Film Institute, PO Box 482 Sentrum, 0105 Oslo. Tel: 2247 4500. Fax: 2247 4599. post@nfi.no. www.nfi.no. Contact: Lise Gustavson.
Norwegian Film Development, Dronningens gt. 16, 0152 Oslo. Tel: 2282 2400. Fax: 2282 2422. mail@nfu.no. Contact: Kirsten Bryhni.
Norwegian Film and TV Producers Association, Dronningens gt. 16, 0152 Oslo, Tel: 2311 9311. Fax: 2311 9316. leif@produsentforeningen.no. Contact: Leif Holst Jensen.
Norwegian Film Workers Association, Dronningens gt. 16, 0152 Oslo. Tel: 2247 4640. Fax: 2247 4689. post@filmforbundet.no. Contact: Sverre Pedersen.
Norwegian Media Authority, Nygata 4, 1607 Fredrikstad. Tel: 6930 1200. Fax: 6930 1201. post@medietilsynet.no. Contact: Tom Thoresen.

TROND OLAV SVENDSEN is a historian from the University of Oslo. He has worked as a newspaper film critic and an editor in the Oslo publishing house of Kunnskapsforlaget. Among his publications is a Theatre and Film encyclopedia.

Pakistan Aijaz Gul

Few films were released in Pakistan during 2011, but what did come out was of better quality than in recent years, which was reflected in the films' healthy performance at the box office. Which is not to say that there weren't a fare share of disasters.

Actress and now producer-director Reema released her second production, **Lost in Love** (*Love Mey Gumm*). It was filmed in Malaysia and other west Asian republics. Most of the film's promotion was online, with its musical numbers appearing everywhere in order to secure a sizable audience. Glossy and aesthetically barren, the film lacked depth, with most of the focus on Reema, whose character is considerably younger than her. The film performed modestly at the box office, despite very poor reviews. In what appears to be a departure from the industry, Reema was married in the US and looks likely to be based there.

Reema's **Lost in Love**

Faisal Bokhari's **Brothers** (*Bhai Log*), which he also performed photographic duties on, performed better than expected. Its portrayal of Karachi's underworld and the social upheaval iit creates was underpinned by strong performances from Nadeem, Javed Sheikh, Babar Ali and Saima.

Shoaib Mansoor's **Bold**

The year's best film was producer-director-screenwriter Shoaib Mansoor's follow-up to *In the Name of God*, **Bold** (*Bol*). Released in nine cities and across 23 screens, it played to packed houses for almost four weeks – box-office gold by any standard. The film deals with a multitude of issues, ranging from child abuse and the travails of parenthood, to domestic abuse, poverty and gender issues related to prostitution, homosexuality and transvestites. This was something very new for a conservative nation like Pakistan.

If Mansoor went overboard with the issues raised, his skills as a filmmaker, from arresting visuals to pacing and magnetic performances from his excellent cast, guaranteed his audience would remain riveted. A special show was even arranged for the diplomats at the American Ambassador's residence. However, Mansoor, who is known to shy away from the limelight was not in attendance at this or any other event. The film has since performed well in India, the UK and Emirates.

Humaima Malik and Mazhar Sehbai made their cinematic debut playing a young girl and her rigid, ultra-conservative father. Pop singer Atif Aslam also made his debut, in a minor role, with the director including his music. Young filmgoers responded enthusiastically to his first appearance on film, as well as to the film's themes.

The Girl (*Jugni*) and **Patriot** (*Eik Ghazi Aur*) failed to do well at the box office and were largely ignored by the critics. Both films were directed by Syed Noor, who suffered a mild stroke in December. It is hoped he will make a full recovery – and one can say the same for his recent work. The films also featured in the lead role popular actress Saima, the director's wife. Their collaboration together, once fruitful, has stalled somewhat in recent years.

Syed Noor's **The Girl**

That said, it is easy to find a soft spot for such films. They may not be imbued with any great cinematic value or craftsmanship but they are still above the average product and are free from the mediocrity and vulgarity of other titles such as Jirar Rizvi's **Son of Pakistan**, Saeed Rana's **Society Girl** and Altaf Hussain's **Silence** (*Khamost Raho*). And even though Saima may have lost some of the star quality of her earlier work, she still shines through. It is a pity that their poor scripts and underwhelming production values, not to mention lacklustre direction, prevented them from bettering their position at the box office or endearing them more with critics, as they are likable films.

Three 3D cinemas opened in Lahore and Karachi, at a time when Hollywood is having second thoughts about the platform. Producers

angered by international imports have called for a quota system to be introduced. Those importing the films and exhibitors profiting from the popularity of foreign fare were unwilling to listen to these calls, instead questioning the quality and merit of local films, most of which remain qualitatively weaker than their foreign counterparts.

Actress Mira was nominated for the President's Pride of Performance Award. This attracted some controversy, as Mira was left with no choice but to address the press, telling them that the honour was genuine and there had been no bribery involved. She certainly has the uncanny ability to remain in the headlines, albeit rarely for the best of reasons.

Last year also saw the passing of Khawaja Pervaiz, who died aged 81. He was best known as a lyricist, with a bent towards the romantic and raunchy, and whose songs were most famously performed by Noorjehan.

Best Films
Bold (Shoaib Mansoor)
Brothers (Faisal Bokhari)

AIJAZ GUL is author of four books on films. He earned his BA and MA in Cinema from USC, Los Angeles. He is member of NETPAC, FIPRESCI and writes regularly on films for Pakistani and foreign publications.

Jira Rizvi's **Son of Pakistan**

لجنة أبوظبي للأفلام
ABU DHABI FILM
COMMISSION

Poland Barbara Hollender

Thanks to the fully-functioning Cinematography Act, the economic crisis has yet to have a significant impact on the Polish film industry. The Polish Film Institute has its own budget, which is supported by television stations (43 per cent), operators of digital television (34 per cent) and cable television (14 per cent), as well as a percentage of the revenue accrued from cinema tickets (8 per cent) and distributors (one per cent). In total, the budget amounts to approximately €28million. This amount is then invested in film production. The Polish Film Institute receives over 500 applications for support of feature and documentary films annually, and about 80 per cent of Polish film productions are made with the assistance of the Institute. Of the remaining 20 per cent, the films are either very commercial or alternative/experimental. On average, around 50 to 60 feature films are made each year.

Antoni Krause's **Black Thursday**

Experienced Polish directors often revisit some of the country's more problematic periods. Antoni Krauze made the modest, yet deeply moving, quasi-documentary **Black Thursday** (*Czarny czwartek*). The film focuses on the so-called December events, when almost fifty people were killed and over 1,000 were injured during workers' rebellions in 1970. Krauze follows the talks held by the state authorities and party officials behind closed doors, where the decision was made to fire on workers. He shows the streets of Gdańsk and Gdynia, where people died on their way to work, were arrested and where the night-time funerals of victims took place.

Agnieszka Holland's **In Darkness**

Agnieszka Holland returned to World War II with **In Darkness** (*W ciemności*). In Lvov, during the Nazi occupation, a simple worker and small-time thief, Leopold Socha, gave shelter to a group of Jews in the sewers. They remained there for 14 months. Initially, he did it for money, but when the Jews ran out of funds he continued to protect them. Though dealing with the nightmare of the Holocaust, Holland has produced a moving and universal testament to the humanity of people, but never forgets our capacity for cruelty.

The major cinematic event in Poland during 2011 was the release of **Rose** (*Róża*) by Wojciech Smarzowski – one of the country's most important filmmakers. It unfolds shortly after World War II has ended, in the region

Wojciech Smarzowski's **Rose**

of Masuria. German inhabitants are being
resettled, Russian marauders are brutally
raping women, Polish repatriates from Russia
are unable to find a place to live in this new
place and are treated as usurpers by the
local population. All the while, the Security
Service is introducing the new communist
order. But amongst the smoldering ruins
there is love, between Róża and Tadeusz. A
Masuria woman, she has been deprived of her
identity and raped. Tadeusz is a former fighter
from Warsaw's uprising. This love – tragic,
distrustful and against all circumstances –
allows the two to retain the last remnants of
their dignity.

Jerzy Hoffman's **1920. The Battle of Warsaw**

The first Polish 3D feature film **1920. The Battle
of Warsaw** (*1920. Bitwa Warszawska*) was
expected to be a great event. A national epic
that detailed Jerzy Hoffman's Polish victory
over Russian forces attempting to invade
Warsaw, the film was decimated by critcs.
Aside of Sławomir Idziak's cinematography, it
is difficult to praise anything: an inconsistent
screenplay, bland and paper-like characters, an

unconvincing love affair and jingoistic pathos not
corresponding to the modern look at history.

Alongside the more traditional period dramas,
these filmmakers are also engaging in a series
of films that attempt to grapple with the
modern condition in Poland. In **Man, Chicks
Are Just Different** (*Baby są jakieś inne*), Marek
Koterski attempted yet another film about the
state of Polish intellectual life. In it, two men
travel in a car and discuss their thoughts on
women. However, beneath these conversations
is a brilliant portrayal of men, detailing their
insecurities, complexes and fears.

Marek Koterski's **Man, Chicks Are Just Different**

Polish cinema also has more recent generation
of directors – 30 to 40-year-olds. Their focus
is on the transformative Poland, the way the
country has changed in their own lifetime.
In **The Mole** (*Kret*) Rafał Lewandowski looks
at how evil committed in the past impacts
subsequent generations. The father, in the past
a leader of miners' strikes, is accused of having
collaborated with the Secret Service. The son,
a grown man, is affected directly. He is forced
to deal with his own feelings for his father and
face the disgrace suffered by his family.

Rafał Lewandowski's **The Mole**

Greg Zgliński's **Courage**

Younger filmmakers look more to the moral dilemmas of faced by people today. The main character of Greg Zgliński's **Courage** (*Wymyk*) has to cope with his guilt over failing to help his brother when he is beaten up by hooligans in front of him. The film's contemporaneity is reinforced by the use of YouTube in the film. Footage of the beating is uploaded, so that everyone can see the young man's 'cowardice'.

Bartosz Konopka's **Fear of Falling**

Bartosz Konopka, whose documentary *Rabbit à la Berlin* was nominated for an Oscar, made his feature debut with **Fear of Falling** (*Lęk wysokości*). It tells the story of a young television journalist whose personal life is in a mess. His father, whom he has not seen for years, suffers a mental breakdown and the son starts to feel pangs of responsibility for him.

Leszek Dawid's **Ki** looks at the world of a young, confused woman. The mother of a two-year-old boy, Ki is barely an adult herself. Crazy, irresponsible and full of dreams,

she is also very lonely. Dawid and actress Roma Gąsiorowska developed the role of Ki together, creating a character whose fear of responsibility is both a credible character and a metaphor for a generation.

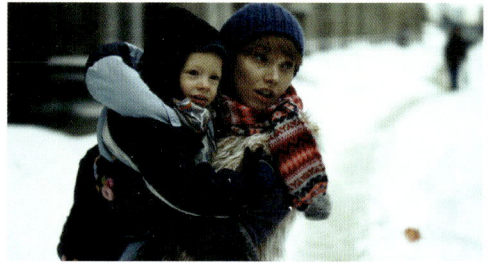

Leszek Dawid's **Ki**

Lewandowski, Dawid and Konopka, who all started out in documentary, are part of a promising generation. Alongside them are a collection of gifted actors, including Robert Więckiewicz (*In Darkness*, *Courage*), Marcin Dorociński (*Rose*, *Fear of Falling*) and Agata Kulesza (*Rose*, *Suicide Room*). Together, they are the current crop of Poland's most sought-after talent.

Form and language is also being played with in a number of new releases. Lech Majewski's **The Mill and the Cross** (*Młyn i krzyż*) is an impressionist take on Breughel's painting *Stations of the Cross*, whilst Łukasz Barczyk's **Italians** offers a near-wordless variation on Shakespear's *Hamlet*. In **Daas**, Adrian Panek's directorial debut, the costume drama is reconfigured as the director tells the story of the self-proclaimed Messiah from the 18th century, Jakub Franek, who became of the founder of the Seventh Day Adventists. And in **Suicide**

Adrian Panek's **Daas**

Room (*Sala samobójców*) Jan Komasa offers an unsettling portrait of the internet age, with characters occupying a space between the real and virtual worlds. A fascinating work, it blends strong performances withexcellent animation.

Of the more commercial productions, the comedies **Letters to M.** (*Listy do M.*) by Mitja Okorn and **O, Charles** (*Och, Karol*) by Piotr Wereśniak dominated the domestic releases at the box office.

Mitja Okorn's **Letters to M.**

Next year is an important one for Polish cinema. A new system of grant allocation will come into force at the Polish Film Institute, which will be based on the decisions of six experts. There are also questions being asked about private funding – in the current economic climate, can many people invest in such a risky industry?

As for forthcoming productions, Andrzej Wajda, who is now 85-years-old, will have completed his film about Lech Wałęsa. The screenplay was written by writer and playwright Janusz Głowacki, with Robert Więckiewicz playing the lead. No less anticipated is the new film about the Warsaw uprising of 1944, directed by 30-year-old Jan Komasa.

BARBARA HOLLENDER is a Warsaw-based journalist and film critic for the daily *Rzeczpospolita*. She covers many major film festivals, and has written, among other works, a study of *Studio Tor* (2000).

The year's best films

Rose (Wojciech Smarzowski)
Courage (Greg Zgliński)
In Darkness (Agnieszka Holland)
The Mole (Rafael Lewandowski)
The Mill and the Cross (Lech Majewski)

Directory

All Tel/Fax numbers begin (+48)

Polish Film Institute, 00-071 Warsaw, ul., Krakowskie Przedmieście 21/23, Tel: (22) 421 0518, Fax: (22) 421 0241. pisf@pisf.pl www.pisf.pl

Polish Filmmakers Association, 00-068 Warsaw, Krakowskie Przedmieście 7. Tel: (22) 556 5440, (22) 845 5132 Fax: (22) 845 3908. biuro@sfp.org.pl www.sfp.org.pl

National Chamber of Audiovisual Producers, ul. Chełmska 21 bud.28 C, 00-724 Warszawa Tel: (22) 840 5901 Fax: (22) 840 5901. kipa@kipa.pl www.kipa.pl

National Film Archive, 00-975 Warsaw, ul., Puławska 61. Tel: (22) 845 5074 Fax: (22) 646 5373. filmoteka@fn.org.pl www.fn.org.pl

Media Desk Poland, 00-724 Warsaw, ul., Chełmska 19/21 p. 229. Tel/Fax: (22) 851 1074, Tel. (22) 559 33 10. biuro@mediadeskpoland.eu www.mediadeskpoland.eu

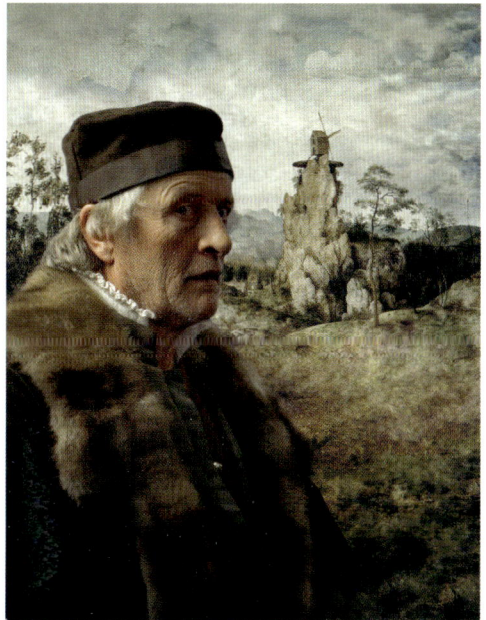

Lech Majewski's **The Mill and the Cross**

Portugal Martin Dale

Optimism has never been one of the strong suits in Portuguese cinema. In 2011, as the country confronted its biggest economic crisis since the 1974 revolution, the main themes addressed in domestic films have been particularly bleak – accompanied by a marked downward trend in admissions figures. Overall admissions in Portuguese cinemas fell by 8 per cent during the year, from 16.6 million in 2010 to 15.3 million in 2011, with gross box-office figures falling from €82million to €78.5million. With Portugal's GDP expected to shrink by 3.2 per cent in 2012 and with VAT on cinema tickets likely to be hiked from 13 to 23 per cent, total admissions are expected to tumble further in 2012. Portuguese cinema's share of overall admissions was only 0.6 per cent in 2011.

Since 2005, there has been at least one annual domestic title with more than 100,000 admissions – typically an erotic drama or local comedy – but in 2011 the biggest local hit only clocked up 20,000 admissions.

One of the main growth signs in terms of admissions was the rising number of successful documentaries – of the 22 domestic features released in 2011, six were feature-length documentaries. Documentaries actually performed better than domestic features, with average admissions of 4,324 spectators per documentary, compared to an average of only 1,074 per Portuguese feature.

The year's top film was João Canijo's brooding urban melodrama **Blood of My Blood** (*Sangue do meu Sangue*), which played in Toronto and won the FIPRESCI award at the 2011 San Sébastian film festival.

Like many Portuguese auteurs, Canijo delights in exploring the dark and sordid underbelly of Portugal's most impoverished neighbourhoods. In it, his long-time collaborator Rita Blanco portrays struggling mother Marcia, who desperately fights to protect her two children.

João Canijo's **Blood of My Blood**

The next biggest local hit was Mário Patrocínio's documentary debut **Complexo: Parallel Universe** (*Complexo: Universo Paralelo*), set in one of Rio de Janeiro's biggest slums, or favelas, known as the Complexo do Alemão. The film garnered 17,100 admissions and won the Human Rights award in the Artivist Film Festival, in Los Angeles. US-trained director Mário Patrocínio and his brother Pedro, spent 3 years living in the slum, where locals struggle to survive in the midst of intense poverty, drug barons, gang warfare and everyday violence.

Mário Patrocínio's **Complexo: Parallel Universe**

Sérgio Trufaut's **The City of the Dead**

Brazilian-born Sérgio Trufaut shot the documentary **The City of the Dead** (*A Cidade dos Mortos*) in Cairo and won the Grand Prize at the 2010 Documenta Madrid festival. It racked up 6,866 admissions in Portugal. The film explores the world's largest inhabited cemetery – Cairo's unique necropolis neighbourhood – where one million people live in tomb houses, shops, schools and workshops nestled next to graves.

Solveig Nordlund's **The Death of Carlos Gardel**

Susana de Sousa Dias's documentary **48** makes innovative use of still photographs, accompanied by victims' voices, as it explores the taboo subject of the brutal imprisonment and torture practises applied during 48 years of fascist dictatorship in Portugal. Solveig Nordlund's **The Death of Carlos Gardel** (*A Morte do Carlos Gardel*) is an adaptation of the homonymous novel by António Lobo Antunes. With a moving poetic structure, the film revolves around a hospitalised young drug addict, as his family try to bring him out of a coma. We flash through episodes of his life, as if entering his comatose mind.

Teresa Vilaverde's **Swan** (*Cisne*), which premiered at Venice, is an existential film poem that flits between lush countryside scenes and dark Lisbon interiors in an exploration of loneliness and the search for human connection. Sérgio Trufaut's **Journey to Portugal** (*Viagem à Portugal*) stars two of Portugal's best-known actresses – Maria de Medeiros and Isabel Ruth. Based on a true story, and shot in stark black and white, the film follows a Ukrainian doctor, who arrives in Portugal, at Faro airport, as a tourist, but is detained by the Border control agency and commences a nightmare journey.

Sérgio Trufaut's **Journey to Portugal**

João Nuno Pinto's debut **America** is an angst-ridden ride through one of Portugal's squalid social sub-cultures – as a group of petty crooks fake passports and mingling with Ukrainians, Russians and immigrants from Portugal's former colonies.

João Nuno Pinto's **America**

José Miguel Ribeiro's **Journey to Cape Verde**

Experimental filmmaker Edgar Pera's gothic monochrome film **The Baron** (*O Barão*) is reminiscent of a 1930s horror film, skilfully blending humour with a palpable sense of dread. José Miguel Ribeiro's stylish animated travel diary **Journey to Cape Verde** (*Viagem a Cabo Verde*) picked up the Best Documentary Director at the 2011 Krakow Film Festival. Meanwhile, Gonçalo Tocha's documentary **It's the Earth Not the Moon** (*É na Terra não é na Lua*), set in the volcanic island of Corvo in the Azores, won the Special Jury Prize at the 2011 Locarno film festival.

Gonçalo Tocha's **It's the Earth Not the Moon**

Other notable films from 2011 include Paulo Rocha's personal odyssey, **If I Were a Thief… I'd Steal** (*Se Eu Fosse Ladrão… Roubava*) and Miguel Gomes' love and crime drama, **Taboo** (*Tabu*).

There is no obvious silver lining to Portugal's current cloud of economic depression, but there are some promising upcoming films for 2012. Bille August will return to Portugal for the first time since 1993's *The House of the Spirits*, once again teaming up with

Jeremy Irons for **Night Train to Lisbon**. Zeze Gamboa is putting the finishing touches to his Angolan drama **The Great Kilapy**, a Portugal-Mozambique co-production, and Flora Gomes is completing **The Children's Republic**, starring Danny Glover, about a futuristic Mozambican city ruled by children in the wake of a tragic civil war.

The year's best films
Blood of My Blood (João Canijo)
Complexo: Parallel Universe (Mário Patrocínio)
Journey to Cape Verde (José Miguel Ribeiro)
The Death of Carlos Gardel (Solveig Nordlund)
The Baron (Edgar Pera)

Directory
All Tel/Fax numbers begin (+351)
Cinemateca Portuguesa, Rua Barata Salgueiro 63, 1269-059 Lisbon. Tel: (21) 359 6200. Fax: (21) 352 3180. www.cinemateca.pt
Institute of Cinema, Audiovisual & Multimedia (ICAM), Rua de S Pedro de Alcântara 45, 1°, 1250 Lisbon. Tel: (21) 323 0800. Fax: (21) 343 1952. mail@icam.pt. www.icam.pt

MARTIN DALE has lived in Lisbon and the north of Portugal since 1994 and works as an independent media consultant and a contributor to *Variety*. He has written several books on the film industry, including *The Movie Game* (1997).

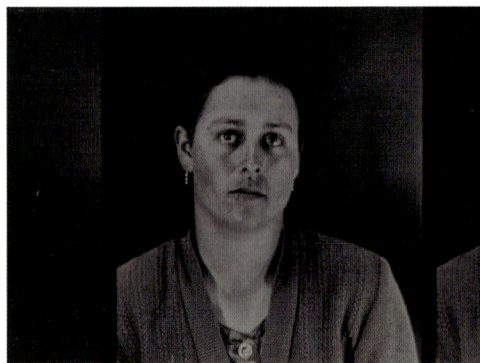
Susana de Sousa Dias's **48**

Romania Christina Corciovescu

2011 was a jubilee year for Romanian cinema: it was the tenth anniversary of Cristi Puiu's *Stuff and Dough* (*Marfa si banii*), considered to be the first film of the so-called 'Romanian New Wave'. It was also ten years since the first edition of the Transylvania International Film Festival (TIFF), the most important event of its kind in the country. In time, TIFF has become a major occasion on the European film festival calendar. I have marked this historic moment with the recent publication of *The New Romanian Cinema: From Comrade Ceausescu to Mr. Lazarescu.*

The last few years have seen Romania release between 15 and 17 features annually, of which almost half were international co-productions. In addition to this, each year has produced approximately twenty shorts and the total number of distributed films has reached around 180. The increase of multiplexes and cinemas – there are now 137 screens in the country – has helped improve audience attendance, although most of these venues are located in cities, with many smaller towns having no facilities. As stated in the last Romanian entry in the 2010 IFG, domestic cinema is greatly disadvantaged by the lack of widespread exhibition. Romanian cinema only ever attracts viewers when films have won international awards, but the multiplexes rarely ever screen these films because they do not generate significant revenue. In the ongoing debate between film as art or industry, the latter argument is still winning.

Some 2011 premieres did not pass unnoticed at international competitions. After its premiere at Cannes, in the 'Un Certain Regard' section, Catalin Mitulescu's **Loverboy** saw Ada Condeescu pick up the Best Actress award at

Sarajevo. The film tells the story of young man who procures innocent girls only to coerce them into a life of prostitution. However, when he falls in love with one of the girls, he is faced with a tough decision – to follow his heart or to continue in his work.

Adrian Sitaru's **Best Intentions**

Adrian Sitaru's new feature, **Best Intentions** (*Din dragoste cu cele mai bune intentii*), witnesses a man's psychotic episode after his mother is admitted to hospital. His condition improves, but cannot face the idea that his life will one day end. Winner of the Best Director and Best Actor (the excellent Bogdan Dumitrache) Awards at Locarno, it is a skilfully executed film.

Catalin Mitulescu's **Loverboy**

Anca Damian's **Crulic: The Path to Beyond**

Anca Damian's **Crulic: The Path to Beyond** (*Crulic: Drumul spre dincolo*) played at numerous international festivals, collecting a handful of awards. It combines documentary and animation in its true story of the injustice meted out to a young Romanian who dies in a prison in Poland after going on hunger strike to protest against his false arrest.

Bogdan George Apetri's **Outskirts**

Of all the films released over the last year, Bogdan George Apetri's debut, **Outskirts** (*Periferic*) garnered the most awards. It details a young woman's futile attempt to create some order in her life and escape from a miserable world. It received the Golden Alexander and Best Actress awards at Thessaloniki; the Special Jury Prize and FIPRESCI awards at Warsaw, the 'New Europe/New Names' award at Vilnius and the FIPRESCI prize at Vienna.

The Romanian New Wave continues in its commitment to documenting the travails of daily life: recording ordinary events about ordinary people and filmed in a minimalist style. The best exponent of this approach in 2011 was Constantin Popescu's **Principles of Life** (*Principii de viata*). This study of parent/ child relations is viewed through the prism of a man who thinks he can bring harmony to his new wife, whilst maintaining his duties towards his other family. It is an astute drama, balancing the central character's domestic problems with wider, societal issues.

Constantin Popescu's **Principles of Life**

Genre filmmaking also made something of a return. Sinisa Dragin's **If the Seed Doesn't Die** (*Daca bobul nu moare*) combines two road-movie narratives, underpinned by mystical and philosophical themes. Two fathers, one Serbian and the other Romanian, leave for a neighbouring country in search of their missing children. Their paths cross geographically, but they never actually meet. The film's tone is bleak and the two intersecting stories are littered with metaphorical allusions.

Alexandru Maftei directed the romantic comedy **Hello! How Are You?** (*Buna! Ce Faci?*). A couple find themselves bored in their marriage and look to the internet for companionship. They each believe that they have found their perfect partner online, only

Alexandru Maftei's **Hello! How Are You?**

ABU DHABI FILM
COMMISSION

Cristi Puiu's **Aurora**

to realise that they are, in fact, talking with each other. It is a light, fairly predictable film – something of a stark contrast to the dark, realistic tone of Cristi Puiu's **Aurora**. Set amidst a crowded city, populated by grey buildings within grubby surroundings, the film details the development of a man's vengeful obsession, which ultimately leads him to commit three murders. Ostensibly an anti-thriller, with a slow pace standing in for suspense, its bizarre situations and strange tone reflect the worldview of the central character.

The year's best films
Crulic: The Path to Beyond (Anca Damian)
Best Intentions (Adrian Sitaru)
Principles of Life (Constantin Popescu)
Outskirts (Bogdan George Apetri)
Aurora (Cristi Puiu)

Directory
All Tel/Fax numbers begin (+4)
Centrul National al Cinematografiei, Str. Dem I Dobrescu nr. 4-6, sector 1, 010026, Bucuresti. Tel: 021 310 43 01. Fax: 021 310 43 00. www. cncinema.ro
Uniunea Cineastilor, Str. Mendeleev nr. 28-30, sector 1, Bucuresti. Tel: 021 316 80 83. Fax: 021 311 12 46. www.ucin.ro
Arhiva Nationala de Filme, Soseaua Sabarului nr. 20, com Jilava. Tel/Fax: 021 450 12 67. anf@xnet.ro

CRISTINA CORCIOVESCU is a film critic and historian, and the author of a number of books on film and the arts.

Russia Kirill Razlogov

The ongoing economic crisis and the parliamentary – and forthcoming presidential – elections did not change the cinematic landscape in Russia too much. The officially launched Forum 2020 – a United Russia Party project – combined, as usual, empty promises and a battle for resources: public funding on the one hand and film heritage on the other. As one of the results of this chess game, the management of the collection of Soviet films (all films produced by the Soviet State, except Mosfilm productions, kept by this non-privatised Studio, now called Film Concern) was transferred by the Ministry of Culture to a specially created state enterprise. Then, following a meeting between local animation filmmakers and Prime Minister Vladimir Putin, it went to the State Film Archive Gosfilmofond. The undercurrent of this fighting was the debate over who would profit from the money earned through potential sales. Finally, it was decided that the sales rights would go to the reorganised Sovexportfilm.

As a result of the economic crisis, private money fled from film production and, for the first time, Russian filmmakers seriously considered international co-production opportunities. Russia became member of Eurimages, festivals featured co-production forums, and a fierce battle ensued for control of the international impact of Russian film industry; some parties opposed Sovexportfilm and the Film Fund, which controls most of the state subsidies to film production and exhibition. That amounts to about US$90million, with half of that left to the Ministry of Culture for art-house features, fiction debuts, documentary and animated films, as well as two film universities and anything else that falls under this umbrella (total state funding is around US$150million).

The first results of the activities of the Film Fund did not have an obvious economic impact, except for a delay in the transfer of money from the state. The overall figure for 2010 showed little change with almost 170 million tickets sold. However, the total box-office for the year was up 27.6 per cent due to higher ticket prices, much of which was linked to revenue from 3D releases. Unfortunately, the domestic share of the box office, which was represented by 80 releases, dropped to 15.4 per cent, compared with 30 per cent in 2008.

Levan Gabriadze's **Lucky Trouble**

Only one Russian film to appear in the top ten box-office earners in 2011 was **Christmas Trees** (*Yolki*, also known as *Six Degrees of Celebration*), a New Year's Eve comedy by Timur Bekmambetov. It grossed almost US$23million. Next in terms of revenue were an animated version of a local legend, **How Not to Rescue a Princess** (*Tri bogatyrya I shamakhanskaya tsarist*), earning US$20million, and **Lucky Trouble** (*Vykrutasy*), another comedy produced by Bekmambetov but directed by the Georgian Levan Gabriadze, which brought in US$12.5million.

The predilection of the Russian public for comedies, as well as the absence of new original ideas was illustrated by the fact that the fourth and the fifth rankings were taken by a remake of great Soviet comedy from the 1970s and a 3D re-issue of a recently released film. Eldar Ryazanov's *Work Place Romance* was updated as **Work Place Romance – Our Time** (*Sluzhebnyi Roman – Nashe Vremya*) and directed by Savik Andreasyan. It managed to pull in US$12million, while another 2008 hit, *The Very Best Film*, took in another US$10million in its new format.

Nikita Mikhalkov's **Burnt by the Sun 2: The Citadel**

The biggest controversy of the year surrounded the candidate for the Best Foreign Language Film candidate for the 2012 Academy Awards. The Russian committee, after long discussions, put forward the second and final part of Nikita Mikhalkov's war-time blockbuster, **Burnt by the Sun 2: The Citadel** (*Utomlennye Solntsem 2: Tsitadel*). The film, which turned a bloody reality into a fairy-tale, received more positive reviews from Russian critics compared with the first part of the sequel, *Exodus*, but lost much of the earlier film's audience, scrapping by on US$1.5million as opposed to to US$7.5million).

The scandal surrounding the film began when the President of the Committee, Vladimir Menshov, who had voted for another film, declared at a press conference his disagreement with the majority decision. The press supported his protest, declaring Mikhalkov's film both an artistic and box-office failure. The decision was not changed, however, but it was decided to reform the Committee. From now on it will comprise

exclusively of producers and directors of Russian films who have either received or been nominated for an Academy Award, or have been the recipient of an award from one of the main 14 festivals identified by FIAPF.

Alexander Sokurov's **Faust**

Other films considered to be the year's best and as such could have been put forward by the committee included **Faust** by Alexander Sokurov. It is a radical re-imagining of the medieval legend that inspired Goethe, which was awarded the top prize at Venice. The film has yet to secure a domestic release. Andrei Zvyagintsev's **Elena**, a modern social drama handled with a Hitchcockian brio, which won an award in the Cannes' 'Un Certain Regard' section, was the film supported by Menshov. Also in the running was last year's *The Fortress of Brest*.

Andrei Zvyagintsev's **Elena**

The main cinematic sensation of the year was Sergei Loban's **Chapiteau-Show**. Shown in competition at the Moscow International Film Festival, the four-hour saga is comprised of a quartet of interlinking stories and was enjoyed by audiences and praised by critics – both

Sergei Loban's **Chapiteau-Show**

domestic and international – as the birth of a new kind of sensibility. It received a special prize at the festival.

Veteran actor-scriptwriter-director Andrei Smirnov's **Once Upon a Time There Lived a Simple Woman** (*Zhila-byla odna baba*) was also a major event in the cinematic calendar. This film was praised mostly by elderly intellectuals as a combined portrait of a woman and a country enduring a series of tragic events in the twentieth century.

A dark kind of realism also characterises **Portrait in Twilight** (*Portret v sumerkakh*) by Russian New Yorker Angelina Nikonova, with the widow of the director Ivan Dykhovichny Olga in the main part of a woman torn between sex and culture. On a lighter note, Andrei Smirnov's daughter Avdot'ya describes a romance between a vice-minister (Fedor Bondarchuk) and a country museum curator (Ksenia Rappoport) in **Two days** (*Dva dnya*).

Fedor Bondarchuk also takes on a younger persona in Oleg Flyangoltz's **Indifference** (*Bezrazlichie*), which took more than ten years to make. This social satire reconstructs the Soviet Union of the 1960s by shrewdly including original documentary footage from that time. The film received the main prize at the national 'Kinotavr' film festival in Sochi. Word then passed around that the decision of the Jury attracted critical remarks from the Prime Minister: wasn't there a really new film to give the award to?

A more recent past – the 1990s – was very much present in **Generation P**, Viktor Guinzburg's adaptation of Viktor Pelevin's grotesque novel, and **Pyrammmid** (*Pirammmida*), in which Eldar Salavatov dramatised the financial wheeler-dealing of Sergei Mavrodi, who created a gigantic ponzi scheme. For some Russian films, the international impact was more important than the domestic one. Bakur Bakuradze's second feature film **The Hunter** (*Okhotnik*), a strange love story set in the far north and featuring non-professional actors, was selected for the 'Un Certain Regard' programme at Cannes.

Alexander Zeldovich's **The Target**

Shown in Berlin, Alexander Mindadze's **Innocent Saturday** (*V subbotu*) reconstructed the first day after the Chernobyl explosion in the neighbouring city of Pripyat. By contrast, Alexander Zeldovich's **The Target** (*Mishen*), which was written by Vladimir Sorokin, portrayed the future from the fantastic perspective of characters with an eternal life.

The artistic diversity of directorial debuts becomes evident when comparing Andrei Bogatyrev's **Buggy** – a dark tale of everyday betrayal – with the brilliant genre exercise **Dosh** (*Bablo*), by Konstantin Buslov, the brother of Petr, the acclaimed director for *Boomer*.

For the first time in the past few years, quality films appeared in popular genres too. Natalia Uglitskikh made a pleasant underwater comedy, **On the Hook** (*Na Kryuchke*). Alexander Gordon adapted his father Harry's novel **Lights of the Brothel** (*Ogni pritona*), a melodrama set in Odessa in 1958 and featuring a brilliant performance by Oxana Fandera.

Vladimir Mirzoev, who works in theatre more than film, proposed a contemporary version of Pushkins's tragedy **Boris Godunov**, played out against modern St. Petersburg settings, while Slava Ross's **Siberia. Mon Amour** (*Sibir'. Monamour*) became a cult film even before its commercial release. Pavel Kostomarov and Alexander Rastorguyev's mockumentary **I Love You** (*Ya tebya lyublyu*) blended reality and fiction with young people given cameras by the directors in order to act out their own lives. It stands in contrast to Elena Demidova's documentary **Cranberry Island** (*Klykvennyi ostrov*), which details the life of a family who live in the rural woods.

Slava Ross's **Siberia. Mon Amour**

Summing up these diverse experiments we can be sure that the overwhelming pessimism about the future of national cinema is more due to the national mentality than to any actual reality. The near future will see an epic TV version of *Burnt by the Sun* which brings together the three theatrical releases and as yet unseen footage. There is also Ilya Khrzhanovsky's **Dau** and Alexei Guerman's **It's Difficult to be God**, each featuring multiple narrative strands and which have been in production for the last few years.

We are also awaiting new films by the Proshkins (father and son), Vasili Sigarev, Alexei Popogrebski and Boris Khlebnikov. There are

also works by at least ten new filmmakers in the pipeline. As for the ongoing controversies and scandals surrounding each new work by Mikhalkov, Sokurov or Zvyagintsev, it could be argued that they are proof of the vitality and productive conflict between generations in a time of great technological, political and spiritual change. Russian cinema, if not entirely healthy all the time, is very much alive.

The year's best films
Chapiteau-Show (Sergei Loban)
Burned by the Sun 2: Citadel
(Nikita Mikhalkov)
Faust (Alexander Sokurov)
Elena (Andrei Zvyagintsev)
The Target (Alexander Zel'dovich)

Directory
All Tel/Fax numbers begin (+7)
Alliance of Independent Distribution Companies, Tel: 243 4741. Fax: 243 5582. felix_rosental@yahoo.com.
Ministry of Culture (without Mass Communications) of the Russian Federation, 7, Maly Gnezdnikovsky Lane, Moscow 103877 Tel: 495-923-2420 and 629-7055
National Academy of Cinema Arts & Sciences, 13 Vassilyevskaya St, Moscow 123825. Tel: 200 4284. fax: 251 5370. unikino@aha.ru
Russian Guild of Film Directors, 13 Vassilyevskaya St, Moscow 123825. Tel: 251 5889. fax: 254 2100. stalkerfest@mtu-net.ru.
Russian Guild of Producers, 1 Mosfilmovskaya St, Moscow 119858. Tel: 745 5635/143 9028. plechev@ mtu-net.ru.
Union of Filmmakers of Russia, 13 Vassilyevskaya St, Moscow 123825. Tel: 250 4114. fax: 250 5370. unikino@aha.ru.

KIRILL RAZLOGOV is Director of the Russian Institute for Cultural Research and Programme Director of the Moscow International Film Festival. He has written 17 books on cinema and culture and hosts Kultura's weekly TV show, *Movie Cult*.

Serbia Goran Gocić

Serbian actors are on the loose. The most active remains Ljubisa Samardzic who has filmed another television series, **Scent of Rain in the Balkans** (*Miris kise na Balkanu*), which unfolds in Sarajevo between 1914 and 1945. A feature of the same name, inspired by the series, is also planned. Actor Lazar Ristovski directed the political farce **White Lions** (*Beli lavovi*). Finally, **Montevideo, God Bless You!** (*Montevideo, bog te video*), the directing debut of actor Dragan Bjelogrlic, is a crowd-pleasing period drama set between the two World Wars, about the formation of a Serbian soccer team, in advance of the first world championship, by a bunch of enthusiasts. It scored well at the box office and a sequel is already planned.

Lazar Ristovski's **White Lions**

Darko Bajic's documentary **Gringo**, whose subject is also soccer, is dedicated to a Serbian player Dejan Petkovic Rambo, the only foreign player to ever achieve success and fame in Brazil. Other notable documentaries included Mila Turlajic's **Cinema Communisto**, which looks at the genre of Yugoslav Partisan films set during World War II – the most successful cinematic genre of the former federation. Zelimir Zilnik's **One Woman – One Century** (*Jedna zena – jedan vek*) is a profile of a 100-year-old woman from Istria, in Slovenia, who witnessed the demise of six states in the Balkan region.

Zelimir Zilnik's **One Woman – One Century**

In his feature **How I Was Stolen by the Germans** (*Kako su me ukrali Nemci*) writer-director Milos Misa Radivojevic tells the story of his own childhood, when he was practically raised by a benevolent German officer during the war, in occupied Belgrade. The more recent civil conflict remains a hotly debated subject for domestic filmmakers. **The Enemy** (*Neprijatelj*) by Dejan Zecevic is a tense horror-thriller set in the earlier stages of the recent wars, about a mysterious, devilish man found by a stray Serbian platoon, who gradually drives each of the soldiers to suicide.

Milos Misa Radivojevic's **How I Was Stolen by the Germans**

Mladen Maticevic's **Together** (*Zajedno*), about a writer who manages to win back his estranged wife, is a low-budget TV family drama that successfully scored festival distribution. **Zduhach Means Adventure**

Miodrag Milinkovic's **Zduhach Means Adventure**

(*Zduhac znaci avantura*) is a teenage comedy shot with a Cannon EOS camera, which enabled writer/director Miodrag Milinkovic to work with a small budget, similarly to Maticevic. **October** (*Oktobar*) is an omnibus film about democratic changes in Serbia.

Srdjan Dragojevic's **Parade**

Parade (*Parada*), a dark comedy about organising a Serbian gay pride parade, features a collection of colourful characters, above all an ex-warlord who runs a small security company, which ends up sandwiched between Belgrade's arty LGBT community and right-wingers who want to beat the hell out of them. Srdjan Dragojevic, who wrote last year's runaway success *Montevideo, God Bless You!*, wrote and directed *Parade*, which looks set to dominate the top of the box-office charts for the season.

Admissions in Serbia in 2010 rose steeply by 22 per cent compared to 2009. Notable regional efforts, such as Macedonian director

Vladimir Blazevski's *Punk's not Dead*, Romanina director Sinisa Dragin's *If the Seed Does Not Die*, Bosnian Danis Tanovic's *Circus Columbia* and Dutch director Sasha Matijevic's *Hij* were all supported by Serbian actors, crew, production facilities and public funds.

The year's best films
Tilva Rosh (Nikola Lezajic)
Parade (Srdjan Dragojevic)
Gringo (Darko Bajic)

Nikola Lezajic's **Tilva Rosh**

Directory
All Tel/Fax numbers begin (+381 11)
The Film Center Serbia, Zagrebacka 9/III, 11000 Belgrade. Tel: 262 51 31, 262 87 47 Fax: 263 42 53. fcs.office@fcs.co.yu www.fcs.co.yu
Yugoslav Film Archive, Knez Mihajlova 19, 11000 Belgrade. Tel/Fax: 262 25 55. kinoteka@eunet.yu www.kinoteka.org.yu
Faculty of Dramatic Arts, Bulevar Umetnosti 20, 11070 Belgrade. Tel: 214 04 19 Fax: 213 08 62. fduinfo@eunet.yu

GORAN GOCIĆ is a broadcast and print journalist whose works have been published by over thirty media outlets in eight languages. He has published works on Warhol, Kusturica, illness in cinema and pornography, and directed two feature-length documentaries.

ABU DHABI FILM
COMMISSION

Singapore Yvonne Ng

Singaporean cinema in 2011 seemed divided more than ever along the lines of mainstream and art-house production. Whereas mainstream movies tended to be grounded in local sensibilities and the time-tested genres of horror and comedy, alternative films favoured drama, documentary and animation, frequently drawing on sources further afield.

The year started with the release of the commercially-orientated **The Ghosts Must Be Crazy**, a split-narrative that attempts to blend both horror and comedy. One is set in the army while the other involves gambling. There are more misses than hits in this reworking of episodes from *Where Got Ghost* by Jack Neo and Boris Boo. Even weaker in plot and characterisation was Gilbert Chan's **23.59**, another army ghost story released at the end of the year.

For the Chinese New Year season, Kelvin Tong directed **It's a Great, Great World** (*Tua Seh Kai*). The film is a nostalgic, though contrived, revisit to Great World, one of the popular amusement parks that thrived in Singapore during the 1950s and 1960s. In it, an elderly man recounts the stories of people who appear in old photographs. The dialogue is spoken in various Chinese dialects that were commonly used during that period – a pleasant surprise as the use of dialects in Singaporean films is restricted today.

Lee Thean-Jeen's **Homecoming** is the first feature produced by Homerun Asia. This Singapore-Malaysia-produced Chinese New Year comedy revolves around different groups attempting to reach home for the annual celebrations. Among them is Jack Neo, in a

Lee Thean-Jeen's **Homecoming**

cross-dressing role as a middle-aged mother caught in a madcap journey home with her bachelor son.

Set further afield is Tan Siok Siok's **Twittamentary**, an innovative documentary made in the United States about the social media platform Twitter and the impact it has had on the lives of its users. The stories, characters and production crew were all sourced via Twitter, with even its narrative shaped by Twitter feedback. The result is a fascinating journey across the US, with the director finding a number of compelling characters.

Yong Mun Chee's **Where the Road Meets the Sun**

Where the Road Meets the Sun is another independent film made in the US. Yong Mun Chee's directorial debut is set in Los Angeles, where the director is currently based. The story introduces the intersecting lives of four men from different backgrounds and cultures, all staying at a run-down hotel. This well-acted though convoluted drama of immigrants, crime and friendship was partly funded by the Singapore Film Commission.

Eric Khoo paid tribute to the life and work of famed manga artist Yoshihiro Tatsumi in his first animated feature, **Tatsumi**. Narrated in Japanese by Tatsumi himself and accompanied by a lyrical, flowing soundtrack, the film weaves the artist's biographical work *A Drifting Life* with five of his short stories, bringing to life his panel drawings, which reveal the darker side of humanity. *Tatsumi* was shown in the 'Un Certain Regard' section at Cannes in 2011 and selected to represent Singapore at the Academy Awards in 2012.

Yoshihiro Tatsumi's **Tatsumi**

One of the most popular sections at the 24th Singapore International Film Festival, which moved from April to September in 2011, was the 'Singapore Panorama' section. Of the nine titles featured, eight played to sold-out venues. Among them was Helmi Ali and Razin Ramzi's **Ignore All Detour Signs**, a music documentary that chronicles the struggles faced by a local rock band during a performance at the 2009 South by Southwest music festival in Texas.

There was welcome news for the film industry when the Media Development Authority (MDA) announced the streamlining of funding programmes from the existing 46 to just five. The new schemes cover development assistance, production, marketing, talent support and enterprise development, and

will apply to all media sectors. Significantly, the government is moving away from the concept of co-investment to the awarding of grants. It is hoped this will allow for better content development and help companies to fully own their intellectual property. Consequently, any profit made need not be shared with the MDA.

Sherman Ong's **I Want to Remember**

The year's best films
Tatsumi (Eric Khoo)
Twittamentary (Tan Siok Siok)
Homecoming (Lee Thean-Jeen)
Comfort (Afiq Omar)
I Want to Remember (Sherman Ong)

Directory
All Tel/Fax numbers begin (+65)
Cinematograph Film Exhibitors Association, 13th & 14th Storey, Shaw Centre, 1 Scotts Rd, Singapore 228208. Tel: 6235 2077. Fax: 6235 2860.
Singapore Film Commission, 140 Hill St, Mita Bldg #04-01, Singapore 179369. Tel: 6837 9943. Fax: 6336 1170. www.sfc.org.sg.
Singapore Film Society, 5A Raffles Ave, #03-01 Marina Leisureplex, Singapore 039801. Fax: 6250 6167. ktan@sfs.org.sg. www.sfs.org.sg.

YVONNE NG is on the editorial board of *KINEMA*. She is the co-author of *Latent Images: Film in Singapore CD-ROM* (2003) and *Latent Images: Film in Singapore* (second edition, 2010).

Slovakia Miro Ulman

Despite a decline in cinema attendance by 10 per cent, Slovak cinema in 2011 was quite successful with the production of features doubling to eight films (excluding international co-productions). Whether there is anywhere to screen them is a different issue. As of 2010, there were only 162 commercial cinemas with 227 screens (66 of which were digital). At the end of 2011, the Minister of Culture granted €340,000 for the digitisation of single-screen cinemas, as so far only nine such venues have been digitised.

After a less successful 2010, last year saw Slovakian films once again screening abroad, but also attracting a more significant domestic audience. Moreover, the narrative features dominated.

Zuzana Liová's **The House**

Zuzana Liová's debut **The House** (*Dom*), an impressive chamber-piece about the clash between two generations, was selected for the Berlinale 'Forum'. The internecine strife between generations was skilfully employed as a metaphor for larger societal problems.

Martin Šulík's **Gypsy** (*Cigán*) walked away with four prizes from Karlovy Vary. Filmed with the director's signature poetic flair and making the most of its non-professional cast, the film

Martin Šulík's **Gypsy**

focuses on the story of a boy whose dreams of love and education are crushed by the cruel reality of Roma life.

Ivan Trojan, the lead actor in Peter Krištúfek's psychological drama **Visible World** (*Viditeľný svet*), picked up the Best Actor award at Bratislava. Trojan plays a misanthrope whose observation of, and irritation with, a local family's happiness results in his attempts to destroy their lives. It is a skilled performance that papers over the cracks in the script.

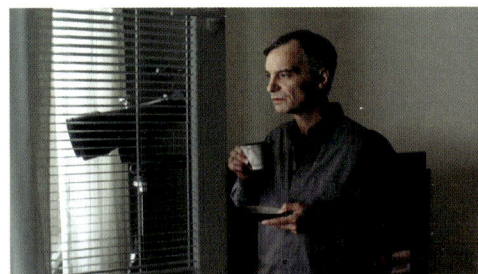

Peter Krištúfek's **Visible World**

Peter Bebjak's **Apricot Island** (*Marhuľový ostrov*) is a film about passion, love and the co-existence of various nationalities in one region in the south of Slovakia. It succeeds in telling a story without words – a unique achievement amongst Slovak films of recent years.

Peter Bebjak's **Apricot Island**

LÓVE, the second film by 24-year-old Jakub Kroner, offers up a story concerning two young thieves and a college girl, and has been seen as the director's defining statement on his generation. It examines the way that Hollywood clichés and contemporary culture's obsession with celebrity dominate these lives. It was seen by 108,000 viewers during its seven-week run and went on to become the fifth-most successful domestic release since the country gained independence in 1993. By contrast, the last of the narrative features, Juraj Nvota's **Confidant** (*Konfident*) is based on a true story from the time when the country was still part of Czechoslovakia, in 1968.

Jakub Kroner's **LÓVE**

Three Slovak documentaries employed fictional elements to complement or illustrate their subject. Peter Dimitrov's **Time of Grimaces** (*Čas grimás*) describes the circumstances surrounding the creation of the famous busts by F. X. Messerschmidt, an eccentric sculptor of the Theresian era. Gejza Dezorz and Jozef Páleník's **Massacre of Devínska** (*Devínsky masaker*) reconstructs scenes that detail the bloodshed in Devinska Nova Ves (part of Bratislava) in 2010. However, the film offers nothing new to the much-discussed topic.

Matej Mináč's **Nicky's Family** (*Nickyho rodina*), a sequel to the Emmy-award winning documentary *Nicholas Winton – The Power of Good*, once again explores the story of Sir Nicholas Winton, who saved the lives of 669 children at the outbreak of World War II by organising Kindertransport from Prague to the UK.

Matej Mináč's **Nicky's Family**

National elections will take place in Slovakia in March 2012. It is an event that could have a major impact on the filmmaking landscape. Before then, eight new films – an equal number of features and documentaries – from young directors are scheduled for release. They include Róbert Šveda's intimate story of love, sacrifice and death, **Angels** (*Anjeli*); Juraj Krasnohorsky's **Tigers in the City** (*Tigre v meste*), which offers some insight into the lives of young people on the threshold of their thirties; Palo Janík's **Take It Easy, or the Third Wheel on a Wagon** (*TAK FAJN, alebo tretie kolo na voze*), a light romantic musical comedy about three friends on a trip to the Croatian coast; and finally, the very first Slovak fantasy feature, **Immortalitas**, directed by Erik Bošňák.

The year's best films
The House (Zuzana Liová)
Gypsy (Martin Šulík)
Visible World (Peter Krištúfek)

MIRO ULMAN is a freelance journalist. He works for the Slovak Film Institute and is a programmer for the Art Film Festival Trenčianske Teplice – Trenčín.

South Africa Martin P. Botha

The current revival in South African cinema has been characterised by a strong emphasis on genre films. With few exceptions, the majority of features are mediocre imitations of various US genre films, especially crime thrillers. Charlie Vundla's **How to Steal 2 Million** is a good example. It tells the story of Jack, a career criminal who has come out of jail to find his best friend married to his ex-fiancée. Wanting to go straight, he attempts to separate himself from old, bad influences, but finds that it's easier said than done and he returns to crime. Young film critic Kavish Chetty described the film as a cliché-ridden trawl through all the signifiers of the US film noir mode. Chetty argued that in South Africa the US no longer has to valorise its culture at the expense of others; its own way of thinking is so internal and permeated in our own that the highest hallmark of achievement is to mimic, no matter how poorly executed. The results are not anachronisms but oddities.

Paul Eilers' **Roepman**

The few outstanding features of the year managed to secure international distribution deals. Paul Eilers' **Roepman** (*The Callman*), an honest insight into the apartheid culture of South Africa in the 1960s, as it was experienced by poor, working-class Afrikaners, secured a contract with the American production and distribution company D Street Media Group, which will see the film released across North America in 2012. To date, it is the fourth highest-grossing Afrikaans drama.

Oliver Hermanus's **Beauty**

Another Afrikaans-language film, **Beauty** (*Skoonheid*), by Oliver Hermanus (*Shirley Adams*), secured a distribution deal with TLA Releasing. The controversial drama is about a middle-aged married man François (Deon Lotz) and his sexual obsession with Christian (Charlie Keegan), a handsome, youthful student. It premiered at the Cannes film festival, where it screened in the 'Un Certain Regard' programme and won the Queer Palm. It has subsequently been sold in the UK, Australia, Germany, Italy, Holland and France. The director's representation of homosexuality divided South African audiences and critics, but Hermanus is undoubtedly a major talent.

Spud, based on John van de Ruit's bestselling novel of the same name, secured distribution deals for release in the UK, Ireland, the Middle East, Turkey, Australia, New Zealand and Scandinavia. Director Donovan Marsh's film,

ABU DHABI FILM
COMMISSION

Donovam Marsh's **Spud**

starring John Cleese, sensitively chronicles 14-year-old John Milton's (Troye Sivan) first year at Michaelhouse, an elite boarding school for boys around the time of Nelson Mandela's release from jail. As with *Roepman*, *Spud* is a lovely coming-of-age drama.

Another highlight that detailed a young boy's coming-of-age during the apartheid years was Lonny Price's **Master Harold… and the Boys**, based on Athol Fugard's early life in South Africa. It is not just a simple retelling of an incident from the playwright's past, but rather Fugard's attempt to extend his experience so that it offers a more universal commentary. Fugard wrote a play about human relationships that are put to the test by societal and personal forces. *Master Harold… and the Boys* focuses on the relationship between a young white boy, his one-legged alcoholic father and the two black men who work in his parents' Tea Room in Port Elizabeth. Through the social humiliation of his father's behaviour

Lonny Price's **Master Harold… and the Boys**

and his friendship with Sam (Ving Rhames), young Hally (a superb performance by Freddie Highmore) learns about respect and tolerance. Some of Athol Fugard's most guarded and shameful memories are brough to the screen in an adaptaion that is often deeply moving.

John Trengrove's **Hopeville**, a major winner at FESPACO, tells the story of Amos, a reformed alcoholic on a mission to forge a relationship with his estranged son, Themba. Arriving in the dusty town of Hopeville, they discover a mean little community where apathy, fear and suspicion are the order of the day. When Amos decides to restore the public swimming pool, so that his son can pursue a swimming career, he is met with scepticism and resistance from the town's authorities and its inhabitants. Through patience, determination and, above all, courage, Amos's selfless act ripples through the town, inspiring others to take action and do what they know is right. Slowly but surely, goodness ripples through Hopeville, transforming the town and its inhabitants.

John Trengrove's **Hopeville**

Where is South African cinema heading? In her study *The representation and mediation of a national identity in the production of post-apartheid South African cinema*, Astrid Treffry-Goatley concluded that while the South African government's development of its film industry is informed by a vision of cultural diversity and an intention to empower the previously disadvantaged, an equally pervasive, if not stronger, trend of neoliberalism is also present that is sometimes at odds with this vision. Neoliberal characteristics in state policy include fiscal prudence, the avoidance of 'direct intervention in product commodification' and an emphasis on production for export. This policy has a continued impact on the production, distribution and consumption of post-apartheid cinema. Furthermore, it affects the economic, cultural and ideological development of the film industry.

From a production point of view, it was found that many films are made primarily for an export market. This has a number of consequences for such works and the development of the industry as a whole. Firstly, these films are ostensibly more expensive to produce than those targeting local audiences and the inflated budgets make it more difficult for such works to recoup costs. Secondly, in terms of distribution, an emphasis on export can be seen to curtail the creative self-expression of the director – a far greater degree of foreign involvement in productions means filmmakers are under pressure with regards to casting, characterisation, content, narrative structure, language and style. Thirdly, there are ideological implications for this cinematic production and consumption model. In order to comply with the expectations of foreign partners and markets, filmmakers tend to perpetuate stereotypical African and South African identities rather than exploring complex, refreshing alternatives. These findings explain the obsession in current South African cinema with US film genres.

MARTIN P. BOTHA has published six books on South African cinema, including *South African Cinema 1896–2010*. He is a professor of film studies in the Centre for Film and Media Studies at the University of Cape Town and a member of FIPRESCI.

Oliver Hermanus's **Beauty**

The year's best films
Roepman (Paul Eilers)
Hopeville (John Trengrove)
Spud (Donovan Marsh)
Skoonheid (Oliver Hermanus)
Master Harold... and the Boys (Lonny Price)

Donovan Marsh's **Spud**

Directory
All Tel/Fax numbers begin (+27)
Cape Film Commission, 6th Floor, NBS Waldorf Bldg, 80 St George's Mall, Cape Town 8001. Tel: (21) 483 9070. Fax: (21) 483 9071. www.capefilmcommission.co.za.
Independent Producers Organisation, PO Box 2631, Saxonwold 2132. Tel: (11) 726 1189. Fax: (11) 482 4621. info@ipo.org.za. www.ipo.org.za.
National Film & Video Foundation, 87 Central St, Houghton, Private Bag x04, Northlands 2116. Tel: (11) 483 0880. Fax: (11) 483 0881. info@nfvf.co.za. www.nvfv.co.za.
South African Broadcasting Co (SABC), Private Bag 1, Auckland Park, Johannesburg 2006. Tel: (11) 714 9797. Fax: (11) 714 3106. www.sabc.co.za.

لجنة أبوظبي للأفلام
ABU DHABI FILM
COMMISSION

South Korea Nikki J. Y. Lee

South Korean cinema held its grip on the domestic market in 2011. There were 117 theatrical releases (by the end of October 2011) and the market share for domestic films remained at around 50 per cent. At the same time, three popular directors with established overseas reputations were all away working on international projects. Park Chan-wook, who presented his co-directed iPhone4 short **Night Fishing** (*Paranmanjang*) at the Berlin Film Festival, is now working on his first Hollywood venture, **Stoker**. (Written by *Prison Break* star Wentworth Miller and produced by Ridley Scott's Scott Free Productions, it stars Mia Wasikowska, Nicole Kidman and Dermot Mulroney.) Bong Joon-ho is directing the futuristic **Snowpiercer**, based upon the French graphic novel, which takes place in a time when extreme cold weather has taken over the Earth; it is currently shooting at the Barrandov Studio in Prague, where the main set – a train – has been constructed. Kim Jee-woon's **The Last Stand**, produced by Lionsgate, casts Arnold Schwarzenegger as a sheriff fighting a drugs cartel on the border of New Mexico and Nevada. These titles will be eagerly anticipated by the directors' Korean and international fans.

Kim Ki-duk's **Arirang**

Auteur Kim Ki-duk, who has been relatively quiet for some time, returned with **Arirang**, a documentary about himself that screened at Cannes, and **Amen**, his no-budget, one-man crafted film, which screened at San Sébastian. **The Day He Arrives** (*Bukchonbanghyang*) by Hong Sang-soo, another internationally renowned auteur who is ceaseless in producing unique films, received warm and favourable comments from fans and critics alike.

Na Hong-jin's **The Yellow Sea**

In late December 2010, when Na Hong-jin's, action thriller **The Yellow Sea** (*Hwanghae*) was released, the domestic success of visceral fare was in doubt. It had been overtaken by comic films like **Hello Ghost** (*Helou Goseuteu*), **Meet the In-laws** (*Wiheomhan Sanggyeonrye*) and **Unstoppable Family** (*Gamuneui Younggwang 4 – Gamuneui Sunan*). This situation appears to reflect local audiences' growing fatigue towards action films, particularly work like Kim Jee-woon's *I Saw the Devil*, which pushed brutal screen violence to the limit.

This year's blockbusters also failed to dominate the box office, even if their returns were still healthy. The big-budget 3D ocean action

Hun Jang's **The Front Line**

adventure **7 Sector** (*Chil Gwangu*), failed to repeat the success of *Tidal Wave*, which was produced by the same company, JK Film. At the time of writing, Hun Jang's **The Front Line** (*Gojijeon*), this year's contribution to the Korean War film, was only in sixth place at the domestic box-office for 2011.

Korean cinema in 2011 instead showcased a broad palette of popular genre films and independent dramas. Romantic comedy, action comedy, melodrama, sports drama, animation and human dramas all featured strongly. In particular, clever genre films, with strong scripts that sported surprising twists, appealed to audiences. **War of the Arrows** (*Choijongbyunggi Hwal*), a period epic, led the way, looking set to stay atop of the year's box-office figures. In third place was **Detective K: Secret of Virtuous Widow** (*Joseon Myungtamjeong: Gaksitugukkocheu Bimil*). Adapted from a popular period detective novel by Kim Tak-hwan, the film successfully blended a manga style with fictional historical settings. Further down the

Kim Seok-yun's **Detective K: Secret of Virtuous Widow**

top ten was **Quick** (*Quig*), a derivative *Speed*-style thriller. **Officer of the Year** (*Chepowang*), a down-to-earth action comedy, was also slickly made, highlighting the technical expertise of the South Korean industry.

Im Chan-ik's **Officer of the Year**

Attempts to broaden the generic scope of Korean films can be found in titles such as **Blind** (*Beulaindeu*) and **The Client** (*Euiroein*). *Blind* is a thriller about a young blind woman who claims she witnessed the kidnapping of another woman by a potential suspect in a serial rape and murder case. Marketed as the first genuine Korean courtroom thriller, *The Client* entertains audiences with its well-crafted sense of suspense and a series of unexpected plot twists.

Sunny (*Sseoni*), the year's second-biggest box-office success is the second feature by Kang Hyung-cheol, whose 2008 comic drama *Scandal Makers* was a surprise hit. With its nostalgic memories of the 1980s (including Boney-M's eponymous track) and a fine sense of humour, the film appealed mostly to middle-aged females.

Other titles that drew a middle-aged demographic included faithful manga adaptation **Late Blossom** (*Geudaereul Saranghapnida*), an adaptation of the popular TV series *The Last Blossom* (*Sesangeseo Gajang Areumdaun Ibyeol*) and **Mama**.

Released in late October, **Punch** (*Wandeugi*), an adaptation of a popular novel, is on course to join the top earners of the year. Thanks to a

Han Lee's **Punch**

strong performance by popular young star Yu A-in, as well as the charismatic Kim Yun-seok, *Punch* delivers a comic, yet touching, story of a young boy's growing pains.

2011 also saw the release of a number of animated films. To everybody's surprise, **Leafie, a Hen into the Wild** (*Madangeul Naon Amtag*), a big-budget adaption of the children's story of the same title, beat its competitors over summer. Diametrically opposed to this family-friendly animation is the independent title **The King of Pigs** (*Doejieu Wang*) – an outstanding and very dark social fable directed by Yeon Sang-ho, whose previous two shorts, *The Hell 1* and *The Hell 2*, were an accurate forecast of what could be expected of the young director.

Yeon Sang-ho's **The King of Pigs**

If just one title represented South Korean cinema in 2011, it would be **Silenced** (*Dogani*). An adaptation of Gong Ji-young's bestselling novel from 2005 – itself based upon the real abuse and sexual assault of handicapped children by their guardians, teachers and principal in an educational institution – the

film became a phenomenon. Gong Yu, the heartthrob from the TV drama *Coffee Prince*, initiated the production, which seemed to have little commercial potential. He also plays the main character, a newly appointed teacher who has to face all the ugly truths buried by those in power. The press coverage of the film, as well as of the real case, resulted in public outrage and the closure of the institution. Revised legislation on rape cases involving handicapped women and children, dubbed the Dogani (the Korean title of the film) Law, was passed in the National Congress in late October.

The year's best films
Alien Bikini (Hong Young-du)
Detective K: Secret of Virtuous Widow
(Kim Seok-yun)
Moby Dick (Park In-je)
Officer of the Year (Im Chan-ik)
The King of Pigs (Yeon Sang-ho)

Hong Young-du's **Alien Bikini**

Directory
All Tel/Fax numbers begin (+82)
Korean Film Archive, 1602 DMC, Sangam-dong, Mapo-gu, Seoul 120-270. Tel: (2) 3153 2001. Fax: (2) 3153 2080. www.koreafilm.or.kr.
Korean Film Council (KOFIC), 206-46 Cheongnyangni-dong, Tongdaemun-gu, Seoul 130-010. Tel: (2) 9587 581~6. Fax: (2) 9587 590. www.kofic.or.kr

---

NIKKI J.Y. LEE is a lecturer at Nottingham Trent University. She mainly writes about South Korean directors and films, and East Asian cinema and popular culture.

Spain Jonathan Holland

'Due to recent budget cuts,' read one poster at Madrid's summer 2011 protests, 'the light at the end of the tunnel has been turned off.' It may not be quite that bad for the Spanish film industry, but at year's end, its problems do remain fairly constant and cutbacks of one form or another loom ever larger. P2P piracy continues to be an unresolved issue, with recent research showing that an astounding 77 per cent of digital content in Spain is downloaded illegally. The resistance to Spanish film of many Spanish cinemagoers, of the opinion that the films are awarded unfairly high government subsidies and that they are all navel-gazing rubbish, continues to represent a problem of perception which the industry is seeking to rectify by making more crowd-pleasers, mostly thrillers. But the decline in cinema audiences continues apace anyway, with four million fewer cinema seats being filled during the first six months of 2011 compared with the same period the year before.

The Government and producers agree that the way forward, in financing terms, is through collaborations with foreign producers, with Spain's ICAA announcing new grants for international co-productions during the

Juan Carlos Fresnadillo's **Intruders**

summer. High-profile Spanish co-productions include Rodrigo Cortés' forthcoming **Red Lights**, starring Robert de Niro and Sigourney Weaver, and Juan Carlos Fresnadillo's **Intruders**. France and Argentina remain Spain's biggest production partners, with new countries coming on board. But it's a decent plan that's only half working, as the number of big-budget projects that might appeal abroad has declined since the credit crunch started.

Commercially, the biggest recent hits have been Woody Allen's Gallic historical romance **Midnight in Paris**, which by mid-November was the fifth highest-grossing Spanish film of all time. But, of course, that project is Spanish only in terms of financing, not artistically. The

biggest Spanish waves of of the year were made by the latest instalment in Santiago Segura's record-smashing grungy cop comedy series **Torrente 4, Lethal Crisis** (*Torrente 4, Crisis Letal*), which had grossed close to US$30million by year's end and which, largely single-handedly, doubled the country's market share during the first half of 2011, compared to the same period in 2010, to nearly 18 per cent. To put that in perspective, Pedro Almodóvar's cold, slick thriller **The Skin I Live In** (*La piel que habito*), featuring Antonio Banderas as a troubled surgeon seeking cosmetic revenge for the rape of his daughter, was Spain's third-highest grossing movie as of November 2011, but made only US$6.5million.

September and October were boom months for Spanish films, with the market share rising to over 20 per cent. Responsible for this were a handful of high-profile productions that displayed the range of quality of Spanish top-end fare. As usual, Almodóvar was partly responsible, with *The Skin I Live In* attracting critical and commercial success internationally, reaffirming his status as practically the only Spanish director whom non-Spaniards can name. Three successful chillers released around the same time, Andi Baiz's Spanish/Colombian co-production **The Bunker** (*La Cara oculta*), about the mysterious sudden disappearance of an orchestra director's girlfriend, and Jaume Balaguero's **Sleep Tight** (*Mientras Duermes*), starring Luis Tosar as a psychopathic janitor taking out his frustrations on one of the residents of the house he tends, showed that Spanish thrillers work

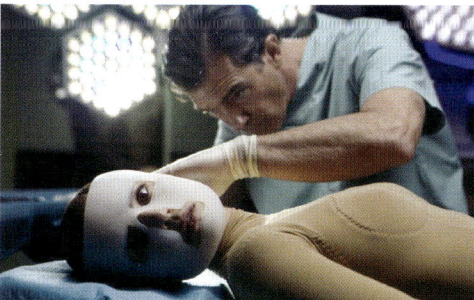

Pedro Almodóvar's **The Skin I Live In**

particularly well when based on character and confined to enclosed spaces. Fresnadillo's *Intruders*, starring Clive Owen, was a slightly underwhelming addition to the canon of Spanish chillers about monster-seeing kids.

Enrique Urbizu's **No Rest for the Wicked**

While Spanish horror continues to make its mark internationally – **Rec 3: Genesis**, the third instalment in the popular trilogy, is set for release in 2012 – advances are being made in other genres. Enrique Urbizu's latest, **No Rest for the Wicked** (*No habrá paz para los malvados*), is a hard-boiled, thoroughly contemporary noir about a bad cop (Jose Coronado) who shoots two people dead in the first ten minutes and spend the rest of the film covering his tracks. Paco Cabeza's derivative but enjoyably muscular **Neon Flesh** (*Carne de neon*), about a Barcelona street kid who sets about making some serious money, was similarly turbo-charged, turning its thriller clichés into an underrated crowd pleasing comedy thriller, with nods to Tarantino, Guy Ritchie and *Trainspotting*. Mateo Gil's revisionist English-language western **Blackthorn**, starring Sam Shepard as an ageing Butch Cassidy, breathed new life into an old genre. And Kike Maillo delivered one of the year's strongest debuts with **Eva**, a rare Spanish incursion into sci-fi, about an android designer and a little girl. That the story was as much about our lost humanity as it was about robots gave it an unexpected depth.

Other debuts included Jonas Trueba (son of Fernando) with the broken-heart drama **Every Song is About Me** (*Todas las canciones* *hablan de mí*), which mixed love, literature and life lessons into an engaging but retro piece, suggesting that the *nouvelle vague* had never left us. Another outstanding debut, Paula Ortiz's **From Your Window to Mine** (*De tu ventana a la mía*), spanned three generations and told the story of ordinary women whose lives are suddenly tainted by an extraordinary tragedy. The film won the Best New Director award at Spain's Valladolid festival. It was also, sadly, the only feature to be directed by a female Spanish filmmaker in 2011.

Montxo Armendáriz's **Don't Be Afraid**

If international waves were mostly being made by escapist genre fare, there was a still a steady flow of social realism on offer. Montxo Armendáriz tackled the difficult topic of child abuse in **Don't Be Afraid** (*No tengas miedo*), and, aided by terrific performances by Michelle Jenner and Lluis Homar as daughter and father, made a film that was both compassionate and profoundly unsettling. Enrique Gabriel's underrated **Small Lives** (*Vidas Pequeñas*) tackled poverty and unemployment head on, examining the interlinked lives of a group of people living in a caravan park on the outskirts of Madrid. Ramón Termens' three-parter, **Catalunya Über Alles**, tackled immigration in various forms with wit, passion and palpable

Ramón Termens' **Catalunya Über Alles**

anger, while Max Lemcke's tragicomic **Five Square Metres** (*Cinco Metros Cuadrados*) explored the phenomenon that has brought the Spanish economy to its knees: property speculation. It took the best film award at the Malaga Festival.

Spanish history perhaps received less attention from filmmakers than it has in other years. Yet it still provided a fair share of turkeys. Among them was Chema de la Peña's **23-F**, an attempt to bring to the screen the near fateful coup of 23 February 1981, and perhaps the year's most emotive piece, Benito Zambrano's **The Sleeping Voice** (*La voz dormida*), which dealt with life in a women's prison in the aftermath of the Civil War and featured a standout performance by María León.

Benito Zambrano's **The Sleeping Voice**

The year also saw some terrific documentaries. Mercedes Alvarez followed up her magnificent *The Sky Turns* with **Futures Market** (*Mercado de futures*), a beautifully-poised but savage attack on property speculation. In **Jacques Leonard, el Payo Chac**, Yago Leonard used photographs taken by his grandfather, Jacques, of the gypsy community under Franco as the basis for a lyrical study of memory and forgetting. Isaki Lacuesta brought two documentaries to the table: **All Night Long** (*La noche que no acaba*), about the mutually adoring relationship between Ava Gardner and Spain during the 1950s and 1960s, and **The Double Steps** (*Los pasos dobles*), which followed Spanish artist Miquel Barcelo to Mali in the footsteps of the French artist Francois Augieras in

Sandra Sanchez' **Behind the Lights**

oder to explore the key Lacuesta themes of myth-making and storytelling. *The Double Steps* won the best film at San Sébastian. Equally compelling, but in a very different way, was **Behind the Lights** (*Tralas luces*), Sandra Sánchez's intimate, affecting study of a gipsy woman struggling to keep her itinerant fairground family going.

The number of Basque-language titles on the release list seems to be rising and for the first time, some of them are worth seeking out. Among them is Immanol Rayo's **Two Brothers** (*Bi Anai*), a lyrical, gorgeous-looking study of a 1950s Basque family. **The Stone** (*Arriya*), an attractive portrait of village life in the Basque country, had two clans fighting over a rock in the village square, and like all the finest work from the area, was suffused with a strong sense of place as it tackled the relationship between tradition and modernity. Altogether more raucous was Telmo Esnal's black comedy **Happy New Year, Grandma!** (*Urte berri on, amona!*), in which a family is broken apart, initially amusingly and then bleakly, by a matriarch's refusal to be sidelined.

The change of government in November 2011 from the Socialists to the centre-right Partido Popular had the film industry quaking in its boots, with a luminary of the stature of Antonio Banderas suggesting that the Partido Popular's cuts would mean the end of industry subsidies. Among proposals mooted by the Partido Popular is one releasing the private TV channels from their obligation to finance Spanish and European cinema. This would lead to a loss of some €60million a year,

which could, in the eyes of industry doomsayers, lead to its collapse. It fell to Enrique González Macho, the recently-elected president of the Spanish Film Academy, to qualify the gloom: 'There will be changes and cuts, but I don't believe this will be a catastrophe for Spanish cinema.' Somehow, the industry has always struggled through crises before, and chances are that it will again – albeit under reduced circumstances.

The year's best films
Behind the Lights (Sandra Sanchez)
Catalunya Über Alles (Ramon Termens)
Don't Be Afraid (Montxo Armendariz)
No Rest for the Wicked (Enrique Urbizu)
The Sleeping Voice (Benito Zambrano)

Directory
All Tel/Fax numbers begin (+34)
Escuela de Cinematografia y de la Audiovisual de la Comunidad de Madrdid (ECAM), Centra de Madrid a Boadilla, Km 2200, 28223 Madrid. Tel: (91) 411 0497. www.ecam.es.
Federation of Associations of Spanish Audiovisual Producers (FAPAE), Calle Luis Bunuel 2-2° Izquierda, Ciudad de la Imagen, Pozuelo de Alarcón, 28223 Madrid. Tel: (91) 512 1660. Fax: (91) 512 0148. web@fapae.es. www.fapae.es.
Federation of Cinema Distributors (FEDICINE), Orense 33, 3°B, 28020 Madrid. Tel. (91) 556 9755. Fax: (91) 555 6697. www.fedicine.com.
Filmoteca de la Generalitat de Catalunya, Carrer del Portal de Santa Madrona 6-8, Barcelona 08001. Tel: (93) 316 2780. Fax: (93) 316 2783. filmoteca. cultura@gencat.net.
Filmoteca Espanola, Calle Magdalena 10, 28012 Madrid. Tel: (91) 467 2600. Fax: (91) 467 2611. www.cultura.mecd.es/cine/film/filmoteca.isp.
Filmoteca Vasca, Avenida Sancho el Sabio, 17 Trasera, Donostia, 20010 San Sebastián. Tel: (943) 468 484. Fax: (943) 469 998. www.filmotecavasca. com. andaluciafilmcom@fundacionava.org.

JONATHAN HOLLAND is a university teacher and journalist based in Madrid. He reviews Spanish films for *Variety*.

Sweden Gunnar Rehlin

A clinical study of black boys robbing white boys and a story about two teenage girls becoming both friends and competitors at a riding school. These were the two international Swedish hits of 2011. Ruben Östlund´s controversial **Play** had its debut in the 'Directors' Fortnight' at Cannes and went on to become a festival darling throughout the year. After winning awards at Sundance and Berlin, Lisa Aschan's **She Monkeys** (*Apflickorna*) also travelled the world. Both films represent new, young Swedish film directors, a generation that dares to do the unexpected and to steer away from the conventional, both in terms of subject matter and narrative style.

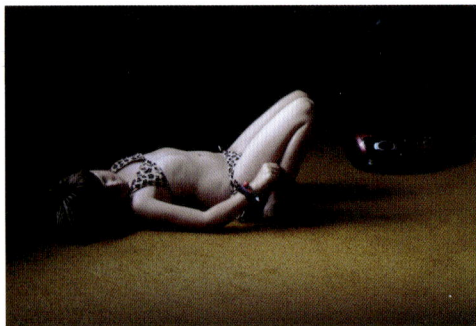

Ruben Östlund's **Play**

Lisa Aschan's **She Monkeys**

Lisa Aschas describes *She Monkeys* as 'a modern western'. There is something in that description, although the film's style owes much to documentary. The same can be said about Ruben Östlund's hugely successful *Play*, which develops themes raised in his previous film, *Involuntary*. The new film is based on the true story of a gang of black teenagers in Gothenburg that employed racial stereotypes to intimidate and rob young white boys. It is an impressive and daring film, provoking us

into asking questions about peer pressure and racism. Östlund shows with the film that he is the heir to Roy Andersson.

Both films opened domestically during the latter half of the year, with the first six months bereft of any great releases, with the exception of Pernilla August's acclaimed literary adaptation **Beyond** (*Svinalängorna*). The film opened late in 2010, after having won the Critics' Prize at Venice, and was picked as the Swedish entry for the 2012 Academy Awards.

Back to the start of 2011, the war film **The Border** (*Gränsen*), directed by Richard Holm, had its defenders. The documentaries **I Am My Own Dolly Parton** (*Jag är min egen Dolly Parton*), directed by Jessica Nettelbladt,

Richard Holm's **The Border**

Göran Hugo Olsson's **The Black Power Mixtape 1967–1975**

and **The Black Power Mixtape 1967–1975**, by Göran Hugo Olsson, also received good reviews, but performed poorly at the box office (though the latter film played well at festivals). Martin Jern and Emil Larsson's **The Beast** (*Odjuret*) and Agnieszka Lukasiak's **Between 2 Fires** were uneven but watchable dramas, while the advance hype for Ella Lemhagen's **The Crown Jewels** (*Kronjuvelerna*) guaranteed the film would disappoint.

The end of summer saw the release of Alexandra Theresa Keinig's striking **With Every Heartbeat** (*Kyssen*). Ruth Vega Fernandez and Liv Möjnes impressed as two young women who meet and fall in love, despite the fact that one of them is about to be married. Partly based on producer Josefin Tengblad's own experiences, the film is a captivating depiction of love prevailing against all odds. It should attract audiences beyond gay festivals and the director and actresses are names to watch.

Autumn began with **I Miss You** (*Jag saknar dig*), directed by Anders Grönros. It is a heartfelt story about teenage twins and what happens when one of them is killed in accident. Henrik J. P. Åkesson and Mattias Olsson's solid thriller **Missing** (*Försvunnen*) showed that Sweden can produce genre product beyond the usual police dramas.

At Venice's Critics' Week, first-time feature director Simon Kaijser da Silva screened **Stockholm East** (*Stockholm Östra*), a captivating low-key romance.

Older directors also turned in some impressive work. Kjell Sundvall has talked for years about a sequel to his action hit *The Hunters*. As the year was drawing to a close, **The Hunters 2** (*Jägarna 2*) reached cinemas. The film features the same lead actor in Rolf Lassgård, as well as the same northern setting. Other than that it had little to do with the original. It received mixed reviews but performed well with audiences.

Richard Hobert's **One Way to Antibes**

Björn Runge presented **Happy End**, the final film in his trilogy about tragic lives and ruined relationships, while Richard Hobert scored a critical hit with his gentle drama **One Way to Antibes** (*En enkel till Antibes*). Runge was attached to direct the film version of the bestseller **Simon and the Oaks** (*Simon och ekarna*), a coming-of-age tale set during World War II, but citing creative differences, Runge left the production and Lisa Ohlin took over. The result was visually impressive, but lacked the punch and drama that Runge might have brought to it.

Simon Kaijser da Silva's **Stockholm East**

The end of the year also saw the release of Kjell-Åke Andersson's **Somewhere Else** (*Någon annanstans i Sverige*), an Altman-esque ensemble piece.

The major box-office hits of the year were local comedies such as Leif Lindblom's **Svensson, Svensson** and Lasse Åberg's **The Stig-Helmer Story**. However, as with many local comedies, whose humour may not travel so well, they are unlikely to have a life outside the domestic market.

Kjell-Åke Andersson's **Somewhere Else**

Leif Lindblom's **Svensson, Svensson**

So 2011 was hardly a great year for Swedish film. A couple of really good films, yes, but in general most of what we saw was quickly forgotten. 2012 looks far more interesting, with Axel Petersén's Toronto winner **Avalon**, Jan Troell's **Truth and Consequence** (*Dom över död man*), Anders Öhman's **Bitch Slap** (*Bitchkram*), Jesper Ganslandt's **Blondie**, Mikael Marcimain's **Call Girl**, Catherine Hardwick's Anita Lindblom biopic starring Noomi Rapace, and Peter Dalle's drama **An Enemy to Die For** (*En fiende att dö för*) all awaiting release.

The new year will also see the premiere of Lasse Hallström's thriller **The Hypnotist** (*Hypnotisören*), his first Swedish film in more than twenty years. Hallström returns home as other creative talent, such as Noomi Rapace, Michael Nyqvist, Daniel Espinosa, Alicia Vikander, Alexander Skarsgård and many others, seek their fame and fortune abroad.

The year's best films
Play (Ruben Östlund)
She Monkeys (Lisa Aschan)
Somewhere Else (Kjell-Åke Andersson)
Stockholm East (Simon Kaijser da Silva)
With Every Heartbeat (Alexandra Therese Keinig)

Directory
All Tel/Fax numbers begin (+46)
Cinemateket, Swedish Film Institute, Box 27126, SE-102 52 Stockholm. Tel: (8) 665 1100. Fax: (8) 666 3698. info@sfi.se. www.sfi.se.
Swedish Film Distributors Association, Box 23021, SE-10435 Stockholm. Tel: (8) 441 5570. Fax: (8) 343 810.
Swedish Film Institute, Box 27126, SE-10252 Stockholm. Tel: (8) 665 1100. Fax: (8) 666 3698. info@sfi.se.
Swedish Film Producers Association, Box 27298, SE-102 53 Stockholm. Tel: (8) 665 1255. Fax: (8) 666 3748. info@frf.net.
Swedish National Archive for Recorded Sound & Moving Images, Box 24124, SE-10451 Stockholm. Tel: (8) 783 3700. Fax: (8) 663 1811. info@ljudochbildarkivet.se.

GUNNAR REHLIN is a Swedish journalist and critic, working for several international media, among them Swedish news agency TT Spektra, Norwegian magazine *Film & Kino* and *Variety*. His four years as a TV host was the subject of a one-hour mockumentary, directed by *Let the Right One In* director Tomas Alfredson.

Switzerland Marcy Goldberg

I n 2011 Swiss cinema succeeded in garnering a satisfying amount of attention, both at home and on the international festival scene. The domestic market share was four per cent, down from five per cent a year ago. However, two significant films on human rights issues captured the public's imagination and generated important debates in the media as well as the political sphere.

Markus Imboden's Swiss-German historical drama **The Foster Boy** (*Der Verdingbub*) reminded local audiences of the systematic mistreatment of foster children hired out as slave workers to farms, a practice that began in the early 1800s and persisted well into the 1950s, thanks to the collusion of local authorities and the Church. Imboden's 'movie of the week' aesthetic and a predictable, not to mention overly melodramatic, script will likely hamper the film's international sales. However, at home *The Foster Boy* topped the box-office chart for several weeks in November, beating international blockbusters like Steven Spielberg's *The Adventures of Tintin*.

Fernand Melgar's hard-hitting documentary **Special Flight** (*Vol spécial*) called attention to a current and highly controversial aspect of Swiss

Fernand Melgar's **Special Flight**

refugee policy that will strike a chord in many other First World countries: detention centres in which asylum seekers and illegal immigrants can be incarcerated for up to 18 months whilst awaiting deportation. In this follow-up to his award-winning *The Fortress*, which had examined the refugee application process, Lausanne-based Melgar spent nine months filming in one of Switzerland's 28 detention centres – the end of the line for those whose applications have been rejected. Shot in direct-cinema style with no commentary, the film powerfully captures both the desperation of the men facing forced expulsion – the 'special flight' cases – back to countries where their lives may be in danger, and the dilemma of the prison wardens charged with ensuring 'humane' conditions for the inmates.

On the festival circuit, Swiss films were present at Berlin, Cannes, Locarno, Venice, San Sébastian and Sundance, mainly with documentaries and international co-productions. For the time being, it seems likely that the country's chances of recognition abroad continue to lie in these areas, rather than in success with domestic features.

The Berlinale 'Forum' saw the debut of Thomas Imbach's self-described 'fictional autobiography' **Day Is Done**. The experimental documentary juxtaposes 15 years' worth of luminous 35mm footage shot from the filmmaker's studio window, with answer-machine messages culled from the same period. Taken together, this material tells the somewhat fictionalised story of T., a filmmaker struggling to build a career as his personal life unravels. Also in Berlin, in the 'Panorama' programme, was **Off Beat**, Jan Gassman's promising feature debut. Shot in a dark and hand-held 'indie' style, it tells the story of an illicit gay love triangle set in the Swiss-German hip hop milieu.

Thomas Imbach's **Day Is Done**

Following a lacklustre period for Switzerland's Italian-language film sector, there has been a growing number of co-productions between the two countries. Cannes' 'Directors' Fortnight' featured the Italian-Swiss co-production **Corpo celeste**, a coming-of-age drama about a teenage girl's return from Switzerland to Italy, written and directed by Alice Rohrwacher (sister of the Italian actress Alba Rohrwacher). **Summer Games** (*Giochi d'estate*), another Italian-language film, premiered out of competition in Venice. This sensitively shot story of a family's summer

vacation gone awry was written and directed by Swiss-Italian Rolando Colla, produced by the Zurich-based Peacock Films and shot in Tuscany with a Swiss and Italian cast and crew. Both films went on to enjoy much success at festivals, which should continue into 2012.

Milagros Mumenthaler's **Back to Stay**

Further proof that Switzerland would do well to increase its focus on international collaborations was provided by the Swiss-Argentine-Dutch co-production **Back to Stay** (*Abrir puertas y ventanas*), a family drama by Swiss-Argentine director Milagros Mumenthaler. It received the Golden Leopard and Best Actress awards at Locarno and was also screened in San Sébastian, before going on to pick up several more awards at Latin American film festivals.

Two of the year's most fascinating documentaries unfolded some way from the Swiss border. Jarreth Merz's **An African Election**, which premiered at Sundance, chronicles the 2008 presidential election in Ghana as it transformed into a tense stand-off between the country's two main political parties. Also on an African theme, Heidi Specogna's **Carte Blanche** follows investigators from the International Criminal Court in the Hague as they research war crimes allegedly committed in the Central African Republic on the orders of Congolese political leader Jean-Pierre Bemba.

Finally, two personal favourites from 2011 marked a departure from more stereotypical Swiss seriousness. **The Sandman** (*Der Sandmann*) by Peter Luisi, a gently surreal

Laurent Nègre's **Opération Casablanca**

comedy in the spirit of Michel Gondry and Spike Jonze, tells the story of an aspiring and eccentric classical music composer who inexplicably leaves a trail of fine sand wherever he goes as his professional and personal life begin to crumble. And **Opération Casablanca**, by Laurent Nègre (a co-production with Canada and France), is a satirical slapstick comedy, poking fun at stereotypes of Muslims and terrorists that manages to be timely, entertaining and witty.

All in all, Swiss cinema – whether in German, Swiss-German, French, Italian or the country's unofficial *lingua franca*, English – continues to show potential for increased success in the years to come. Last year also saw veteran producer and film festival director Ivo Kummer replace the controversial Nicolas Bideau as the head of the Federal Film Office, a change that observers hope will serve to reunify the linguistically and regionally fragmented film industry. At the same time, Kummer's post as longtime head of the Solothurn Film Festival, the influential annual showcase for Swiss cinema, has now been filled by Seraina Rohrer.

As a representative of a younger generation, and the first woman to hold the position, Rohrer is the focus of much anticipation as to how she will make her mark on Swiss film culture.

The year's best films
The Sandman (Peter Luisi)
Opération Casablanca (Laurent Nègre)
Back to Stay (Milagros Mumenthaler)
Special Flight (Fernand Melgar)
Day Is Done (Thomas Imbach)

Peter Luisi's **The Sandman**

Directory
All Tel/Fax numbers begin (+41)
Swiss Films, Neugasse 6, P.O. Box, CH-8031 Zurich. Tel: (43) 211 40 50. Fax: (43) 211 40 60. info@swissfilms.ch www.swissfilms.ch.
Swiss Films Genève, Maison des Arts du Grütli, 16, rue Général Dufour, CH-1204 Genève. Tel: (22) 308 12 40, Fax: (22) 308 12 41. geneva@swissfilms.ch www.swissfilms.ch.

MARCY GOLDBERG is a film historian and independent media consultant based in Zurich.

لجنة أبوظبي للأفلام
ABU DHABI FILM
COMMISSION

Taiwan Luna Lin

Perhaps the biggest significance of 2011 for the Taiwanese film industry is that the term 'Taiwanese Film Renaissance' is no longer a government publicity slogan or part of a marketing stunt for promoting a single film; rather, it has become an actuality for the entire entertainment industry. The film market over the last year saw a 23 per cent increase on the previous year's total box-office gross, whilst revenues for domestic productions actually doubled. Taiwanese films finally returned to being a profitable business and investors saw their confidence in local filmmakers restored. That is, a new generation of filmmakers who continued in a humanist vein but also aimed for more market-driven productions.

Yeh Tian-lun's **Night Market Hero**

Night Market Hero (*Ji Pai Ying Xiong*) was the first film to herald this a box-office turnaround. The debut of Yeh Tian-lun and starring Blue Lan and Alice Ko, the film deals with a journalist's encounter with a group of night-market vendors. Touched by their warm-hearted hospitality, she is determined to fight alongside them against a real estate group that covets the land other work on.

Vividly representing the unique night-market culture of Taiwan, the film emanates the same vibrant energy present in its subject's real-life counterpart. The resulting success saw it pull in around US$4.6million.

Lien Yi-chih's **Make Up**

Drawing a distinction between their work and that of the Taiwanese auteur filmmakers of the 1980s, such as Hou Hsiao-hsien and Edward Yang, the new generation of directors are more willing to tackle genres such as horror and thriller. Nowhere is this more apparent than in Lien Yi-chih's successful attempt at a thriller with **Make Up**, an exquisite debut that was welcomed by both the audiences and critics. The film offers up a love triangle that escalates out of control when a mortuary beautician is faced with the dead body of her young lesbian lover.

Make Up's success was followed by Lin Yu-hsien's Eddie Peng vehicle **Jump Ashin**, a true story about a man's journey from street gangster to medal-winning gymnast. Peng's strong performance and the impressively choreographed action scenes, for which South Korean action directors were employed, made for an entertaining film.

Lin Yu-hsien's **Jump Ashin**

The war epic **Warriors of the Rainbow: Seediq Bale** was also dependent on the help of South Korean experts. Starring Vivian Hsu, along with Da-Ching, Lo Mei-ling and Japanese actor Ando Masanobu, the film is set in the 1930s in central Taiwan and tells the true story of the Wushe Incident, in which the Seediq tribal warrior Mouna Rudo led his people to rebel against Japanese occupation. Director Wei Te-sheng demonstrates the brutality of a war that saw guns raised against swords, but also highlights the spiritual and cultural divide between Japanese civilisation and the indigenous hunter culture, and the the the conflict between colonialism and the resistance to it.

Wei Te-sheng's **Warriors of the Rainbow. Seediq Bale**

Despite certain flaws in character development, Wei's ambition paid off. Not only was it one of the few epic films made locally in the past ten years, when released locally in two parts, it earned a healthy US$25million at the box office. The film also won the Best Picture prize at the Golden Horse Awards, Taiwan's equivalent of the Academy Awards.

The biggest surprise of 2011 came with novelist and debut filmmaker Giddens Ko's sleeper hit **You Are the Apple of My Eye**. Adapted by Ko from his autobiographical novel and starring Michelle Chen and first-time actor Ko Chen-tung, the film is a high-school love story set in the 1990s in south Taiwan. The US$1.25milion budget drama swept aside most titles released in its wake, taking US$14.64million at the local box office and a further US$7.86million in Hong Kong. Ko's quirky humour and the refreshing on-screen chemistry between Ko and Chen were key to the film's success.

Giddens Ko's **You Are the Apple of My Eye**

The string of box-office successes has increased the market share of Taiwanese productions against foreign films. The domestic share of the market increased from 7.1 per cent to 18.4 per cent, the biggest increase in the last two decades. As a result, this group of new young filmmakers also attracted great interest from investors outside of the industry. During the 2011 Taipei Golden Horse Film Festival, over ten venture capitalist companies participated in the festival's film financing forum for the first time, looking for the 'next big thing' from the film world.

Eyeing on China's ever-expanding film market, Taiwanese filmmakers also began to partner with mainland Chinese companies for Taiwan-China co-productions. Tom Lin's **Starry Starry Night** is a callaboration with Beijing's Huayi Brothers. Based on an illustrated novel by Taiwanese author Jimmy Liao, Lin presents a fantasy love story between two alienated teenagers who find each other when they both escape the city to the mountains. The skilfully rendered computer graphic work gives the film a sophisticated fairy-tale look. Employing the perspective of a 13-year-old girl, Lin tells a convincing tale about growing up and the loss of innocence.

Tom Lin's **Starry Starry Night**

Another collaboration with mainland China is the documentary **Hometown Boy**, directed by Yao Hong-yi and produced by Hou Hsiao-hsien's 3H Productions. It tells the story of Chinese artist Liu Xiaodong, recounting his youthful days in his hometown of Jincheng in northeast China, and its dramatic transformation into a factory, with its land overrun by apartment blocks full of unemployed workers. The fluid narrative and Liu's calm reflection on the changes in Chinese society makes for a quiet but powerful story.

LUNA LIN is a Beijing-based journalist and consultant who contributes to the Beijing *City Weekend magazine* and consults several Beijing-based film companies.

Yao Hong-yi's **Hometown Boy**

The year's best films

Hometown Boy (Yao Hong-yi)
Make Up (Lien Yi-chih)
Starry Starry Night (Tom Lin)
Warriors of the Rainbow: Seediq Bale (Wei Te-sheng)
You Are the Apple of My Eye (Giddens Ko)

Directory

All Tel/Fax numbers begin (+886)

Chinese Taipei Film Archive, 4F, 7 Chingtao East Rd, Taipei. Tel: (2) 2392 4243. Fax: (2) 2392 6359. www.ctfa.org.tw.

Government Information Office, Department of Motion Picture Affairs, 2 Tientsin St, Taipei 100. Tel: (2) 3356 7870. Fax: (2) 2341 0360. www.gio.gov.tw.

Motion Picture Association of Taipei, 5F, 196 Chunghwa Rd, Sec 1, Taipei. Tel: (2) 2331 4672 Fax: (2) 2381 4341.

Taipei Film Commission, 4F, #99, Section 5, Civic Blvd., Taipei. Tel: (2) 2528-9580 Fax: (2) 2528-9580. www.taipeifilmcommission.org

ABU DHABI FILM
COMMISSION

Thailand Anchalee Chaiworaporn

2011 is likely to be seen as a rich year for the Thai film industry. Politically, the country saw some stability after a tumultuous 12-month period. Seven of the top ten films at the box office were all released in the first half of the year. There was a brief sojourn in the middle of the year, to make way for the national elections in July. Business should then have returned to normal.

However, extreme weather hit the country, just as a number of blockbusters were to be released over the October school holidays. Around twenty multiplexes were temporarily closed, new releases were postponed and all production was cancelled as the country was affected by severe storms and flooding. As a result of people being unable to work, the economy turned sour, with no one able – or able to afford – to go to the cinema, let alone carry on with their lives. The likelihood is that cinema in 2012 will be deeply affected, particularly as much money will be needed to rebuild the country's infrastructure.

Around fifty titles were released in 2011, many of which were comedies. Of the top ten box-office titles, two were the continuation of Prince Chatreechalerm Yukol's epic series: **King Naresuan 3** and **4** (*Tamnan Somjej Phra Naresuan 3* and *4*). Originally planned to end at the third sequel, the true life of King Naresuan, who liberated the Siamese from Burmese control during the 16th century, has now been extended to a fourth sequel. These films would eventually become the highest grossing domestic films of 2011. Another major earner was Sophon Sakdaphisit's horror film **Ladda Land**. One of three horror films released last year, it attracted audiences with its portrayal of an actual haunting that took place in northern

Sophon Sakdaphisit's **Ladda Land**

Thailand two decades ago. The film brought in US$3.2million and looks set to pick up many awards.

As for the remaining popular films, there was slapstick, horror comedy, teen comedy and, especially, romantic comedy – a popular new genre that has emerged in recent years thanks to a growing thirty-something audience. Young audiences are no longer the main target group they were in the past, with more attention being paid to a new generation of baby boomers. Films such as Rirkchai Puangphet's **Lucky Loser** (*Sudkhot Salodpod*), Puttipong Promsaka na Nakorn's **30+** (*30 buak sode on sales*) and Somjing Srisuphab's **Fabulous 30** (*30 kamlangjaew*) all made their way into the year's top ten. *Lucky Loser* details the attempt by an indie musician to be accepted by a music studio and to win the heart of a woman he has fallen for. Both *30+* and *Fabulous 30* tell the stories the attempts by women in their mid-thirties to get married after leaving a long-term relationship. Even Chayanop Boonprakob's **Suck Seed** (*Suck seed huay khan thep*), which details the lives of three high school losers who try to set up their own rock band, had to change its marketing plan by focusing on the cameo appearances of several thirty-something rock singers in the movie, after its poor performance at the box-office during the first week of its release.

Very few films from the last year deserve overt praise. The highly anticipated release of Pen-Ek Ratanaruang's **Headshot** (*Fon tok khuen fah*) was something of a let down as it became clear the film had reverted to the style of the director's early work. Released in November, the film is an adaptation of Win Lieuwarin's nourish thriller *Rain Fallying Up the Sky*, about a cop-turned-hitman who sees things upside down after he comes out of a coma. A formulaic genre film grossing just US$97,000 after a three-week run, it should break even following its sale to US and French markets.

Yuthlert Sippapak's **Friday Killer** (*Mah kae antarai*), the first of three stories about assassins, was finally released after a year's delay. The film follows an ageing assassin who is released from prison and hunted by former enemies. Director Barry Levinson and his fellow jury members at Shanghai International Film Festival awarded it the Special Jury and Best Cinematography awards, but it failed to help the film at the box office.

Aditya Assarat's semi-biographical feature **Hi-So**, about a man living in two cultures, and Sivaroj Kongsakul's **Eternity** (*Tee rak*), which looked at the director's parent's romance, were finally released at the end of the year and should feature as potential awards winners.

Sivaroj Kongsakul's **Eternity**

Pen-Ek Ratanaruang's **Headshot**

Kongdej Jaturanrasmee's **P-047** (*Tae piang phu deaw*) looked at the strange lives of a would-be locksmith and writer who enjoy their lives in someone else's home, while internationally-acclaimed visual artist Rirkrit Tiravanij's debut **Lung Neaw Visits His Neighbours**, is an experimental documentary about the daily life of a man who lives in the north of the country. Both films were entered into the Venice Film Festival and will be released locally in 2012.

The year's best films
Headshot (Pen-Ek Ratanaruang)
Eternity (Sivaroj Kongsakul)
Hi-So (Aditya Assarat)
Friday Killer (Yuthlert Sippapak)
Ladda Land (Sophon Sakdaphisit)

Directory
All Tel/Fax numbers begin (+66)
Federation of National Film Association of Thailand, 31/9 UMG Theatre 2 Fl., Royal City Avenue, New Petchburi Road, Bangkapi, Bangkok 10310. Tel: (2) 6415917-8. www.thainationalfilm.com.
National Film Archive, 93 Moo 3, Phutthamonthon Soi 5 Phutthamonthon, Nakorn Prathom 73120. Tel: (2) 4822013-5. www.nfat.org.
Office of Contemporary Arts and Culture, Ministry of Culture, 666 Baromrajchonnanee Road, Bangplad, Bangkok 10700. Tel: (2) 4228819-20. http://www.ocac.go.th.

ANCHALEE CHAIWORAPORN is a film-critic based in Thailand. She won the 2000 Best ML Bunlua Thepphayasuwan Film Critic and the 2002 Best MR Ayumongkol Article Writer awards.

Tunisia Maryam Touzani

It is impossible to refer to film production in Tunisia this year without acknowledging the revolution that irrefutably changed many of the country's realities. The Arab Spring has, at the moment, shaped the nature of many films produced and set the foundations of imminent change, whose effects in the long term should provide a vital impulse to the sector.

Mourad Ben Cheikh's **No More Fear**

As a reaction to the revolution, a large number of documentaries have been produced. One of the first films to look at the events of 14 January is Mourad Ben Cheikh's **No More Fear** (*Plus Jamais Peur*), which screened at the Cannes Film Festival. The film reveals the revolution through the fates of three different people: Lina Ben Mhenni, a blogger who dared to challenge the Ben Ali regime since the beginning of the uprising; Radhia Nasraoui, a lawyer and fervent human rights defender; and finally Karem Sharif, a journalist who tried to defend his neighbourhood with the support of his family during the terrible days that followed the dictator's departure. These stories have a common denominator: fear. However, through the post-revolutionary voice of this film, there is a unanimous cry: 'No more fear!'

The filming of Franco-Tunisian Nadia El Fani's documentary **Secularism, Inch'Allah!**

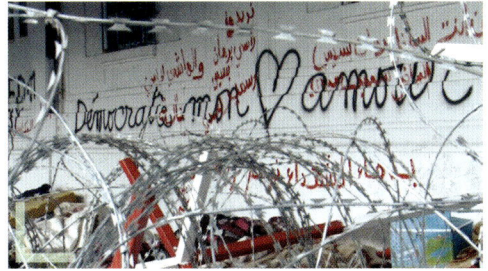

Nadia El Fani's **Secularism, Inch'Allah!**

(*Laïcité, Inch'Allah!*), began before the Tunisian uprisings. During Ramadan and despite heavy censorship under the rule of Ben Ali, the filmmaker depicts a country that appears open to freedom of conscience and its relationship with Islam. Three months later, El Fani witnessed the outburst of the Tunisian revolt and wonders in his film if, through the desire of the people, a Muslim country could – and should – opt for a secular constitution. A film about tolerance, it saw its title changed following the huge controversy provoked by the original – *Neither Allah nor Master!*

In the same light, Elyes Baccar's feature documentary **Rouge Parole** recounts the story of the popular revolution and the eviction of President Ben Ali, sensitively told by its heroes, as it registers Tunisia's first steps towards democracy.

Elyes Baccar's **Rouge Parole**

Moving away from politics, Ridha Behi's **Always Brando** (*Dima Brando*) is inspired by his passion for the American actor. It is the tale of Anis, whose destiny turns toward tragedy after his resemblance to the star promises success and fame in Hollywood. Following his encounter with the young Tunisian actor, Behi decided to write a film starring both of them. He succeeded in gaining Brando's interest, with whom he collaborated closely on the project. But Brando died shortly before the film was scheduled to go into production. Behi perseveres in his dream and years later his fictional narrative, chronicling his fascinating encounter with Brando and his young doppelganger, sees the light of day.

Latifa Robbana Doghri's first documentary, **Boxing With Her** (*Banet El Boxe*) explores the world of female boxing in Tunisia. The film questions the taboos surrounding a woman's body, particularly in Arab society, as it follows eight Tunisian female boxing champions in their daily life, showing the challenges they encounter as women practicing a 'male' sport.

Walid Tayaa's **Life**

This year has witnessed an increase in short films, which have been produced with very little means and have consequently developed a certain freedom of tone. In Walid Tayaa's **Life** (*Vivre*), a 40-year-old widow working as a telephone operator at a French call centre and who lives with her elderly mother and aunts winesses her life pass by uneventfully.

Ridha Behi's **Always Brando**

In **The Bottom of the Pit** (*Kaa El Bir*) Moez Ben Hassen recounts the story of desperate Lotfi, who is considering suicide. However, he finds himself engulfed in a nightmare in which he sees his mother suffer through his decision. Meriem Riveill's **Tabou** (*Baydha*) is the story of eighteen-year-old Leila who, during a lonely Ramadan night, recalls what happened to her as a child.

Tunisian cinema seems to be in the middle of its own revolution. After the historic uprisings, the decision by the Ministry of Culture to finally create the National Centre for Cinema and Image (Centre National du Cinéma et de l'Image) is an unprecedented breakthrough. The institution's mission will be to establish a real cinematographic industry in the country, contributing to the support, creation, production and distribution of new films by young as well as established filmmakers. Long demanded by the country's filmmakers. As such, the CNCI could finally see the emergence of a Tunisian cinema that has for too long lagged behind its neighbours.

The year's best films

Secularism, Inch'Allah! (Nadia El Fani)
No More Fear (Mourad Ben Cheikh)
Always Brando (Ridha Behi)

MARYAM TOUZANI is a freelance journalist based in Morocco and working internationally, specialising in cinema.

Turkey Atilla Dorsay

I t was once again a very good year for Turkish cinema. The box-office revenue for 2011 came close to 42 million sold tickets. Admittedly, the Turkish share was down to just under 40 per cent. However, this is easily accounted for, due to the absence from the screen of films by mainstream comedians such as Cem Yilmaz and Yilmaz Erdogan, as well as singer-turned director Mahsun Kirmizigül, whose popularity guarantees greater returns in the years that he is active.

The most popular films were TV serial adaptations. Zübeyr Sasmaz's **Valley of Wolves – Palestine** (*Kurtlar Vadisi - Filistin*) featured the Turkish equivalent of Rambo, this time sorting out problems in the Israeli-occupied territories. It is little more than efficiently produced nationalist propaganda. The same dearth of quality could be found in Serdar Akar's **Behzat C**, about a Turkish cop chasing down a serial killer, and Ömer Vargi's action blockbuster **The Anatolian Eagles** (*Anadolu Kartallari*), about a group of teenagers who enter the military and whose experiences are more in the style of *Top Gun*. Box-office honours ultimately went to cherished comedian Ata Demirer, with **Oh God 2** (*Eyvah Eyvah-2*). Directed by Hakan Algül, the sequel, which Demirer also wrote, was the year's outstanding earner.

There was a marked abundance of political films throughout the year. They mainly dealt with issues Turks would prefer to forget, or at least not to remember in the way they should. Veteran director Orhan Oguz's **Hayda Bre** focused on a family divided in their loyalties between Turkey and Macedonia and grappled with Turkey/Balkan relations. Mehmet Tanrisever's **The Free Man** (*Hür Adam*)

detailed the life and times of Said-i Nursi, an almost forbidden name in official histories, who was a Kurdish clergyman (1876–1960) that the State presents as a radical enemy of Atatürk, but who in fact was a reformer of Islam and a wise and illuminated figure from those harsh times.

Sedat Yilmaz's **Press**

Haluk Ünal's **Sakli Hayatlar** (*Hidden Lives*) depicts the life of an Alevide (Shi'ite) family after they fled the massacre in Çorum in the late 1970s, settling in Istanbul, and the problems they faced there. Sedat Yilmaz's feature debut **Press** provided an account of the problems faced by a local newspaper in Diyarbakir in the early 1990s when authorities attempted to put pressure on it to withdraw its defence of the rights of the Kurdish minority. And Dervis Zaim, with **Shadows and Faces** (*Gölgeler ve Suretler*), looks at the early days of the Cyprus problem, going back to 1963, when the first struggles erupted on the island. A native of Cyprus, he offered an objective overview of that incendiary topic.

The most impressive film to look back to the past was directed by Cagan Irmak, who had already attracted acclaim for *My Father, My*

Cagan Irmak's **My Grandfather's People**

Son. **My Grandfather's People** (*Dedemin Insanlari*), took us back to the early 1920s when, after the Turkish war of independence, more than two million people, from both Turkey and Greece, were forced to leave their native lands. Irmak shows the plight of a Turkish family forced to leave Crete and follows them over the ensuing sixty years. With its impressively constructed narrative and beautiful imagery, it is one of the director's – and the year's – most memorable films.

Elsewhere, there were some fine new features. Nuri Bilge Ceylan's **Once Upon a Time in Anatolia** (*Birzamanlar Anadolu'da*) was awarded the Grand Jury Prize at Cannes and will represent Turkey at the 2012 Academy Awards. A far from typical outing for the director, it also bears little resemblance to Sergio Leone's epic, to which it shares a similar title. Instead, it is a tremendous and rewarding expression of the director's desire to renew and enrich his art. His longest, most talkative film, and certainly the richest in terms of characterisation, it revolves around the search for a murdered man.

Tolga Örnek's **The Loser's Club**

Yavuz Turgul tried his hand at contemporary noir with **The Hunting Season** (*Av Mevsimi*), an enigmatic story about the search for a killer,

with his usual actor Sener Sen taking on a very dark role. Tolga Örnek's **The Loser's Club** (*Kaybedenler Kulübü*) depicts, with great charm and humour, the lives of two controversial DJs at a private radio station in the early 1990s. Tayfun Pirselimoglu's **Hair** (*Saç*) completed his trilogy of 'death and conscience', which began with *Riza* and *Haze*. Once again, it is the story of little men lost in the big city.

Tolga Karacelik's **Toll Booth**

Tolga Karacelik's feature debut **Toll Booth** (*Gişe Memuru*) ingeniously depicts the descent of an ordinary tollbooth attendant on the Bosphorus Bridge into a world of fantasy and folly. Seyfi Teoman, after his successful *Summer Book*, slightly disappoints with Berlinale competitor **Our Grand Despair** (*Bizim Büyük Caresizligimiz*), which follows the disintegration of the friendship between two bachelors when a young woman comes into their lives.

Two sophomore features disappointed. Özcan Alper followed up the impressive *Autumn* with **The Future Lasts Forever** (*Gelecek Uzun Sürer*), about a young female researcher's trip to Eastern Turkey, which draws on Kurdish-Armenian issues, while *Takva* director Özer Kiziltan offered up a forgettable love story with **Don't Forget Me** (*Beni Unutma*).

İlksen Basarir's second film **Merry-Go-Round** (*Atli Karinca*) sensitively tackles the taboo subject of incest, producing a film of compassion. Another female director, Belma Bas employed documentary techniques for her feature debut, **Zephyr** (*Zefir*). A beautifully-shot film, particularly the vistas of the Black Mountains, it is a heart-felt family drama about strained relations between a young girl, her mother and grandparents.

Among the last releases of the year, Onur Ünlü's **The Extremely Sad Story of Celal Tan and His Family** (*Celal Tan ve Ailesinin Asiri Acikli Hikayesi*) is a brave attempt at a black humourous drama, but ends up being grotesque (although it does have its fans). Yüksel Aksu's second film **Intellectuals Versus Peasants** (*Entelköy Efeköy'e Karşı*) shows far more maturity with his story of a group of intellectuals from the metropolis who attempt to stop the construction of a thermal centre in an Aegean village. It is a slick and intelligent comedy that has proven popular with audiences.

Yüksel Aksu's **Intellectuals Versus Peasants**

The government has passed a new law that will offer help to foreign productions working in Turkey, an acknowledgement of the country's increased popularity as a location. Over the last few months, Turkey has seen Nicolas Cage in Capadoccia to shoot scenes for *Ghost Rider – Spirit of the Vengeance*; Liam Neeson for *Taken 2*; Ben Affleck shooting long sequences of *Argo* in Istanbul; Bahman Ghobadi visiting on two occasions with Monica Bellucci for *Rhinos Season*. And finally, the new James Bond will feature old Istanbul, with the Saint Sophia area closed to all traffic while filming takes place.

Turkish cinema is looking forward optimistically, with the local production growing both in quantity (2011 will have seen 75 features produced) and quality, as can be seen in the number of international awards, positive reviews and the interest from festivals around the world.

Nuri Bilge Ceylan's **Once Upon a Time in Anatolia**

The year's best films

Once Upon a Time in Anatolia
(Nuri Bilge Ceylan)
My Grandfather's People (Cagan Irmak)
Toll Booth (Tolga Karacelik)
The Loser's Club (Tolga Örnek)
Intellectuals Versus Peasants (Yüksel Aksu)

Directory

All Tel/Fax numbers begin (+90)
CASOD (The Association of Actors), Istiklal Caddesi, Atlas Sinemasi Pasaj- C Blok 53/3 - Beyoglu/ Istanbul. Tel: 212 251 97 75 Fax : 212 251 97 79. casod@casod.org.
FILM-YÖN (The Association of Directors), Ayhan Isik Sokak, 28/1- Beyoglu/ Istanbul. Tel: 212 293 90 01
IKSV- Istanbul Kültür ve Sanat Vakfi (The Istanbul Culture and Arts Foundation), Sadi Konuralp Caddesi No 5/ Deniz Palas, Evliya Çelebi Mahallesi- 34433, Sishane/ Istanbul. Tel: 212 334 07 00- Fax: 212 334 07 02. film.fest@istfest.org
SIYAD- Sinema Yazarları Dernegi (The Association of Film Critics), Erol Dernek Sokak No 7/1-A, Beyoglu 80600/ Istanbul. Tel: 212 251 56 47/ Fax: 212 251 63 27. denizyavuz@superonline.com
TÜRSAK (The Turkish Cinema and Audiovisual Culture Foundation), Gazeteci Erol Dernek Sokak, 11/ 2 Hanif Han- Beyoglu/ Istanbul. Tel: 212 244 52 51/ Fax 212 251 67 70. tursak@superonline.com

---

ATILLA DORSAY is the author of over forty books, mostly on cinema. He is the founder and honorary president of SIYAD, the Turkish critics' association, and one of the founders of the Istanbul Film festival.

Ukraine Volodymyr Voitenko

2011 saw the largest budget for cinema support in twenty years: US$14million, of which US$9million was for film production. Also, at the first publicly held film projects competition, 37 were entitled for partial or full funding, including 16 features.

The new International Film Festival was held for the second time in Odessa, which since the 1920s has been the cradle of Ukrainian cinema – legendary Ukrainian filmmaker Aleksandr Dovzhenko began his career here. It is now seen as the main platform for the burgeoning national film renaissance.

However, the machinations of President Yanukovych's government, which has resorted to the politically motivated persecution of opponents, threaten the nation's integration into the European Community, with the fallout having a severe impact on the potential of the country's film industry. It is also being recorded in front of the camera. **Ukraine, Goodbye!** is a portmanteau of short films detailing the country's woes.

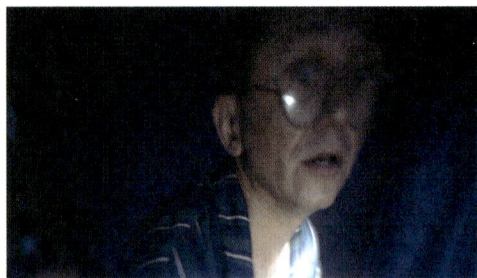

Ihor Podolchak's **Delirium**

Ihor Podolchak's bold hallucinatory artistic experiment, **Delirium**, is an piercing enquiry into the state of existence. That perilous state, particularly the precariousness of life, is also

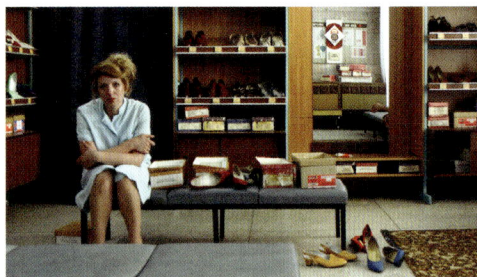

Alexander Mindadze's **Innocent Saturday**

documented by Russian filmmaker Alexander Mindadze in **Innocent Saturday** (*V subbotu*), which was made to commemorate the 25th anniversary of the Chernobyl disaster. It competed at the 2011 Berlinale, offering a powerful portrait of the world since the plant's meltdown.

Two feature debuts deal with the subject of growing-up. Oleg Sentsov's **Gamer** adopts a documentary style in its tale of a teenager who discovers himself through his passion for computer games. Although it doesn't always convince, it is a solid calling card for this new director. Dmytro Prikhodko's **Rock'n'Ball** looks forward to the Euro 2012 football tournament, which takes place in Ukraine and Poland, whilst commenting on the history of Ukrainian-Polish relations.

Oleg Sentsov's **Gamer**

Valeriy Yamburskiy directed the country's first 3D feature. The romantic comedy **Love. Full Stop** (*Lyublyu i tochka*) may have had lofty ambitions, but it is let down by technical imperfections.

From an older generation of Ukranian filmmakers, Mykhaylo Illenko returned with the historical fantasy **Firecrosser** (*Toyschoproyshovkrizvohon*), about a Soviet military pilot subjected to repression in the USSR who became chief of an indigenous tribe. The film was a victim of state underfunding, taking over four years to make. However, it's main problem lies in its unevenness as a drama. Valentyn Vasyanovych faced similar problems with his feature debut **An Ordinary Case** (*Zvychayna sprava*), but this time caused by the delays caused by the director attempting to perfect the film's script and its relevance to public discourse.

Maryna Vroda's **Cross**

The outstanding achievement of 2011 was Maryna Vroda's short **Cross**, which followed in the footsteps of Igor Strembitsky's 2005 film *Wayfarers*, by winning the Best Short Film award at Cannes. Another coming-of-age story, it is also an effective metaphor for the state of the Ukraine.

The state budget for 2012 was approved, with even more money (US$10million) allocated for film production. But such optimism over the increased resources available for production is undermined by continuing pessimism regarding the state of the country's political order and its drift toward Putin's Russia.

Valeriy Yamburskiy's **Love. Full Stop**

The year's best films
Cross (Maryna Vroda)
An Ordinary Case (Valentyn Vasyanovych)

Directory
All Tel/Fax numbers begin (+380)
National Oleksandr Dovzhenko Center (State Film Archives), 1 Vasylkivska St, Kyiv 03040. Tel: 257 7698 Fax: 201 6547.
Central State Archives of Film, Photo & Sound Documents, 24 Solomyanska St, Kyiv 03601. Tel: 275 3777 Fax: 275 3655. tsdkffa@archives.gov.ua.
Institute of Screen Art, Kyiv National University of Theatre, Cinema and Television, 40 Yaroslaviv Val St, Kyiv 01034. Tel: 272 1032 Fax: 272 0220. info@knutkt.kiev.ua http://knutkt.kiev.ua.
Ukrainian Cinema Foundation, 6 Saksahansky St, Kyiv 01033. Tel/Fax: 287 6618. info@ucf.org.ua www.ucf.org.ua
Ministry of Culture and Tourism of Ukraine, State Cinema Service, 19 Ivan Franko St, Kyiv 01601. Tel/Fax: 234 4094, 234 6951. ros@mincult. gov.ua http://dergkino.gov.ua/
Kyiv International Film Festival Molodist, 6 Saksahansky St, Kyiv 01033. Tel/Fax: 461 9803. info@molodist.com www.molodist.com.
Krok International Animated Film Festival, Suite 208, 6, Saksagansky St, Kyiv 01033. Tel/Fax: 287 52 80. krokfestival@gmail.com www.krokfestival.com

VOLODYMYR VOITENKO is a film critic and editor-in-chief of www.kinokolo.ua and www.screenplay.com.ua. He also presents the weekly programme *1+1*, about art cinema, on the national TV channel.

United Kingdom Jason Wood

Following the shock announcement in July 2010 that the UK Film Council was to be abolished, the British Film Institute (BFI) duly became the lead body for film in the UK on 1 April 2011. Most of the UK Film Council's core functions were transferred, including the distribution of National Lottery funding for the development and production of new British films, as well as audience development activity through supporting film distribution and exhibition.

The BFI also took over responsibility for the certification of UK films (which enables filmmakers to access the UK film tax relief for film production); film education; the Research and Statistics Unit; overseeing support for film in the English Regions; liaising with the National Screen Agencies in the devolved Nations; funding skills development for the film workforce in partnership with Skillset; and supporting First Light and MEDIA Desk UK. The responsibility for oversight of the BFI itself, previously held by the UK Film Council, has now transferred to the Department for Culture, Media and Sport (DCMS). Also from 1 April, the UK Film Council's role in encouraging inward investment into the UK moved across to Film London, in a public/private partnership with Warner Bros., Pinewood Studios Group, the Production Guild, UK Screen Association and others.

To ensure a smooth transition, the BFI simultaneously announced a new transitional Lottery Film Fund to support organisations across the UK dedicated to delivering audience development activities for specialised and British film. The €2million fund will provide transitional financial support for one year, to enable bodies such as independent cinemas, film festivals, film clubs and societies, arts centres and regional archives to continue their vital work in delivering film to audiences. At the same time, the fund is designed to give organisations stability and continuity during this year of transition; to cope not only with challenging finances, but also with structural change in public funding across film.

The Minister for the Creative Industries, Ed Vaizey, sounded a triumphant note: 'The transfer of UKFC activities has been concluded with no disruption to filmmakers. The BFI will be administering British film certification; taking over as the Lottery distributor; and overseeing a 60 per cent increased share of Lottery proceeds for British films. In retaining key industry expertise and building on the wealth of knowledge already in the BFI, the future of British film is in safe hands.'

The 1 April date could have been unfortunately prophetic, but thankfully the transfer seems to have proved painless and there are already signs of a prudent approach to the management of resources and a genuine commitment to cinema in the UK. Although the UK Film Council grant-in-aid was cut by 50 per cent before it transferred to the BFI, the agreed Lottery funding priorities for distribution and exhibition, as outlined in the UK Film Council's three-year plan until 31 March 2012, are to be honoured, with the exception of the Innovation Fund. Funding film development remains a priority, with the Film Fund and the Prints and Advertising Fund continuing to accept and assess applications for funding, with the respective Heads of the funds also continuing to green-light awards to films in development, production and distribution. Significantly, the BFI increased the Lottery fund for film by 20 per cent, from €15million to €18million in 2011/12.

With British films such as **Wuthering Heights**, **We Need to Talk About Kevin**, **Shame** and **Two Years At Sea** delivering a strong showing at international film festivals, British film found itself firmly in the spotlight on the world's stage, precipitating the announcement of fast-tracking support for Britain's film industry internationally. In recognition of the need for immediate action whilst the industry awaits the Government's new Film Policy Review and the BFI's own Forward Plan for Film, the BFI made available funds to promote British film and talent internationally, including activity at Sundance, Berlin and Cannes. Financial support was also given to the Film London Production Market, which took place at October's BFI London Film Festival. Amanda Nevill, the CEO of the BFI commented: 'This is a powerful moment for the British film industry and I want to congratulate our British film talent who are excelling on the world's stage. Ahead of us we have major international markets and the awards seasons and it is crucially important that the BFI supports the industry now in this transitional period. Going forward we will be developing an international strategy as one of the key priorities in the BFI's five year Forward Plan for Film, which launches next year, informed by the recommendations from the Review of Film Policy. It's enormously exciting that the BFI will spearhead this new phase for British film around the world.'

Tom Hooper's **The King's Speech**

Audience figures would also suggest that on home soil British cinema is indeed in rude health and that there is cause for industry optimism. Statistics for UK Box Office results are not published until after this editon of the IFG will have has gone to press but the half-year report from the BFI's Research and Statistic Unit offers encouraging reading. UK cinema admissions for the first six months of 2011 were 80.7million, up 0.7 per cent on the first half of 2010. This represents the second-highest first half admissions of the last five years. The year began with the release of Tom Hooper's multi-Academy Award-winning **The King's Speech** (mentioned in the 2010 overview), which topped the box office charts for three weeks and remained in the top ten for almost three months. Grossing over €45million at the UK box office, a record for an independent UK film, this rousing if rather predictable royal drama helped lift admissions by almost 16 per cent in February. Ticket sales in March and April were down almost 24 per cent on the same period in 2010, but June admissions saw a marked increase on the equivalent month last year, when the World Cup had a major impact on release schedules and box office. Average weekly admissions were three million in June, up from two million in 2010. In terms of predicting the remainder of the year, admissions at the end of October were up one per cent on the previous year and November looks set to better it too. According to Sean Perkins, Acting Head of Research and Statistics Unit at the British Film Institute, 'I'd be very surprised if it didn't conform to the

Andrea Arnold's **Wuthering Heights**

David Yates' **Harry Potter and the Deathly Hallows: Part 2**

"plateau" we've seen since 2002 – in other words just one or two per cent up or down on the previous year'.

There were numerous other box-office behemoths. The concluding part of the *Harry Potter* franchise, a cash cow Warners Bros. will find difficult to replace (a loss not cushioned by Christopher Nolan's imminent sign-off from Batman with **The Dark Knight Rises**), David Yates' 3D **Harry Potter and the Deathly Hallows: Part 2** pleased critics and Potterites alike. There has been much recent debate about a perceived audience loss of appetite for the 3D format (though this year interestingly saw the release of three of the most interesting exponents of the format yet: *TT3D Closer to the Edge*, *Cave of Forgotten Dreams* and *Pina*), but Yates' final showdown between Potter and the evil Lord Voldermort grossed a staggering €73million. Perhaps more of a bolt from the blue was the popularity of the big screen spin-off of **The Inbetweeners**.

Ben Palmer's **The Inbetweeners**

Taking its four naïve suburban heroes on a Mediterranean jaunt in search of sexual fulfilment (with a few sharp observations about Brits abroad offsetting some of the more bawdy moments), the film doesn't stray far from the small-screen version, a move which saw an impressive box-office haul of just under €45million (a smidgeon behind *The King's Speech*); never did the adage 'if it ain't broke don't fix it' seem so apt. Though directed by a Swede, **Tinker Tailor Soldier Spy** has been warmly embraced as a British success. An intricate, classy and immaculately designed adaptation of John Le Carré's much loved espionage thriller, Tomas Alfredson marshals an impressive cast including Colin Firth, John Hurt, Mark Strong and Benedict Cumberbatch. Returning to a leading man role, Gary Oldman excels as George Smiley, the British intelligence officer brought out of forced retirement to hunt down a Soviet mole. The film's current box office stands at over €13million. The commercial success of the other Brit spy film **Johnny English Reborn** was altogether more predictable and dispiriting.

Tomas Alfredson's **Tinker Tailor Soldier Spy**

Following up a phenomenon like *Slumdog Millionaire* was always going to be a tall order, but Danny Boyle went about it with quiet assurance with **127 Hours**. Featuring a sensational performance from James Franco as Aron Ralston, the hiker forced to amputate his arm to free it from a trapped boulder, the film sustains an impressive tension despite awareness of the outcome. Another veteran director returning to the filmmaking fray this year, Ken Loach's **Route Irish** was a characteristically committed and abrasive affair that nonetheless left a slight feeling of disappointment. The tale of private security contractors working in the Middle East, the film felt a little didactic. Thankfully, the Digital reissue of *Kes* was on hand to remind us of Loach's greatness. Other reissue highlights included *The Great White Silence*, *Deep End* and *Whiskey Galore*.

Ken Loach's **Route Irish**

Hanna, the fourth feature from Joe Wright, was a total misfire. The account of a feral teenage assassin (Saoirse Ronan) being tracked down by a ruthless intelligence operative (Cate Blanchett), it was slick, shallow and instantly forgettable. Other directors entering the more established period of their careers fared better. Returning to the screen after a prolonged absence and production difficulties on *The Lovely Bones* (which was eventually directed by Peter Jackson), Lynne Ramsey teamed up with Tilda Swinton and novelist Lionel Shriver to compelling effect with *We Need to Talk About Kevin*. Swinton is Eva, a mother coping with a tragic event that has torn her family apart. Through a series of flashbacks, Eva questions her suitability as a mother, wondering if her parenting skills were the reason for the disaffected relationship she had with her son and how much responsibility she should shoulder for his actions.

With only her third feature Andrea Arnold has established herself as one of the brightest (and loudest) voices in contemporary British

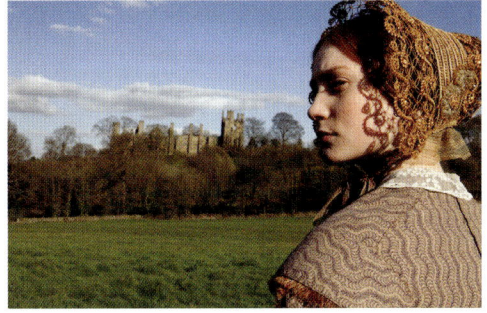
Cary Fukunaga's **Jane Eyre**

filmmaking. A radical treatment of Emily Brönte's novel, *Wuthering Heights* uses mostly non-professional actors and a black Heathcliff to capture the spirit of life on the Yorkshire moors and the dangers of illicit romance. The film is beautifully shot by Robbie Ryan who makes the most of the harsh climate and misty landscape. A refreshing take on a familiar story, Arnold's vision is poles apart from Cary Fukunaga's more traditional tilt at Charlotte Brönte's **Jane Eyre**.

Though only the second feature from Joanna Hogg, **Archipelago** establishes her as a filmmaker of the highest order. Adored by critics – though it precipitated a furious debate on the web pages of the *Guardian* following Peter Bradshaw's five star review – the film follows the gathering of a dysfunctional upper-class family on a remote British island for an increasingly strained vacation. A devastating portrait of emotional crisis that gradually brings anxiety and torpor into sharp focus, the film is immaculately constructed with Hogg's painterly eye.

Lynne Ramsay's **We Need to Talk About Kevin**

Terence Davies' **The Deep Blue Sea**

2011 saw the welcome return to the screen of perhaps Britain's greatest living filmmaker, Terence Davies. An exquisite adaptation of Terence Rattigan's play, **The Deep Blue Sea** offers a richly rewarding evocation of life in 1950s London, which provides the backdrop to an illicit love affair between Hester Collyer (Rachel Weisz) and battle-scarred RAF pilot Freddie Page (Tom Hiddleston). Influenced by Vermeer and featuring a characteristic use of popular 1950s tunes, this affectionate homage to the melodramas of the era is also an astute depiction of raw passion and sincere love that cannot be reciprocated.

Asif Kapadia's **Senna**

In a world blighted by economic crisis, war and the imminent destruction of the planet, British documentaries provided both commentary and escape. By far the most visible documentary of the year, Asif Kapadia's **Senna**, was also the most successful (it's three million-plus box office puts it in the top five most successful documentaries of all time in this country).

Senna began its run by winning the Best Documentary award at Sundance. A pulsating and poignant celebration of the physical and spiritual achievements of Ayrton Senna, the film is comprised entirely of archive footage.

Another film about sport that turns out to not really be very much about sport at all, Stevan Riley's **Fire in Babylon** is a remarkable account of how the West Indies cricket team triumphed over England to become one of the most successful sporting teams in history. Narrated by members of the legendary team, the film contextualises their achievements and highlights the players' role in confronting racism and undermining stereotypes.

Over the last five years an independent record shop has closed in the UK every three days. **Sound it Out** looks at the very last surviving vinyl record shop in Teesside, North East England. A cultural haven in one of the most deprived areas in the UK, director Jeanie Finlay, who grew up three miles from the shop, documents a place that is thriving against the odds and the local community that keeps it alive. This is a distinctive, funny and intimate film about men, the North and the irreplaceable role music plays in our lives. Also music related, Paul Kelly's **Lawrence of Belgravia** offered a revealing portrait of former Felt front-man Lawrence as he seeks to get his life and musical career back on track. The film enjoyed three sell-out performances at the London Film Festival, the last under the excellent tenure of departing Artistic Director Sandra Hebron. Her replacement is Claire Stewart. Edinburgh also gets a new Artistic

Jeanie Finlay's **Sound It Out**

ABU DHABI FILM
COMMISSION

Director in Chris Fujiwara. Let's hope he can revive the festival's flagging fortunes.

In **Project Nim** James Marsh presents the moving story of a life hijacked by science. Nim was raised as a human child at Columbia University in order for those following his every action to ascertain whether chimpanzees had the skills to communicate with the complexity of humans. Featuring remarkable archive footage and interviews with everyone involved in Nim's life, Marsh offers a provocative contribution to the nature/nurture debate. Sadly, the film proved to be one of the final releases from Icon, who suffered closure in November this year. Their loss will be keenly felt.

Carol Morley's **Dreams of a Life**

James Marsh's **Project Nim**

Nobody noticed when 38-year-old Joyce Vincent died in her bedsit above a shopping centre in North London in 2003. When her skeleton was discovered three years later, her heating and television were still on. Newspaper reports offered few details of Joyce's life, not even a photograph. Who was Joyce Vincent? And how could this happen to someone in our day and age, the so-called age of communication? **Dreams of a Life** is Carol Morley's quest to discover who Joyce was and how she came to be so forgotten. Morley placed adverts in newspapers, on the Internet and on the side of a London taxi. As a result she discovered Joyce's former friends, lovers and colleagues. Their testimonies, together with re-imagined scenes from Joyce's life, form a haunting, multilayered portrait of Joyce, and an insight into the world she inhabited.

Due for release next year as part of Soda's consistently laudable New British Cinema Quarterly strand (2011's highlight being Jamie Thraves' **Treacle Jnr.**), Grant Gee's **Patience (After Sebald)** is a multi-layered essay film on landscape, art, history, life and loss. It offers a unique exploration of the life, work and influence of W. G. Sebald via a long walk through coastal East Anglia, tracing the thematic and narrative thread of his most famous book, *The Rings of Saturn*. Visually and aurally innovative, the film features contributions from Tacita Dean, Rick Moody, Andrew Motion, Chris Petit, Iain Sinclair and Marina Warner.

2011 witnessed the gratifying emergence of a high number of new voices. A follow-up to *Down Terrace*, **Kill List** saw Brighton-based Ben Wheatley cement his reputation as an incredibly original talent. Jay is an ex-soldier-turned-assassin; following a botched job in Russia, he returns home, depressed, to an assignment travelling the country, despatching

Ben Wheatley's **Kill List**

people whose names appear on a list. Assuming that they had it coming, Jay soon begins to suspect that there is a darker force at work. Evocative of *The Wicker Man*, but if anything more unnerving, the film packs a powerful punch to the gut that doesn't diminish, even with repeated viewings.

Richard Ayoade's **Submarine**

An affecting coming-of-age comedy from British TV comedy *IT Crowd* actor Richard Ayoade, **Submarine** offered one of the brightest and most cine-literate British features of the year. Adapted from Joe Dunthorne's cult novel, this tale of fifteen-year-old Swansea schoolboy Oliver Tate's obsession with losing his virginity and his desperate attempt to save his parents' marriage is a touching look at the trials of adolescence.

After playing a drippy mystic for Ayoade, actor Paddy Considine stepped behind the camera for his first feature as director with emotionally bruising **Tyrannosaur**. Influenced by Alan Clarke and Gary Oldman's *Nil By Mouth*, the film features a sensational turn by Olivia Coleman as Hannah, a woman desperately trying to find a way to escape her abusive husband James (a truly terrifying Eddie Marsan). When she meets Joseph (Peter Mullan) she finds some possibility of happiness, but he also has his own demons to deal with.

A one-night stand turns into something altogether more unexpected in Andrew Haigh's heartfelt **Weekend**. One of the most positively reviewed films of the year, this

naturalistic study of two men (excellently played by Tom Cullen and Chris New) falling in love with each other deftly depicts a new relationship unfolding whilst astutely articulating the contemporary gay experience. Achingly romantic, the film achieved a sizeable following, both in Britain and in the US.

Of a more experimental bent, **Two Years At Sea** saw artist/filmmaker Ben Rivers return to the character of Jake Williams, a man first portrayed in Rivers' *This Is My Land*. Jake lives alone in a ramshackle house in the middle of the forest. He goes for walks whatever the weather and takes naps in the misty fields and woods. He builds a raft to spend time fishing in a loch and drives a beat-up old jeep to pick up supplies of wood. Seen across the seasons, surviving frugally and passing the time with strange projects, he is living the radical dream he had as a younger man, a dream he spent two years working at sea to realise. Winner of a FIPRESCI Prize at Venice, this is a beguiling, contemplative work.

Ben Rivers' **Two Years At Sea**

Evolving as a series of drawings, **This Our Still Life** offers a beguiling and expansive portrait of 'Louyre', the remote tumbledown Pyrenean hidey-hole that one-man filmmaking industry Andrew Kötting shares with his partner Leila McMillan and their daughter, Eden. A family of artists for whom creativity flows like blood, life in this part-time rural idyll is elemental, rudimentary, fun and intimate. Filmed over a twenty-year period, the film explores notions of nostalgia, memory, isolation and love, as it offers snatched insights into the minutiae of the Kötting family's everyday life.

Joe Cornish's **Attack the Block**

Ben Rivers, Andrew Kötting, Joanna Hogg, Paddy Considine, Joe Cornish (whose **Attack the Block** was tremendous fun) and Andrew Haigh are evidence of the current vitality to be found in British cinema, a vitality that prompted the Guardian's Andrew Pulver to pronounce that we are currently experiencing 'a golden age' in the medium. Pulver certainly has a point, but the next step is to ensure that audiences get to experience this vitality for despite the support across the industry from producers, distributors, exhibitors and critics, many of the less obviously commercial titles regularly fail to chime with a British public who still seem resistant to move outside of their comfort zone (*Weekend* being the one notable exception). Considine's *Tyrannosaur* is a good case in point. Rapturously received by the press and released with significant fanfare by its distributor, it met with what can best be described as mediocre success. *Kill List* suffered a similar fate, so it is imperative to ensure that if these films are getting made and are supported by the industry, then they also need to receive the backing of the British public. The films are there, but to ensure that they continue to be, people have to go and see them.

Peering ahead into the early part of 2012, a number of significant British releases stand out in terms of their likely impact on the cinematic landscape. Phyllida Lloyd's **The Iron Lady** is powered by an awards-friendly performance by Meryl Streep as Margaret Thatcher. There is no doubting Streep's astonishing transformation into one of the most iconic figures in British politics, but

the film, scripted by Abi Morgan, pulls its punches, presenting Thatcher as a befuddled geriatric pining for her dear departed Dennis (Jim Broadbent). It would no doubt have been too much to expect a more frank portrayal of Thatcher's ruinous policies, but the film's refusal to offer any kind of analysis of Tory rule is perplexing and infuriating.

Phyllida Lloyd's **The Iron Lady**

Morgan redeems herself, however, with a co-writing credit on **Shame**, Steve McQueen's stunning follow-up to *Hunger*. Featuring the ubiquitous Michael Fassbender (the hands down British actor of the year) as a successful New York broker with a debilitating sex addiction, this impeccably executed and performed drama brilliantly picks at existential angst and emotional crisis, and is adult in every sense of the word.

Steve McQueen's **Shame**

A bold directorial debut from Ralph Fiennes, **Coriolanus** is a muscular version of Shakespeare's play about power. Drawing parallels with modern-day events, Fiennes sets

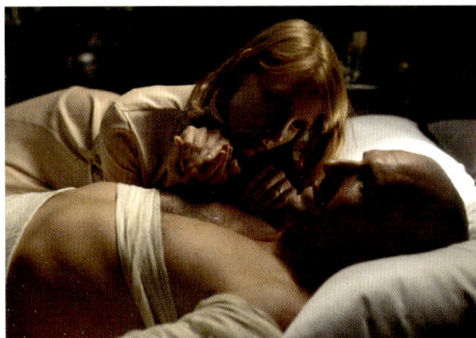

Ralph Fiennes' **Coriolanus**

the action against the backdrop of a modern Balkan war zone and takes on the role of the eponymous war hero-turned-politician. Barry Ackroyd's cinematography and the visceral battle scenes are tremendous.

Sources
Sean Perkins, Acting Head of Research and Statistics Unit, British Film Institute.
Andrew Pulver, *Britain's Golden Age is Now*, The Guardian, October 13, 2011.

The year's best films

Archipelago (Joanna Hogg)
Kill List (Ben Wheatley)
Dreams of a Life (Carol Morley)
We Need to Talk About Kevin (Lynn Ramsey)
Two Years At Sea (Ben Rivers)

Joanna Hogg's **Archipelago**

JASON WOOD is a film programmer and contributor to *Sight and Sound* and *The Guardian*. He has also published several books on cinema.

```
            1996 Modem Festival
    http://1996modfest.blogspot.com

            to be continued
```

Directory

All Tel/Fax numbers begin (+44)

British Academy of Film & Television Arts (BAFTA), 195 Piccadilly, London, W1J 9LN. Tel: (20) 7734 0022. Fax: (20) 7734 1792. www.bafta.org.

British Actors Equity Association, Guild House, Upper St Martins Lane, London, WC2H 9EG. Tel: (20) 7379 6000. Fax: (20) 7379 7001. info@equity.org.uk. www.equity.org.uk.

British Board of Film Classification (BBFC), 3 Soho Square, London W1D 3HD. Tel: (20) 7440 1570. Fax: (20) 7287 0141. webmaster@bbfc.co.uk. www.bbfc.co.uk.

British Film Institute, 21 Stephen St, London, W1T 1LN. Tel: (20) 7255 1444. Fax: (20) 7436 7950. www.bfi.org.uk.

Directors Guild Trust & DGGB CIC Ltd, Studio 24, Royal Victoria Patriotic Building, John Archer Way, London, SW18 3SX. Tel: (20) 8871 1660. guild@dggb.org. www.dggb.org.

Film London, The Tea Building, 56 Shoreditch High Street, London E1 6JJ. Tel: (20) 7613 7676. Fax: (20) 7613 7677. info@filmlondon.org.uk.

National Film & Television Archive, British Film Institute, 21 Stephen St, London W1P 1LN. Tel: (20) 7255 1444. Fax: (20) 7436 0439.

Scottish Screen Archive, 1 Bowmont Gardens, Glasgow G12 9LR. Tel: (141) 337 7400. Fax: (20) 337 7413. archive@scottishscreen.com. www.scottishscreen.com.

United States Curtis Woloschuk

A glance at 2011's top-grossing films would suggest that this was the year that the 'idea factories' feeding Hollywood closed their Research & Development divisions and focused on churning out proven sellers. How else does one explain that the year's top ten earners consisted of seven sequels, one prequel, and two comic book adaptations?

And while the paucity of original ideas had many cinephiles grumbling, the studios were bemoaning the lack of revenue coming their way. Even with an increase in ticket prices (from US$7.85 to US$7.96) and the promise of an eleventh-hour injection of box-office spoils from money-makers like Steven Spielberg and Tom Cruise, projections put the year's revenue at approximately US$9.92billion, a considerable 4 per cent decline from 2010.

Once again, Hollywood banked on 3D to rescue it from its woes. The summer movie season saw 18 features released in the format, up from only seven on 2010. Despite the US$5premium to be paid for watching one's entertainment through plastic glasses, there was a mere one per cent bump in ticket revenue. However, the most alarming statistic was that the season's US$4.38billion haul was collected from the lowest number of tickets purchased since the summer of 1997.

Ben Stiller and Eddy Murphy in **Tower Heist**

With ticket sales for the calendar year poised to be the lowest since 1995, one studio declared its intention to explore new revenue streams. With the November theatrical release of **Tower Heist** imminent, Universal announced that the Ben Stiller/Eddie Murphy caper comedy would be made available in living rooms through video-on-demand a scant three weeks later (albeit in two trial markets only). Potential viewers scoffed at the exorbitant US$59.99 price tag and irate exhibitors threatened the studio with a boycott of the film. Universal blinked first in the standoff and advised that they were delaying their experiment.

Video-on-demand may have become increasingly contentious amongst the heavy hitters, but it was being hailed as the future of independent film distribution. Relieved of the prohibitive promotional and print traffic costs associated with large-scale theatrical releases, smaller companies like Magnolia and IFC suddenly had a relatively low-risk distribution model through which they stood a reasonable chance of seeing considerable returns on wise investments.

Perhaps it was this thinking that fuelled an unexpected shopping spree at the Sundance Film Festival. Despite losing some of its lustre in recent years, Sundance remains the place where tastemakers seek out the new voices of American cinema. This year, they went looking with their wallets in hand. After only a handful of films were purchased in 2010, 38 features were snatched up in January 2011.

Of course, headlines were generated when one party opted not to sell – and made a big production of it. Crowned an indie darling at Sundance in 1994 with *Clerks*, Kevin Smith returned to Park City to debut **Red State**, an uncharacteristic (and not terribly successful) stab at horror. At a post-screening auction, Smith denounced traditional distributors, snapped up the rights to his own film for US$20, and unveiled plans for a national road show. Much to his detractors' annoyance, Smith's gamble paid off. He'd reportedly turned a profit on *Red State* by early April.

Sean Durkin's **Martha Marcy May Marlene**

Fortunately, Smith's theatrics didn't overshadow an exceptional Sundance for emerging talent. Sean Durkin deservedly won a directing award for **Martha Marcy May Marlene**, a disquieting, fragmented portrait of a young woman who escaped a cult. A horror story in its own right, J. C. Chador's tightly scripted **Margin Call** offers an incisive depiction of the cataclysmic 24 hours at a Lehman Brothers-like investment bank that ushered in the 2008 financial crisis.

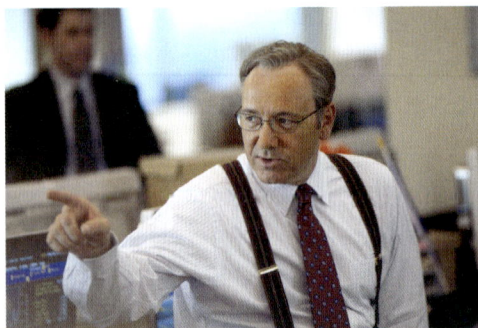

J. C. Chador's **Margin Call**

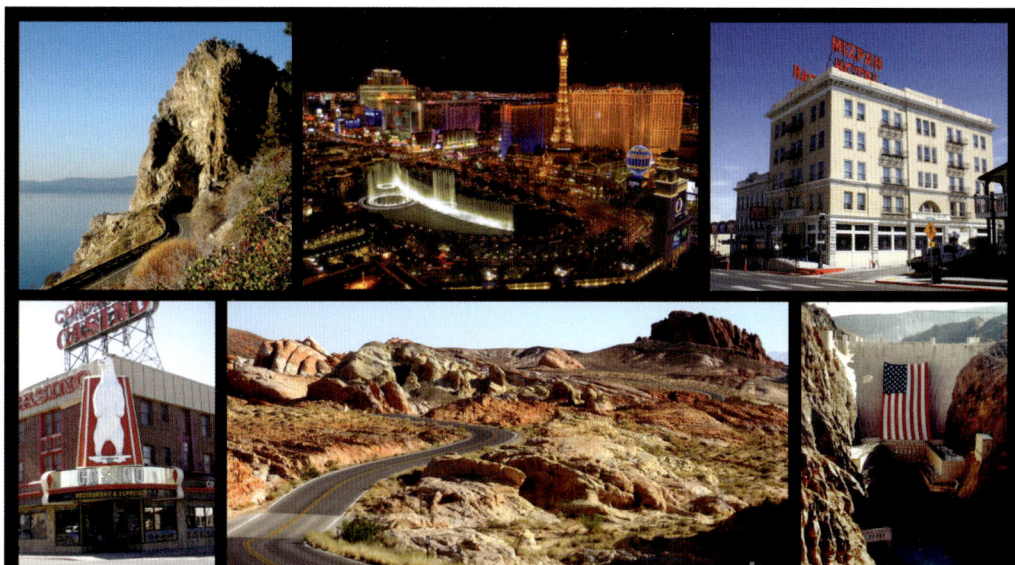

NEVADA FILM OFFICE

Your Imagination. Our Locations.

877.638.3456 • 702.486.2711 • nevadafilm.com

The Nevada Film Office (NFO) has been promoting Nevada as a film-friendly location for films, commercials, television, music videos, documentaries and other multi-media projects to the international production community for 30 years. We connect productions and clients world-wide to Nevada's state-of-the-art production facilities, support services, resources and local professional crews and vendors.

The NFO provides a variety of services free of charge for hundreds of productions annually including permitting needs and requirements, research and customized location scouting tailored to specific project needs and inter-governmental coordination and liaison assistance. Customer service is at the core of our philosophy; we do our utmost to ensure that all your production needs are met with the type of hospitality that is synonymous with Nevada to make your experience as enjoyable as possible.

Our motto at the Nevada Film Office is "Your Imagination. Our Locations" as Nevada boasts a variety of unique and one-of-a-kind locations. If your next production is searching for neon and glitter, ghost towns, miles of scenic roads,

majestic mountains, desert landscape or picturesque lakes, your camera will find it in Nevada. Our interactive website (nevadafilm.com) allows productions 24/7 access to hundreds of diverse location photos through our online database.

The annually published Nevada Production Directory is the number one resource tool used by industry professionals planning or conducting a shoot in Nevada. The Nevada Production Directory serves as a "yellow pages" for productions and includes a vast amount of information to obtain talent and professional crews, world-class accommodations, state-of-the-art production equipment, facilities and supplies, stages and studios and support services. In addition, the Nevada Film Office publishes "Nevada: A Visual Guide to Locations" which features the Reno/Tahoe areas, Las Vegas and Southern Nevada locales, Roads of Nevada and Nevada's Countryside to showcase the variety of locations throughout Nevada.

For a free copy of the Nevada Production Directory or visual guides, please email us at
lvnfo@nevadafilm.com

Mike Cahill's **Another Earth**

Mike Cahill's **Another Earth** and Evan Glodell's **Bellflower** both witness the collision between high-concept storytelling and lo-fi filmmaking. Cahill touchingly details the hope instilled in a troubled young woman by the discovery of a parallel Earth. Conversely, Glodell's apocalyptic romance sees a troubled young man sewing the seeds of his own destruction. Building both a fire-spewing muscle car and his own cameras, Glodell emerged as the preeminent poster boy for the current crop of DIY directors (particularly those who had watched *Mad Max* one too many times).

No other indie filmmaker executed their vision with the authority or artistry of **Take Shelter**'s Jeff Nichols. Tormented by harrowing visions of catastrophic storms, a desperate everyman constructs an elaborate shelter in his backyard, all the while fearing for his mental stability. Bolstered by pitch-perfect performances by Michael Shannon (an actor with endless reserves of repression and rage) and Jessica Chastain (far and away 2011's

Jeff Nichols' **Take Shelter**

break-out star), *Take Shelter* intermingled the intimate with the epic and scored Nichols the highest of honours – Terrence Malick comparisons.

It wasn't long before Malick had made his grand return, unveiling his long-gestating opus, **The Tree of Life** at May's Cannes Film Festival. Boasting all of Malick's trademark lyrical ruminations and resplendent visuals (courtesy of cinematographer Emmanuel Lubezki, whose camera fluttered about like a restless spirit), it was also the enigmatic auteur's most experimental offering. Furthermore, it registered as a deeply personal work, with the striking scenes of three young boys torn between their domineering father and beatific mother feeling like echoes of Malick's own upbringing.

Terrence Malick's **The Tree of Life**

Capturing the Palme d'Or, it was the first Malick effort that critics didn't rush to declare a masterpiece. Some were left cold by the piece's overt spirituality. Others were flummoxed by a 20-minute interlude in which Malick – in league with special effects pioneer Douglas Trumbull – charted the origins of the universe. Indeed, it is an audacious film that hardly lends itself well to immediate assessments. However, it seems likely that posterity will find it standing shoulder-to-shoulder with Malick's other masterworks.

Published in late April, Dan Kois' *New York Times* editorial, 'Eating Your Cultural Vegetables,' didn't have the chance to mention *The Tree of Life* by name. In addressing his conflicted feelings about

Kelly Reichardt's **Meek's Cutoff**

'challenging' work, Kois instead focused on Kelly Reichardt's **Meek's Cutoff**. Told with a strong feminist slant, Reichardt's enthralling revisionist western features assured turns from Michelle Williams and Bruce Green-wood, and a minimalist plot that sees pioneers fending off death as they traverse an imposing Oregon desert.

After years of actively seeking out such 'slow-moving, meditative drama', Kois, a film critic for various outlets, now publicly questioned the value of such 'aspirational viewing', which offered little in the way of escapism or entertainment. Sparking a furore in the critical community, his peers vehemently argued the relative merits of supposedly 'boring' work. Meanwhile, the paying public (or what was left of it) were too busy queuing up for the blockbuster *du jour* to pay the debate much mind.

Harry Potter and the Deathly Hallows: Part 2 emerged as the year's top-grossing film by some distance, with domestic receipts tallying over US$381million. The final entry in the eight-film series (and the first to be released in 3D) was lavished with praise by critics, who also took the opportunity to acknowledge one of the most ambitious undertakings in Hollywood history.

Pundits were less kind to **Transformers: Dark Side of the Moon** (US$352million), **Pirates of the Caribbean: On Stranger**

Tides (US$254million) and **Fast Five** (US$209million), the third, fourth and fifth chapters in their respective series. Michael Bay proved no closer to understanding visual composition; Johnny Depp had rarely looked more disinterested; and *The Fast and the Furious* franchise served notice that it still wasn't finished dumbing itself down.

A more unexpected target caught in the critical cross-hairs was **Cars 2**. Granted, the reviews were hardly scathing for John Lasseter and Brad Lewis's automobiles-as-espionage-agents goof. However, it was a far cry from the unreserved adulation that typically meets a Pixar release.

At least Lasseter and his Pixar collaborators had US$190million to console themselves with. Parent company Disney were left to lick some ugly wounds when **Mars Needs Moms** recouped only US$21million of its US$150million budget. While nothing else came close to rivalling the animated interstellar rescue mission as the year's biggest bomb, **Kung Fu Panda 2**, **Happy Feet Two** and Shrek-spinoff **Puss in Boots** all struggled to turn a profit on the home front. Easily the most imaginative animated feature was Gore Verbinski's **Rango**. As a duplicitous chameleon talked his way into becoming sheriff of a desert town, the spaghetti western (with a side of noir) became a delirious amalgam of every stray idea and off-beat impulse that entered its creative team's orbit.

Gore Verbinski's **Rango**

Duncan Jones' **Source Code**

Contrary to expectations, the top dog in the animal kingdom was **Rise of the Planet of the Apes**. Audiences and reviewers alike were enchanted by Andy Serkis's brilliant performance-capture work as the mutated, revolutionary primate Caesar that they were willing to turn a blind eye to the hokey dialogue and clunky story mechanics. More well-conceived sci-fi offerings were **Source Code**, Duncan Jones' pacy time travel thriller, and **Contagion**, Steven Soderbergh's chilling depiction of a global pandemic. Methodically amping-up its dread, the latter had viewers flinching every time one of their neighbours coughed or sneezed.

Trying desperately to launch their own *Iron Man*, Warner Bros. drafted Ryan Reynolds to play the cocksure **Green Lantern**. Regrettably, a super hero whose powers are only limited by his imagination found himself in a film with a dearth of creativity and an overabundance of shoddy CGI. Elsewhere, Joe Johnston's **Captain America** and Kenneth Branagh's **Thor** were graced with

Joe Johnston's **Captain America**

enough directorial flourishes – retro futurist production design for the World War II super-patriot and pseudo-Shakespearean bellowing for the Norse thunder god – to mask the fact that they weren't so much their own movies as the final pieces of the foundation for 2012's mega-blockbuster, *The Avengers*.

Serving as counter-programming to the abundant fare for kids, teenagers, and man-children was **The Help**, Tate Taylor's laborious adaptation of Kathryn Stockett's novel. Clumsily juggling broad humour and overwrought drama, Taylor recounted a sassy white woman's efforts to reveal the endemic racism that plagued the American South in the 1960s. Its only unqualified success was confirming that Viola Davis and Octavia Spencer were far too talented for pap like this. Consequently, their performances appeared to evince both the characters' and their own frustrations.

Paul Feig's **Bridesmaids**

Somewhat surprisingly, it was producer Judd Apatow (synonymous with bromances) who shepherded **Bridesmaids** to the screen. Demonstrating that it wasn't just boys who could behave badly (read: projectile vomit), the female-fronted comedy saw a maid-of-honour (star/co-writer Kristen Wiig) lapse into a downward spiral of pettiness and passive aggression as her best friend's 'big day' approached. A wholly believable central friendship afforded the film some uncommon emotional stakes without ever hampering its ability to generate more laughs than any other comedy this year.

Jason Reitman's **Young Adult**

The most fearless comedic performance of 2011 was delivered by Charlize Theron in **Young Adult**, the reunion of *Juno*'s director Jason Reitman and screenwriter Diablo Cody. Theron played a less-than-successful ghostwriter who returns to her hometown, determined to 'rescue' her ex from his happy family life. Female protagonists so deluded and irredeemable are rare commodities, as are black comedies boldly willing to adhere to their bleak worldview.

The Hangover 2 may have equalled its predecessor's financial success but it also shamelessly and cynically recycled its plot, simply dumping three amnesia-ridden friends in Bangkok. Such rank laziness was endemic in buddy comedies, with **The Change-Up** (best friends switch bodies) and **Thirty Minutes or Less** (a bank heist goes bad), suggesting that 'original' screenplays needn't possess even a hint of invention. While certainly more novel, **Your Highness** – a US$50million medieval stoner comedy – also ranked as one of the most inexplicable endeavours in years.

Someone who definitely suffered buyer's remorse was a ticket holder for **Drive**, Danish genre-bender Nicolas Winding Refn's first effort on American soil. Perturbed that the film wasn't the *Fast and Furious* knock-off promised by its trailers, a Michigan woman sued distributors FilmDistrict for false advertising. One couldn't help but wonder how she would've gone about accurately

encapsulating this formally adventurous 'action movie' in a mere two-minute preview.

Purportedly inspired by star Ryan Gosling driving a cold medication-addled Refn around Los Angeles, *Drive* unfolds as a fairy-tale distorted by a druggy haze. When a stuntman/getaway driver runs afoul of low-rung mobsters, the semblance of a plot only serves to facilitate the director's fetishes for heady moods, flamboyant visuals and abstract violence. In turns brutal and operatic, it was reminiscent of Michael Mann's synth-scored, neon-tinted 1080s films like *Thief*.

Nicolas Winding Refn's **Drive**

It must be said that Refn was hardly the only filmmaker who spent 2011 looking back longingly. In this vein, two old hands adjourned to Paris to deliver very different takes on nostalgia.

Woody Allen's **Midnight in Paris** focused on a contemporary American writer (Owen Wilson, who brilliantly translated Allen's

Woody Allen's **Midnight in Paris**

neurotic, nattering dialogue into lilting musings) prone to escaping his overbearing fiancée by time-travelling back to 1920s Paris and hobnobbing with idols like F. Scott Fitzgerald and Ernest Hemingway. The film's ultimate moral – indulging in nostalgia is just a way of avoiding the present's problems – may have been straightforward but it was also charmingly conveyed. *Midnight in Paris* brimmed with the sort of whimsy that few suspected Allen was still capable of.

Martin Scorsese's **Hugo**

Martin Scorsese's **Hugo** similarly transports us back to the Paris of 1931, whirling us about until we settle in with the film's eponymous hero (Asa Butterfield), a young orphan who lives in the walls of a train station, melancholically spying on the comings and goings of strangers. That is, until he stumbles upon Georges Méliès (Ben Kingsley), the groundbreaking 'cinemagician' responsible for *A Trip to the Moon*, and becomes determined to help the visionary filmmaker once again embrace the art form he has forsaken.

Fans didn't have to look hard to see the parallels between Hugo and Scorsese. Having also endured an isolated childhood, Scorsese would later seek out and befriend his hero, Michael Powell, and help reintroduce his work to the world. 'The movie that plays in my heart', is how Scorsese has lovingly referred to Powell's *The Red Shoes*. Odds are, many a cinephile will come to speak of *Hugo* in similarly fond terms. Collaborating with masterful cinematographer Robert

Richardson, Scorsese offers us not just a testament to how wondrous cutting-edge 3D can be when wielded by expert hands, but also a reminder of how awe-inspiring the filmgoing experience was in its earliest days. Above all, Scorsese celebrates the salvation that cinema still offers the world's dreamers, be they named Georges, Hugo or Martin.

Understandably, younger nostalgists didn't look quite so far into the past for inspiration. Actor Jason Segel almost single-handedly orchestrated the return of Jim Henson's beloved vaudevillians to the big-screen in **The Muppets**. Despite some wrong-headedness in its scripting, the film (directed by James Bobin) still emerged as the highest-grossing *Muppets* film in history. Granted, all evidence pointed to those numbers being attributed to adult converts rather than legions of new pint-sized fans.

Other filmmakers set their retro sights on Steven Spielberg's heyday. After helping dictate the course of the horror genre with the *Saw* franchise, James Wan directed **Insidious**, a *Poltergeist*-indebted haunted-house yarn that regrettably spiralled into silliness in its final reels. Similarly, a solid grasp of tone eluded Greg Mottola's **Paul**, a *Close Encounters of the Third Kind* spoof. Ultimately, J. J. Abrams' **Super 8** was the strongest of the lot. With the added advantage of having Spielberg serve as its producer, Abrams' alien encounter possessed a heart as big as its set pieces. A sublimely devised train

J. J. Abram's **Super 8**

derailment was undeniably spectacular, but it was the disarming sweetness with which a grade-school kid assured his crush – 'I'm just doing the best I can to save you' – that truly took our breath away.

With the stage adequately set, Spielberg descended on the multiplexes with two new features released only days apart: **War Horse** and **The Adventures of Tintin**. Charting a majestic steed's labyrinthine path through World War I, *War Horse* saw Spielberg so eager to wring drama from every moment that he practically suffocated the material. Decidedly minor but notably more successful, *The Adventures of Tintin* – a foray into 3D performance-capture animation – reacquainted us with Spielberg the consummate entertainer. Scripted by a trio of young writers reared on his popcorn flicks, it was an old-fashioned swashbuckler laden with intricately choreographed action sequences and clever visual details.

Steven Spielberg's **The Adventures of Tintin**

Not only did Cameron Crowe and Alexander Payne return from protracted absences, they both did so with films about a father haphazardly guiding his children through the grieving process. Contrived and pandering, Crowe's **We Bought a Zoo** irksomely suggested that purchasing a wildlife park could heal all wounds. Refreshingly, Payne's **The Descendants** allowed its characters' emotions to run wild. As his comatose wife is being removed from life support, Matt King (George Clooney, convincingly coming apart at the seams) discovers that

Alexander Payne's **The Descendants**

she's been having an affair. Thrust into such unforeseeable, unthinkable circumstances, King and his daughters abandon all standard codes of conduct. As they rage inarticulately and behave inadvisably, they become all the more humorous and humane. Payne's potent cocktail of dark comedy and compelling drama was intoxicating.

Performing a similarly skilful balancing act was Mike Mills' largely-autobiographical **Beginners**. Occasionally burdened by its own tweeness, it was nevertheless a poignant look at a son taking posthumous inspiration from a father who had only achieved self-actualisation when he came out at 75. As chronologically jumbled, son-celebrating-dad fare goes, it is certainly preferable to Steven Daldry's **Extremely Loud and Incredibly Close**, a manipulative, pretentious account of a young boy's recovery from losing his father on 9/11. Oscar bait didn't come any more blatant.

Mike Mills' **Beginners**

George Clooney's **The Ides of March**

A more commendable brand of polished entertainment could be found in **The Ides of March** and **Moneyball**. However, while the Clooney-directed political thriller packed some well-crafted plot twists and Bennett Miller's behind-the-scenes baseball flick was buoyed by Aaron Sorkin's sharp dialogue, both seemed destined to fade from memory until the awards season rolls around.

David Fincher's **The Girl with the Dragon Tattoo**

Speaking of which, after watching *The King's Speech* win Best Picture and Best Director (along with two other Oscars) at the Academy Awards in February, David Fincher – director of the far superior *The Social Network* – devoted his considerable talents to an unnecessary remake of the lurid murder mystery **The Girl with the Dragon Tattoo**. Undeniably top-tier genre fare, it nevertheless left Fincher's more demanding admirers hoping that he'd take on a real challenge with his next film.

Whatever that next project might be, it will undoubtedly face a major hurdle in getting

green-lit. If 2011 laid bare one contradiction, it's that while filmmaking equipment had never been more accessible or inexpensive, it had conversely never been more difficult to get a film made in the studio system. And it seemed like no one was immune to this hardship. Even after the billions Gore Verbinski and Johnny Depp generated with the *Pirates of the Caribbean* franchise, Disney still saw fit to shut down production on the duo's *Lone Ranger* project until they trimmed 14 per cent from its budget. With 'sure thing' December sequels **Sherlock Holmes: A Game of Shadows** and **Alvin and the Chipmunks: Chip-Wrecked** falling well short of expectations, it seemed unlikely that the purse strings are going to loosen in 2012.

If the state of the industry was decidedly gloomy at year's end, there was one inspiring story for those who still deigned to view films as art rather than investments. Quite unexpectedly, the source of such hope was the tragic tale (both on- and off-screen) of **Margaret**, Kenneth Lonergan's long-awaited follow-up to *You Can Count on Me* from 2000. Dealing with a mercurial young woman's descent into an emotional quagmire after accidentally causing a traffic fatality, Lonergan commanded one of the most complex, compelling performances of the year from Anna Paquin. The catch being: said performance was filmed back in 2005.

In the ensuing six years, *Margaret* became subject of an embittered feud between Lonergan and Fox Searchlight, with

Kenneth Lonergan's **Margaret**

ugly arguments over the running time escalating into lawsuits being hurled in either direction. After reportedly receiving editing assistance from Martin Scorsese and Thelma Schoonmaker and a cash influx from Matthew Broderick (who appears in the film), Lonergan finally completed *Margaret*, bringing it in twenty seconds under the maximum allowable running time. Fox Searchlight responded by unceremoniously dumping it into a handful of theatres in the fall.

However, that was not the end of *Margaret*. The hashtag #teammargaret began to appear on Twitter as film critics – soon to be followed by film lovers of all stripes – embarked on a grass roots movement to champion Lonergan's sprawling, provocative, frequently brilliant and occasionally frustrating film. By year's end, Fox Searchlight had been pressured into setting up critics' screenings in several cities, opening up the possibility of awards consideration, and rekindling hope that the film might yet find the wider audience it so rightfully deserved.

In a year dominated by concerns about viewer indifference, it was heartening to see impassioned cinephiles take up the cause of a film in which they truly believed. And it wouldn't have happened if there weren't still committed filmmakers like Lonergan who were willing to risk their entire career in order to make the one film they need to make: a film worth fighting for.

The year's best films
Hugo (Martin Scorsese)
The Tree of Life (Terrence Malick)
The Descendents (Alexander Payne)
Take Shelter (Jeff Nichols)
Margaret (Kenneth Lonergan)

CURTIS WOLOSCHUK is a member of the Vancouver Film Critics Circle and serves as Associate Editor and Programming Consultant for the Vancouver International Film Festival.

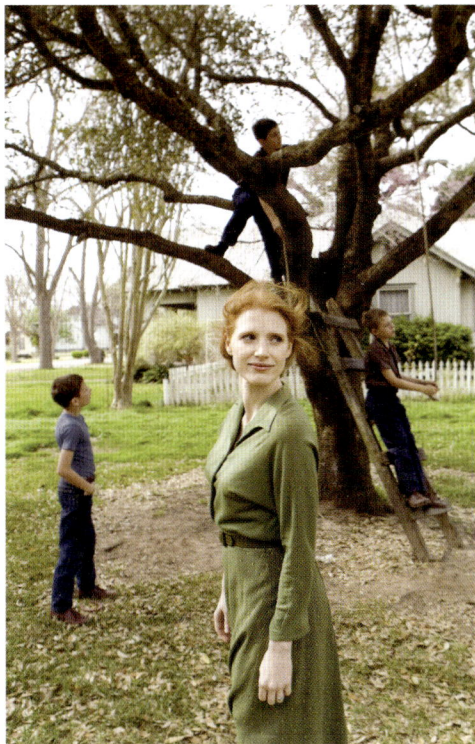

Terrence Malick's **The Tree of Life**

Directory
All Tel/Fax numbers begin (+1)
Academy of Motion Picture Arts & Sciences, Pickford Center, 1313 North Vine St, Los Angeles, CA 90028. Tel: (310) 247 3000. Fax: 657 5431. mpogo@oscars.org. www.oscars.org.
American Film Institute/National Center for Film & Video Preservation, 2021 North Western Ave, Los Angeles, CA 90027. Tel: (1 323) 856 7600. Fax: 467 4578. info@afi.com. www.afi.com.
Directors Guild of America, 7920 Sunset Blvd, Los Angeles, CA 90046. Tel: (1 310) 289 2000. Fax: 289 2029. www.dga.org.
Independent Feature Project, 104 W 29th St, 12th Floor, New York, NY 10001. Tel: (1 212) 465 8200. Fax: 465 8525. ifpny@ifp.org. www.ifp.org.
International Documentary Association, 1201 W 5th St, Suite M320, Los Angeles, CA 90017-1461. Tel: (1 213) 534 3600. Fax: 534 3610. info@documentary.org. www.documentary.org.
Motion Picture Association of America, 15503 Ventura Blvd, Encino, CA 91436. Tel: (1 818) 995 6600. Fax: 382 1784. www.mpaa.org.

Additional Countries

BURKINA FASO

The film that made the most impact in 2011, both in terms of quality and subject matter, was **Bayiri, the Homeland** (*Bayiri, la patrie*), the sixth feature by Pierre Yaméogo, now celebrating his 27th year as a filmmaker. The film follows a young Burkinabe fleeing the war in neighbouring Cote d'Ivoire, where she lived and became pregnant after being raped. The other outstanding production was Kollo Sanou's **The Weight of the Oath** (*Le poids du serment*). A woman attempts to leave her husband and the grip of a Christian group that saved his life. It details the conflict between traditional and more recent religious practices, although is unfortunately marred by an irrelevant subplot.

Eléonore Yaméogo's **Paris My Paradise**

The new generation of filmmakers was well represented by Eléonore Yaméogo's documentary **Paris My Paradise** (*Paris mon paradis*), about young Burkinabes living in France. Yaméogo depicts the harsh living conditions of African immigrants in Europe. In particular, it is very rare to hear Africans talk about their 'hell' so openly.

The Pan-African Festival of Cinema and Television of Ouagadougou, the most important film event in Africa, was held from February 26 to March 5, which attracted large crowds and international organisations. Burkina Faso won the Jury Award thanks to the Sarah Bouyain's 2010 film *The Place in Between*.

HONORÉ ESSOH is a journalist and filmmaker who works for various media outlets in West Africa. He is also an associate in a film production company in Ivory Coast.

CAMBODIA

2011 saw the foundations of a future film industry finally put in place. Since the creation of the Cambodia Film Commission, whose role includes training film crews, the number of domestic film productions of an international technical standard has climbed from one or two in 2010 to five or six in 2011, reported commission CEO Cédric Eloy. And for the very first time, a production with international funding was shot with a crew almost entirely comprised of Cambodians, he said.

This was the latest feature film by world-renowned French-Cambodian director Rithy Panh. Taking place in 1972, **Shiiku, The Catch**

Rithy Panh's **Shiiku, The Catch**

(*Gibier d'élevage*) is the first film to capture the terror that Cambodian farmers felt as US B-52 bombers turned their fields into infernos during the Vietnam conflict. Unfolding at a stately pace, the film, which is about a US pilot taken prisoner by the Khmer Rouge and put under the surveillance of village boys, quietly captures the Khmer Rouge's harsh violence, which would later turn Cambodia into a graveyard.

French director Davy Chou released his feature documentary **Golden Slumbers** (*Le Sommeil d'or*), which focused on the vibrant Cambodian film industry of the 1960s and early 1970s. This young director, whose grandfather was the leading Cambodian film producer of that era, has single-handedly created a huge interest among a new generation in their cinematic heritage.

MICHELLE VACHON is a journalist based in Cambodia who mainly covers archaeology, history, culture and the arts.

CAMEROON

This year was marked by a number of activist films that attracted government censure. Franck Bieleu's documentary **Big Banana** denounced the difficult working conditions of employees at a multinational French-American fruit firm. However, in April, on the grounds that the film was officially censored, the police evacuated the venue where the first screening was due to take place. The film was screened outside Cameroon.

A few months later, the journalist and film-maker Henri Fotso experienced a similar situation with his medium-length film **The Correspondent** (*Le Correspondant*). This is the story of a French radio correspondent covering disputed elections in an African country. This subject was reportedly considered as 'sensitive' in this presidential election year in Cameroon.

On a lighter note, Alphonse Béni realised **Volunteer Widows** (*Les Veuves Volontaires*) where three friends decide to do everything possible to kill their husbands. A film well-served by the experience of talented actors like Gérard Essomba and Jean-Pierre Dikongué Pipa but marred by a few inappropriate erotic scenes.

The major innovation of the fifteenth edition of Black Screens Festival that took place from 18 to 25 June 2011 was three new prizes including best film of Central Africa.
– *Honoré Essoh*

CHAD

Closed for almost 30 years, like most theatres in the country, the Normandie, located in the capital city of N'Djamena, was re-opened on January 8, 2011. The renovation of the 500-seat cinema was funded with €1.8million by the Chadian government, under the guidance of filmmakers including Issa Serge Coleo, who took on the role of director of the cinema.

The re-involvement of the state in the film industry also resulted in the re-opening of other cinemas, the creation of a training centre and also a production fund. Such actions will help strengthen local production, which has mostly been limited to a few TV series.

The only national film event, the Euro-African Film Festival, took place between June 18 to July 2. The fifth edition saw an extensive programme of African and European films, screened at venues across the capital.

Mahamat Saleh Haroun's **A Screaming Man**

Outside the country, Chad's greatest cinematic icon, Mahamat Saleh Haroun, picked up the Silver Stallion for *A Screaming Man* at the Pan African Film and Television Festival in Ouagadougou, Burkina Faso (FESPACO). The film was previously awarded the Jury Prize at the 2010 edition of the Cannes Film Festival.
– *Agnes Thomasi*

Oscar Castillo's **The Compromise**

COSTA RICA

Film production hit a new high in 2010, with five films released – the most ever achieved in Costa Rica.Last year remained stable, with three films released: Paz Fábrega's **Cold Water of the Sea** (*Agua fría de mar*), Oscar Castillo's **The Compromise** (*El compromiso*) and Hernán Jiménez's **The Return** (*El regreso*).

Paz Fábrega's **Cold Water of the Sea**

Cold Water of the Sea had already been screened in festivals and picked up a number of awards, among which was the 'Tiger V Pro' at Rotterdam. The story focuses on the meeting between two women, a girl and a young woman from different social classes, who spend the year-end on a beach, where they are joined by something magical. The film is full of symbolism blending the feminine and the natural. However, for a country more used to consuming Hollywood product, neither critics nor the public liked the film.

The Compromise received mixed reviews and a similar response from audiences. Oscar Castillo is the most experienced director in the region, but this was his most personal film. The first part of the story is about two men who, in

their youth, dreamed of changing all the social injustices in the world. Although their dreams are never fulfilled, a child conquers their hearts and changes them. The other story deals with the Central American revolutions of the 1970s and 1980s, in which the older one may possibly have participated.

Jiménez's *The Return* proved to be the year's runaway success. The story focuses on the return of young Antonio – played by the director – from New York to Costa Rica. He witnesses the disorder, waste, bureaucracy, noise and violence of his former home, as well as the way his family have been torn apart. Antonio wants to flee immediately, but bureaucratic problems prevent him from doing

Hernán Jiménez's **The Return**

so. The film touches on fundamental issues such as family, friendship and love.

The Return also shows a realistic Costa Rica, not the postcard image that is presented abroad. Audiences tired of such stereotypes of 'Central America Switzerland', so *The Return*, with its sense of humour, was appreciated by audiences and critics nationwide.

Next year sees the release of Miguel Gomez's **The End**, a comedy about the end of the world.

MARIA LOURDES CORTÉS teaches film at the Universidad de Costa Rica and directs the Film and Television School of the Veritas University and the Cinergia audiovisual foundation. Her most recent book, *La pantalla rota. Cien años de cine en Centroamérica*, was on Costa Rican and Central American cinema.

GABON

Veteran director Henry Joseph Koumba finally returned to the screen after a ten-year absence with the long-awaited **The Collar of the King** (*Le collier du Makoko*), which premiered in Libreville in September 2011. The film tells an adventure story in which a queen goes in search of a necklace to legitimise the king's power. The beautiful scenery of Gabon is one of the strengths of this film that advocates protection of the environment and traditional values.

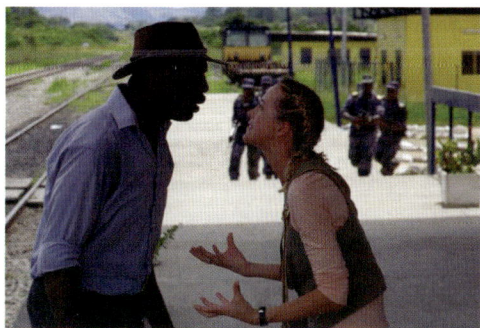

Henry Joseph Koumba's **The Collar of the King**

Alice Atérianus's **New Writings of Oneself**

The new generation was mainly present through short films. Two documentaries were also released, produced by the State-backed Image and Sound Institute. Murphy Ongagna's **Home Studio** traces the twenty years of rap in Gabon, featuring a series of testimonials by members of the movement, as well as performances and archive footage. Alice Atérianus's documentary, **New Writings of Oneself** (*Nouvelles écritures de soi*), focuses on the slam poetry scene, presenting a portrait of four Libreville slammers.

Young director Vincent Mbindzou completed shooting on his second feature. Little is known of the film, but it is said to be an adventure film.

On a sad note, it was announced on 3 June that director Charles Mensah had died. He one of the pioneers of cinema in Gabon and was an inspiring figure to younger generations of filmmakers. – *Agnes Thomasi*

GUATEMALA

During 2010, 14 films were produced. Except for Julio Hernandez's *Marimbas from Hell*, which picked up more than 15 international awards, the rest had little impact internationally. In 2011, only four films were released.

Sergio Ramirez's **Distance** (*Distancia*) won several international awards. Based on a true story, it describes the native aboriginal world of the country's highlands and details the reunion between indigene Tomás Choc and his daughter Lucía, twenty years after the

Guatemalan army kidnapped her. To meet her he has to travel 150km. Tomás has written a book on his struggle, resistance and survival, with the hope of one day giving it to his daughter. The film, spoken in Quiché, one of the most widely spoken indigenous languages in the country, details Tomás's long journey; one that is as much emotional as it is physical. The film's purpose is also twofold – to narrate the tale of these characters, but also highlight how widespread such stores are. There are 45,000 missing people from the conflict.

Alejo Crisóstomo's **Fé**

Another young filmmaker, Alejo Crisóstomo, directed **Fé**. It deals with the rise of evangelical Christianity in the region, focusing on Arturo Herrera, an evangelical minister who questions his life and religious calling. Whilst giving a service at a prison, he meets Beto, a young fisherman from a village in the Guatemalan Caribbean, who is accused of killing a 13-year-old girl. When Beto is released, Arturo takes him in, but a subsequent crime in the neighbourhood tests his faith. Through the film's drama, Crisóstomo reflects on the principles that people hold on to in violent cities like the country's capital.

Elias Jiménez's *Toque de queda* is the latest zombie film, a popular genre in Central America and the Caribbean. Filmmakers have used the living dead as a metaphor for social malaise of violence within a given country. The latest edition deals with residents of a citadel who decide to arm themselves against the zombie hordes, but eventually start to fight amongst themselves.

Playwright Fran Lepe's **Trip** is a very personal take on drug addiction. Based on the 2005 stage play *Delirium Tremens*, which in 2010

also became the musical *Pasos de vida*, it has been seen by over 60,000 people, a high figure for Guatemala.

There are several films in the process of completion, which will be premiered in 2012. However, there is still little sign of government support for the industry. – *Maria Lourdes Cortés*

IRAQ

The third edition of Baghdad International Film Festival (BIFF), held in October, was one of a number of cultural activities that raised awareness of the work of Iraqi filmmakers.

Koutaiba Al-Janabi's debut **Leaving Baghdad** was shot in Iraq, Hungary and the UK. Set in the 1990s, it is a docu-drama that follows paranoid Sadik, who attempts to escape the Iraqi secret police across Europe. In his memoirs, Sadik reveals that he had been keeping footage of the atrocities committed by the regime when he was serving as the personal cameraman to Saddam Hussein. Al-Janabi wrote, directed and digitally shot it after working on a number of documentaries and shorts. With a background in still-photography and drawing on some of his own personal experiences, Al-Janabi succeeds in creating a bleakly realistic drama. The film was selected by Dubai and the Gulf Film Festivals, picking up the Best Film Award at the latter. After its European premiere at Raindance Film Festival in London, it screened at Ghent Film Festival in Belgium.

Atia and Mohamed Al-Daradji's **In My Mother's Arms**

Shot in Baghdad's toughest district, Al-Sadr City, **In My Mother's Arms** is another docu-drama by Iraqi brothers Atia and Mohamed Al-Daradji. It focuses on Husham, who handles a small orphanage that keeps more than thirty homeless boys off the street. When his landlord gives him notice to vacate, the children gather for a cathartic stage performance of the play 'In My Mother's Arms', which reflects their aspirations for a better tomorrow. – *Sherif Awad*

IVORY COAST

Even if Ivory Coast's cinematic year was under-mined by the country's post-election crisis in the country, a few good productions were produced.

The best of these, **The Ideal Man** (*Le Mec Idéal*), was a feature by a young Ivorian director based in France, Owell Brown. In this romantic comedy, a young man earning a modest living finds himself competing with his wealthy friend for the heart of the girl he likes. Winning awards at festivals in Burkina Faso, Morocco and China, it has repositioned Ivorian cinema, giving it a profile on the world stage that it has been absent from for twenty years.

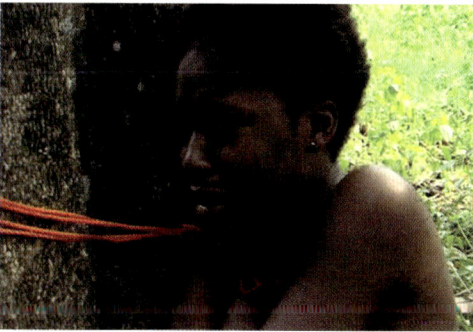

André Marouni's **In the Woods**

Another young filmmaker, André Marouni, directed his second feature **In the Woods** (*Dans les bois*). The story of a young executive revolted by moral depravity transforms into a criminal. The violence of certain scenes shocked some, but the fight sequences and special effects were impressively executed.

An association of young filmmakers founded in late 2010 started operating this year, with the scheduling of screenings and debates, as well as training sessions in screenwriting and direction. The organisation is preparing production of a series of shorts, with filming due to start early in 2012. – *Honoré Essoh*

KYRGYZSTAN

There were a significant number of films for commercial purposes made in Kyrgyzstan this year – more than twenty. Mostly amateur in nature, but aimed squarely at the market and made with a profit in mind, the films come under the title 'Film made for one million somov,' meaning they were produced for a budget of approximately US$20,000.

The most popular melodrama over summer was **How to Make Gu Chjun Pe Your Husband?** directed by Daniyar Abdykerimov. Gu Chjun Pe (Lee Min Ho) is the hero of Korean TV. He is an idol for Aliya, as well as for thousands of other Kyrgyz girls who, like her, dream of becoming his wife. The enormous popularity of film saw renewed appreciation of Kyrgyz films, with more widespread screenings, including new places in the centre of the country's capital, such as the National Historical Museum.

Ernest Abdyzhaparov, one of the key figures in widening the distribution of Kyrgyz cinema and whose *Saratan* participated at Berlinale in 2005, directed a new film, **Shakherezada from Kukushkino**. The film tells the story of

Ernest Abdyzhaparov's **Shakherezada from Kukushkino**

a girl who loses her memory after trying to commit a suicide. The film then traces what happened to bring her to such a state.

Graduates of the American-Kyrgyz University, including Aleksander Tsai, Eldar Supataev, Ruslan Akun, Stepan Golovash and Saule Alymbekova, produced the comedy **Bishkek, I Love You**. It features ten short stories detailing the problems of Kyrgyz youth, from broken love to unemployment. It was made for a specialist audience and as such was not exhibited in normal venues.

Aleksander Tsai, Eldar Supataev, Ruslan Akun, Stepan Golovash and Saule Alymbekova's **Bishkek, I Love You**

On the background of such success, popular filmmakers are awaiting the financing for a number of ambitious projects, but in the meantime are producing shorts and teaching. Marat Sarulu directed the excellent short **Mothers**, which details the story of Osh city over the last year, which saw the deaths of a significant number of Kyrgyzs and Uzbeks. In November, Aktan Arym Kubat organised the Third Festival of Art House Cinema, during which forty short films where screened. These show that there is boom of cinematic activity that will develop further, perhaps even progressing to an international level. – *Gulnara Abikeyeva*

LEBANON

With the support of Fonds Sud in Europe and Doha Film Institute in Qatar, numerous Lebanese films made their way into competitions at international film festivals over the last year. Many of these films reflected regional struggles, but also echoed universal themes.

Shortly after appearances in Georges Hachem's *Stray Bullet* and Italian director Ricky Tognazzi's *The Father and the Stranger*, Nadine Labaki returned to the director's chair for her second feature **Where Do We Go Now?** The film premiered in the 'Un Certain Regard' programme at Cannes. The story takes place in a small Lebanese village in the countryside where sectarian conflict looms over its inhabitants. This turmoil drives the women, young and old, Christian and Muslim, to reunite in their efforts in finding inventive, even comical, schemes to save their families from descent into violence. Labaki, who co-wrote the script and co-stars, interweaves dramatic scenes with symbolic musical numbers that occasionally undermine the seriousness of the subject; Labaki the filmmaker cannot hide her adoration for Labaki the beautiful actress.

Nadine Labaki's **Where Do We Go Now?**

Lebanese visual artist and filmmaker Laila Hotait's **Crayons of Askalan** is a docu-drama that re-enacts the powerful story of Palestinian painter Zuhdi Al-Adawi, who was imprisoned inside the high security jail of Askalan, Israeli, in 1975. With the help of his fellow prisoners and their families, 15-year-old Al-Adawi kept his spirit alive through painting and drawing, using colour crayons smuggled into prison. His artwork mostly reflected his physical confinement and state of mind. The works were smuggled out of prison in pillowcases and exhibited while he was still behind bars. Like the protagonist of her film, Hotait employs an expressionistic use of colour and CGI, highlighting the alternate world Al-Adawi created for himself. In the film's final moments, there is a touching interview with the real Zuhdi Al-Adawi, now middle-aged, in his own home.

Jean-Claude Codsi's **A Man of Honour**

Jean-Claude Codsi's thrilling drama **A Man of Honour** depicts 'honour crimes', the old tribal Middle Eastern practice that still drives family members to kill women if they are suspected of committing adultery. A discrete salesman hiding in Lebanon, Brahim (Majdi Machmouchi) was a victim of such a legacy that made him leave Jordan twenty years earlier. However, his troubled past comes back to haunt him in the form of Leila (Caroline Hatem), a mysterious woman who suddenly appears in his life in order to convince him to return to his former, deeply traditional community. In his second feature as writer-director, Codsi draws strong performances from his protagonists, elevating the film above the many Arab TV soaps that usually deal with such subjects. – *Sherif Awad*

MALAYSIA

2011 was the most prolific year for Malaysian cinema, with over 40 films released. Local films are also gaining more support from audiences, with a number attaining a degree of success.

The most succesful Malaysian film of 2011 was Syamsul Yusof's **KL Gangster**, an action film about two brothers caught up in a world of

Syamsul Yusof's **KL Gangster**

crime. This film broke all box-office records for a local film. It overtook Syamsul's horror film **The Superstition** (*Khurafat*), which was also one of the year's top-grossing local films.

Syamsul Yusof's **The Superstition**

The increase in production saw more filmmakers drawing on genre elements, with horror emerging as the most popular. Almost half of the films released last year were either horror or a mix of horror and comedy. Interestingly, the genre continues to generate heated debate. The former Prime Minister of Malaysia, Dr. Mahathir Mohamad's claim that local horror films are 'counter-productive' to building a progressive and developed society, prompted a flurry of reactions from industrial practitioners, filmmakers, academics, critics and religious figures.

Chiu Keng Guan's **Great Day**

Among the other interesting films released last year was Chiu Keng Guan's Cantonese-language comedy-drama **Great Day** which performed well at the box office. The film focuses on two grumpy old men who sneak out of their old people's home in order to meet their children in Kuala Lumpur, intent upon proving whose children are the most successful and loving. The beguilingly simple story is visually stunning, good humoured and heart-warming.

Khir Rahman's **…In a Bottle**

Khir Rahman's **…In a Bottle** (*…Dalam Botol*) is a dark and pessimistic melodrama about a gay man undergoing a sex change operation in a misguided attempt to please his lover, who no longer cares for him. While showcasing Khir's meticulous direction, the film sparked controversy over its representation of sexuality, a topic considered taboo in Malaysian society.

Yusry Abdul Halim's big-budget, CGI-dominated **The Malay Chronicles: Bloodlines** (*Hikayat Merong Mahawangsa*) is adapted from an ancient Malay epic, *Hikayat*, which recounts the deeds of a renowned naval captain and traveller, who founded the Malaysian state of Kedah. In effect, the film emulates the style and action of Hollywood swashbuckling epics such as *Pirates of the Caribbean*.

The phenomenal success of *KL Gangster* and other action films such as *The Malay Chronicles: Bloodlines*, Farid Kamil's **Kongsi** and Ismail Bob Hasim's **My Gangster Wives** (*Bini-Biniku Gangster*), augurs well for more genre films. In particular, audiences appear to delight in the type of film that highlights physical action, young masculinity and violence. This may be the direction Malaysian cinema is travelling towards.

NORMAN YUSOFF teaches film studies at Universiti Teknologi MARA, Malaysia. He is currently pursuing his PhD at the University of Sydney, Australia, with his research focusing on questions of genre in contemporary Malaysian cinema.

MALI

Few feature films were produced over the last year. Those that were released received financing from the state-backed National Centre for Cinematography of Mali (CNCM).

After last year's *Da Monzon, The Battle of Samanyana*, directed by Sidi Diabaté, the CNMC produced Ibrahim Touré's **Spider Webs** (*Toiles d'araignée*). It is an adaptation of an autobiographical novel by Ibrahim Ly, a young teacher who was active in the fight against the dictatorial regime of President Moussa Toure in the 1970s. Arrested by the police, the teacher spent four difficult years in prison. The film's tempo is aided considerably by a soundtrack featuring Malian composer Cheick Tidiane Seck.

The other major production of the year was Bata Diallo's documentary **Djeneba: The Lifeworld of a Minyanka Woman of Southern Mali** (*Djeneba une femme Minyanka du Sud du Mali*). The director, who studied filmmaking in Norway, documents the daily life of Djeneba, from the Minyanka community, who remains optimistic despite the hard circumstances of raising nine children in a small village.

Daouda Coulibaly's **Tinye So?**

Malian cinema was the recipient of three awards at the 2011 edition of Pan-African Festival of Cinema and Television, in Ouagadougou: two prizes for *Da Monzon, The Battle of Samanyana* and third for Daouda Coulibaly's short **Tinye So?** – *Honoré Essoh*

MAURITANIA

The increase in the number of women in cinema was the major story of the year. Local film production reached around fifty, mostly dominated by documentary shorts.

In her documentary **Dimi**, Salma El Sheikh Welly pays tribute to the famous Mauritanian singer Dimi Mint Abba, nicknamed the diva of the desert, who died on June 4, 2011. The filmmaker focused on the humility and sincerity of the artist, despite her popularity.

Mohamed Iddoumou's **Ahmedou**, is an intimate film shot over two years, during which the director learned sign language in order to record the life of the deaf art teacher Ahmedou, who is himself an artist.

In **The Wound of Slavery**, young director Ousmane Diagana deals with slavery, which is still a reality in the country. It is the story of an impossible love between a slave child and a descendant of a noble family. It was awarded one of the top prizes at the country's National Film Week. The fifth edition was held from 23 to 29 October, during which 67 films were screened.
– Agnes Thomasi

NEPAL

The Nepalese film industry saw huge ups and downs over the last year. Most significantly, the number of films produced was the best for a decade, with over seventy released. Sadly, despite their quality, none were successful commercially, so the early excitement of filmmakers was somewhat dampened by the end of the year.

Narayan Rayamajhi's **Gorkha Troop** (*Gorkha Rakshyak*), based on the story of Nepalese working in the Indian army, managed to attract some success at the beginning of the year. Rayamajhi, famed as a folk singer, infused a folk flavour into his first film.

Sudarshan Thapa's **Is This Love?**

Young director Sudarshan Thapa, who became the talk of town last year, released two love stories. Sadly, both **My Love Story** (*Mero Love Story*) and **Is This love?** (*Ke Yo Maya Ho*) were not received well by audiences.

Established director Ujawal Ghimire's **Speculation** (*Aandaj*) was released in August. Despite good notices, the tragic love story failed to fare any better commercially. Likewise, Prashant Raishainli's **Acharya** drew widespread attention for its huge investment, which failed to translate into box-office revenue. It is based on the life of famous singer Bhakta Raj Acharya and starred his son Satya Raj Acharya in the lead role.

After waiting a decade, audiences could finally see the new film by Nir Sah. Based on the classic story of Gopal Prasad Rimal, Sah's **Cemetery** (*Masan*) was released in November. However, the heartfelt story failed to make a profit.

In September, Film South Asia, the festival of South Asian documentaries, was held in Kathmandu. Anand Patwardhan's Indian documentary **Jaya Bhim Comrade** picked up the first prize. Similarly, Nepali film audiences had the opportunity to see Himalayan-related films at the Kathmandu International Mountain Film Festival in December.

The reason for the number of high quality films being produced with significant investment was to fight the domination Bollywood. However, Nepalese films do not have access to the international market and producers struggled to raise investment due to intense competition. As a result, filmmakers are left to wait and see what lies in store.

PRABESH SUBEDI is a freelance journalist and documentary maker. He is also the editor of the e-magazine *Filmnepal.com*.

PALESTINE

While Palestinian filmmakers continued to explore human relationships against the backdrop of unrest across the Palestinian territories, other international filmmakers depicted the Palestinian-Israeli conflict from a different context.

Tawfik Abu Wael's **Last Days in Jerusalem**

Premiering at Locarno and Toronto, Tawfik Abu Wael's **Last Days in Jerusalem** (*Tanathur*) revolves around an upper-middle-class Palestinian couple who plan to emigrate to Paris in the hope of starting a new life. However, on their way to the airport, Dr. Iyad (Ali Badarni), a successful surgeon, receives an emergency call urging him to go back and help the victims of a bus accident. His wife Nour (Lana Haj Yahia), a rising stage actress who has been offered her first leading role, voluntary accepts to delay their departure for a few days. Following his first feature *Thirst*, writer-director Abu Wael continues to examine the difficulties in detaching oneself from life in East Jerusalem, a city under siege.

Susan Youssef's **Darling, Something's Wrong With Your Head**

German-Palestinian actor Kais Nashif (*Paradise Now*) who has a supporting role in *Last Days in Jerusalem*, plays the lead in writer-director Susan Youssef's **Darling, Something's Wrong With Your Head** (*Habibi Rasak Kharban*). A modern retelling of the Bedouin story of star-crossed lovers Qays and Layla, the romantic comedy follows Layla (Maisa Abd Elhadi), who lives in Khan Younis, and Qays (Nashif), who comes from a neighbouring refugee camp. When they meet in college and fall in love, they face the disapproval of their conservative families. Youssef quickly asserts the right tone for a romantic comedy, while offering an accurate depiction of the Arab society in Gaza and its desire for love and not violence. The film premiered at Venice and also screened at the Dubai Film Festival, which had also supported the film in post-production.

Guy Davidi and Alexandre Goetschmann's Swiss-produced **Interrupted Streams** details the survival stories of West Bank villagers who are struggling from a lack of drinking water. The camera follows several characters from

Guy Davidi and Alexandre Goetschmann's **Interrupted Streams**

the village of Bil-in, which relies on a damaged infrastructure of pipelines controlled by the Israeli government. The ancient technique of collecting rainwater by digging pits eventually becomes the villagers' own way expressing independence and hope.

Screened at the Sao Paulo Film Festival, the Brazilian documentary **Football and Barriers** (*Sobre Futebol e Barreiras*) was shot in Israel and Palestine during the TV coverage of the South African World Cup, in 2010. The four filmmakers, João Carlos Assumpção, Arturo Hartmann, Lucas Justiniano and Jose Menezes interviewed Palestinians and Israelis, drawing out their feelings on life, sport and their own future. – *Sherif Awad*

QATAR

After popularising Al-Jazeera TV channels worldwide, Qatar is now keen to establish a regional film industry that can make an impact on the international stage.

This has been achieved through the Doha Film Institute (DFI), which hosts a year-long programme of film initiatives, including education and workshops with established filmmakers, financing through two annual grants, and the Doha Tribeca Film Festival (DTFF), in Katara Cultural Village.

For its third edition, the festival received hundreds of filmmakers and stars from all over the world, including Omar Sharif, Robin Wright, Bosnian filmmaker Jasmila Zbanic and Robert De Niro, co-founder of Tribeca Festival in New York. The festival opened with the US$55million-budget **Black Gold**, a co-production between the DFI and Tunisian producer Tarek Ben Ammar. Jean-Jacques Annaud's film takes place in the Arab desert at the beginning of the twentieth century, when two Arab countries go to war following the discovery of oil in the land across their border. Although the main characters are Arabs, the leads were given to Spanish star Antonio Banderas, playing Sheikh

Jean-Jacques Annaud's **Black Gold**

Nassib, British actor Mark Strong, playing Nassib's nemesis Sheikh Amar, and French-Algerian rising star Tahar Rahim, playing Prince Auda.

While *Black Gold* has been hyped as a big-budget Qatari production, it is difficult to see it as an Arab film given its Western cast and crew. Rahim delivers a good performance in the first half of the film as the bookworm Auda, who is taken from his father Amar and raised by Nassib, only to become the saviour of the two nations. Banderas rarely appears on screen and his casting seems to have been made to secure better distribution in Europe and the US. The Spanish star missed the opening, but was warmly welcomed half-way through the festival, when he arrived for an on-stage discussion, followed by the premiere of *Puss in Boots* and a special tribute screening of the first *Spy Kids* film. Currently, DFI financing has a dozen projects by Arab filmmakers in development, or at the post-production stage,

Michel Kammoun's **Beirut Hold'em**

and are set for release in 2012. Among them is Lebanese filmmaker Michel Kammoun's **Beirut Hold'em**, Syrian filmmaker Mohamed Malas's **Mosqui Cinema**, Egyptian filmmaker Tamer Ezzat's **When We Are Born** and Jordanian filmmaker Mais Darwazah's **My Love Awaits Me By the Sea**. – *Sherif Awad*

SENEGAL

Featuring a fair number of twists and some beautiful imagery, Moussa Touré's **The Pirogue** (*La Pirogue*) was the country's most acclaimed release. This film follows the perilous journey by a pirogue (a flat-bottomed boat) to Europe with young Senegalese immigrants aboard. It is an impressive film by a filmmaker who, for the last 25 years, has mostly made documentaries.

Moussa Touré's The Pirogue

Also dealing with the issue of illegal immigration is **The Point of View of the Lion** (*Le Point de vue du lion*), the directorial debut of the famous Senegalese rapper Didier Awadi. The documentary is a rich work, featuring interviews with a host of African personalities, such as Malian activist Aminata Traoré and former Senegalese President Abdou Diouf. Yet at ninety minutes, the film does outstay its welcome.

Based on a moving love story between two young people, Hubert Laba Ndao's **Dakar Sidewalks** (*Dakar Trottoirs*) explores the side of Dakar that tourists rarely see; a city of violence and misery. Were it not for some of the surreal characters that populate the film, it

could easily be mistaken for a documentary. The Senegalese government announced that in 2012 it would launch an ambitious project called the Dakar Pan-African Centre for Film and Audiovisual. The complex will include screening and post-production spaces, a development laboratory, film sets and a training centre. – *Honoré Essoh*

TAJIKISTAN

The Tajikistan film industry, which has been in operation for eighty years in 2012, has developed little since the country achieved its independence, twenty years ago. The main reason behind this has been the civil war. The conflict has also affected the development of the exhibition circuit. Not only are films produced solely on video, Dushanbe city only has two cinemas, both of which are only capable of screening DVDs. There are no cinemas in less urban areas of the country.

Filmmakers have tried to compensate for this shortage of venues. With the release of his latest film **Ormonkho**, Mukhiddin Dzhuraev took his projector and a mobile screen across the country. The film tells the story of the son of a prosecutor who hits a passerby on a road. The prosecutor fails to act in the case and as a result, when the case reaches trial, the prosecutor is forced to resign. The film's budget was US$50,000.

In discussing the state of Tajik cinema, Safar Khakdodov, Chairman of Unite of Filmmakers of Tajikistan stated, 'Tajik cinema of today requires, first of all, A-class management'. For the last seven years, he has organised the Didor International Film Festival which programmes screenings in Dushanbe's cinemas and is also responsible for the education of aspiring filmmakers. The 2011 edition saw the premiere of Shakhzoda Radzhabova's **The Wheel**. It is a psychological drama about an old man who teaches his grandson Tajik traditions and traits, while seeing his son become too urbanised.

Looking to the future, there are two potentially interesting projects. Iskander Usmonov's **Love Orbit** tells of the encounter between two people journeying across the entire country: a woman going to pick her nephew and a man who is travelling to his mother's funeral. Akhmal Khasanov's **Knock to the Closed Door** is about the destiny of young village-woman who lives with a man she does not love, but is unwilling to change. – *Gulnara Abikeyeva*

UZBEKISTAN

The 20th anniversary celebrating Uzbekistan's independence saw the commencement of the first international film forum, the Golden Gepard, which resurrected the Tashkent Film Festival of Asian, African and Latin American countries. Also, during the celebration of independence, Djasur Uskhakov's **The Day of Truth** was exhibited across the country. Tashkent is seen through the eyes of foreigners in the film, as they are guided through the sights by a tour guide. 'We see Uzbekistan of the 21st century – modern architecture, a wonderful city, where people live and build their happy future', wrote Uzbek media about the film.

The Grand Prix of Golden Gepard, whose deciding jury was presided over by Moritz de Hadeln, ex-director of the Berlinale, was awarded to Zulfikhar Musakov's **The Lead**.

The story takes place in the 1950s, on the eve of Stalin's death and details events that spiral out of control for two KGB clerks.

The film that attracted the highest profile internationally was 20-year-old Ruslan Pak's Uzbekistan-South Korean co-production **Hanaan**. It was premiered at the Locarno Film Festival and then at a number of international film festivals. It tells the story of a group of young South Koreans living in Tashkent. They run a small business concern and in their spare time smoke marijuana. Ruslan himself graduated from a film school in Seoul, where he teamed up with the film's Korean producer.

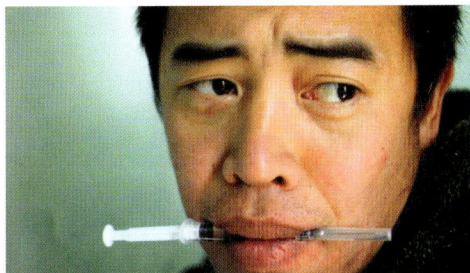

Ruslan Pak's **Hanaan**

Over the last twenty years of independence, Uzbekistan has become self-sufficient in film production and distribution, with eighty films produced last year and which dominated the local market to an unprecedented degree. No surprise, then, that the country is referred to as the Central Asian Bollywood.
– *Gulnara Abikeyeva*

Festival News

European Film Awards

This year's European Film Awards returned to the European Film Academy's (EFA) home in Berlin, with the prestigious ceremony unfolding in the immense Tempodrom, a spectacular venue close to Potsdammerplatz, where the Berlinale and European Film Market unfolds every February. The awards are the culmination of the EFA's year and are a chance to showcase the best and brightest of the continent's talent and output.

A quick glance over the nominations for the 17 categories shows what a remarkable year it has been for European film, both artistically and in terms of commercial success. The list featured filmmakers old and new, and films that challenged and entertained. The winners also reflected this spectrum, and were voted for by the 2,500 members of the EFA.

Both Denmark and the UK fared well on the evening. The standout film was Lars Von Trier's *Melancholia*, which picked up three awards,

The 24th European Film Awards. Photo: Franziska Krug/Action Press

including Best European Film. Von Trier was not present for the ceremony, a guarantee that the director would not overshadow his film, as he did in Cannes. Two other Danes, Susanne Bier and Mads Mikkelsen also won awards: Best Direction for *In a Better World* and European Achievement in World Cinema for the acclaimed actor. *The King's Speech* continued to trailblaze its way through every award ceremony of the last year. Tom Hooper accepted the Peoples' Choice Award, the only prize not voted for by the EFA, while Tariq Anwar picked up the European Editor award. Colin Firth added another accolade to what must be an overpopulated mantelpiece, with the European Actor award for his portrayal of King George VI. Another Brit, Tilda Swinton received the European Actress prize for her searing performance in *We Need to Talk About Kevin*.

This year's Lifetime Achievement Award also went to a British filmmaker, Stephen Frears. One of the graduates of the golden age of British television, Frears accurately characterised British society during the Thatcher years of the 1980s with films such as *Bloody Kids* and *My Beautiful Laundrette*. He then moved on to the world stage with *Dangerous Liaisons* and *The Hi-Lo Country*, but frequently returned to the UK for films such as *Dirty Pretty Things*, *The Queen* and *Tamara Drewe*.

One of the highlights of the evening was an appearance by the charming and gracious Michel Piccoli, who accepted the EFA Special Honorary Award. His career spans the last fifty years of European film and runs the gamut from artistic endeavours to mainstream hits. It is a career that reflects the diversity of the EFA and its annual awards ceremony.

The European Film Awards 2011 were presented by the European Film Academy e.V. and EFA Productions gGmbH with the support of the Capital Cultural Fund, FFA German Federal Film Board, the German State Lottery Berlin, the German State Minister for Culture and the Media, the MEDIA Programme of the EU, Medienboard Berlin-Brandenburg, CinePostproduction, Hôtel Concorde Berlin, PanAm Lounge, Pinewood Studio Berlin, ŠKODA AUTO Deutschland GmbH, Tempodrom and TNT Express.

European Film
Melancholia, (dir. Lars von Trier, Denmark/Sweden/France/Germany)
European Director
Susanne Bier for *In a Better World* (Hævnen)
European Actress
Tilda Swinton in *We Need to Talk About Kevin*
European Actor
Colin Firth in *The King's Speech*
European Screenwriter
Jean-Pierre & Luc Dardenne for *The Kid with a Bike* (*Le Gamin au velo*)
Carlo Di Palma European Cinematographer Award
Manuel Alberto Claro for *Melancholia*
European Editor
Tariq Anwar for *The King's Speech*
European Production Designer
Jette Lehmann for *Melancholia*
European Composer
Ludovic Bource for *The Artist*
European Discovery – Prix FIPRESCI
Oxygen (*Adem*) (dir. Hans Van Nuffel, Belgium/Netherlands)

Susanne Bier (European Director 2011 for In a Better World*)*
Photo: Franziska Krug/Action Press

EFA Documentary – Prix ARTE
Pina (dir. Wim Wenders, Germany)
EFA Animated Feature Film
Chico & Rita (dir. Tono Errando, Javier Mariscal & Fernando Trueba)
EFA Short Film
The Wholly Family (dir. Terry Gilliam, Italy)
European Co-Production Award – Prix EURIMAGES
Mariela Besuievsky, Spain
European Achievment in World Cinema
Mads Mikkelsen, Denmark
EFA Lifetime Achievement Award
Stephen Frears, UK
EFA Special Honorary Award
Michel Piccoli, France
The People's Choice Award
The King's Speech (dir. Tom Hooper, UK)

THE 25th EUROPEAN FILM AWARDS
1 December 2012 in Malta

The Human Rights Film Festival Celebrates its 10th Anniversary

To mark its 10th anniversary, the International Film Festival and Forum on Human Rights (FIFDH) is celebrating peace-makers: the women and men helping to advance the cause of human rights, as well as the young generations around the world who are mobilising themselves for the respect of their dignity. The festival will pay a special tribute to the Syrian people. At its opening, the festival is hosting a solidarity evening that will feature discussion with the Syrian resistance.

The 10th edition, which will take place 2–11 March, will also feature previously unscreened films and debates on current crucial issues, such as the future of the Arab Spring; Europe's neo-populist drift; the sudden civic awakening in Russia; opposition to the dominance of financial markets; international justice in action; peace-builders and reconciliators working behind the scenes to promote human rights.

FIFDH is a unique opportunity to meet with revolutionaries, activists, bloggers, political personalities, committed filmmakers and artists. Among this year's guests: Indian writer, editor and journalist Tarun Tejpal; Indian novelist Shumona Sinha; French Ambassador Stéphane Hessel; Europe Ecologie parliamentarian Daniel Cohn-Bendit; French sociologist Edgar Morin; Ambassador for Palestine at UNESCO Elias Sanbar; Israeli politician Yaël Dayan; UN High Commissioner for Human Rights Navi Pillay; lawyer and member of the UN

Debate at the FIFDH, Geneva 2011. Photo: Miguel Bueno.

Commission of Enquiry on War Crimes in Sri Lanka Yasmin Sooka; former Minister of Economy of Argentina (who said 'no' to the IMF) Roberto Lavagna; Syrian writer Samar Yazbeck; Tunisian blogger Lina ben Mhenni; Belgian film director Thierry Michel and Cambodian filmmaker Rithy Panh.

A decade of commitment and engagement for human rights is something to be shared. To conclude the 2012 edition, FIFDH is inviting the public to participate in a Human Rights Night – an exceptional event for an exceptional anniversary!

« See it. Film it. Change it. »
WITNESS

FIFDH | GENEVA
INTERNATIONAL FILM FESTIVAL AND FORUM ON HUMAN RIGHTS
10TH EDITION | 2 TO 11 MARCH 2012 | GENEVA | MAISON DES ARTS DU GRÜTLI

www.fifdh.org

Festival Director Profiles

Tiina Lokk –
Tallinn Black Nights Film Festival (PÖFF)

In its 15-year existence, Tallinn Black Nights Film Festival (PÖFF) has become one of the most expansive in Europe. It was created by Tiina Lokk, who remains the key to its continued success. What it has helped achieve is a complete transformation of a national cinema. 'PÖFF was born at a difficult time for the Estonian film industry,' Lokk commented in a recent interview. 'State support for the industry (both film production as well as distribution and exhibition) had withered away and mainstream movies were taking over the film landscape in Estonia. We wanted people to start asking questions: Where had all the cinemas disappeared to? What had happened to films from different countries? What had happened to Estonian film? It seemed that the best way to do it was by organising a film festival – so with support from Nordic embassies, we put together a programme that included films from Nordic and a few other European countries. This small venture (mostly run by the team of the art-house distribution company Filmimax) eventually grew into the big international festival that PÖFF is today.'

Today the festival features the main section, which screens over 200 films from around 70 countries, many of which are in competition. There are also the many sub-sections – individual festivals under the main umbrella of Black Nights – such as animation ('Animated Dreams'), films for children and youth ('Just Film'), student films ('Sleepwalkers') and a host of other programmes championing documentary, American independent film, retrospectives and prize-winning films from other festivals. Lokk's aim is 'is to create a versatile yet quality-driven programme that would be interesting for both audiences and juries. Because of our geographical and historical position, we have access to many cultures and markets that are not common in the rest of the Europe. For example, our EurAsia competitive programme features outstanding films, many of which cannot be seen anywhere else.'

The festival also prides itself on an extensive industry platform. 'Black Market Industry Screenings is a film market for industry professionals,' comments Lokk. 'It includes a seminar programme, 'Industry Days', as well as the literary rights market, 'Books To Films'. There's also the co-production market 'Baltic Event' that's become very important for the region.'

The industry side of the festival is also moving online throughout the year, with 'Black Market Online'. 'It is a truly unique enterprise, comments Lokk enthusiastically. 'It will be an online B2B environment for film industry that includes industry contacts, country profiles and statistics, co-production projects and online screening rooms for buying and selling film rights in Baltic, Scandinavian, Central-Asian, Caucasian and Russian territories.'

In 2012 Estonia celebrates 100 years of its national cinema. PÖFF will be at the forefront of this, as it was last year, when Tallinn was named the European City of Culture. There are plans afoot to look back over the century of Estonian film and a desire to place Estonian film within the larger context of Europe's rich cinematic past. Whatever form these celebrations come in, Tiina Lokk knows that 'PÖFF is absolutely ready to help realise these common ideas'.

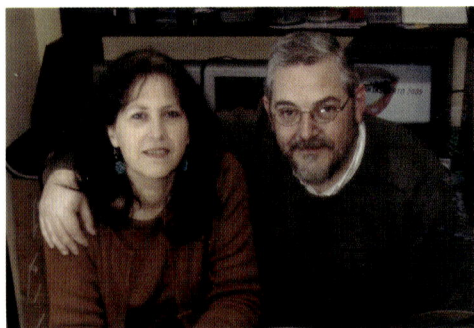

Mário Dorminsky and Beatriz Pacheco Pereira – Oporto International Film Festival – Fantasporto

For an event that began with the aim of championing fantasy, sci-fi and horror, Fantasporto, the city of Oporto's International Film Festival, has changed a great deal in its 32-year existence. It is now a major film event that screens the best cinema from around the world.

For its 32nd edition, Festival Directors Mário Dorminsky and Beatriz Pacheco Pereira have a rich and varied programme for the 80,000 audience who attend each year: 'Outside of the three competitions, we will screen a number of retrospectives, celebrating the work of Antonio-Pedro Vasconcelos, Alain Robbe-

Grillet and Karen Shaknazarov. There is also a tribute to Mike Hodges with a celebration of the 40th anniversary of *Get Carter*, and the 30th anniversary of *Blade Runner*, which received its premiere in Fantasporto in 1983.'

All this at a time when the Portuguese economy remains in a perilous state. It is a situation that has obviously impacted on all areas, the festival notwithstanding. As Pacheco Pereira comments, 'We have obviously been affected. Some private sponsors fled, the State has downsized their support. But we come from the time when we needed to be resourceful, whether it was because of censorship rather than the economy, and we have re-invented the festival many times, according to its needs.'

Re-invention is key to the festival's identity. When it began in the early 1980s, it was a small, non-competitive event. It then changed its status, offering prizes for the best sci-fi, fantasy or horror films of the year. Previous winners included *Scanners* (David Cronenberg, 1982), *A Chinese Ghost Story* (Si-Tung Ching, 1988) and *Black Rainbow* (Mike Hodges, 1990).

Then, in 1991, the festival expanded its format, presenting the 'Directors' Week', a round-up of the most exciting talent in world cinema. The first year was won by Tom Stoppard and subsequent winners have included Tom Kalin, Lodge Kerrigan, Mark Van Diem, Paul Greengrass, Michael Cuesta and Andrea Arnold.

Acknowledging the importance of Asian cinema over the last decade, the 'Orient Express' competition was introduced in 2004. As Dorminsky points out, 'They are so imaginative that we created a competition some years ago dedicated to Asia alone'. Winners have included Ringo Lam, Johnnie To, Tsui Hark, Chan Wook Park and Park Ki-Hyeong.

There are numerous other events, including the Special Programme, which Pacheco Pereira is particularly proud of. 'The Special Programme was introduced in 2009, re-organising the many non-film events that were traditionally created around the festival every year, in order to draw people's attention to the variety of cultural events on offer at Fantasporto. Mixing films with music, theatre and the arts, or discussing what the future holds in store, widened the range of the festival and gave visitors a chance to take a break from the many screenings. It also allowed us to champion our home city, offering tours around Oporto, a World Heritage City.'

Roman Gutek – New Horizons International Film Festival and American Film Festival

In 2001, Roman Gutek created New Horizons International Film Festival. It was very much an extension of his distribution company, Gutek Film, which had been responsible for championing world cinema in Poland, releasing between 18 to 20 films each year. The festival enabled audiences in Poland to see a wider array of films from around the world.

New Horizons quickly grew from its humble beginnings. 'The first edition took place in Sanok', comments Gutek. 'During the first day of the festival we quickly realised that the town was too small for this kind of event. We moved to Cieszyn the following year. It had a better infrastructure which was suitable for the next four years.' Then, in 2006, the festival was invited to Wrocław, one of the country's largest cities. 'Thanks to the move the festival gained stability and room for growth.' Since

then, it has become one of the key events in the European festival calendar.

Anyone who visits New Horizons knows that it is not merely a festival of film, something its founder is always keen to stress: 'During the festival, we not only feature music concerts, but also exhibitions, performances and video installations, as well as silent films with live music. These extra events are always linked to the films that we screen. We are trying to show how various art forms merge. We welcome artists who are active in many fields.'

And now New Horizons has a younger sibling – the American Film Festival. 'It was the awareness of the richness and diversity of American cinema and limited chances to present it at New Horizons that made us create the American Film Festival', says Gutek. 'To a large extent, we want to look at the history of American cinema and its influence on world culture in general. We felt that we had a mission to educate younger audiences about great American filmmakers and to offer the chance to discover the country and its social, political, cultural complexities.'

Like New Horizons, the American Film Festival also features a strong industry platform. For Gutek, it is an essential part of both festival's make-up: 'Currently, more than 200 film professionals visit [New Horizons] every year. The festival brings excellent opportunities to meet, discuss and exchange ideas, find co-producers and discover new talent. Several industry events are organised – most recently the New Horizons Studio (workshops for young filmmakers) and co-production forums (in 2011, a Polish-Norwegian Co-production Forum). We hope the status of the American Film Festival will grow and allow us to access the filmmakers easier. This will partly be achieved through projects selected for 'Gotham in Progress', now called 'US in Progress'. That may also help us build the position as a great forum for the discussion of the many facets of US filmmaking and convince American talent to visit Poland and our festivals in Wrocław.'

Film Festivals Calendar

May

June

July

August

September

October

Leading Festivals

Abu Dhabi Film Festival
October 11–20, 2012

The Abu Dhabi Film Festival was established in 2007 with the aim of helping to create a vibrant film culture throughout the region. The event, presented each October by the Abu Dhabi Authority for Culture and Heritage (ADACH), under the patronage of HE Sheikh Sultan Bin Tahnoon Al-Nahyan, Chairman of ADACH, is committed to curating exceptional programmes to engage and educate the local community, inspire filmmakers and nurture the growth of the regional film industry. With its commitment to presenting works by Arab filmmakers in competition alongside those by major talents of world cinema, the Festival offers Abu Dhabi's diverse and enthusiastic audiences a means of engaging with their own and others' cultures through the art of cinema. At the same time, a strong focus on the bold new voices of Arab cinema connects with Abu Dhabi's role as a burgeoning cultural capital in the region and marks the Festival as a place for the world to discover and gauge the pulse of recent Arab filmmaking. *Inquiries to:* Abu Dhabi Film Festival, PO Box 2380, Abu Dhabi, UAE. Tel: (971 2) 556 4000; e: contact@adff.ae; web: www.abudhabifilmfestival.ae.

Antalya Golden Orange Film Festival
October 2012

Turkey's oldest festival celebrates its 49th edition in 2012 and will screen over 190 films at twelve venues across the city. The basic mission of the Festival is 'to give material and moral support to the Turkish film sector, to form the basis for Turkish cinema to be viewed by an international audience by provoking Turkish film producers to produce qualified masterpieces'. *Inquiries to:* Antalya Foundation for Culture and Arts (AKSAV), Sakip Sabanci Bulv, Ataturk Kultur Park Ici, Antalya, Turkey. Tel: (90 242) 238 5444; e: info@aksav.org.tr; web: www.aksav.org.tr.

AWARDS 2011
Best Film: **Journey of No Return** (Germany/Turkey), Güclü Yaman, Marcel Miller and Aljoscha Sena Zinflou.
Best First Film: **Zenne Dancer** (Turkey).
Turkish Film Critics Association Award: **Zenne Dancer** (Turkey).

Internationale Filmfestspiele Berlin
February 9–19, 2012

Over 20,000 accredited visitors from 115 countries, including 3,825 journalists, attended the 61st Berlin International Film Festival in 2011. Approximately 484,000 cinemagoers came to the Festival, with roughly 300,000 tickets sold. Altogether, 385 films were shown in 965 screenings. Besides the regular sections 'Competition', 'Panorama', 'Forum', 'Generation', 'Perspektive Deutsches Kino' and 'Berlinale Shorts', special events including the 'Ingmar Bergman Retrospective' and the 'Homage to Armin Müller-Stahl', as well as the 'Berlinale Special' and 'Culinary Cinema' sidebars, were almost sold out. The European Film Market (EFM) and the associated Co-Production Market offered a wide range of prospects for industry professionals, as did the Berlinale Talent Campus for up-and-coming filmmakers. Under Jury President Isabella Rossellini, the jurors Jan Chapmann, Nina Hoss, Aamir Khan, Guy Maddin and Sandy Powell brought glamour, passion and expertise to the 2011

Journalists at the Red Carpet 2012
© Internationale Filmfestspiele Berlinale, Photo: Alexander Janetzko

Berlinale. Iranian director Jafar Panahi, who was also invited to serve on the International Jury, was sentenced in December 2010 to six years imprisonment and banned from filmmaking for the next twenty years. The verdict was met with worldwide protest against this violation of freedom of opinion and expression. The Berlinale held Panahi's place open in the Jury to symbolise the Festival's support for his struggle for freedom. The EFM, one of the top three international markets in the world, is the business centre of the Berlin International Film Festival. Over a period of nine days, running parallel to the Festival, the EFM, with almost 7,000 registered participants, is the focal point for international film buyers and sellers, producers, world sales agents, distributors, cinema operators, film financiers, as well as representatives of the global television, home entertainment and new media market. The EFM provides the opportunity to discover the best quality products in the film business, but also new talents and the latest trends in the film industry during the first international market of the year. Under the auspices of the EFM, the Berlinale Co-Production Market offers producers an opportunity to present new projects to financiers and potential co-production partners during a two-and-a-half-day event. *Inquiries to:* Internationale Filmfestspiele Berlin, Potsdamer Str 5, D-10785

Berlin, Germany. Tel: (49 30) 259 200; e: info@ berlinale.de; web: www.berlinale.de.

AWARDS 2011
Golden Bear: **A Separation: Nader and Simin** (Iran), Asghar Farhadi.
Jury Grand Prix Silver Bear: **The Turin Horse** (France, Germany, Hungary, Switzerland), Béla Tarr.
Silver Bear for Best Director: Ulrich Köhler for **Sleeping Sickness** (Germany).
Silver Bear for Best Actress-ensemble: **A Separation: Nader and Simin** (Iran), Asghar Farhadi.
Silver Bear for Best Actor-ensemble: **A Separation: Nader and Simin** (Iran), Asghar Farhadi.
Golden Bear for Best Short: **Night Fishing** (South Korea), Park Chan-wook and Park Chan-Kyong.
Silver Bear for Best Short: **Broken Night** (South Korea), Yang Hyo-joo.

Golden Bear for Best Film: **A Separation: Nader and Simin** – *Festival Director Dieter Kosslick, the President of the International Jury Isabella Rossellini, director Asghar Farhadi. Photo: Andreas Teich © Berlinale 2011*

Bilbao Documentary & Short Film Festival
Late November 2012

Celebrating its 54th edition in 2012 and established for its speciality on the international film festival circuit. It features over 2,500 films from over eighty countries, with an international competition that encompasses three categories for fiction, documentary and animation. *Inquiries to:* Bilbao Documentary & Short Film Festival, Colón de Larreátegui 37, 48009 Bilbao, Spain. Tel: (34 94) 424 8698; e: festival@zinebi.com; web: www.zinebi.com.

Bogota Film Festival
October 2012

'International Competitive' section, 'National Competitive' section and side bars. Features, animation, shorts, documentary. Entries must be subtitled in Spanish and must not have been previously screened in Colombia. *Inquiries to:* Bogota Film Festival, Residencias Tequendama, Centro Internacional Tequendama, Cra 10 Suite 27-51 Of 325, Bogotá, Colombia. Tel: (57 1) 341 7562; e: prensa@bogocine.com; web: www.bogocine.com.

Brussels International Festival of Fantastic Film
April 2012

Competitive international and European selection for shorts and features. *Inquiries to:* 8 Rue de la Comtesse de Flandre, 1020 Brussels, Belgium. Tel: (32 2) 201 1713; e: info@bifff.net; web: www.bifff.org.

AWARDS 2011
Grand Prix Golden Raven: **I Saw the Devil** (South Korea), Ji-Woon Kim.
Silver Raven: **Midnight Son** (USA), Scott Leberecht, and **Detective Dee and the Mystery of the Phantom Flame** (China/Hong Kong), Tsui Hark.
Silver Mélies: **Transfer** (Germany), Damir Lukacevic.
Pegasus Audience Award: **Rare Exports: A Christmas Tale** (Finland/France/Norway/Sweden), Jalmari Helander.

Busan International Film Festival
October 2012

In 2011 the second-largest city in South Korea changed its English name from Pusan to Busan, so the Festival has now become known as the Busan International Film Festival. In addition, the project market formerly known as the Pusan Promotion Plan (PPP) was renamed the Asian Project Market (APM). BIFF is known as the most energetic film festival in the world and has become the largest film festival in

Asia. The 17th edition, in 2012, aims to further expand the programme so that Festival attendees can more actively participate. As well as the Citizen Reviewers, cultural-artistic professionals from diverse backgrounds will be able to participate as principal agents of cinema discourse. Films must have been produced within the year prior to the Festival and must be subtitled in English. BIFF screens over 300 films from over seventy countries, of which around 150 are world and international premieres. Also, retrospectives, special programmes in focus, seminars and master classes. In addition, its project market has been a platform for moving Asian film projects forward in the international marketplace, along with its own talent campus, Asian Film Academy (AFA), offering various filmmaking programmes for young talent from all over Asia. *Inquiries to:* BIFF, Seven Bldg, 13–21 Namsan-dong 3-ga, Jung-gu, Seoul 100-043, Korea. Tel: (82 2) 3675 5097; web: www.biff.kr.

Cairo International Film Festival
Late November/early December 2012

The Festival is organised by the General Union of Arab Artists and is the oldest film festival in the Middle East with the aim of promoting the Egyptian, Arab and African film industries. Competitions for feature films, feature digital films and Arab films. *Inquiries to:* Cairo International Film Festival, 17 Kasr el Nile St, Cairo, Egypt. Tel: (20 2) 2392 3562; e: info@cairofilmfest.com; web: www.cairofilmfest.com.

Cannes International Film Festival
May 9–20, 2012

Cannes remains the world's leading festival and the best known, attracting key films, personalities and industry professionals. The official selection includes the 'Competition', films out of competition, special screenings, 'Un Certain Regard', short films in competition, 'Cinéfondation' and 'Cannes Classics' (created 2004). The Marché du Film (Producers' network, Short Film Corner) is part of the

Dede Gardner, Bill Pohlad - Palme d'Or - **The Tree of Life** *by Terrence Malick © AFP*

official organisation. *Inquiries to:* Festival de Cannes, 3, rue Amélie 75007 Paris, France. Tel: (33 1) 5359 6100; e: festival@festival-cannes.fr; web: www.festival-cannes.com.

AWARDS 2011

Palme d'Or Feature Film: **The Tree of Life** (USA), Terrence Malick.
Grand Prix: **The Kid with a Bike** (Belgium/France/Italy), Jean-Pierre and Luc Dardenne, and **Once Upon a Time in Anatolia** (Turkey), Nuri Bilge Ceylan.
Best Director: Nicolas Winding Refn for **Drive** (USA).
Best Screenplay: Joseph Cedar for **Footnote** (Israel).
Best Actress: Kristen Dunst for **Melancholia** (Denmark).
Best Actor: Jean Dujardin for **The Artist** (USA).
Jury Prize: **Polisse** (France), Maïwenn Le Besco.
Caméra d'Or: **Las Acacias** (Argentina/Spain), Pablo Giorgelli.

Cartagena International Film Festival

February 23–29, 2012

Established in 1960, Cartagena is the only festival in the region that specialises in Ibero-American movies and exhibits the best audio-visual work of Latin America. It encourages the presentation of cultural expressions of Latin American identity through films and is a true audio-visual showcase of Colombia and the countries in the region,

gaining worldwide attention and recognition for the territory's filmmakers. *Inquiries to:* Cartagena International Film Festival, Centro, Calle San Juan de Dios, Baluarte San Francisco Javier, Cartagena, Colombia. Tel: (57 5) 664 2345; e: info@ficcifestival.com; web: www. ficcifestival.com.

Cinema Jove International Film Festival

June 15–22, 2012

Promotes the work of young filmmakers and has two competitive sections, feature films screened for the first time in Spain and another for the best shorts on the international scene. These constitute the thrust of a programme that also embraces tributes to veteran filmmakers, young 'cult movie' directors, exhibitions and professional meeting points. *Inquiries to:* Cinema Jove International Film Festival, La Safor 10-5, 46015 Valencia, Spain. Tel: (34 96) 331 1047; e: info@cinemajove.com; web: www.cinemajove.com.

Clermont-Ferrand Short Film Festival

January 27–February 4, 2012

The Festival has become the world's premiere cinema event dedicated to short films. It is the second-largest film festival in France after Cannes in terms of audience, circa 140,000, and profesional attendance with around 3,000 delegates. 'International', 'National' and 'Lab' competitions for 35mm films and digital works on DigiBeta and Beta SP, all completed after July 1, 2010, of forty minutes or less. *Inquiries to:* Clermont-Ferrand Short Film Festival, La Jetée, 6 Place Michel-de L'Hospital 63058 Clermont-Ferrand Cedex 1, France. Tel: (33 4) 7391 6573; e: info@clermont-filmfest.com; web: www.clermont-filmfest.com.

AWARDS 2011
Grand Prix
International: **Kawalek Lata** (Poland), Marta Minorowicz.
National: **Tremblay-en-France** (France), Vincent Vizioz.
Lab: **Night Mayor** (Canada), Guy Maddin.

Cork Film Festival
November 4–11, 2012

Cork Film Festival is one of Ireland's most important cultural events, and its longest-running film festival. Now in its 57th year, there is a defined aesthetic drive to the Festival, which includes 'World Cinema', 'Documentary Panorama', 'Irish Cinema Platform', comprehensive 'Short Film' competitions and innovative explorations in live cinema and experimental work. A popular filmmakers' festival for many years; in 2011 Cork introduced a Filmmaker Development Programme, bringing industry partners together and providing opportunities for emerging filmmakers. In particular the Festival celebrates the art of the short film with over 45 programmes of short films in competition and in special programmes. Awards include Best International Short, Best European Short and Best Irish Short. *Inquiries to:* Cork

Cork Film Festival Jury and the winner of the Best Irish Short Award (l-r) Tom Climent, Alexandra Gramatke, Phil Harrison (Director of **Even Gods***), Felim Mac Dermott.*

At the premiere of **The Baron** *at Cork Film Festival (l-r) Actor Nuno Melo, Festival Director Mick Hannigan, and Director, Edgar Pera.*

Film Festival, Emmet House, Emmet Place, Cork, Ireland. Tel: (353 21) 427 1711. e: info@corkfilmfest.org. Web: www.corkfilmfest.org.

AWARDS 2011
Best Irish Short: **Even Gods**, Phil Harrison.
Claire Lynch Award for Best First-Time Irish Director: **The Art of Making Friends**, Paul McNulty.
Best International Short: **Aglaée** (France), Rudi Rosenberg.
Cork Short Film Nominee for the European Film Awards: **Two Hearts** (Ireland), Darren Thornton.
Audience Award for Best International Short: **Silent River** (Romania), Anca Miruna Lazarescu.
Audience Award for Best Irish Short: **Even Gods**, Phil Harrison.
Award of the Festival for Best Short: **The Wind Is Blowing On My Street** (Iran/USA), Saba Riazi.
Outlook Award for Best LGBT Short: **I Don't Want To Go Back Alone**, (Brazil), Daniel Ribeiro.
'Made In Cork' Award for Best Short: **Rats' Island**, Mike Hannon.

Report 2011

The 56th edition attracted approximately 24,000 admissions to a wide-ranging programme of screenings, talks, masterclasses and special events. The Festival devoted a special focus to Edgar Pera, director of The Baron; presented People Like Us – a live performance of 'The Magical Misery Tour'; and hosted a retrospective on Romanian short films amongst the 'Explorations' section. Filmmakers attended from over twenty countries; including Edgar Pera and Nuno Melo (director and actor The Baron and special focus), Buharov brothers (special focus), F. J. Ossang (director of Dharma Guns), P. V. Lehtinen (director of Soul Catcher), John Henry Summerour (director of Sakhanaga) and Andrew Haigh (director of Weekend). Cork also welcomed many international festivals, programmers and industry professionals.
– **Sean Kelly**, Festival Manager.

Courmayeur Noir Film Festival

December 2012

International film and literary mystery festival showing the best of cinema and literature in the field of thriller, mystery, spy story, horror and film noir, held in the picturesque ski resort of Courmayeur, in Val d'Aosta, in the shadow of Mont Blanc. The twelve films in competition are all premières of the year and compete for the Mystery Award for Best Film and the Napapijri Prize for the Best Performance. The Festival also features a documentary section, retrospectives exploring the history of the genre, discovering cult authors, as well as a TV Noir section and the Festival for young audience, Mini Noir. *Inquiries to:* Courmayeur Noir in Festival, Via Panaro, 17-00199 Rome, Italy. Tel: (39 06) 860 3111; e: noir@noirfest.com; web: www.noirfest.com.

Crossroads Film Festival

April 13–15, 2012

The Crossroads Film Festival is the premiere film festival in central Mississippi, now celebrating its thirteenth anniversary in

*Cindy Meehl, Director of award-winning film **Buck** and Chris Myers interact with Crossroads Film Festival sold-out audience. (April 2011, Madison, Miss) Photo: Art Minton*

2012. Founded in 1999 in the capital city of Jackson – 'The Crossroads of the South' – the Festival is known as a venue where the strands and influences of art, theme, and culture come together. Every year the event celebrates film, music, and food, along with the great culture and heritage of Mississippi. The Festival provides a cross-cultural backdrop of screenings, concerts and receptions in addition to dynamic workshops and filmmaker forums. Over the years, Crossroads has celebrated filmmakers with ties to Mississippi, from Robert Altman and Morgan Freeman, to resident Joey Lauren Adams and Vicksburg's own Charles Burnett. Crossroads is a top Mississippi stop for many films made in the state: *Prom Night in Mississippi, Ballast, Big Bad Love, O Brother, Where Art Thou?, The Rising Place, I'll Fly Away, Cries of Silence, Red Dirt* and *Blossom Time* among them. *Inquiries to:* Crossroads Film Festival, PO Box 22604, Jackson, MS 39225-2604, USA. Tel: (1 601) 345 5674; e: info@crossroadsfilmfestival.com; web: www.crossroadsfilmfestival.com.

AWARDS 2011

Best Experimental Film: **In Between** (Israel), Tamar Shippony.
Best Animated Film: **The Thomas Beale Cipher** (USA), Andrew Allen.
Adam Ford Youth Award: **How Could She?** (USA), Kevin Rieg.
Best Student Film: **God of Love** (USA), Luke Matheny.
Best Music Video (Juried): **The Language** (Dead Snares) (USA), Jeffrey Cain.

Best Short Narrative: **Checkpoint** (France), Ruben Amar.
Best Short Documentary: **Loy Krathong** (Thailand), Jeffrey Waldron.
Best Feature Documentary: **Buck** (USA), Cindy Meehl.
Best Feature Narrative: **Der Sandmann (The Sandman)** (Switzerland), Peter Luisi.
Programmer's Choice Award: **Murderabilia** (USA), David Matthews.
Ruma Award (Most Promising Mississippi Filmmaker): **Bearanoid** (USA), Wade Acuff.
Transformative Award: **Mississippi Innocence** (USA), Joe York.
Audience Choice Award for Best Film: **La Hora Cero (The Zero Hour)** (Venezuela), Diego Velasco.
Audience Choice Award for Best Music Video: **Crack Kills** (Green Seed) (USA).

Report 2011

Notable screenings for the 2011 Crossroads Film Festival included *Buck*, followed by Q&A with Mississippi native director Cindy Meehl; *La Hora Cero*, followed by Q&A with Diego Velasco, a graduate of the University of Southern Mississippi Film School; a packed workshop – 'Acting With Frank Vitolo' – and the Music Video Showcase, featuring nearly two dozen regional bands. An international 14-member panel made up of film critics, directors, filmmakers, and actors juried the films in competition to select the award winners. **– Nina Parikh**.

Eurasia International Film Festival
September 19–24, 2012

Eurasia is an international film festival in Almaty, Central Asia, screening both Eastern and Western films and supported by the Kazakhstan Government. In recent years, the Festival focused on films from Central Asia and the Turkic world, but this year the remit was broadened to encompass films from Europe, Asia and the CIS countries. In 2011, the Festival featured the following programmes: dynamic Kazakh cinema, special events (screenings of film that won awards at various international festivals), virtual West and changing East, Echo of Venice, USA

documentary showcase, and a competition programme, which included films from the Philippines, Russia, Romania, France, Iran and Kazakhstan. *Inquiries to:* Eurasia International Film Festival, 176 Al-Farabi Ave, 050023 Almaty, Kazakhstan. Tel: (7 727) 302 1642; e: info@eurasiaiff.kz; web: www.eurasiaiff.kz.

AWARDS 2011

Best Film: **The First Rains of Spring** (Japan/Kazakhstan), Erlan Nurmukhambetov and Sano Shinju.
Best Director: Nariman Turebaev for **Sunny Days** (Kazakhstan).
Best Actor: Theodor Juliusson for **Volcano** (Iceland).
Best Actress: Olga Simonova for **The Bedouin** (Russia).
FIPRESCI Prize: **Busong** (Philippines), Auraeus Solito.
NETPAC Prize: **The Lead** (Uznekistan), Zulfikar Musakov.

Report 2011

Among the most notable events was the screening of Zeze Takahisa's film *Heaven's Story*, dedicated to the spring tragedy in Japan. The pitching session for the best Kazakh project for Kazak-European co-production was organised for the first time. The winner was young film director Emir Baigazin with *Harmony Lessons*. Two books were also presented: 'Film Encyclopaedia of Kazakhstan' by Tamara Smailova and 'Princiles and Facilities of Financing French Cinematography' by Joel Chapron and Priscilla Jessati. The jury president was South Korean director Kim Ki-Duk **– Gulnara Abikeyeva**, Artistic Director.

(l-r) Artistic director Gulnara Abikeyeva, jury members – Jilles Marchand, Kim Ki-Duk, Vladimir Khotinenko. Photo: Isturgan Aduev.

Fajr International Film Festival
February 1–11, 2012
Iranian International Market for Films and TV Programmes
February 2–6, 2012

In the international programme of the Festival, there are three different competitive sections: 'International Competition', 'Competition of Films from Islamic Countries' (emphasising cinema's role as a way for salvation) and 'Competition of Asian Cinema' (organised with the aim of promoting film art and industry in Asian countries). The non-competitive sections include 'Festival of Festivals' (a selection of outstanding films presented at other international festivals), 'Special Screenings' (films of documentary or narrative content which introduce cinema or cultural developments in certain geographical regions), retrospectives, etc. Coinciding with the international programme, the Iranian Film Market (IFM) provides not only a friendly

Fajr International Film Festival 2011

atmosphere for cutting deals, but also a unique showcase for new Iranian productions with English subtitles or simultaneous translation, premiered for the international participants. In the national programme, there are different competitive sections as well. Director: Mohammad Khazaie. *Inquiries to:* Fajr International Film Festival, No. 13, 2nd Floor, Delbar Alley, Toos St, Valiye Asr Ave, Tehran 19617-44973, Iran. Tel: (98 21) 2274 1250/1251. Fax: 2273 4801; e: office@fajrfestival.ir; web: www.fajrfestival.ir.

30th Fajr International Film Festival

February 1st/11th
2012
Tehran-Iran

Organization of Fajr Int'l Film Festival
13, Delbar Alley, Toos St., Valiye Asr Ave.,Tehran 19617 Iran.
Tel:+98 21 22741250-1/+98 21 22735090
Fax:+98 21 22734801
E-mail:office@fajrfestival.ir

AWARDS 2011

International Competition:

Best Film: **Lola** (France/Philippines), Brillante Mendoza.

Best Director: Dariush Mehrjui for **Beloved Sky** (Iran).

Best Script: **Honey** (Germany/Turkey), Semih Kaplanoglu and Orcun Koksal.

Special Jury Prize: **The Facing Mirrors** (Iran), Negar Azarbaijani.

Best Performance: Anita Linda and Rustica Carpio for **Lola** (France/Philippines).

Best Artistic Achievement: **How I Ended This Summer** (Russia), Pavel Kostomarov.

Special Mention: **Son of Babylon** (Iraq), Mohamad Al-Daradji.

Competition of Asian Cinema:

Best Film: **My Mongolian Mother** (China), Ning Cai.

Best Director: Liu Jie for **Deep in the Clouds** (China).

Best Script: **My Mongolian Mother** (China), Lo Jianfan and Ning Cai.

Special Jury Prize: **The One Man Village** (Lebanon), Simon El Habre.

Best Performance: Mahtab Keramati, Faramarz Gharibian, Mehran Ahmadi and Mehdi Hashemi for **Alzheimer** (Iran).

Best Artistic Achievement: **The Maritime Silk Road** (Iran), Parvin Safari and Bahram Badakhshani.

Interfaith Award: **Golchehreh** (Iran), Vahid Mousaian.

Human Rights Special Mention: **33 Days** (Iran), Jamal Shoorjo.

Golden Flag/Moustapha Akkad Special Prize: **Alzheimer** (Iran), Ahmad Reza Motamedi.

Report 2011

In the 29th edition of the Festival, Rustam Ibragimbekov (screenwriter/Azerbaijan), Nikolay Burlyaev (actor/Russia), Anne Demy-Geroe (film academic and festival curator/Australia), Pouran Derakhshandeh (filmmaker/Iran) and Donald Ranvaud (producer/UK) were the members of the International Jury, while Mohamed Al-Daradji (filmmaker/Iraq), Salma Al-Masri (actress/Syria), Jabbar Patel (festival

February 2nd to 6th, 2012 / Tehran

iifm

2012

15TH

IRANIAN INTERNATIONAL

MARKET

FOR
Films and TV Programs

Organization of Fajr Int'l Film Festival
13, Delbar Alley, Toos St., Valiye Asr Ave.,Tehran 19617, Iran.
Tel: +98 (21) 22741252-4, 22734939
Fax: +98 (21) 22734953
E-mail: fcf1@dpi.net.ir

director and filmmaker/India), Nosir Saidov (filmmaker/Tajikistan) and Alireza Shojanoori (producer and distributor/Iran) served on the jury of the 'Competition of Asian Cinema'. The success of Asian Films was a landmark in Fajr 2011. **– Amir Esfandiari**, Head of International Affairs.

Fantasporto
February 24–March 3, 2012
February 22–March 2, 2013

The Oporto International Film Festival – Fantasporto, the most important film festival in Portugal takes place every year in Oporto, a UNESCO World Heritage City. The Festival was founded in 1981 and still has the same team running it. It is state- and privately-funded. It began with one competition, 'Fantasy – Shorts and Features', evolving in 1991 to a general festival with the new competition, the 'Directors Week'. Now a third competition, dedicated to Asian films, 'Orient Express', adds further depth to the programme. It screens premieres and previews and always has a showcase of the latest Portuguese Cinema, called 'Panorama do Cinema Português'. There are also retrospectives and animated films, on-stage interviews, press conferences, workshops and several sidebars. The 'Retrospective' section includes a focus on emerging talent, as well as established names. The newest addition to the programme is the 'Special Programme', which intertwines Cinema and the Arts and Sciences. With the presence of specialists, both national and

Festival Director, Beatriz Pacheco Pereira, with International Film Guide Editor, Ian Haydn Smith. Photo: Lauren Maganete.

foreign, the Festival already discussed Cinema and Architecture (2009), Robotics and Special Effects (2010) and the Fine Arts in 2011. In 2012 the subject will be Science Fiction and the Performing Arts. Fantasporto screens around 250 films every year and the event closes with an all-night party called the Vampires' Ball. Directors: Beatriz Pacheco Pereira and Mário Dorminsky. *Inquiries to:* Fantasporto, Rua Anibal Cunha 84, Sala 1.6, 4050-048 Porto, Portugal. Tel: (35 1) 222 058 819; e: info@ fantasporto.com; web: www.fantasporto.com.

AWARDS 2011
Official Fantasy Section
Best Film Award Grand Prix: **Two Eyes Staring** (The Netherlands), Elbert Van Strien.
Jury's Special Award: **A Serbian Film** (Serbia), Srdjan Spasojevic.
Best Direction: **I Saw the Devil** (South Korea), Kim Jee-won.
Best Actor: Axel Wedekind for **Iron Doors** (Republic of Ireland).
Best Actress: Seo Yeong-hee for **Bedevilled** (South Korea).
Best Screenplay: Elbert Van Strien and Paulo van Vlietfor for **Two Eyes Staring** (The Netherlands).
Best Special Effects or Cinematography: **La Herencia Valdemar II: La Sombra Prohibida** (Spain), José Luís Alemán.
Best Short Film: **Brutal Relax** (Spain), David Muñoz.
21st Director's Week
Best Film Award/Manoel de Oliveira Award: **The Housemaid** (South Korea), Im Sang-soo.
Jury's Special Award: **Miyoko** (Japan), Yoshifumi Tsubota.

The outside of the Rivoli Theatre at the 31st Fantasporto. Photo: Lauren Maganete.

Best Director: **Carancho** (Argentina), Pablo Trapero.
Best Screenplay: **Miyoko** (Japan), Yoshifumi Tsubota.
Best Actor: Jeon Do-yeon for **The Housemaid** (South Korea).
Best Actress: Lee Jung-jae for **The Housemaid** (South Korea).
Orient Express Official Section
Best Film Award: **I Saw the Devil** (South Korea), Kim Jee-won.
International Film Guide Inspiration Award and Special Jury Award: **Enemy at the Dead End** (South Korea), Park Soo-young.
Critics Award: **Rabies** (Israel), Aharon Keshales and Navot Papushado.
Audience Award: **The Extraordinary Adventures of Adèle Blanc-Sec** (France), Luc Besson.
Career Awards: Mick Garris (USA), Maria de Medeiros (Portugal), Paulo Trancoso (Portugal), João Menezes (Portugal).

Report 2011

Fantasporto screened seventeen documentaries about painters and sculptors (part of its special programme dedicated to the Fine Arts) and created two new awards for Portuguese cinema. Elbert van Strien's *Two Eyes Staring* won the Best Film Award. It was voted for by a jury comprised of directors Mick Garris (USA) and Julian Grant (Canada), and the Spanish journalist Raoul Gil Toural. The film also picked up the Award for Best Screenplay. The 21st Directors' Week was dominated by Asian cinema. *The Housemaid* by Im Sang-soo left no one indifferent and was awarded Best Film by a jury consisting of

Festival Director Mario Dorminsky outside one of the screenings. Photo: Lauren Maganete.

actress Maria de Medeiros (*Pulp Fiction*), and filmmakers Tiago Guedes (Portugal) and Stefan Le Lay (France). In the 'Orient Express' Official Section Kim Jee-woon won again. After his success with *The Tale of Two Sisters*, he won the Orient Express Best Film Award for *I Saw the Devil*. The Jury of the 'Official Fantasy' section gave it the Best Director Award, while the Jury of the 'Orient Express' (Xosé Carlos Fernandez, Spanish producer; Stephan Weiz, German distributor; François Casales – Belgian journalist) awarded it the Best Film prize. *A Serbian Film* won the Special Jury Prize. The 21st Week also had an Asian accent. The Directors' Week/Manoel de Oliveira award went to *The Housemaid*, which also picked up the best actor and actress awards. The audience of Fantasporto 2011 voted for the latest film by French director and producer Luc Besson. *The Extraordinary Adventures of Adèle Blanc Sec* is an adventure film about an intrepid journalist who, besides writing, is also part of the news, fighting mummies in Egypt as in Paris. **– Beatriz Pacheco Pereira and Mário Dorminsky**, Festival Directors.

Far East Film Festival
April 20–28, 2012

Born in 1998, the Far East Film Festival is the most highly anticipated annual event in Udine. A popular festival, a celebration of cinema that has cut a truly unique place for itself, presents international and European premieres of films from Japan, China, Hong Kong, Thailand, Philippines, Indonesia, Malaysia, South Korea, Taiwan, Vietnam and Singapore. With an overall attendance of over 50,000 people, Far East Film Festival has seen, year after year, an increase in interest from the international, national and local public, as well as over 1,200 accreditation requests from journalists and buyers coming from Europe, Asia and America. Far East Film is now considered the most important showcase for Asian cinema in Europe. *Inquiries to:* Centro Espressioni Cinematografiche, Via Villalta 24, 33100 Udine, Italy. Tel: (39 04) 3229 9545; e: fareastfilm@ cecudine.org; web: www.fareastfilm.com.

AWARDS 2011
The Festival doesn't have a jury so all the awards are voted for by the audience. The Audience Awards are voted for by the regular audience as well as by the White Dragon Accreditation Holders. The Black Dragon Awards are voted for by the Black Dragon Accreditation holders that support the Festival paying a higher price for the accreditation. The MyMovies Award is voted for by the users of the MyMovies website.
Audience Award First Prize: **Aftershock** (China), Feng Xiaogang.

Michael Hui on satge receiving the Golden Mulberry Award for his Career Achievement. Photo: Rick Modena.

Audience Award Second Prize: **Under the Hawthorn Tree** (China), Zhang Yimou.
Audience Award Third Prize: **Here Comes the Bride** (Philippines), Chris Martinez.
Black Dragon Award First Prize: **Confessions** (Japan), Nakashima Tetsuya.
Mymovies Award: **Confessions** (Japan), Nakashima Tetsuya.
Technicolor Asia Award: **A Crazy Little Thing Called Love** (Thailand), Sakonnakorn Puttipong Promsakha Na and Pokpong Wasin.

Report 2011
In the most recent edition the Festival organised two retrospectives: 'Asia Laughs!', a survey of Asian comedy films, and 'Pink Wink', a tribute to Asakura Daisuke and to the Japanese Pink movies. Ms Asakura Daisuke was present in Udine for the screenings. For the first time this year the Far East Film Festival gave the Golden Mulberry Award for Career Achievement to Michael Hui, who was one of the guests invited for the comedy retrospective 'Asia Laughs!' – **Linda Carello**, Executive Manager.

Festival International du Film Francophone de Namur
Late September/early October 2012

The Festival promotes French-speaking film and diffuses French-speaking feature-length and documentary films and tries, for this purpose, to gather in Namur all the directors, producers, screenwriters, actors and distributors involved in French-speaking cinema. The Festival also contributes to the education and the training of young people, offering activities and space to develop. The Bayards offer prizes for competition winners in the following sections: feature films, short films and first works. *Inquiries to:* Festival International du Film Francophone de Namur, 175, Rue des Brasseurs, 5000 Namur, Belgium. Tel: (32 81) 241 236; e: info@fiff.be; web: www.fiff.be.

Festroia
June 2012

Festroia (Festival Internacional de Cine de Setubal) will feature around 180 films from forty countries. This year's Festival features the usual competitive sections – 'Official Section', 'First Works' and 'Man and Nature'. *Inquiries to:* Festroia, Rua Antonio J da Silva, 11, 2900-430 Setúbal, Portugal. Tel: (351 265) 525 908; e: info@festroia.pt; web: www.festroia.pt.

Giffoni International Film Festival (Giffoni Experience)
July 2012

Founded in 1971 by Claudio Gubitosi to promote films for young audiences and families, the Festival is located in a small town about forty minutes from Naples. It includes five competitive sections: 'Elements +6' (animated and fiction feature-length films and shorts that tell fantastic stories, juried by 500 children aged 6 to 9); 'Elements +10' (animated and fiction feature-length films and shorts, mainly fantasy and adventure, juried by 500 children aged 10 to 12); 'Generator +13' sees 450 teenagers (aged 13 to 15) assessing features and shorts about the pre-adolescent world; 'Generator +16' has 400 jurors (aged 16 to 19) and focuses on films for young people. 'Troubled Gaze' has 100 jurors (from 19 years old) and looks at films that explore the relationship between children and parents. *Inquiries to:* Giffoni Film Festival, Cittadella del Cinema, Via Aldo Moro 4, 84095 Giffoni Valle Piana, Italy. Tel: (39 089) 802 3001; e: info@giffoniff.it; web: www.giffonifilmfestival.it

Gijón International Film Festival
Late November 2012

Celebrating its 50th edition in 2012, Gijón is now at the peak of its popularity. Having firmly established itself as a barometer of new film trends worldwide, it draws a large and enthusiastic public. Gijón has built on its niche as a festival for young people, programming innovative and independent films made by and for the young, including retrospectives, panoramas, exhibitions and concerts. Alongside the lively 'Official Section', sidebars celebrate directors who have forged new paths in filmmaking. *Inquiries to:* Gijón International Film Festival, Casa de la Palmera, 82 Calle Cabrales, 33201 Gijon, Spain. Tel: (34 98) 518 2940; e: info@gijonfilmfestival.com; web: www.gijonfilmfestival.com.

goEast Festival of Central and Eastern European Film
April 18–24, 2012

Every year since goEast was founded by Deutsches Filminstitut in 2001, the Festival has provided an annual showcase for filmmaking in Central and Eastern Europe. A wealth of cinematic breadth and variety unfolds in the course of the seven days of the Festival: current tendencies, experimental positions,

From left to right: Maria Schrader (German Actress and Director), Stefan Adrian (Executive Director), Gaby Babić (Festival Director) at the goEast-Matinee. Photo: Kristin Stock.

and historical rarities, always against the background of socio-political, film-aesthetic and film-theoretical debates. Conceived as a forum of East-West dialogue, the Festival also sees itself as an agent and disseminator of creative interaction: panels and workshops, film series and discussions, co-operative agreements with other cultural and social institutions. The Festival pursues a cultural mission: to provide a public platform for remarkable, unusual and engaged films unlikely to find distribution on the commercial cinema circuit. Carefully compiled programmes successfully blend art-house cinema with mainstream films. Festival visitors – filmmakers and industry specialists from Germany and abroad, local film enthusiasts and international guests – are invariably enthused by the quality and special atmosphere of a festival that facilitates the exchange of skills and knowledge. Young filmmakers and children and young people from the region particularly profit from the emphasis goEast places on creative exploration and educational offerings. The Festival hosts FIPRESCI Jury. *Inquiries to:* Deutsches Filminstitut - DIF, goEast Film Festival, Schaumainkai 41, 60596 Frankfurt M, Germany. Tel: (49 611) 236 843-0; e:info@filmfestival-goeast.de; web: www.filmfestival-goeast.de.

AWARDS 2011

Competition
The Škoda Award for Best Film – the 'Golden Lily': **A Stoker** (Russia), Alexey Balabanov.
Award of the City of Wiesbaden for Best Director: **Morgen** (Romania), Marian Crişan.

Documentary Award – 'Remembrance and Future': **The Last Days of Summer** (Poland), Piotr Stasik.
Award of the Federal Foreign Office: **Gorelovka** (Georgia), Alexander Kviria.
FIPRESCI Prize: **A Stoker** (Russia), Alexey Balabanov.
Student Competition
The BHF-BANK Foundation Award: **Through Glass** (Poland), Igor Chojna.
Audience Awards
Documentaries: **August 2008** (Georgia) Anna Cherkezishvili.
Animated and Experimental Films: **B-1033** (Poland), Paweł Kryszak.
Fiction Shorts: **Through Glass** (Poland), Igor Chojna.
Co-Production Prize of the Robert Bosch Stiftung
Category Animated Film: **Breaking News** (Germany/Kosovo/Russia, Alexandra Lukina.
Category Documentary Film: **Roma Rally** (Germany/Hungary), Gabór Hörcher.
Category Short Feature Film: **Pepsi** (Germany/Romania), Peter Kerek.

Report 2011

'And the Golden Lily goes to...' Announcing the Main Prize winner in Caligari FilmBühne, Wiesbaden, was the last official act by goEast Jury President Želimir Žilnik and his co-jurors. Guests then flocked to the City of Wiesbaden's traditional closing reception in Wiesbaden town hall, which was followed by a memorable party in the Kulturpalast venue. By the end of the festival week, more than 9,000 visitors had viewed 127 short and full-length films from thirty different countries, among them numerous German and international premieres. New festival director Gaby Babić introduced a new section to goEast 2011: 'Beyond Belonging', which also heralded an expansion of the Festival's geographical range. Over the course of three days the goEast Symposium 'Marching Into the Picture – The New Right in Eastern European Film', curated by Grit Lemke, offered searching insight into the phenomenon of right-wing extremism in Central and Eastern Europe.

The films and lectures brought home to the audience the alarming speed at which old and new prejudices and resentments have blended into a form acceptable to far too much of the electorate. The homage to Jan Švankmajer as well as a workshop discussion with his principal animator Bedřich Glaser were further festival highlights, alongside the comprehensive Students' Section. Another guest of honour at goEast 2011 was actress Maria Schrader, who enchanted the Sunday Matinée audience when interviewed by Rudolf Worschech, editor-in-chief at EPD-film.
– **Stefan Adrian**, Executive Director.

Haugesund – Norwegian International Film Festival

New Nordic Films: August 15–18, 2012
The Amanda Awards Ceremony: August 17, 2012
The Norwegian International Film Festival:
August 17–23, 2012

Situated on the west coast of Norway, this charming festival, often called the 'Nordic Cannes', is a gateway to the Norwegian film industry. With Liv Ullmann as Honorary President, The Norwegian Film Festival brings together the complete Norwegian film industry and press corps, who participate in red carpet screenings, festival parties and events, along with our most famous actors and actresses. The Amanda Awards ceremony – the Norwegian Oscar™ – will celebrate the previous year's Norwegian film production during a live TV show. The market programme consists of films at three different levels in the production phase; screening of the best

completed Nordic films from 2012, a showcase for works in progress of upcoming films and a successful co-production and film financing forum. Festival Director: Gunnar Johan Løvvik. Programme Director: Tonje Hardersen. *Inquiries to:* Norwegian International Film Festival, PO Box 145, N-5501 Haugesund, Norway. Tel: (47 52) 743 370; e: info@ filmfestivalen.no; web: www.filmfestivalen.no.

The red carpet in front of Edda kino, Haugesund, where Festival Director Gunnar Johan Løvvik (left) is greeting Swedish actress Lena Endre and Kantinka Farago (right). Photo: Helge Hansen.

AWARDS 2011

Norwegian Film Critics Award: **Oslo, August 31st** (Norway), Joachim Trier.
Ray of Sunshine: **The Help** (USA), Tate Taylor.
Audience Award: **The Help** (USA), Tate Taylor.
Andreas Award: **The Tree of Life** (USA), Terrence Malick.

Report 2011

A total of 93 films, including 15 films during New Nordic Films, were screened during the Festival. There were presentations of 14 works in progress, 21 Nordic co-productions and

five Nordic screenplays. In all, more than 140 productions were screened or presented in Haugesund during the ten days of the Festival. Some 1,410 professionals from 25 countries visited the Festival. A number of seminars for film professionals were held in co-operation with the various industry organisations and the National film school. The Festival's focus on screenwriters was reflected in a number of interesting encounters between the screenwriters, the industry and audiences. – **Nina Mari Bræin**, Head of Press.

Hof International Film Festival/ Internationale Hofer Filmtage
October 23–28, 2012

The Hof International Film Festival – often nicknamed 'The German Telluride' – was founded in the northern Bavarian town of Hof in 1968 by current festival director Heinz Badewitz and several up-and-coming filmmakers of the day (Wim Wenders, Volker Schloendorff, Werner Herzog and Rainer Werner Fassbinder among them) and has since gone on to become one of the most important film festivals in Germany, concentrating both on German films by the new filmmaking generation and independent films from abroad. There are also retrospectives that have so far celebrated the work of Monte Hellman, Mike Leigh, John Sayles, Brian de Palma, Peter Jackson, Roger Corman, John Cassavetes, Costa-Gavras, Wayne Wang, Bob Rafelson and David MacKenzie. It is a festival that not only attracts cinema goers and critics, but also filmmakers, producers, distributors and the media. *Inquiries to:* Hof International Film Festival, Altstadt 8, D-95028 Hof, Germany. Fax: (49) 9281 18816; e: info@hofer-filmtage.de. Web: www.hofer-filmtage.com.

Report 2011
The 45th Hof International Film Festival centred on young English filmmaker David Mackenzie, who received his first career retrospective. The programme included all seven of his feature films – including his very

*Jazz legend and composer Klaus Doldinger (**Das Boot***) with festival director Heinz Badewitz and US director Ramin Niami (**Babe's and Ricky's Inn***) at Hof IFF. Photo: Dieter Neidhardt.*

latest production, *You Instead* – as well as four of his shorts. In all, 117 films were screened at the Festival's latest edition, 74 of which were full-length features. Twenty films were documentaries and more than fifty were international productions. As for prizes, they ate traditionally not awarded by the Festival itself, since all films are judged to be of equal importance and quality. The City of Hof Award is given to a German director or actor close to the Festival. This year the award – a locally crafted porcelain sculpture – went to the Austrian director, actor and writer Peter Kern. The Young German Cinema Award is given by Bavaria Film, Bavarian Broadcasting (BR) and HypoVereinsbank, in recognition of an outstanding work of artistic merit in a German-language film screened in Hof and is given to a young person in any production category (excluding directors and actors). The award which includes prize money of €10,000, went to cinematographer Lars Petersen for his work on *Bastard* (directed by Carsten Unger) and to Julian Wagner for the production design in *Colour of the Ocean* (directed by Maggie Peren). The Eastman Award for Young Talents is awarded by Kodak Germany and includes €4,000's worth of film stock. It was awarded to Felix Charin for *Leben Lassen*. **– Rainer Huebsch**.

International Film Festival and Forum on Human Rights (FIFDH)
March 2–11, 2012

The inspiration and impetus behind the International Film Festival and Forum on Human Rights (FIFDH) came from Human Rights defenders, filmmakers, representatives from the media and the University of Geneva. The FIFDH coincides with the UN Human Rights Council and is a platform for all public and private actors defending human dignity. The Festival is an International Forum on Human Rights that informs and denounces violations wherever they take place. Situated in the heart of Geneva, the International Capital for Human Rights, the Festival also serves as a go-between for all human rights activists. For ten days, it offers debates, original film screenings and solidarity initiatives. With its concept '*a film, a subject, a debate*', the aim of the FIFDH is to denounce attacks on human dignity and to raise public awareness through films and debates in the presence of filmmakers, defenders of human rights and recognised specialists. *Inquiries to:* Leo Kaneman, Director General and Jeffrey Hodgson, Deputy Director, Maison des Arts du Grütli, 16 rue Général Dufour, CP 5251 CH 1211 Geneva 11, Switzerland. Tel: (41 22) 809 6900; e: contact@fifdh.ch; web: www.fifdh.ch.

Debate at the FIFDH, Geneva 2011. Photo: Miguel Bueno.

AWARDS 2011

Grand Prix FIFDH: **Rainmakers** (The
Netherlands), Floris-Jan Van Luyn.
Special Mention: **The Devil Operation**
(Canada/Peru), Stephanie Boyd.
*Barbara Hendricks Foundation for Peace and
Reconciliation Award:* **Granito** (Guatemala/
Spain/USA), Pamela Yates.
OMCT Award: **Qui A Tue Natacha** (France),
Mylène Sauloy.
Special Mention: **Impunity** (Colombia/France/
Switzerland), Juan José Lozano and Hollman
Morris.
Youth Jury Award: **The Green Wave**
(Germany), Ali Samadi Ahadi.

Report 2011

Once again, the International Film Festival and
Forum on Human Rights (FIFDH) in Geneva
raised awareness through its concept *'a film,
a subect, a debate'*, on the struggle for human
rights worldwide. By the time this year's
edition ended, more than 20,000 festival-
goers had attended the films and participated
in accompanying debates. The Festival was
organised around current pressing topics such
as 'Human rights are not negotiable', 'Europe
under the boot of populism', 'Arab uprisings
and after?', 'Development which kills', 'The
right to be a Roma', 'The combat of women
against sexual crimes', 'The oppression
of the Sahraoui', 'Journalists – targets of
terrorism', 'Violence at the polls', 'Justice
facing history', 'Are private security firms
above the law?', among others. They provoked
enormous interest and involvement. Among

the Festival's ninety guests, Judge Garzón,
Viviane Reding, Stephane Hessel, Adam
Michnik, Ruth Dreifuss, Robert Guédiguian,
Axelle Red and Antonio Tabucchi, were some
of the high-profile personalities who attracted
large crowds, keen to debate crucial civil
liberties issues with them – precisely the kind
of exchange needed if people are to mobilise
in support of human-rights victims and further
the cause of human rights. The 2011 jury
was comprised of: Spanish French writer,
scriptwriter and politician Jorge Semprun,
French actress, film and theatre director Zabou
Breitman, French Tunisian historian, researcher
and Deputy Secretary General of the FIDH
Sophie Bessis, Iranian film director Jafar
Panahi (who was not present due to his being
under house arrest in Iran) and Turkish film
director Hüseyin Karabey. – **Jeffrey Hodgson**,
Deputy Director.

International Film Festival of India
Late November/early December 2012

In 2004, IFFI was moved to Goa. Since then
it has been an annual competitive event. It
is government-funded, recognised by FIAPF
and held under the aegis of India's Ministry of
Information and Broadcasting. It features the
comprehensive 'Cinema of the World' section,
foreign and Indian retrospectives and a film
market, plus a valuable panorama of the year's
best Indian films, subtitled in English. *Inquiries
to:* The Directorate of Film Festivals, Sirifort
Cultural Complex, August Kranti Marg, New
Delhi 110049, India. Tel: (91 11) 2649 0457;
e: iffifilms@gmail.com; web: www.iffi.nic.in.

Isfahan International Festival of Films
for Children and Young Adults
October 2012

International Festival of Films for Children and
Young Adults includes different competitive
sections: the 'International Competition of
Short and Feature Films' and the 'International
Competition of Short and Feature Animated
Works'. Three international juries judge the
films: International Jury, International Youth

Jury and CIFEJ Jury. Also there are some non-competitive sections such as out of competition, special screenings, tributes and retrospectives. In the national section, new Iranian children films and videos are screened in the competitive sections. Director: Seyed Ahmad Mir-Alaee. *Inquiries to:* International Children Film Festival Office, 13, 2nd Floor, Delbar Alley, Toos Street, Valiye Asr Avenue, Tehran, 19617-44973, Iran. Tel: (98 21) 2274 1250/1251. Fax: (98 21) 2273 480; e: office@ icff.ir; web: www.icff.ir.

Isfahan International Festival of Films for Children and Young Adults

AWARDS 2011
International Sections
International Competition of Animated Works
Golden Butterfly Award for the Best Short Film: **Monster Sacre** (France), Jean-Pierre Lemouland.
Golden Butterfly Award for Special Jury Prize: **Little Voices** (Colombia), Jairo Eduardo Carrillo.
Golden Butterfly Award for the Best Feature Film: **Leafie, A Hen into the Wild** (South Korea), Eun Lee, Jaemyung Dhim and Sunku Kim.
International Competition of Live Action Works
Golden Butterfly Award for Best Film: **Wind & Fog** (Iran), Naser Dehghani Poudeh.
Golden Butterfly Award for Best Director: **Winter's Daughter** (Germany/Poland), Johannes Schmid.
Golden Butterfly Award for the Best Script: Salman Aristo for **The Dreamer** (Indonesia).
Golden Butterfly Award for Special Jury Prize: **On the Sly** (Belgium/France), Olivier Ringer.

Golden Butterfly Award for the Best Short Film: **Mokhtar** (Canada), Halimeh Ouardiri.
Golden Butterfly Award for the Best Asian Feature Film: **Harun-Arun** (India), Vinod Ganatra.
Golden Butterfly Award for the Best Creative Technical or Artistic Achievements: **A Tale of Ululu's Wonderful Forest** (Japan), Osamu Fujiishi.
Golden Butterfly Award for the Best Young Performer: Aldo Tansani for **Garuda in My Heart** (Indonesia).
Jury Honour Diploma: **The Sound of My Foot** (Iran), Mehrdad Khoshbakht.
CIFEJ PRIZE: **The Dreamer** (Indonesia), Riri Riza.

Report 2011
After spending four years in Hamedan, one of the oldest cities in Iran, the International Film Festival for Children and Young Adults (held November 14–18, 2011) once again moved to the historic city of marvels, Isfahan, on its 25th anniversary. In the presence of more than seventy international guests and some 370 national film figures, the Festival focused on two competitive international sections: 'Competition of Live-Action Films' and 'Competition of Animated Works'. The International Jury of the Festival, presided over by Polish filmmaker and CIFEJ board member, Andrzej Roman Jasiewicz, working with Buster Film Festival director, Fusun Eriksen, president of Pandora, Rie Nakano, artistic director of Zagreb Film, Simon Bogojevic Narath, Syrian animator, Sulafa Hijazi, Iranian veteran filmmaker, Pouran Derakhshandeh, and Iranian actor, Alireza Khamseh, watched eleven feature films and fourteen short films in this section. There were some 150 feature and around a hundred short live-action films submitted to the Festival this year. In the 'Competition of Animated Works', 23 members of the International Youth Jury (from Armenia, Bangladesh, India, Italy, South Korea, Spain, Tajikistan, Tunisia, Venezuela and Iran) decided about nine features and twenty short animations selected from some 150 submissions. **– Amir Esfandiari**, Head of International Affairs.

Istanbul Film Festival
March 31–April 15, 2012

The only film festival to take place on two continents, the Istanbul Film Festival boasts the largest attendance in for a festival in Turkey, with 150,000 in 2011. In its 31st edition, the Festival will be part of the celebrations of two anniversaries: the 400th year of Turkish-Dutch diplomatic relations, and the 'China Year' in Turkey. In parallel to these celebrations, special sections will be curated, including sections on Dutch animation and children's films, also contemporary film from China. In addition to panel discussions and an exhibition, a co-production and project exchange workshop will also take place. The 2012 edition will feature the seventh edition of its industry event, Meetings on the Bridge, and the fifth edition of the award-giving feature-film development workshop. The Festival programme focuses on features dealing with the arts and the artist, and literary adaptations, in its main competition, the Golden Tulip: selections from world festivals, with other thematic sections such as, 'Human Rights in Cinema' with the Council of Europe Film Award – FACE, 'Mined Zone', 'Documentary Time', 'Young Masters', 'Midnight Madness' and a competitive showcase of Turkish cinema with emphasis on new talents and innovative approaches. *Inquiries to:* Ms Azize Tan, Istanbul Foundation for Culture and Arts, Sadi Konuralp 5, Sishane 34433, Istanbul, Turkey. T: (90 212) 334 0720; e: film.fest@iksv.org; web: film.iksv.org.

AWARDS 2011
International Competition
Golden Tulip: **Microphone** (Egypt), Ahmad Abdalla.
Special Prize of the Jury: ex-aequo to **Our Grand Despair** (Germany, The Netherlands, Turkey), Seyfi Teoman and **Useful Life** (Spain, Uruguay), Federico Veiroj.
FIPRESCI Prize: **Norwegian Wood** (Japan), Tran Anh Hung.
FACE Award: **As If I'm Not There** (Macedonia, Republic of Ireland, Sweden), Juanita Wilson.
FACE Award Special Prize of the Jury: **Press**

(Turkey), Sedat Yılmaz.
People's Choice Awards: **Our Grand Despair** (Germany, The Netherlands, Turkey), Seyfi Teoman.

Jeonju International Film Festival
Late April/early May 2012

JIFF is now recognised as one of the most important film festivals in Asia, screening independent and experimental films from around the world. It presents a variety of contemporary films to an appreciative audience. Since 2000, a number of new filmmakers have been introduced on to the world stage through JIFF. The Festival's wide range of programmes include masterclasses, various retrospectives and special screenings. The two main projects of the Festival are the Jeonju Digital Project and Short! Short! Short! *Inquiries to:* Jeonju International Film Festival, 5F Girin Officetel, 155-1 Gosa Dong, Wansan Gu, Jeonju 560-706, South Korea. Tel: (82 63) 288 5433; e: media@ jiff.or.kr; web: www.jiff.or.kr.

Jerusalem International Film Festival
July 5–14, 2012

Celebrating its 29th Anniversary this year, the Jerusalem International Film Festival, Israel's most prestigious cinematic event, offers an alternative Middle East headline – that those of all faiths, ethnicities and political positions have the opportunity to sit side-by-side in the shadow of the silver screen – to be moved, to share discourse and yes, to hope. Our Opening Gala event attracts over 6,000 spectators, under the stars, in the shadow of the ancient Jerusalem Walls. During the Festival over 70,000 people increase their awareness of contemporary world cinema. The Festival's programme will present 150 films in a wide spectrum of themes and categories, focusing on the best of international cinema; best of new Israeli cinema; human rights and social justice. Other categories include: documentaries; animation; Jewish themes; retrospectives; avant garde; restorations; special tributes and classics. The Festival has become the largest local market for international films, where distributors from all over the world have the opportunity to bring the finest of world cinema to the growing and increasingly influential Israeli audience. Israeli filmmakers have the world premiere of their films at the Festival knowing that a strong local reaction is key to a new Israeli film's success throughout Europe and the world. The Festival offers dozens of professional events and seminars, designed to promote and assist local filmmakers and to connect Israel to the European and international Industry. The Festival has become not only the harbinger and launching point for new and cutting edge Israeli cinema, but also an active and proud promoter. Past examples include, The Jerusalem Pitch Point – for the sixth year running, the Festival has held a meeting place for Israeli filmmakers and producers with key members of the European and international film industry whose aim is to encourage and promote co-productions with Europe, and beyond, of Israeli full-length feature films. Submission deadline: April 1, 2012. *Inquiries to:* Jerusalem Film Festival, Hebron Road 11, Jerusalem 91083, Israel. Tel: (972 2) 565 4333; e: daniel@jff.org.il; web: www.jff.org.il.

Karlovy Vary International Film Festival
July 1–9, 2012

Founded in 1946, Karlovy Vary is one of the most important film events in Central and Eastern Europe. It includes an 'Official Selection' – 'Competition', 'Documentary Films in Competition', 'East of the West' – 'Films in Competition' and other programme sections which give the unique chance to see new film production from all around the world. Film entry deadline: April 1, 2012. *Inquiries to:* Film Servis Festival Karlovy Vary, Panská 1, CZ 110 00 Prague 1, Czech Republic. Tel: (420 2) 2141 1011; e: festival@kviff.com; web: www.kviff.com.

AWARDS 2011
Grand Prix – Crystal Globe: **Restoration** (Israel), Joseph Madmony.
Best Director: Pascal Rabaté for **Holidays by the Sea** (France).

Best Actress: Stine Fischer Christensen for **Cracks in the Shell** (Germany).
Best Actor: David Morse for **Collaborator** (Canada/USA).
Best Documentary Film Under 30 Minutes: **Declaration of Immortality** (Poland), Marcin Koszałka.
Best Documentary Film Over 30 Minutes: **The Good Life** (Denmark), Eva Mulvad.
East of the West Award: **Punk's Not Dead** (Macedonia/Serbia), Vladimir Blaževski.
Crystal Globe for Outstanding Artistic Contribution to World Cinema: Judi Dench (UK).

International Film Festival of Kerala
December 7–14, 2012

The Festival boasts an extremely popular competition section for films produced or co-produced in Asia, Africa and Latin America within the last year. The usual sections include world cinema, a focus on Malayalam cinema, the latest in Indian cinema, retrospectives, homages and tributes. *Inquiries to:* International Film Festival of Kerala, Kerala State Chalachitra Academy, Mani Bhavan, Sasthamangalam, Trivandum, Kerala 695010, India. Tel: (91 471) 231 0323; web: www.iffk.in.

Kolkata Film Festival
November 2012

Celebrating its 18th edition in 2012, the Festival has grown over the years with ever-increasing numbers of visitors. This year it will screen over 150 films at eleven venues across the city. In earlier editions, legendary filmmakers such as Miguel Littin, Fernando Solanas, Ali Ozgenturk, Amos Gitai, Krzysztof Zanussi, Catherine Breillat, Jeon Soo-il, Gus Van Sant, Jafar Panahi, Tehmina Milani and others have graced the Festival with their presence. Recognised as a major film event in India and overseas, the Festival will once again showcase a host of quality movies from around the world in the presence of prominent guests and enthusiasts. *Inquiries to:* Kolkata Film Festival, 1/1 A J C Bose Road, Kolkata 700020, India. Tel: (91) 33 2223 1210. e: info@kff.in. Web: www.kff.in.

www.iffk.in

17th

INTERNATIONAL
FILM FESTIVAL OF KERALA
7-14 DECEMBER 2012
THIRUVANANTHAPURAM, KERALA, INDIA

iffk

attractive competition for films produced in
africa, asia and latin america

Recognised by
FIAPF, NETPAC

FIAPF

NETPAC

organized by
The Kerala State Chalachitra Academy on
behalf of the Govt of Kerala

e-mail: info@iffk.in, iffkoffice@gmail.com

Krakow Film Festival
May 28–June 3, 2012

One of the oldest film events dedicated to documentary, animated and short fiction films in Europe. Visitors have an opportunity to watch around 250 films from Poland and abroad. Films are presented in competitions and in special sections like retrospectives, thematic cycles and archive screenings. The Festival is accompanied by exhibitions, concerts, open-air screenings and meetings with the filmmakers. Every year, the Festival hosts over 500 Polish and international guests: directors, producers and film festival programmers. The Festival is divided into three sections: 'International Documentary Film Competition' (new), 'International Short Film Competition' and the 'National Competition'. The diverse programme also includes retrospectives, themed platforms and tributes. The Festival is accompanied by the Krakow Film Market and Dragon Forum (pitching) – an industry magnet that draws many film professionals to Krakow. *Inquiries to:* Krakow Film Festival, Ul Basztowa 15/8A, 31-143 Krakow, Poland. Tel: (48 12) 294 6945; e: info@kff.com.pl; web: www.kff.com.pl.

Festival del film Locarno
August 1–11, 2012

Founded in 1946, located right in the heart of Europe in a Swiss-Italian town on Lake Maggiore, the Festival del film Locarno is one of the world's top film events offering a panoramic view of the full range of current cinematic expression. With its three competitive sections 'Concorso internazionale' (International Competition), 'Concorso Cineasti del presente' (Filmmakers of the Present), 'Concorso Pardi di domani' (Leopards of Tomorrow), the Festival takes stock of new approaches and perspectives in filmmaking; throughout its 64-year history, Locarno has often discovered or confirmed directors who now enjoy a widespread recognition. The Festival also provides a showcase for major new films of the year from around the world: every night the famous open air screenings offer prestigious

premieres to an audience up to 8,000 people in the extraordinary setting of Piazza Grande. The Festival del film Locarno has also established itself in recent years as an important industry showcase for auteur filmmaking, a perfect networking opportunity for distributors, buyers and producers from all countries with over 3,000 film professionals and 900 journalists attending – together with 150,000 film-goers. *Inquiries to:* Festival del film Locarno, Via Ciseri 23, CH-6601 Locarno, Switzerland. Artistic Director: Olivier Père. Tel: (41 91) 756 2121; e: info@pardo.ch; web: www.pardo.ch.

AWARDS 2011
Concorso internazionale
Pardo d'oro (Golden Leopard): **Back To Stay** (Argentina/Switzerland), Milagros Mumenthaler.
Premio speciale della giuria (Special Jury Prize): **Tokyo Koen** (Japan), Shinji Aoyama.
Pardo per la migliore regia (Best Director): Adrian Sitaru for **Best Intentions** (Hungary/Romania).
Pardo per la miglior interpretazione femminile (Best Actress): María Canale in **Back To Stay** (Argentina/Switzerland).
Pardo per la miglior interpretazione maschile (Best Actor): Bogdan Dumitrache in **Best Intentions** (Hungary/Romania).
Concorso Cineasti del presente
Pardo d'oro – Premio George Foundation (Golden Leopard): **L'Estate Di Giacomo** (Belgium/France/Italy), Alessandro Comodin.
Premio speciale della giuria CINÉ CINÉMA (Special CINÉ CINÉMA Jury Prize): **The Student** (Argentina), Santiago Mitre.
Opera prima
Pardo per la migliore opera prima (Best First Feature): **Nana** (France), Valérie Massadian.

BFI London Film Festival
October 2012

The UK's largest and most prestigious public film festival presented at the BFI Southbank, West End venues, and at cinemas throughout the capital. The programme comprises around 200 features and documentaries as well as showcasing over 100 short films. There is a

British section and a very strong international selection from Asia, Africa, Europe, Latin America, US independents and experimental and avant-garde work. More than 1,600 UK and international press and industry representatives attend and there is a buyers/sellers liaison office. *Inquiries to:* London Film Festival, BFI Southbank, Belvedere Road, South Bank, London SE1 8XT, UK. Tel: (44 20) 7815 1305; e: emilie.arnold@bfi.org.uk; web: www.bfi.org.uk/lff.

AWARDS 2011

Best Film in Partnership with American Express: **We Need To Talk About Kevin** (UK/USA), Lynne Ramsay.
Grierson Award for Best Documentary: **Into the Abyss: A Tale of Death, A Tale of Life** (USA) Werner Herzog.
Best British Newcomer: **Junkhearts** (UK), Tinge Krishnan.
Sutherland Trophy Winner: **Las Acacias** (Argentina/Spain), Pablo Giorgelli.
BFI Fellowship: David Cronenberg and Ralph Fiennes.

Los Angeles Film Festival
June 14–24, 2012

Now in its eighteenth year, the Los Angeles Film Festival is widely recognised as a world-class event, showcasing the best in new American and international cinema and providing the movie-loving public with access to some of the most critically acclaimed filmmakers, film industry professionals, and emerging talent from around the world. The Festival features unique signature programmes including the Filmmaker Retreat, Ford Amphitheatre Outdoor Screenings, Poolside Chats, and more. Additionally, the Festival screens short films created by high school students and has a special section devoted to music videos. Over 200 features, shorts, and music videos, representing more than forty countries, make up the main body of the Festival. *Inquiries to:* Los Angeles Film Festival, 9911 W Pico Blvd, Los Angeles, CA 90035, USA. Tel: (1 310) 432 1200; e: lafilmfest@filmindependent. org; web: www.lafilmfest.com.

AWARDS 2011
Best Narrative Feature: **Familiar Ground** (Canada), Stéphane Lafleur.
Best Documentary Feature: **Wish Me Away** (USA), Beverly Kopf and Bobbie Birleffi.
Audience Award for Best Narrative Feature: **Attack the Block** (UK), Joe Cornish.
Audience Award for Best Documentary Feature: **Beats, Rhymes & Life: The Travels of a Tribe Called Quest** (USA), Michael Rapaport.
Audience Award for Best International Feature: **Senna** (UK), Asif Kapadia.

Mar del Plata International Film Festival
Mid-November 2012

The Festival is the only A-grade film festival in Latin America with an official competition, usually comprising around fifteen movies, with an average of two from Argentina. Other sections include 'Latin American Films', 'Out of Competition', 'Point of View', 'Near Darkness', 'Soundsystem', 'Heterodoxy', 'Documentary Frame', 'Argentine Showcase', 'Memory in Motion' and 'The Inner Look'. *Inquiries to:* Mar del Plata IFF, Hipólito Yrigoyen 1225 (C1085ABO), Buenos Aires, Argentina. Tel: (54 11) 4383 5115; e: info@ mardelplatafilmfest. com; web: www.mardelplatafilmfest.com.

Minsk International Film Festival (Listapad)
November 2012

Listapad brings together many interesting films and internationally recognised representatives of the movie industry. Some 38 countries were represented at the 18th edition in 2011, including Russia, Croatia, Hungary, the Philippines, Thailand, Belgium, the Netherlands, Austria, Estonia, Poland, Serbia, France, Germany, Bulgaria, Ukraine, Latvia, Georgia, Armenia, Mongolia, Belarus, Kyrgyzstan, Israel, Turkey, Italy, Slovakia, South Korea, Sweden, Azerbaijan, Czech Republic, Rumania, Brazil, Mexico and others. The programme consists of three sections: features (the main competition and the debut film competition), documentaries (the main competition and the competition among young directors) and films for children. Inquiries to: Minsk International Film Festival, Nezavisimosti Ave 25A, Minsk, Belarus. Tel: (375 17) 321 2477; e: info@listapad.com; web: www.listapad.com.

Molodist International Film Festival (Kiev)
October 2012

FIAPF accredited, this is a specialised international film festival of first films of directors. The Festival's main goal is to discover new young filmmakers from around the world. The competition programme consists of student films, short first films (animation, documentary, fiction film) and first feature-length narrative films. Programme director: Denis Nikitenko. *Inquiries to:* 6 Saksahanskoho St, Kiev 01033, Ukraine. Tel: (380 44) 461 9803; e: so_happy@molodist.com or program@molodist.com; web: www.molodist.com.

AWARDS 2011
Grand Prix Best Feature Film of the Competition Programme: **Breathing** (Austria), Karl Markovics.
Best Feature Film: **Las Acacias** (Argentina/Spain), Pablo Giorgelli.
Best Short Film: **The Runaway** (Spain), Victor Carrey.
Best Student Film: **Coral** (Argentina), Ignacio Chaneton.
Yves Montand Prize for the Best Young Actor/Actress: Alicia Vikander for **Pure**.
Audience Prize: **Paris Shanghai** (France), Thomas Cailley.

Montreal World Film Festival
August 23–September 3, 2012

The goal of the Festival is to encourage cultural diversity and understanding between nations, to foster the cinema of all continents by stimulating the development of quality films, to promote filmmakers and innovative works, to discover and encourage new talents, and to encourage meetings between cinema professionals from around the world. The Festival includes the 'World Competition', 'First Films World Competition', 'Hors Concours' (World Greats), 'Focus on World Cinema', 'Documentaries of the World', as well as tributes to established filmmakers and a section dedicated to Canadian student films. *Inquiries to:* Montreal World Film Festival 1432 de Bleury St, Montreal, Quebec, Canada H3A 2J1. Tel: (1 514) 848 3883 e: info@ffm-montreal.org. Web: www.ffm-montreal.org.

AWARDS 2011
Feature Films
Grand Prix des Americas: **Come As You Are** (Belgium), Geoffrey Enthoven.
Special Grand Prix of the Jury: **Chronicle of My Mother** (Japan), Masato Harada.
Best Director: **The Fire** (Germany), Brigitte Maria Bertele.
Best Actress: Fatehmeh Motamed-Arya for **Here Without Me** (Iran).
Best Actor ex-aequo: Boris Szyc for **The Mole** (Poland), and Danny Huston for **Playoff** (France/Israel).
Best Screenplay: **The Art of Love** (France), Emmanuel Mouret.
Best Artistic Contribution: **Tatanka** (Italy), Giuseppe Gagliardi.
Innovation Award: **Life Back Then** (Japan), Takahisa Zeze.

Moscow International Film Festival
June 21–30, 2012

More than 200 guests from all over the world attend, including noted filmmakers, journalists and film critics, along with over 200,000 visitors. The large competition remains international in scope, covering Europe and the CIS, South East Asia, and Latin and North America. The 'Media-Forum' (panorama and competition) is devoted to experimental films and video art. There is also a wide panorama of recent Russian films, a documentary films competition and special documentary cinema programme, 'Free Thought'. *Inquiries to:* Moscow International Film Festival, Sadovnicheskaya Ulitsa, 72-2, Moscow 115035, Russia. Tel: (7 495) 725 2622; e: info@moscowfilmfestival.ru; web: www.moscowfilmfestival.ru.

AWARDS 2011

Golden George Film Award: **The Waves** (Spain), Alberto Morais.

Silver George Film Award: **Chapiteau-Show** (Russia), Sergey Loban.

Special Mention of the Jury: **Sneakers** (Bulgaria), Valeri Yordanov and Ivan Vladimirov.

Silver George Film Award for the Best Direction: Wong Ching Po for **Revenge: A Love Story** (Hong Kong).

Silver George Film Award for the Best Actor: Carlos Alvarez-Novoa for **The Waves** (Spain).

Silver George Film Award for the Best Actress: Urszula Grabowska for **Joanna** (Poland).

Silver George Film Award for the Best Film of the Perspectives Competition: **Anarchy in Zirmunai** (Hungary/Lithuania), Saulius Drunga.

Silver George Film Award for the Best Film of the Documentary Competition: **Hell and Back Again** (UK/USA), Danfung Dennis.

Special Prize for Outstanding Contribution to World Cinema: John Malkovich.

Special Prize for Outstanding Achievement in the Career of Acting and Devotion to the Principles of K. Stanislavsky's School: Helen Mirren.

Mumbai Film Festival
October 2012

The only independent film festival in India divided into nine sections: 'International Competition for the First Feature Films of Directors', 'World Cinema', 'Indian Frame', 'Dimensions Mumbai', 'Celebrate Age', 'Retrospectives', 'Above the Cut', 'New Faces in Indian Cinema' and 'The Real Reel'. Running alongside the Festival is the Mumbai Film Mart, during which some of the biggest entertainment industry players, from India and abroad, meet over three days with senior decision-makers from leading film production houses, buyers, sellers, festival programmers and independent filmmakers. *Inquiries to:* Mumbai Film Festival, Mumbai Academy of the Moving Image (MAMI), 49/50 Maruti Chambers, 3rd Floor, Fun Republic Lane, Andheri (W), Mumbai 400 053, India. Tel: (91 22) 4106 8223; e: mumbaifilmfest@gmail.com; web: www.mumbaifilmfest.com.

AWARDS 2011

International Competition

Golden Gateway Award for Best Film: **My Little Princess** (France), Eva Ionesco.

Silver Gateway Award Jury Grand Prize: **The Salesman** (Canada), Sebastien Pilote.

Silver Gateway Award for Best Director: Eva Ionesco for **My Little Princess** (France).

Silver Gateway Award for Best Actress: Isabelle Huppert and Anamaria Vartolomei for **My Little Princess** (France).

Silver Gateway Award for Best Actor: Gilbert Sicotte for **The Salesman** (Canada).

International Lifetime Achievement Award: Morgan Freeman.

New Horizons International Film Festival
July 19–29, 2012

New Horizons International Film Festival is the largest film festival in Poland and regarded as one of the most important film events in Central Europe, visited each year by an increasing number of cinema lovers from Poland and abroad. New Horizons presents films that go beyond the borders of conventional cinema. Its main objective is to present uncompromising, innovative and original cinema from all over the world. The Festival's name suggests an exploration of new horizons in film language, expressions and storytelling. The Festival belongs to the elite group of festivals accredited by FIAPF. *Inquiries to:* New Horizons International Film Festival, 1 Zamenhofa Street, 00-153 Warsaw, Poland. Tel: (48 22) 530 6640; e: festiwal@nowehoryzonty. pl; web: www.nowehoryzonty.pl.

AWARDS 2011

International Competition

Grand Prix: **Attenberg** (Greece), Athina Rachel Tsangari.

FIPRESCI Jury Prize: **Gravedigger** (Hungary), Sándor Kardos.

Audience Prize: **The Prize** (France/Germany/Mexico/Poland), Paula Markovitch.

IFG Inspiration Award: **Brownian Movement** (The Netherlands), Nanouk Leopold.

Films on Art International Competition

Best Film Award: **Arirang** (South Korea), Kim Ki-duk.
New Polish Films Competition
Wrocław Film Award Founded by the President of the City: **It Looks Pretty From a Distance** by Anka and Wilhelm Sasnal.

Visions du Réel, International Film Festival – Nyon Doc Outlook-International Market
April 20–27, 2012

Visions du Réel is a unique international festival providing an overview of the best of *cinema du réel*, with films challenging the boundaries of the genres, made by independent filmmakers and producers taking risks in radical aesthetical choices, original writing and new forms of storytelling. Thanks to the excellent reputation of its programming, Visions du Réel is considered a benchmark and a must for world-renowned filmmakers. At the same time, it is a launch-pad for young filmmakers. The Doc Outlook-International Market ensures excellent working conditions for producers, buyers, decision-makers and distributors, supported by optimum facilities and cutting-edge tools. It fosters contacts for the funding and promotion of films, as well as for networking and for acquiring film rights. More than 900 participants from approximately 35 countries took part in 2011. Entry deadline Festival: 10 January 2012. Entry deadline Media Library: 10 January 2012. Submission deadline Pitching du Réel: 20 January 2012.

*Awards Ceremony 13/04/2011 with Luciano Barisone and the winner of the Grand Prix La Poste Tatiana Huezo Sánchez (***El lugar mas pequeño***). In the background are film directors and members of the jury Jennifer Fox and Michael Madsen. Photo: Miguel Bueno.*

Inquiries to: Visions du Réel, Place du Marché 2CH-1260 Nyon, Switzerland. Tel: (41 22) 365 4455; e: programme@visionsdureel.ch; web: www.visionsdureel.ch.

AWARDS 2011
International Competition
Grand Prix La Poste Suisse for the Best Feature Length Film: **El Lugar Mas Pequeño** (Mexico), Tatiana Huez Sánchez.
Grand Prix La Poste Suisse for the Best Director of a Feature Length Film: **Ikuisesti Sinun** (Finland), Mia Halme.
Special Mention for the Feature Length Film: **Epilogue** (Belgium), Manno Lanssens.
Prize George Foundation for the Best Middle Length Film: **Ein Brief Aus Deutschland** (Germany), Sebastian Mez.
Prize George Foundation for the Best Director of a Middle Length Film: **People I Could Have Been and Maybe Am** (The Netherlands), Boris Gerrets.
Special Mention for the Middle Length Film: **Aranda** (Finland), Anu Kuivalainen.
Prize Visions du Réel for the Best Short Film: **Anne Vliegt** (The Netherlands), Catherine Van Campen.
Prize Visions du Réel for the Best Director of a Short Film: **Territorios** (Portugal), Monica Baptista.
Special Mention for the Short Film: **Fini** (Denmark), Jacob Secher Schulsinger.
Prize of the Interreligious Jury for a Feature Length Film: **El Lugar Mas Pequeño** (Mexico), Tatiana Huez Sánchez.
Special Mention for the Feature Length Film: **Scheich Ibrahim, Bruder Jihad** (Germany), Andres Rump.
Prize Buyens-Chagoll for the Feature Length Film: **Peace** (Japan), Kazuhiro Soda.
Young Audience Prize of the Société des Hôteliers de la Côte: **Hula and Natan** (Israel) Robby Elmaliah.
Special Mention for the Middle Length Film: **Sonor** (Germany), Levin Peter.
Cinéma Suisse (Swiss Films):
Prize SRG SSR Idée Suisse for the Best Swiss film: **Raising Resistance** (Germany/Switzerland), David Bernet and Bettina Borgfeld.

VISIONS DU RÉEL
INTERNATIONAL FILM FESTIVAL
DOC OUTLOOK-INTERNATIONAL MARKET
NYON, 20–27 APRIL 2012
VISIONS DU RÉEL
THE ONLY DOCUMENTARY FESTIVAL IN SWITZERLAND AND ONE OF THE MOST IMPORTANT WORLDWIDE WITH ITS EXCLUSIVE DOC OUTLOOK-INTERNATIONAL MARKET.
NYON: A MUST FOR PROFESSIONALS AND FILM LOVERS
WWW.VISIONSDUREEL.CH
IMAGE: JOSÉ LUIS GUERIN – EN LA CIUDAD DE SYLVIA DESIGN: BONTRON&CO
SPONSORS PRINCIPAUX:
LA POSTE
La Mobilière
Assurances & prévoyance
PARTENAIRES:
SRG SSR
Etat de Vaud
NYON
Loterie Romande
MEDIA
DOC ALLIANCE

Festivalgoers enjoying the beautiful spring weather while waiting for the next screening. Photo: Thierry Kleiner.

Prize Suissimage and Société Suisse des Auteurs SSA: **Les Lessiveuses** (France/Switzerland), Yamina Zoutat.
État d'Esprit
Public Prize of the city of Nyon: **An African Election** (Switzerland/USA), Jarreth Merz.
Prize Regard Neuf of the Canton of Vaud: **Mercado de Futuros** (Spain), Mercedes Alvarez.
Special Mentions: **Eine Ruhige Jacke** (Switzerland), Ramón Giger and **Koniec Rosji** (Poland), Michal Marcak.
Premiers Pas (First steps):
Prize Loterie Romande Vaud et Genève: **Con la Licencia de Dios** (Switzerland), Simona Canonica.

Report 2011
The first edition under the supervision of new director Luciano Barisone will be remembered for its rigour and innovative programming. It took place in a spirit of continuity, respecting the achievements of an event that has grown over the years. Apart from the geographical changes that have allowed attendees to enjoy a new festival centre located in the centre of town, the line-up was marked by profound humanism, a sense of discovery and a significant platform for films of the South. The reorganisation of the various sections has produced more clarity. Three international competitions were introduced for full-length, medium-length and short films, which consisted entirely of premieres (world, international or European). New sections, such as 'Etat d'Esprit', showcased the finest world productions that were receiving their Swiss premiere. There was also 'Port-Franc', a highly successful thematic section that compared personalities from various walks of life with films touching on this year's theme, La Trace. There were also the traditional 'Ateliers' (workshops) hosted José Luis Guerín (Spain) and Jay Rosenblatt (USA). The 'Séances Spéciales' were dedicated to Marília Rocha (Brazil) and Giovanni Cioni (Italy), and Colombia was represented in the *Focus* section. **– Brigitte Morgenthaler**, Communication and Partnerships.

Oberhausen International Short Film Festival
April 26–May 1, 2012

The International Short Film Festival Oberhausen, one of the leading short film festivals in the world, is known for its open attitude towards short formats and its focus on experimental works. The competitions – international, German, regional, children's shorts and music video – provide an extensive overview of current international short film and video production. The curated programmes feature a wide selection of films on a topic that changes annually. 'Shooting Animals' looked at the history of animal films, while the 2012 programme will concentrate on the 50th anniversary of the Oberhausen Manifesto, featuring archive and contemporary films. Retrospectives of individual artists or groups complete the line-up. In 2011, programmes were dedicated to Grzegorz Krolikiewicz and William E Jones. Oberhausen also continues its 'Podium' series of lively and very well-attended discussions. Deadline for entries: 13 January 2012. Entry forms and regulations can be downloaded at www.kurzfilmtage.de from October 2011. Festival Director: Dr Lars Henrik Gass. *Inquiries to:* Oberhausen International Short Film Festival, Grillostrasse 34, D-46045 Oberhausen, Germany. Tel: (49 208) 825 2652; e: info@kurzfilmtage.de; web: www.kurzfilmtage.de; Facebook: www.facebook.com/kurzfilmtage

AWARDS 2011

International Competition

Grand Prize of the City of Oberhausen: **Sans-Titre** (France), Neil Beloufa.

Principal Prize: **The Artist** (UK), Laure Prouvost.

Principal Prize: **Mercúrio** (Portugal), Sandro Aguilar.

ARTE Prize for a European Short Film: **TSE** (Israel), Roee Rosen.

Prize of the Jury of the Ministry for Family, Children, Youth, Culture and Sport of North Rhine-Westphalia: **Sans-Titre** (France), Neil Beloufa.

FIPRESCI Prize: **Handebol** (Brazil), Anita Rocha da Silveira.

Prize of the Ecumenical Jury: **Atrophy** (South Africa), Palesa Shongwe.

Prize of the International Short Film Festival Oberhausen: **Kengere** (Uganda), Peter Tukei Muhumuza.

German Competition

Prize for the best contribution to the German Competition: **Traces of an Elephant** (Germany/UK), Vanessa Nica Mueller.

3sat Promotional Award: **Marxism Today (prologue)** (Germany), Phil Collins.

NRW Competition

First Prize: **How To Raise the Moon** (Denmark/Germany), Anja Struck.

Second Prize: **Der Mond Ist Ein Schöner Ort** (Germany), Anne Maschlanka and Viktoria Gurtovaj.

Children's and Youth Film Competition

Prize of the Children's Jury: **Mobile** (Germany), Verena Fels.

Prize of the Youth Jury: **Little Children, Big Words** (Sweden), Lisa James-Larsson.

Oulu International Children's and Youth Film Festival
November 19–25, 2012

Annual festival with a competition for full-length feature films for children and youth, screening recent titles and retrospectives. Oulu is located in northern Finland, on the coast of the Gulf of Bothnia. *Inquiries to:* Oulu International Children's and Youth Film Festival, Hallituskatu 7, FI-90100 Oulu, Finland. Tel: (358 8) 881 1293; e: eszter.vuojala@oufilmcenter.fi; web: www.oulunelokuvakeskus.fi/lef.

AWARDS 2011

Kaleva Award: **Iris** (Finland), Ulrika Bengts.

CIFEJ-Prize: **Lost in Africa** (Denmark), Vibeke Muasya.

ECFA Prize: **On the Sly** (Belgium/France), Olivier Ringer.

The Church Media Foundation's Prize: **The Little Snow Animal** (Finland), Miia Tervo.

The Northern Film and Media Foundation POEM's Little Bear Award: Mikael Wahlforss.

For Tomorrow Youth Prize: **Skyscraper** (Denmark), Rune Schjött.

Report 2011

The 30th anniversary Festival was a success with over 19,000 admissions. The patron of the Festival was President Tarja Halonen. The opening film was the French film *Nicostratos*. The focus this year was on Danish children's and youth film and Danish media education. There were twelve films in the international children's competition. The other sections were: 'Youth Film Competition', 'Finnish

The Danish reception at Oulu city hall. From left to right: Director Olivier Horlait, Director Raimo O Niemi and festival Co-Ordinator Mika Anttolainen. Photo: Elena Alaniska.

Competition', 'Kaleidoscope', 'Danish Classics', 'Documentaries' and 'Shorts'. The Friends of the Young organisation founded a youth prize entitled 'For Tomorrow'. The European Children's Film Association also gave the first ECFA Prize at the Festival. **– Eszter Vuojala**, Festival Director.

Pordenone Silent Film Festival
October 6–13, 2012

The world's first and largest festival dedicated to silent cinema, now celebrating its 31st year. The event sees an annual invasion by archivists, historians, scholars, collectors and enthusiasts from around the world, along with cinema students chosen to attend the internationally recognised 'Collegium'. Year-on-year, the Festival consistently succeeds in rediscovering lost masterpieces from the silent years, all accompanied by original live music. Festival Director: David Robinson. *Inquiries to:* Le Giornate del Cinema Muto c/o La Cineteca del Friuli, Palazzo Gurisatti, via Bini 50, 33013 Gemona (UD), Italy. Tel: (39) 0432 980458; e: info.gcm@cinetecadelfriuli.org; web: www. giornatedelcinemamuto.it.

Report 2011
The 30th edition brought dramatic historic rediscoveries: Alfred Hitchcock's earliest credited work, on Graham Cutts' *The White Shadow*; Robert Paul's long-lost first British film *The Soldier's Courtship* (1896), a never-before-seen Garbo kiss (an out-take from Victor Sjöström's *The Divine Woman* from 1929), and the only known and painstakingly restored coloured print of Méliès' *A Trip to the Moon*. There were live orchestral shows of Chaplin's *The Circus*, Sjöström's *The Wind*, and Kozintsev and Trauberg's *The Overcoat*

Hungarian filmmaker István Szabó at the 30th Pordenone Silent Film Festival. Photo: Paolo Jacob.

and *New Babylon* – the last two as part of the innovative series, 'Shostakovich and the Factory of the Eccentric Actor'. Further programmes were dedicated to Georgian cinema, Japanese animation, the earliest Disney films, newly discovered early Italian cinema, Michael Curtiz before Hollywood, and the popular 'Canon Revisited' feature, reviving masterworks by Friedrich Ermler, Marcel L'Herbier and Joe May. **– David Robinson**, Festival Director.

Portland International Film Festival
February 9–25, 2012

Portland International Film Festival will be an invitational event presenting more than 100 films from thirty or more countries to 35,000 people from throughout the Northwest. Along with new international features, documentaries and shorts, the Festival will feature showcases

Portland International Film Festival screening of **How to Die in Oregon** *with director Peter Richardson (left) and PIFF staff member Thomas Phillipson (right).*

surveying Hispanic film and literature, Pacific Rim cinema and many of the year's foreign-language Oscar submissions. *Inquiries to:* Northwest Film Center, 1219 SW Park Ave, Portland, OR 97205, USA. Tel: (1 503) 221 1156; e: info@nwfilm.org; web: www.nwfilm.org.

Reykjavík International Film Festival
September 27–October 7, 2012

The Festival is one of the most exciting film events in Northern Europe as well as Iceland's major annual film event. The main purpose of the Festival is to offer a wide selection of alternative, independent cinema. The Festival celebrates cultural diversity, provoking the public's interest in independent cinema

Pack your bags… "RIFF Is Where I Roll" Photo: reykjavikdesignlaboratory.com.

and imparting film's social importance. The Festival emphasises the relationship between film and other art forms with art exhibitions, concerts etc. The Festival's main award for 'the Discovery of the Year' – the Golden Puffin Award – is dedicated to new filmmakers. *Inquiries to:* Reykjavík International Film Festival, Tjarnargata 12, 101 Reykjavík, Iceland. Tel: (354) 411 7055; web: www.riff.is.

AWARDS 2011
The Golden Puffin, Discovery Award: **Twilight Portrait** (Russia), Angelina Nikonov.
FIPRESCI Award: **Volcano** (Denmark/Iceland), Rúnar Rúnarsson.
The Church of Iceland Award: **Volcano** (Denmark/Iceland), Rúnar Rúnarsson.
RIFF Audience Award: **Le Havre** (Finland/France/Germany), Aki Kaurismaki.
RIFF Environmental Award: **The Pipe** (Republic of Ireland), Risteard Ó Domhnaill.
RIFF 2011 RIFF TransAtlantic Talent Lab Encouragement Award: **Auf Wiedersehen Papa** (Germany), Sandra Nedeleff.
Best Short Icelandic Film Award: **Come To Harm**, Börkur Sigthorsson.

Report 2011
RIFF broke the attendance records this year by screening the world's most important independent films. Head of jury was the Danish actor Ulrich Thomsen and guests of honour were Béla Tarr, Lone Scherfig and James Marsh. Romania was the country in focus and the emerging master platform celebrated the work of Romanian director, Adrian Sitaru. RIFF held discussions on various subjects, including David Suzuki's

Reykjavík International Film Festival

RIFF.IS

27. SEPTEMBER– 7. OCTOBER 2012

talk about the environmental situation. The Go Indie workshops included lectures on cinematography, indie screenwriting and animation. The Swim-In this year was extremely popular, along with the opening film *Inni*, the new musical film on Sigur Rós. **– Hrönn Marinósdóttir**, Festival Director.

St Petersburg International Film Festival
June 2012

Non-competitive, showcasing the best films from around the world, will be celebrating its 20th edition in 2012. *Inquiries to:* St Petersburg International Film Festival, 10 Kamennostrovsky Ave, St Petersburg 197101, Russia. Tel: (7 812) 237 0072; e: info@filmfest. ru; web: www.filmfest.ru

San Sebastian International Film Festival
September 21–29, 2012

Held in an elegant Basque seaside city known for its superb gastronomy and beautiful beaches, the San Sebastian Festival remains the Spanish-speaking world's most important event in terms of glamour, competition, facilities, partying, number of films and attendance (1,866 production and distribution firms, government agencies and festival representatives from 53 countries, and accredited professionals and 986 journalists from 36 countries). Events include the Official Competitive section, 'Zabaltegi', with its €90,000 award, 'Kutxa – New Directors' for first or second features, 'Horizontes Latinos' with its €35,000 award and various retrospectives. In partnership with the Rencontres Cinémas Amérique Latine in Toulouse, the 'Films in Progress' industry platform aims to aid the completion of Latin American projects. 'Cinema in Motion 6' is a rendezvous point for discovering projects by filmmakers from the Magreb as well as the Portuguese-speaking African countries, and developing Arab countries, presented to professionals in partnership with Amiens Film Festival and Fribourg Film Festival. *Inquiries to:* San Sebastian International Film Festival,

Glenn Close receives the Donostia Award at the Kursaal.
© San Sebastian International Film Festival.

Apartado de Correos 397, 20080 Donostia, San Sebastian 20080, Spain. Tel: (34 943) 481 212; e: ssiff@sansebastianfestival.com; web: www.sansebastianfestival.com.

AWARDS 2011
Official Selection
Golden Shell for Best Film: **The Double Steps** (Spain),Isaki Lacuesta.
Special Jury Prize: **Skylab** (France), Julie Delpy.
Silver Shell for Best Director: Filippos Tsitos for **Unfair World** (Greece).
Silver Shell for Best Actress: María León for **The Sleeping Voice** (Spain).
Silver Shell for Best Actor: Antonis Kafetzopoulos for **Unfair World** (Greece).
Jury Award for Best Cinematography: Ulf Brantas for **Happy End** (Sweden).
Jury Award for Best Screenplay: Hirokazu Kore-eda for **I Wish** (Japan).
Kutxa – New Directors Award: Jan Zabeil for

All award winners at the Kursaal stage at the end of the closing ceremony. © San Sebastian International Film Festival.

The River Used To Be a Man (Germany).
Horizontes Award: **Las Acacias** (Argentina/
Spain), Pablo Giorgelli.

Report 2011
The past edition of the San Sebastian
International Film Festival, under the new
direction of José Luis Rebordinos, saw
an increase in the number of industry and
audience members. A new section, 'Culinary
Zinema', in collaboration with Berlinale's
'Culinary Cinema' began. Some of the Festival
highlights were the Donostia Award to Glenn
Close and the visit of Catherine Deneuve
on the occasion of the Jacques Demy
retrospective. – **Gemma Beltran**, International
Press.

Sarajevo Film Festival
July 6–14, 2012

The Festival presents a wide selection of
both competitive and non-competitive films.
The main competitive focus covers the
region of Southeast Europe (Albania, Austria,
Bosnia and Herzegovina, Bulgaria, Croatia,
Cyprus, Greece, Hungary, Macedonia, Malta,
Montenegro, Romania, Serbia, Slovenia,
Turkey), with platforms for features, shorts
and documentaries. The Festival also aims
to present important and innovative films of
high artistic value made throughout the world.
Inquiries to: Sarajevo Film Festival, Zelenih
Beretki 12/1, 71000 Sarajevo, Bosnia and
Herzegovina. Tel: (387 33) 209 411; e: press@
sff.ba; web: www.sff.ba.

Shanghai International Film Festival
June 16–24, 2012

If there is one gateway to the vast Chinese
Film Market, it's SIFF. As China's only 'A'
category international film festival, it is
becoming increasingly important in the
industry chain. SIFF is mainly composed
of the competition section (Golden Goblet
Award and Asian New Talent Award), SIFF
Mart ('Film Market', 'China Film Pitch and
Catch', 'Co-production Film Pitch and Catch'),

'SIFFORUM and Film Panorama', and 'MOBILE
SIFF' (SIFF's platform for new media). Sign up
your films or projects, or book a place in the
market to access the world's biggest market
of Chinese film and discover an abundance of
resources. *Inquiries to:* Shanghai International
Film Festival, 11F, B, STV Mansions, 298 Wei
Hai Road, Shanghai 200041, China. Tel: (86 21)
6253 7115; web: www.siff.com.

AWARDS 2011
Golden Goblet Awards
Best Feature Film: **Hayde Bre** (Turkey), Orhan
Oguz.
Jury Grand Prix: **Mr Tree** (China), Han Jie.
Best Director: Han Jie for **Mr Tree** (China).
Best Screenplay: Zhang Ming for **The Young
Man Sings Folk Song in the Opposite Door**
(China).
Best Actor: Sevket Emrulla for **Hayde Bre**
(Turkey).
Best Actress: Lv Xingchen for **The Young
Man Sings Folk Song in the Opposite Door**
(China).
Best Cinematography: Tiwa Moeithaisong for
Friday Killer (Thailand).
Best Music: Wen Zi for **The Young Man Sings
Folk Song in the Opposite Door** (China).
Jury Award: Yuthlert Sippapak for **Friday Killer**
(Thailand).
*For details of Asian New Talent and Mobile
SIFF Awards please visit www.siff.com*

Sheffield Doc/Fest
June 13–17, 2012

For five days, Sheffield Doc/Fest brings the
international documentary family together to
celebrate the art and business of documentary
filmmaking. Combining a film festival, industry
sessions and market activity, the Festival offers
pitching opportunities, controversial discussion
panels and in-depth filmmaker masterclasses,
as well as a wealth of inspirational documentary films from across the globe. The
Festival opens with the 'Crossover Summit',
the place to learn about new models of
funding, production and distribution across the
digital landscape. Around 140 documentary

films are screened, mainly from a call for entries made in November. Over fifty debates, discussions, case studies, interviews and masterclasses are presented and there are a number of well-attended social and networking events. The 'MeetMarket' takes place over two days of the Festival. It is a highly effective initiative; pre-scheduled one-on-one meetings where TV commissioning editors, executive producers, distributors and other financiers meet with independent producers and filmmakers to discuss documentary projects in development that are seeking international financing. The film programme is also open to the public. Previously held in November, Doc/Fest has now moved to the summer with the 19th Sheffield Doc/Fest taking place in June 2012. *Inquiries to:* Sheffield Doc/Fest, The Workstation, 15 Paternoster Row, Sheffield, S1 2BX, UK. Tel: (44 114) 276 5141; e: info@sidf. co.uk; web: www.sheffdocfest.com.

AWARDS 2011

Special Jury Award: **The Interrupters** (USA), Steve James.
Sheffield Innovation Award: **Welcome to Pine Point** (Canada), Paul Shoebridge and Michael Simons.
Sheffield Youth Jury Award: **We Are Poets** (UK), Alex Ramseyer-Bache and Daniel Lucchesi.
Sheffield Green Award: **You've Been Trumped** (UK), Anthony Baxter.
Sheffield Student Doc Award: **Eight Eight** (UK), Josh Bamford, Seb Feehan and Hannah Bone.
The Sheffield Doc/Fest Audience Award: **Give Up Tomorrow** (USA/UK), Michael Collins.
Sheffield Inspiration Award: Nick Broomfield

Albert Maysles receiving the inaugural Sheffield Doc/Fest Lifetime Achievement Award, Friday 10th June 2011, Sheffield City Hall. Pictured (left to right): Hussain Currimbhoy, Film Programmer; Albert Maysles; Heather Croall, Festival Director. Photo: Jacqui Bellamy, Pixelwitch Pictures.

Doc/Fest Lifetime Achievement Award: Albert Maysles.

Report 2011

Doc/Fest 2011 presented Morgan Spurlock's *POM Wonderful Presents The Greatest Movie Ever Sold* as its opening night film, with Morgan himself in attendance. A live Q&A, across two screens, followed the sell-out screening, and was followed by an opening night reception. Doc/Fest's free public outdoor screening programme was launched in 2011. The day of documentaries open to all included *Encounters at the End of the World*, a series of shorts and *Grey Gardens*, preceded by a parade through Sheffield city centre and attended by director Albert Maysles, the inaugural recipient of the Doc/Fest Lifetime Achievement Award. **– Lisa Brook**, Publications and Promotions Manager.

Sitges International Fantastic Film Festival of Catalonia

October 2012

Celebrating its 45th edition, Sitges is one of the leading fantasy film festivals and is a stimulating universe of encounters, exhibitions, presentations and screenings of fantasy films from all over the world. It is an essential rendezvous for movie lovers and audiences eager to come into contact with new tendencies and technologies in film and the audiovisual world. The 'Noves Visions' section is dedicated to the most innovative and challenging approaches in contemporary cinema. *Inquiries to:* Sitges Festival Internacional de Cinema Fantastic de Catalunya, Calle Joan Maragall 36, CP:08870 Sitges, Barcelona, Spain. Tel: (34 93) 894 9990; e: festival@sitgesfilmfestival.com; web: www.sitgesfilmfestival.com.

Sofia International Film Festival

March 2012

Competitive festival showcasing new Bulgarian and Balkan films to international audiences. It includes the following sections: official programme (international competition for first or second features and special screenings), documentary programme (competition), Bulgarian feature films, Balkan films showcase, European screen, World screen, Bulgarian shorts competition, shorts, retrospectives, tributes and special events. Sofia Meetings: Co-production Market for first, second or third features of the director takes place during the Festival. *Inquiries to:* Sofia International Film Festival, 1 Bulgaria Sq, Sofia 1463, Bulgaria. Tel: (359 2) 952 6467; e: office@sofiaiff.com; web: www.siff.bg.

Solothurn Film Festival

January 19–26, 2012

Since 1964, the Solothurn Film Festival has presented a wide selection of recent Swiss productions along with many premieres. Each year it attracts over 50,000 spectators from

47ᵗʰ Solothurn Film Festival
19 – 26 January 2012   www.solothurnfilmfestival.ch

within Switzerland and abroad. The Festival has become the most important annual meeting for the Swiss film and media industry. In addition to recent productions, a retrospective dedicated to a renowned filmmaker or actor is presented. Alongside, the Festival widens its scope by inviting films from across the globe. Numerous panels, masterclasses, and one-to-one meetings enrich the film programme. Finally, the Festival hosts the announcements of the Swiss film nominees for the Swiss Film Prize. *Inquiries to:* Solothurn Film Festival, PO Box 1564, CH-4502 Solothurn, Switzerland. Tel: (41 32) 625 8080; e: info@solothurnfilmfestival.ch; web: www.solothurnfilmfestival.ch.

Rainer-Maria Brandauer and Sebastian Koch at the Festival opening, presenting **Manipulation** *by Pascal Verdosci.*

Report 2011

The 46th Solothurn Film Festival hosted around 1,200 professionals, and attracted 55,000 cinemagoers. The Festival programme with around 300 films highlighted the thematic and stylistic spectrum of Swiss filmmaking, with works ranging from political documentaries (*Aisheen – Still Alive in Gaza* by Nicola Wadimoff) to comedies (*The Sandman* by Peter Luisi) and social dramas (*La dernière Fugue* by Léa Pool). The Festival lived up to its reputation as the showcase of Swiss film productions. Panels, special programmes and controversial discussions about film politics framed the Festival. The retrospective was dedicated to the Swiss producer Ruth Waldburger, who has worked with directors such as Jean-Luc Godard, Alain Resnais, Béla Tarr, Robert Frank and Gianni Amelio. The jury prize 'Prix de Soleure' of 60,000 Swiss Francs was awarded to Jean-Stéphane Bron for his film *Cleveland vs. Wall Street*. The Public Award went to the feature film *Sommervögel* by Paul Riniker. – **Seraina Rohrer**, Festival Director.

Stockholm International Film Festival
November 2012

The Festival's focus is the new and cutting-edge, and the competitive section is exclusively for directors making their first, second or third feature film. The Festival, in its 23rd edition, continues to strengthen its position as one of the leading competitive film festivals in northern Europe for uncompromising artistry in contemporary filmmaking, and will present over 180 films from fifty countries. Some 130,000 visitors and 1,000 accredited journalists and industry officials, as well as around a hundred directors, actors and producers attend the Festival. The Festival is recognised by FIAPF and hosts a FIPRESCI jury. It is also a member of the European Coordination of Film Festivals. Distinguished guests over the years have included Gus Van Sant, Susan Sarandon, Wong Kar-Wai, David Lynch, Lauren Bacall, Quentin Tarantino, Dennis Hopper, Roman Polanski, Ang Lee, David Cronenberg and

Charlotte Rampling. *Inquiries to:* Stockholm International Film Festival, PO Box 3136, S-103 62 Stockholm, Sweden. Tel: (46 8) 677 5000; e: info@stockholmfilmfestival.se; web: www.stockholmfilmfestival.se.

Sydney Film Festival
June 6–17, 2012

The Sydney Film Festival is one of the longest-running events of its kind in the world. Each year the Festival brings the best new films from around the world to audiences in Sydney. The 2012 edition will screen the best of the world's cinema, with over 160 films from more than forty countries, including features, documentaries, short films, retrospectives, films for families and animations. When the Festival is over, the Travelling Film Festival continues, taking mini-festivals to 15 venues across regional NSW, the Northern Territory and rural Queensland. *Inquiries to:* Sydney Film Festival, PO Box 96, Strawberry Hills, NSW 2012, Australia. Tel: (61 2) 9690 5333; e: info@sff.org.au; web: www.sydneyfilmfestival.org.

Tallinn Black Nights Film Festival (PÖFF)
PÖFF Main Programme November 16–28, 2012
Children and Youth Film Festival Just Film: November 15–25, 2012
Animation Film Festival Animated Dreams: November 14–18, 2012
AnimaCampus Tallinn November 13–17, 2012
Student and Short Film Festival Sleepwalkers: Spring 2012
Baltic Event Co-Production Market: November 26–28, 2012
Black Market Industry Screenings: November 26–28, 2012

Tallinn Black Nights Film Festival (PÖFF) has grown to be one of the largest and most distinctive film events in the Northern Europe. During its 15th edition, the Festival screened more than 500 films (including 260 features), bringing over 650 screenings to a record-breaking audience of more than 70,000 people, as well as over 500 industry guests and journalists. In 2012, the Festival

30th November, Closing Ceremony of the 2011 Tallinn Black Nights Film Festival (PÖFF), Friðrik Þór Friðriksson receiving a Lifetime Achievement Award from the Estonian Minister of Culture Rein Lang and Black Nights Film Festival Director Tiina Lokk. Photo: Ruwe Saare.

will celebrate 100 years of Estonian Cinema. Recognised by FIAPF, PÖFF embraces a cluster of events, accommodating two full-blown sub-festivals (Animated Dreams and Just Film) as well as international industry gatherings ('Black Market' and 'Baltic Event').

PÖFF includes three international competitive programmes ('EurAsia', 'Tridens Baltic', and 'North-American Indie Films'), a traditional film festival programme with documentaries and feature films, as well as a programme for short films. The Festival hosts a special programme in co-operation with *Screen International* – 'Critics' Choice'; several retrospectives; a programme for prize-winning films from other festivals, and a host of special programmes.

Animated Dreams has established itself as the biggest animation film festival in North-Eastern Europe, screening an international competition of short animations alongside non-competitive programmes, filmmaker retrospectives and a country focus. In 2011 it included a new networking and training event, AnimaCampus Tallinn, with applicants from five continents and more than thirty countries. The Festival also plans to launch an online talent and project market in the first quarter of 2012.

Just Film is the biggest children and youth film festival in the region. It includes a programme called 'streetCULTure', consisting of fiction and documentary films that tackle the topics of modern subcultures among young people.

The industry events bring important industry players to PÖFF, including producers, industry leaders and distributors from Europe, Asia and beyond. 'Black Market' is the regional film market, focusing mainly on new films from neighbouring regions and smaller film industry countries from as Central and Eastern Europe, Nordics, CIS and Russia. 'Black Market' is also home to sub-events, such as the literary rights market 'Books to Films', which introduces an annual selection of books for film adaptation and has been growing in popularity. The seminar programme 'Industry Days' recently focused on the changing economies of the film industry and how different countries are dealing with the seismic shifts in changes in funding and finance.

The film and co-production gathering 'Baltic Event' screens the latest feature films from the Baltic countries, along with a co-production market open for projects from the Baltic countries, Central and Eastern Europe, Russia and Scandinavia. Events and panel discussions are also available on Black Market Online – an online B2B environment for the film industry that includes industry contacts, country profiles and statistics, co-production projects and an online screening room for buying and selling film rights in Baltic, Scandinavian, Central-Asian, Caucasian, and Russian territories. Inquiries to: Tallinn Black Nights Film Festival (PÖFF), Telliskivi 60A, 10412 Tallinn, Estonia. Tel: (372) 631 4640. e: poff@poff.ee. Web: www.poff.ee.

30th November, Closing Ceremony of the 2011 Tallinn Black Nights Film Festival (PÖFF). Mart Taniel, cinematographer of feature film The Idiot (Estonian) and members of the Tridens Baltic Feature Film Competition Jury (from left): Dita Rietuma, Xavier Garcia Puerto, Laufey Guðjónsdóttir. Photo: Ruwe Saare.

30th November, Closing Ceremony of the 2011 Tallinn Black Nights Film Festival (PÖFF). PÖFF people in the spotlight. Photo: Tanel Murd.

AWARDS 2011

International competition programme EurAsia
Grand Prix: **A Simple Life** (China/Japan), Ann Hui.
Best Director: Lynne Ramsay for **We Need To Talk About Kevin** (UK).
Best Actor: Sven Nordin for **Sons of Norway** (Norway).
Best Actress: Deanie Ip for **A Simple Life** (China/Japan).
Jury Prize for Outstanding Performance in Cinematic Language: Cocco and Shinya Tsukamoto for **Kotoko** (Japan).
Special Mention for First Time Director: Gabriel Achim for **Adalbert's Dream** (Romania).
Special Mention: **Rose** Wojciech Smarzowski (Poland).
Tridens Baltic Feature Film Competition
Best Film: **BarZakh** (Finland/Lithuania), Mantas Kvedaravicius and **33 Animals of Santa Claus** (Latvia), Laila Pakalnina.
Heav(i)en Estonian Film Award: **Graveyard Keeper's Daughter** Katrin Laur.
Best Cinematographer: Mart Taniel for **The Idiot** (Estonia).

FIPRESCI Award for Best Baltic Film: **BarZakh** (Finland/Lithuania), Mantas Kvedaravicius.
North American Independent Film Competion
Best Film: **Starbuck** (Canada), Ken Scott.
FICC Jury Award: **A Simple Life** (China/Japan), Ann Hui.
NETPAC Jury Award: **Mourning** (Iran), Morteza Farshbaf.
Audience Award: **Superclásico** (Denmark), Ole Christian Madsen.
Lifetime Achievement Awards: Rein Raamat (Estonia), Rein Maran (Estonia), Fridrik Thor Fridriksson (Iceland) and Aleksandr Sokurov (Russia).

Report 2011

Record audiences came to Tallinn to celebrate the 15th Anniversary of PÖFF. Alongside the exceptional programme of films – ranging from popular hits such as *The Artist* and world premieres, including the Kazakh film *Akkyz* – the Festival also focused on Icelandic cinema and hosted a high-profile panel for film professionals – 'Industry Days'. Among the panellists were former head of the Irish Film Board, Simon Perry, President of the Think Tank on European Film and Film Policy, Henning Cammre and Takenari Maeda, the head of international co-production at UNIJAPAN. Significant festival guests in 2011 included Oscar-nominated directors Fridrik Thor Fridriksson (Iceland) and Juanita Wilson (Ireland), actress Fiona Shaw (Ireland), film producer Jim Stark (USA) and director Sergei Loznitsa (Russia) who served as head of the International Jury. – **Tiina Lokk**, Festival Director.

Tampere Film Festival
March 7–11, 2012

The Festival is the oldest and largest short film festival in Northern Europe and celebrates its 42nd anniversary in 2012. The Festival programme consists of the International and Finnish short film competitions and a special thematic programme. It is famous for its excellent and innovative programming, magnificent atmos-phere and of course, the Finnish Sauna Party. Besides the 120 screenings, the Festival is bursting with various seminars, panel dis-cussions and meetings for film professionals and enthusiasts. The Festival promotes up-and-coming filmmakers – it is an event to find future masters of cinema. The high quality 'Film Market' has over 4,000 titles from all over the world. The special thematic programmes for the 42nd edition include the highlights of Nepalese and Estonian short film, films for children, a retrospective of Michael Glawogger, new student films and new films from Scandinavia. *Inquiries to:* Tampere Film Festival, PO Box 305, FI-33101 Tampere, Finland. Tel: (358 3) 223 5681; e: office@tamperefilmfestival.fi; web: www.tamperefilmfestival.fi.

AWARDS 2011
International Competition
Grand Prix: **Incident By A Bank**, Ruben Östlund (Sweden).
Best Animation: **The External World**, David O'Reilly (Germany).
Best Fiction: **Incident By A Bank**, Ruben Östlund (Sweden).
Best Documentary: **How To Pick Berries**, Elina Talvensaari (Finland).
EFA Nominee: **Silent River**, Anca Miruna Lazarescu (Romania).
Audience Award: **Incident By A Bank**, Ruben Östlund (Sweden).

Thessaloniki International Film Festival
November 2012

In its 53rd year, the oldest and the most important film event in South-East Europe targeted a new generation of filmmakers as well as independent films by established directors. The International Competition Jury comprised of Laurence Kardish (President), Hisami Kuroiwa, Frederic Boyer, Sitora Alieva and Constantine Giannaris. Other sections comprising this year's edition included 'Open Horizons', 'Balkan Survey', 'Greek Films', workshops, round table discussions, exhibitions and parties. Three tributes were also held, celebrating the work of Ole Christian Madsen, Paolo Sorrentino, Sara Driver and Constatine Giannaris. As always, the Festival's market, Agora, acted as an umbrella service for film professionals who benefited from the services of 'Agora Film Market', 'Crossroads Co-production Forum' and 'Works in Progress'. Festival Director: Dimitri Eipides. *Inquiries to:* Thessaloniki International Film Festival, 9 Alexandras Ave, 114 73 Athens, Greece. Tel: (30 210) 870 6000; e: info@filmfestival.gr; web: www.filmfestival.gr.

AWARDS 2011
Golden Alexander: **Twilight Portrait** (Russia), Angelina Nikonova.
Silver Alexander: **Eighty Letters** (Czech Republic), Vaclav Kadrnka.
Bronze Alexander: **Porfirio** (Argentina/Colombia/France/Spain/Uruguay), Alejandro Landes.
Best Director Award: Mark Jackson for **Without** (USA).
Best Screenplay Award: John McIlduff for **Behind the Lamb** (UK).
Best Actress Award: Stefania Gouliotia for **J.A.C.E** (Greece/Portugal/The Netherlands/Turkey).
Best Actor Award: Wotan Wilke Moehring for **The Fire** (Germany).
Artistic Achievement Award: The cast of **The Flood** (Canada/France/Germany/Israel), Guy Nattiv.

Tokyo International Film Festival
October 2012

Celebrating its 25th anniversary in 2012, it is the only FIAPF-accredited festival in Japan and welcomes over 130,000 visitors each year.

TIFF has played an integral role in Japan's film industry and cultural scene since its establishment in 1985. During the Festival, films from a variety of genres will be shown in several intriguing sections: 'Competition', which selects the 'Tokyo Sakura Grand Prix' from a carefully chosen ensemble of premieres, directed by talented first-timers and recognised directors; 'Special Screenings', which premieres highly entertaining films prior to their public release in Japan; 'Winds of Asia – Middle East', which boasts the largest number of films and audience attendance in all of the TIFF screenings; 'Japanese Eyes', which showcases a broad range of independent Japanese films for worldwide audiences, and 'Natural TIFF' highlights films that deal with the 'coexistence of mankind and nature'. TIFFCOM, an entertainment business market affiliated with TIFF, has established its position as one of the major industry opportunities in Asia. *Inquiries to:* Unijapan/TIFF Office, 5F Tsukiji Yasuda Building, 2-15-14 Tsukiji Chuo-ku, Tokyo 104-0045, Japan. Tel: (81 3) 3524 1081; e: tiff-pr@tiff-jp.net; web: www.tiff-jp.net.

AWARDS 2011

Tokyo Sakura Grand Prix: **Untouchable** (France), Eric Toledano and Olivier Nakache.
Special Jury Prize: **The Woodman and the Rain** (Japan), Shuichi Okita.
Best Director: Ruben Östlund for **Play** (Denmark/France/Sweden).
Best Actor: François Cluzet and Omar Sy for **Untouchable** (France).
Best Actress: Glenn Close for **Albert Nobbs** (Ireland).
Audience Award: **When Pigs Have Wings** (Belgium/France), Sylvain Estibal.

Torino Film Festival
November 2011

The Festival celebrates its 30th anniversary this year and is recognised as one of Europe's most important film events, known for its discoveries as well as for its unique retrospectives. The programme includes competitive sections for international features, Italian and international documentaries and Italian shorts, as well as spotlights and premieres. The main competitive section of the Festival is reserved for directors making their first, second or third films with a focus on 'young' cinema, and concentrates primarily on searching out and discovering innovative talent that expresses the best contemporary trends of international independent cinema. *Inquiries to:* Torino Film Festival, Via Montebello 15, 10124 Torino, Italy. Tel: (39 011) 813 8811; e: info@torinofilmfest. org; web: www.torinofilmfest.org.

Toronto International Film Festival
September 2012

The Toronto International Film Festival is the leading public film festival in the world, screening more than 300 films from 65 countries every September. The event attracts thousands of Canadian and international industry delegates as well as approximately 1,200 journalists. From TIFF's inception 36 years ago, the vision has been to present the best of international and Canadian cinema and provide a unique context in which to understand and enjoy this work – in effect, to use the moving image to transform the way people see the world. In 2010, TIFF opened TIFF Bell Lightbox, a breathtaking five-storey complex located in central Toronto that offers programming year-round and provides a permanent home for film lovers to celebrate cinema from around the world. *Inquiries to:* TIFF, Reitman Square, 350 King Street West, Toronto, Ontario, M5V 3X5 Canada. Tel: 1-888-599-8433; e: proffice@tiff.net; web: www.tiff.net/festival

AWARDS 2011

SKYY Vodka Award for Best Canadian First Feature Film: **Edwin Boyd**, Nathan Morlando.
The City of Toronto Award for Best Canadian Feature Film: **Monsieur Lazhar**, Philippe Falardeau.
Best Canadian Short Film: **Doubles With Slight Pepper**, Ian Harnarine.
The Prize of the International Critics (FIPRESCI Prize) for the Discovery Programme: **Avalon** (Sweden), Axel Petersén.

The Prize of the International Critics (FIPRESCI Prize) for Special Presentations: **The First Man** (Algeria/France/Italy), Gianni Amelio.
The Cadillac People's Choice Award: **Where Do We Go Now?** (Egypt/France/Italy/Lebanon), Nadine Labaki.
The Cadillac People's Choice Documentary Award: **The Island President** (USA), John Shenk.
The Cadillac People's Choice Midnight Madness Award: **The Raid** (Indonesia), Gareth Evans.

Transilvania International Film Festival
June 1–10, 2012 (Cluj); June 13–17, 2012 (Sibiu)

Founded in 2002, TIFF has grown rapidly to be the most important film-related event in Romania and one of the most spectacular annual events in the region. Over the years, TIFF has invited, as recipients of the Lifetime Achievement Award or special guests of the event, important figures from world cinema, including Wim Wenders, Claudia Cardinale, Catherine Deneuve, Julie Delpy, Fanny Ardant, Michael Radford, Annie Girardot, Udo Kier, Vanessa Redgrave, Nicolas Roeg and Franco Nero. In 2011, over 55,000 people attended the screenings in the 13 venues of Cluj-Napoca, eager not to miss over 240 features and short films presented in the competitive and show-case sections. Having become a traditional premiere hub for domestic features, which are now landmarks of the evolution of the so-called Romanian New Wave of filmmakers, TIFF has also developed a market of Romanian works-in-progress, featuring narrative and documentary projects, scheduled in the frame of the 'Romanian Days', which take place during the Festival. *Inquiries to:* Transilvania International Film Festival, Popa Soare 52, Sector 2, 023984 Bucharest, Romania. Tel: (40) 21 326 6480; e:info@tiff.ro; web: www.tiff.ro.

Valladolid International Film Festival
October 20–27, 2012

One of Spain's key events, the Festival spot-lights the latest work by established directors as well as newcomers. Competitive for features, shorts and documentaries. Also offers

*Closing Ceremony 29/10/2011. From left to right: Pierre de Clercq (Screenwriter/***Hasta la Vista***), Gonzalo Miró (Son of Pilar Miró), Mariano Vanhoof (Producer/***Hasta la Vista***), Geoffrey Enthoven (Director/***Hasta la Vista***), Maribel Verdú (Spike of Honour), Benjamin Murray (Director/***Unfinished Spaces***) and Ken Scott (Director/***Starbuck***).*

retrospectives, a selection of recent Spanish productions and a congress of new Spanish directors. *Inquiries to:* Valladolid International Film Festival Office, Teatro Calderón, Calle Leopoldo Cano, s/n 4ª Planta, 47003 Valladolid, Spain. Tel: (34 983) 426 460; e:festvalladolid@seminci.com; web: www.seminci.com.

AWARDS 2011
International Jury Awards
Golden Spike for Feature Film: **Hasta La Vista** (Belgium), Geoffrey Enthoven.
Silver Spike for Feature Film: **The Snows of Kilimanjaro** (France), Robert Guédiguian.
Special Jury Prize: Maryam Keshavarz and the actresses for **Circumstance** (France/Iran/Lebanon/USA).
Best Director: Agnieszka Holland for **In Darkness** (Canada/Germany/Poland).
Pilar Miró Prize for Best New Director: Paula Ortiz for **De Tu Ventana a la Mía** (Spain).
Best Actress: Zhou Dongyu for **Under the Hawthorn Tree** (China).
Best Actor ex aequo: Brendan Gleeson for **The Guard** (Ireland/UK) and Patrick Huard for **Starbuck** (Canada).
Miguel Delibes Award for Best Screenplay: Philippe Falardeau for **Monsieur Lazhar** (Canada).
Best Director of Photography Award: Robbie Ryan for **Wuthering Heights** (UK).
Cultural Diversity Award: **Family Portrait In Black And White** (Canada), Julia Ivanova.

FIPRESCI Award: **Monsieur Lazhar** (Canada), Philippe Falardeau.
Golden Spike for Short Film ex aequo: **Ticket** (Hungary), Ferenc Rófusz and **Il Respiro Dell'Arco** (Italy), Enrico Maria Artale.
Silver Spike for Short Film: **Courte Vie** (Morocco), Adil El Fadili.
Best European Short: **Superman, Spiderman Or Batman** (Romania), Tudor Giurgiu.
Meeting Point Section Best Feature: **Volcano** (Denmark/Iceland), Rúnar Rúnarsson.
Meeting Point Section Best Short: **The Extraordinary Life of Rocky** (Belgium), Kevin Meul.
Meeting Point Section Best Spanish Short: **The Red Virgen** (Spain), Sheila Pye.
Best Documentary: **Murandak Songs of Freedom** (Australia), Natasha Gadd and Rhys Graham.

Report 2011
The 56th edition of Valladolid International Film Festival kicked off with Nanni Moretti presenting the Spanish première of *Habemus Papam* and ended with Christian Ole Madsen unveiling his latest film *Superclásico*, the Danish candidate for this year's Oscars. Aside from the eighty features, shorts and documentaries screening in the Festival's competitive sections, one of the highlights of this year's event was 'Swedish Film Is Here', a retrospective of Swedish productions from the past two years. Despite extensive cutbacks to the budget, this year's Festival maintained a high level of films on show and also offered various round tables, including a masterclass in cinema direction by Fernando Leon de Aranoa,

which was packed out with young people. Both visitor attendance and audience participation were on the increase. **– Denise O'Keefe**.

Venice International Film Festival
August 29–September 8, 2012

The Venice Film Festival offers an overview of world cinema, in a spirit of freedom and tolerance. The Festival includes competitive and out-of-competition sections, in addition to retrospectives, tributes, and exquisite art exhibitions around downtown Venice. The official line-up of the 69th edition will be announced in a press conference that will take place in Rome at the end of July 2012. *Inquiries to:* La Biennale di Venezia, Mostra Internazionale d'Arte Cinematografica. San Marco 1364/A, Ca' Giustinian, 30124 Venice, Italy. Tel (39 041) 521 8711; e: foreignpress@labiennale.org; web: www.labiennale.org/en/cinema.

AWARDS 2011
VENEZIA 68 Section
Golden Lion for Best Film: **Faust** (Russia), Aleksandr Sokurov.
Silver Lion for Best Director: Shangjun Cai for **Ren Shan Ren Hai** (China/Hong Kong).
Special Jury Prize: **Terraferma** (Italy), Emanuele Crialese.
Coppa Volpi for Best Actor: Michael Fassbender for **Shame** (UK).
Coppa Volpi for Best Actress: Deanie Yip for **A Simple Life** (Hong Kong).
Marcello Mastroianni Award for Best New Young Actor or Actress: Shôta Sometani and Fumi Nikaidô for **Himizu** (Japan).

The Sala Grande of the Palazzo del Cinema (the chief screening theatre of the Venice Film Festival). © La Biennale di Venezia

Osella for Best Cinematography: Robbie Ryan for **Wuthering Heights** (UK).
Osella for Best Screenplay: Yorgos Lanthimos and Efthimis Filippou for **Alpis** (Greece).
ORIZZONTI Section
Award for Full-length Film: **Kotoko** (Japan), Shinya Tsukamoto.
Special Jury Prize for Full-length Film: **Whores' Glory** (Austria/Germany), Michael Glawogger.
Award for Medium-length Film: **Accidentes Gloriosos** (Denmark/Germany/Sweden), Mauro Andrizzi and Marcus Lindeen.
Award for Short Film: **In Attesa dell'Avvento** (Italy), Felice D'Agostino and Arturo Lavorato.
CONTROCAMPO ITALIANO Award for Narrative Feature-Length Film: **Scialla!** (Italy), Francesco Bruni.
Controcampo Award for Short Film: **A Chjàna** (Italy), Jonas Carpignano.
Controcampo Doc Award for Documentary: **Pugni chiusi** (Italy), Fiorella Infascelli.
Lion of the Future – 'Luigi de Laurentiis' Venice Award for a Debut Film: **Là-Bas** (Italy), Guido Lombardi.
Golden Lion for Lifetime Achievement: Marco Bellocchio.
Jaeger-LeCoultre Glory to the Filmmaker Award 2011: Al Pacino.
Persol 3D Award for the Most Creative Stereoscopic Film of the Year: Zapruder Filmmakers Group (David Zamagni, Nadia Ranocchi, and Monaldo Moretti).
L'Oréal Paris Award for Cinema: Nicole Grimaudo.

Report 2011

The Festival's opener in 2011 was George Clooney's *The Ides of March*. The competition section included 23 features. The main jury was chaired by Darren Aronofsky and included Todd Haynes, David Byrne and André Téchiné among others. The out-of-competition section saw Madonna and Al Pacino on the red carpet. A discussion panel on Nicholas Ray took place celebrating the centennial of his birth, and a screening of the reconstructed version of Ray's *We Can't Go Home Again* was included in the Festival's line-up. The retrospective was dedicated to Italian experimental cinema 1960–1978. **– Giovanni Alberti**, Press Department.

VIENNALE – Vienna International Film Festival

October 25–November 7, 2012

The Viennale is Austria's most important international film event, as well as being one of the oldest and best-known festivals in the German-speaking world. It takes place every October in beautiful cinemas in Vienna's historic centre, providing a festival with an international orientation and a distinctive urban flair. A high percentage of the approximately 96,000 visitors to the Festival are comprised of a decidedly young audience. In its main programme, the Viennale shows a carefully picked selection of new films from all over the globe, as well as new films from Austria. The choice of films offers a cross section of bold filmmaking that stands apart from the aesthetics of mainstream conventionality and is politically relevant. Aside from its focus on the newest feature films of every genre and structural form imaginable, the Festival gives particular attention to documentary films, international short films, as well as experimental works and crossover films. The Viennale receives regular international acclaim for its annual organisation of large-scale retrospectives, in collaboration with the Austrian Film Museum, its numerous special programmes, and its tributes and homages.
Inquiries to: Viennale, Siebensterngasse 2, 1070 Vienna, Austria. Tel: (43 1) 526 5947; e: office@viennale.at; web: www.viennale.at.

Harry Belafonte and Viennale Director Hans Hurch at a press conference in the Vienna Hilton am Stadtpark on Oct 22, 2011. Photo: Robert Newald

Report 2011

2011 saw 750 people giving standing ovations to Harry Belafonte at the screening of the documentary film *Sing Your Song*, at the Gartenbaukino. A great Q&A with the enthusiastic singer, actor and political activist followed. There was a wonderful get-together between director David Cronenberg and Jeremy Thomas at a gala for this outstanding British producer. Nanni Moretti appeared at the three sold-out screenings of his film *Habemus Papam*. Other guests included

Bertrand Bonello, Milagros Mumenthaler, Mathieu Demy, Pierre Schoeller, André Wilms, Azazel Jacobs and Soi Cheang, who came to Vienna to witness his first tribute/retrospective at a festival. The programme of a dozen new Austrian films was a huge success, completely selling out. **– Fredi Themel**, Head of Press Department.

Warsaw International Film Festival
October 12–21, 2012

The 28th edition of the Festival will play host to nearly 110,000 visitors and showcase the latest and most interesting trends in world cinema. Since 2005, the 'CentEast Market' has run alongside the Festival, which provides a meeting place for professionals interested in films from Eastern Europe. The programme of the WFF is divided into five competitive and five non-competitive sections for which full details are available on our website. *Inquiries to:* Warsaw Film Foundation, PO Box 816, 00-950 Warsaw 1, Poland. Tel: (48 22) 621 4647; e: media@wff.pl; web: www.wff.pl.

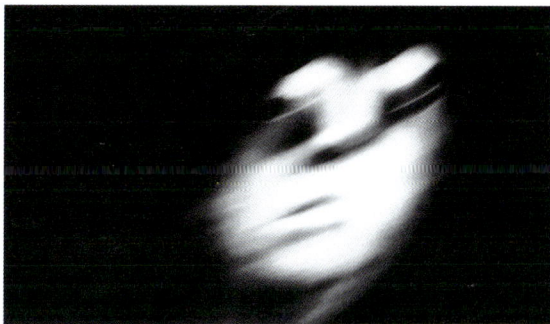

VIENNALE
VIENNA INTERNATIONAL FILM FESTIVAL

OCTOBER 25 – NOVEMBER 7, 2012
www.viennale.at

Festivals and Markets of Note

American Film Festival (AFF), Zamenhofa 1, 00-153 Warsaw, Poland. Tel: (48 22) 530 6640; e: aff@snh. org.pl; web: www.americanfilmfestival.pl. *The festival enables Polish audiences to become acquainted with contemporary American cinema, as well as the culture and reality of the United States – Nov.*

American Film Market, 10850 Wilshire Blvd, 9th Floor, Los Angeles, CA 90024-4311, USA. Tel: (1 310) 446 1000; e: afm@ifta-online.org; web: www.americanfilmmarket.com. *The business of independent motion picture production and distribution – a truly collaborative process – reaches its peak every year at the American Film Market. Over 8,000 leaders in motion picture production and distribution – acquisition and development executives, agents, attorneys, directors, financiers, film commissioners, producers and writers – converge in Santa Monica for eight days of screenings, deal-making and hospitality. The AFM plays a vital role in global production and finance. Each year, hundreds of films are financed, packaged, licensed and green lit, sealing over $800 million in business for both completed films and those in pre-production. With the AFM-AFI FEST alliance, attendees capitalise on the only festival-market combination in North America – Nov.*

Amiens International Film Festival, MCA, Place Léon Gontier, 80000 Amiens, France. Tel: (33 3) 2271 3570 e: contact@filmfestamiens.org; web: www.filmfestamiens.org. *A competitive festival in northern France for shorts, features, animation and documentaries. Also, retrospectives, tributes and the 'Le monde comme il va' series, which includes works from Africa, Latin America and Asia. 'Europe, Europes' presents new works from Young European Talents (Shorts, Documentaries and Animation) – Nov.*

Amsterdam-International Documentary Film Festival (IDFA), Frederiksplein 52, 1017 XN Amsterdam, Netherlands. Tel: (31 20) 627 3329; e: info@idfa.nl; web: www.idfa.nl. *The world's largest documentary festival, will celebrate its 25th Anniversary in 2012. The festival screens over 300 documentaries and sells some 180,000 tickets. Apart from regular sections, IDFA has several competition programmes. In addition to the screenings there are daily talk shows, debates and masterclasses. IDFA has two markets: the FORUM, a market for international co-financing, and Docs for Sale, which stimulates the sales and distribution of creative documentaries. Docs for Sale also boasts an online marketplace where new, as well as older, documentaries can be viewed all year long. Docs for Sale Online is a place where sales agents and producers can show their documentaries to potential buyers and exhibitors online, even after IDFA is over – Nov.*

Anima: Brussels Animation Film Festival, Folioscope, Ave de Stalingrad 52, B-1000 Brussels, Belgium. Tel: (32 2) 534 4125; e: info@folioscope.be; web: www.animatv.be. *The festival will screen over 150 films in the international competition (shorts and features, commercials, music videos). Retrospectives, exhibitions, lessons, workshops for the kids, the Futuranima professional days, round table discussions, numerous guests and film concerts make Brussels an international appointment not to be ignored. It is also the place to find out about Belgian animation with a national competition and screenings in panorama – Feb. 17–26, 2012.*

Anim'est International Animation Film Festival, Strada Dr. Taberei 92, Bl. C 7, Sc. F, Ap. 235 Sector 6, Bucharest 061406, Romania. Tel: (40) 7467 85180; e: contact@estenest.ro; web: www.animest.ro. *With a smart and nonconformist audience, Anim'est has become Bucharest's most loved film festival and a growing name on the European animation scene. Our presentations, workshops, masterclasses and round table discussions provide the perfect opportunity to get in touch with the latest creations and make contacts – Oct.*

Ann Arbor Film Festival, PO Box 8232, Ann Arbor, MI 48107, USA. Tel: (1 734) 995 5356; e: info@aafilmfest.org; web: www.aafilmfest.org. *Celebrating its 50th edition the festival is the longest-running independent and experimental film festival in North America. It presents 40 programmes with more than 180 films from over 20 countries, of all lengths and genres, including experimental, animation, documentary, narrative, hybrid and performance based works – Mar. 27–Apr. 1, 2012.*

Annecy/International Animation Film Festival and International Animation Film Market (MIFA), CITA, c/o Conservatoire d'Art et d'Histoire, 18 Avenue du Trésum, BP 399, 74013 Annecy Cedex, France. Tel: (33 4) 5010 0900; e: info@citia.org; web: www.annecy.org. *Features and short films in or out of competition, TV films and graduation films, as well as tributes, retrospective and special programmes. MIFA is the animation industry's foremost showcase in terms of co-producing, purchasing, selling, financing and distributing animation content for all broadcasting platforms – Festival: Jun. 4–9, 2012; MIFA: Jun. 6–8, 2012.*

Atlantic Film Festival, 1601 South Park St, Halifax, NS, B3J 2L2, Canada. Tel: (1 902) 422 3456; e: festival@atlanticfilm.com; web: www. atlanticfilm.com. *The festival screens some of the best International, Canadian and Atlantic Canadian films from inspiring documentaries and off-beat film noir to beautifully crafted animation and the latest Hollywood has to offer. In addition, the Music & Image Conference provides musicians and filmmakers alike with an engaging educational and networking opportunity to help bring together these two very connected industries. Strategic Partners, an International Film, TV and Multiplatform co-production market kicks off the festival and brings top national and international industry players together to discover and develop compelling projects, create long-term relationships and make investment happen – all set against the backdrop of the vibrant coastal city of Halifax, Nova Scotia – Sep.*

Augsburg Children's Film Festival, Filmtage Augsburg, Schroeckstrasse 8, 86152 Augsburg, Germany. Tel: (49 821) 158 083; e: filmbuero@t-online.de; web: www.filmtage-augsburg.de. *International features for children – Mar. 16–25, 2012.*

Austin Film Festival & Conference, 1801 Salina Street, Austin, TX 78702, USA. Tel: (1 512) 478 4795; e: info@austinfilmfestival.com; web: www.austinfilmfestival.com. *The festival presents an outstanding programme of narrative, animation and documentary features and shorts, including premieres, advanced screenings, independent films and retrospective screenings. Film screenings are complemented by lively and informative Q&A sessions with filmmakers and cast members. The conference provides over 80 inspiring and interactive panels, round tables and 'get to know you sessions' with established screenwriters and filmmakers – Oct. 18–25, 2012.*

Bergen International Film Festival, Georgernes Verft 12, NO-5011 Bergen, Norway. Tel: (47) 5530 0840; e: biff@biff.no; web: www.biff.no. *Norway's beautiful capital of the fjords launches the 13th BIFF in 2012 and has a main International Competition of about fifteen films, as well as an International Documentary Competition. The prestigious Checkpoints' Award focuses on Human Rights and is given to the people the film is portraying. The documentary section makes BIFF one of the Nordic countries' largest annual documentary events. The festival has sidebars with international art-house films, the Norwegian Shorts Competition and premieres of the upcoming Winter and Christmas theatrical releases, the result of extensive collaboration with Norway's distributors – Oct.*

Bermuda International Film Festival, Somers Bldg, 15 Front St, Hamilton HM11, Bermuda. Tel: (441) 293 3456; e: info@biff.bm; web: www.biff.bm. *The festival features the best of independent film from around the world in three competition categories: features, documentaries and shorts, screening between 65 and 75 films – Mar.*

Big Sky Documentary Film Festival, 131 South Higgins Ave, Suite 3-6, Missoula, Montana 59802, USA. Tel: (1 406) 541 3456; e: info@bigskyfilmfest. org; web: www.bigskyfilmfest.org. *Celebrating its 10th edition, the festival has become the largest* cinema event in Montana and the premiere venue for non-fiction film in the American West. It screens more than 125 films, including world and US premieres, classics, rare and experimental works on Montana's largest screen at the historic Wilma Theatre in downtown Missoula, Montana. The competitive event is open to non-fiction films and videos of all genres, subject matter, lengths and production dates – Feb. 17–26, 2012.

Black Movie Film Festival, 16 rue du Général-Dufour, 1204 Geneva, Switzerland. Tel: (41) 22 320 8387; e: presse@blackmovie.ch; web: www.blackmovie.ch. A pioneering film festival that swims against the tide of conventional film fare with its annual programme of emerging talent and established filmmakers from Asia, Africa and Latin America. The festival reflects current aesthetic and social trends via a thematic approach, ranging from social topics or current affairs, popular cinema, new urban cultures, genres or filmmakers of note, while Black Movie for Kids is dedicated to children. We screen all formats with the one requirement that each film has its own authentic voice, freedom of tone, and great cinematographic quality. The growing recognition within the industry internationally, as well as amongst the public, has seen a 10 to 20% annual rise in attendance – Feb. 17–26, 2012.

Boston Film Festival, 126 South St, Rockport, MA 01966, USA. Tel: (1 617) 523 8388; e: info@bostonfilmfestival.org; web: www.bostonfilmfestival.org. Showcasing a selection of feature films, documentaries and shorts. Filmmakers, actors and supporters have the opportunity to network at various events and a variety of awards are given out annually – Sep.

St George Bank Brisbane International Film Festival, St George Bank BIFF, GPO Box 15094, Brisbane City East, Queensland 4002, Australia. Tel: (61 7) 3224 4114; e: biff@biff.com.au; web: www.biff.com.au. Celebrating its 21st Anniversary in 2012, BIFF provides a focus for film culture in Queensland by showcasing the best and most interesting cinema from around the world. It offers the best in world cinema, documentaries, retrospectives, late night thrillers,

animation, a short film competition within its diverse programme. – Nov.

Buenos Aires International Independent Film Festival, Avenue Roque Saenz Peña 832, 6 Piso, 1035AAQ, Buenos Aires, Argentina. Tel: (54 11) 4393 4670; e: info@festivales.gob.ar; web: www.bafici.gov.ar. The 14th edition of BAFICI offers an extensive programme, including the world premiere of feature films, as well as Argentine and foreign shorts, in the official competition, retrospectives and thematic sections. It brings together acclaimed directors and new talent in a dynamic environment. Attendees can enjoy a series of special activities that connect film with other artistic disciplines: concerts, book presentations, free outdoor movies for children (Little Bafici) and adults, workshops and business meetings such as 'Buenos Aires Lab', 'Talent Campus' and 'Industry Office' – April.

BUFF Film Festival, PO Box 4277, SE 203 14 Malmö, Sweden. Tel: (46 40) 302505. e: info@buff.se. Web: www.buff.se. The 29th edition will screen about a hundred films in the following sections: Best Children Film Competition, Best Youth Film Competition, Short Film Competition, New Nordic Film, Panorama, School Cinema, Shorts and Pre School Film Screenings. The SCREEN section of the festival features seminars and workshops for up-and-coming filmmakers. In 2012 we will organise the sixth edition of BUFF Financing Forum. Mar. 13–17, 2012.

Buster, Tagensvej 85F, DK-2200 Copenhagen N, Denmark. Tel: (45) 3312 0005; e: buster@buster.dk; web: www.cphfilmfestivals.dk. International film festival for children and youth – Sep.

Cape Winelands Film Festival, 1 Waterkant, 52 Arum Road, Bloubergrant, Cape Town 7441, South Africa. Tel: (27 21) 556 3204; e: films_for_africa@telkomsa.net; web: http://films-for-africa.co.za. The festival (CWFF) is one of the largest film events on the African continent, has grown significantly in size and international participation since its first edition. The 2012 edition will feature more than 300 screenings in Oude Libertas open air amphitheatre, in the scenic Winelands district of

Stellenbosch, as well as in the historic independent art cinema of the Labia Theatre in the beautiful city centre of Cape Town. The main objective of the CWFF is to provide a window on world cinema and now offers 180 features, documentaries and shorts from more than fifty countries, including the work of around 25 South African filmmakers. The festival remains an important forum for South African cinema. The 2012 edition will open with a 35mm screening of the reconstructed (150 minute) version of Fritz Lang's Metropolis with the participation of the Cape Town philharmonic orchestra in our opera house in the city centre of Cape Town – Mar. 14–24, 2012.

Chicago International Children's Film Festival, Facets Multimedia Inc, 1517 W Fullerton, Chicago, IL 60614, USA. Tel: (1 773) 281 9075; e: kidsfest@ facets.org; web: www.cicff.org. North America's largest film festival devoted to films for and by children, featuring over 250 of the best films and videos from over forty countries. The festival screens a wide range of projects, from live-action and animated feature films to shorts, TV series, documentaries, and child-produced works. More than 100 filmmakers, media professionals and celebrities attend the festival to lead interactive workshops with children – Oct. 26–Nov. 4, 2012.

Chicago International Film Festival, 30 E Adams St, Suite 800, Chicago, IL 60603, USA. Tel: (1 312) 683 0121; e: info@chicagofilmfestival com; web: www.chicagofilmfestival.com. Now in its 48th year it is the longest-running competitive film festival in North America. Known for highlighting the latest work by established international directors and fresh talent, it presents more than 150 films from over 50 countries. Films are exhibited in our competitions, which make up the defining core of the Festival (International Feature Film, New Directors, Docufest, and Short Subject), as well as programmes that showcase new trends in international and independent filmmaking (World Cinema and After Dark) and that highlight the work of under-represented filmmakers and alternative viewpoints (Black Perspectives, Cinema of the Americas, ReelWomen and OUTrageous.) The festival bestows its highest honour, the Gold Hugo, on

the best feature in the International Competition, with separate prizes for new directors, documentaries, and shorts – Oct. 11–25, 2012.

Cinekid Festival, Kleine Gartmanplantsoen 21,1017 RP Amsterdam, Netherlands. Tel: (31 20) 531 7890; e: info@cinekid.nl; web: www.cinekid.nl. Annual Film, Television and New Media festival for Children. Every year more than 50,000 children are given an opportunity to attend one or more of the 500 media productions that Cinekid presents: feature films, children's documentaries, short films, animations, TV series and single plays, cross-media productions, interactive installations and set-ups and workshops. The main festival is held in Amsterdam, but approximately thirty satellite festivals are held in cities all over the Netherlands. Cinekid for Professionals brings together broadcasters, networks, entertainment companies, distributors, producers, directors, academics and journalists, who focus on quality children's media. They meet for four days to discuss major issues in kids' media, debate the future of the industry, and meet like-minded professionals from the global children's media community. Key components of the Cinekid for Professionals programme take place in the two day conference, ScreeningClub, co-production markets and daily network events – Oct.

Cinéma du Réel, BPI Centre Georges Pompidou, 25 rue du Renard, 75197 Paris Cedex 04, France. Tel: (33 1) 4478 4516; e: cinereel@bpi.fr; web: www.cinemadureel.org. Since 1978, the Cinéma du Réel international documentary film festival has been an outstanding international meeting point, where public and professionals discover the films of experienced directors as well as new talent, the history of documentary cinema and contemporary works. The festival programmes around 100 films for its various sections, screened at the Centre Pompidou, the Centre Wallonie-Bruxelles, the MK2 Beaubourg film theatre, the Paris City Hall and several other theatres in the Ile-de-France area. Submissions open in September for films with a 2011 copyright – Mar. 22–Apr. 1, 2012.

Cinéma Tous Ecrans, Maison des Arts du Grütli, 16 rue Général Dufour, CP 5730, CH-1211

Geneva 11, Switzerland. Tel: (41 22) 809 6920; e: info@cinema-tous-ecrans.ch; web: www. cinema-tous-ecrans.ch. *International film festival screening Swiss and international productions made for cinema, television, the web and mobile phones. We provide a platform on which to highlight and promote the constantly evolving nature of filmmaking. The only one of its kind in Switzerland, the festival celebrates the evolution of cinema, welcoming films which are presented on a variety of different screens, but have equal artistic worth, employing visual media formats from the past, present and future – Nov.*

Cinequest, PO Box 720040, San Jose, CA 95172-0040, USA. Tel: (1 408) 295 3378; e: contact@cinequest.org; web: www.cinequest.org. *The festival remains one of the last strongholds for the discovery of new and emerging film artists and presents a dynamic event of 200 international films with over 600 film artists, technologists, and professionals from 44 attending countries – Feb. 28–Mar. 11, 2012.*

Cleveland International Film Festival, 2510 Market Ave, Cleveland, OH 44113-3434, USA. Tel: (1 216) 623 3456; e: marshall@clevelandfilm.org; web: www.clevelandfilm.org. *Ohio's premiere film event features more than 150 feature films and over 130 shorts originating from close to seventy countries. Organised by the Cleveland Film Society, whose aim is to help the world discover the power of the film arts to educate, entertain and celebrate the human experience – Mar. 22–Apr. 1, 2012.*

FilmFestival Cottbus: Festival of East European Cinema, Friedrich-Ebert-Strasse 18, D-03044 Cottbus, Germany. Tel: (49) 355 431 0724; e: info@filmfestival-cottbus.de; web: www.filmfestival-cottbus.de. *In the past twenty years FilmFestival Cottbus has developed as the world's leading festival of East European cinema. Each year, it offers a representative survey of contemporary films from the entire Central and Eastern European area. While the programme is centred around the competitions for feature and short films, there are a variety of other sections: National Hits, Spectrum,*

Retrospectives, and Children's and Youth films. A Focus every year casts a spotlight upon a special region or topic (2012: Eastern Europe by Religions). With over 19,000 visitors in 2011 and a total prize value of 76,500 Euros, the festival attracts film professionals who also gather at the Cottbus receptions in Berlin, Karlovy Vary and Sarajevo. Parallel to the festival, the East-West Co-production Market, Connecting Cottbus, will be held from Nov. 8–9 – Nov. 6–11, 2012.

CPH:DOX, Tagensvej 85F, DK-2200 Copenhagen N, Denmark. Tel: (45) 3312 0005; e: info@cphdox.dk; web: www.cphfilmfestivals.dk. *International documentary film festival – Nov.*

CPH:PIX, Tagensvej 85F, DK-2200 Copenhagen N, Denmark. Tel: (45) 3312 0005; e: info@cphpix.dk; web: www.cphfilmfestivals.dk. *Feature (fiction) film festival – Apr. 12–29, 2012.*

Crossing Europe Film Festival Linz, Graben 30, 4020 Linz, Austria. Tel: (43 732) 785700; e: info@crossingeurope.at; web: www.crossingeurope.at. *The festival presents around 140 high-quality European productions and cinematic highlights of the past festival season, granting a central place to the diversity and richness of the cultural distinctiveness of young European cinema – Apr. 24–29, 2012.*

Cyprus Film Festival, PO Box 70, Anapafseos & Anonymou, Agioi Theodoroi, Corinthia, Greece. Tel: (357) 9979 8112; e: ciff@cyiff.com; web: www.cyprusfilmfestival.org. *The festival offers new and upcoming directors the opportunity to showcase their talent in front of a jury of internationally acclaimed cinema experts, directors and actors. Animation, feature films, music videos, short films and video art – Oct.*

Day for Night Festivals*, 154D St Paul's Rd, London N1 2LL, UK. Tel: (44) 07876 796735; e: hello@day-for-night.org; web: www.day-for-night.org. *Day For Night* curates, programmes and produces film festivals for venues, cultural institutes, NGOs and commercial organisations. With its own festivals (past festivals include Through an Exile Lens, Tibet Film Festival) and*

Filmmaker Tran Anh Hung and actress Rinko Kikuchi in conversation with the Day for Night* team prior to Norwegian Wood *premiere.* © Day for Night*

also commissioned by external organisations, Day for Night* has a range of curatorial projects taking place in the UK in 2012. Day For Night* has been commissioned to curate the Pan-Asia Film Festival for the second year running (March 2012) and will be launching the Scandinavia Film Festival (Dec 2012) – the only film festival in the UK with a focus on Scandinavia's thriving film scene. Day For Night* will also be introducing a new touring film series entitled 'Screen Now'. The first two projects are 'Screen Now: Peace & Conflict', provoking discussions on conflict resolution, and 'Screen Now: South East Asia', celebrating one of the most vibrant areas of independent world cinema today (Summer 2012.) Through these projects, Day For Night* is curating a library of selectively chosen titles available to venues and other organisations, and is particularly keen to support emerging filmmakers, whilst developing audiences for niche films deserving of wider exposure.

Starz Denver Film Festival, Denver Film Society at the Starz FilmCenter, 900 Auraria Parkway, Denver, Colorado 80204, USA. Tel: (1 303) 595 3456; e: dfs@denverfilm.org; web: www.denverfilm.org. *Cinema's potential to transform as well as reflect society in all its diversity is what the Denver Film Society aims to recognise and realise. Celebrating its 35th edition, the festival presents more than 200 films from around the world and plays host to over 150 filmmakers. Including new international features, cutting-edge independent fiction and non-fiction works, shorts and a variety of special programmes, the festival also features the best in student work with the* inclusion of the First Look Student Film section. The Denver Film Society also programmes the Starz FilmCenter, Colorado's only cinematheque, daily throughout the year – Nov. 2012.

Dhaka International Film Festival, c/o Rainbow Film Society, BS Bhaban, Level 3, Room 105, 75 Science Laboratory Rd, Dhaka-1205, Bangladesh; e: ahmedshovan@yahoo.com; web: www.dhakafilmfest.org. *The festival will screen approximately 150 films from more than forty countries with the festival theme being 'Better Film, Better Audience, Better Society'. Competitive section for Asian cinema and categories include: Retrospective, Tributes, Cinema of the World, Children's Film, Focus, Bangladesh Panorama, Women Filmmakers, Independent Films Section and Spiritual Films Section - Jan. 12–20, 2012.*

Divercine, Canelones 2226 Apt 102, Casilla de Correo 5023, 11200 Montevideo, Uruguay. Tel: (59 82) 401 9882; e: ricardocasasb@gmail.com; web: www.divercine.com.uy. *International festival celebrating its 21st edition, which showcases about a hundred titles from thirty countries films for Children and Youth – Jul.*

Doclisboa, Largo da Madalena 1, 1°, 1100-317 Lisbon, Portugal. Tel: (351 21) 8 883 093; e: doclisboa@doclisboa.org; web: www.doclisboa.org. *Competitive, with the international section featuring around 180 of the best documentaries from around the world, which were produced last season (2011–12.) Some have already won awards and received critical acclaim. For others it will be their first screening – Oct.*

Doha Tribeca Film Festival, web: www.dohatribecafilm.com. *The festival will showcase more than 50 films from 35 countries, screening before an expected audience of more than 50,000 people. Internationally acclaimed Arab films, plus a cross-section of comedies, family-oriented films, epics, political biopics, thrillers and documentaries, screened at Doha's celebrated Museum of Islamic Art and in cinemas across Doha. While uniquely Qatari in its identity, the festival is modelled on the success of Tribeca*

Film Festival's dedication to engaging the local community and helping to promote and support filmmaking talent – Oct.

Dubai International Film Festival, Dubai Media City, PO Box 53777, Dubai, United Arab Emirates. Tel: (971 4) 391 3378; e: diffinfo@ dubaimediacity.ae; web: www.dubaifilmfest. com. *The festival was launched in 2004 with the theme of 'Bridging Cultures/Meeting Minds'. DIFF reflects Dubai's cosmopolitan and multicultural character and its mission to promote global understanding and intercultural dialogue. The festival showcases a wide selection of features, shorts and documentaries from around the world, in and out of competition. The festival continues to act as a platform for showcasing excellence in Arab cinema and contributing to the development and growth of the regional industry and talent. The Dubai Film Market is the most comprehensive film market in the Arab world and a multi-faceted initiative that works 'from script to screen', covering every aspect of cinema from conceptualisation to distribution. It houses the Dubai Film Connection, a successful co-production market; the Dubai Film Forum, a popular hub for talent development, funding, workshops and networking; Enjaaz, the dedicated post-production support programme; and Dubai Filmmart, specialising in content trade, acquisition and distribution. As the only gateway of its kind between the major film centres of Europe and South East Asia, the Dubai Film Market represents the interest of the more than 70 nations in the wider region. DIFF screens over 160 films from more than 50 nations; an influx of A-list talent from Europe, the Americas, the Middle East and Asia; and a thriving industry operation – Dec.*

Durban International Film Festival, Centre for Creative Arts, University of KwaZulu-Natal, Durban 4041, South Africa. Tel: (27 31) 260 2506; e: cca@ukzn.ac.za; web: www.cca.ukzn.ac.za. *South Africa's longest-running film festival will present over 250 screenings of current films from around the world, with strong focus on South African and African cinema at venues across Durban and in surrounding communities. Alongside the screenings of films, the festival*

offers an extensive workshop and seminar programme as well as training and industry events – Jul. 19–29, 2012.

Early Melons International Student Film Festival, Tupolevova 18, 85101 Bratislava, Slovakia. Tel: (421 9) 1093 8268; e: info@ earlymelons.com; web: www.earlymelons. com. *Dedicated to different aspects of student cinematography the festival focuses on the latest European film production and aims to become a free platform for people who desire to understand the world through film, video-art and photography. Competitive with workshops supervised by film professionals connected with student film production – Mar.*

East End Film Festival (EEFF), The Brady Arts Centre, 192-196 Hanbury St, London, E1 5HU, UK. Tel: (+44) 020 7364 7917; e: film@eastendfilmfestival.com; web: www. eastendfilmfestival.com. *Held across numerous cinemas and music venues in London's East End the programme reflects the multi-cultural make-up of East London, with a strong emphasis on local, grassroots film exhibition showcasing alongside the 'new wave' of British, Asian and Eastern European cinema blended with an innovative mix of video art, music and cross-platform live events – Apr.*

Edinburgh International Film Festival, 88 Lothian Rd, Edinburgh EH3 9BZ, Scotland. Tel: (44 131) 228 4051; e: info@edfilmfest.org.uk; web: www.edfilmfest.org.uk. *EIFF has developed into a crucial business hub for the UK and international film industry, a key attraction for Edinburgh, and one of the world's best-loved audience festivals. With an emphasis upon new talent, discovery and innovation, EIFF's vibrant programme of films and events combines a commitment to audience edification and pleasure with a strong ongoing stake in the development the UK and Scottish film industries – Jun. 20–Jul. 1, 2012.*

Edmonton International Film Festival, Edmonton International Film Society, Suite 201, 10816A-82 Ave, Edmonton, Alberta, T6E 2B3, Canada. Tel: (1 780) 423 0844;

e: info@edmontonfilmfest.com; web: www.
edmontonfilmfest.com. *The festival screens
cinematic gems of all genres from around
the globe and celebrates the unique voices in
moviemaking such as directors, writers and
producers. The schedule includes 55 feature-
length slots and 110 short films programmed into
feature-length packages. All films screened at EIFF
must be Edmonton premieres – Sept 21–29, 2012.*

Emden International Film Festival, An der
Berufschule 3, 26721 Emden, Germany; web:
www.filmfest-emden.de. *The main focus is on
current film productions from North-Western
Europe. Due to its extensive programme of
new British and Irish films, the festival has also
come to be regarded as a showcase for these
productions in Germany. With over 100 films on
seven screens, it is primarily an audience festival
for its 22,000 visitors and has developed into
a meeting place for numerous representatives
of the German and North-West European film
industry – Jun. 6–12, 2012.*

Espoo Ciné International Film Festival, PO Box
95, FI-02101 Espoo, Finland. Tel: (358 9) 466 599;
e: office@espoocine.fi; web: www.espoocine.fi.
*Showcase of contemporary European, primarily
long feature, films in Finland. The traditional
section should appeal to movie buffs, and the
growing fantasy selection should attract those
hungry for stimulation of the imagination. Annual
special programmes present, for example, French
and Spanish gems, films from Eastern Europe,
documentaries, gay films and US indies, not to
forget the best of contemporary Finnish cinema,
outdoor screenings, retrospectives, sneak previews,
seminars and distinguished guests. Estimated to
screen 150–200 films – Aug. 17–26, 2012.*

European Film Forum Scanorama, Ozo Strasse
4, Vilnius 08200, Lithuania. Tel: (370 5) 276 0367;
e: info@kino.lt; web: www.scanorama.lt. *The
festival screens a variety of genres, including
features, documentaries, shorts and experimental
films from new and emerging talents that
represent contemporary European film in the
three biggest towns in Lithuania: Vilnius, Kaunas
and Klaipėda – Nov.*

Festival Dei Popoli, Borgo Pinti 82 Rosso,
50121 Firenze, Italy. Tel: (39 055) 244 778;
e: festivaldeipopoli@festivaldeipopoli.191.it;
web: www.festivaldeipopoli.org. *International
documentary film festival focusing on social,
anthropological, historical and political issues. It
includes the following sections: Official Selection,
Italian Panorama, tributes/retrospectives,
seminars, panel discussions, special events
– Nov.*

Festival Des 3 Continents, 7 rue de l'Héronnière,
BP 43302, 44033 Nantes Cedex 1, France. Tel: (33
2) 4069 7414; e: festival@3continents.com; web:
www.3continents.com. *The festival provides a
showcase for eighty to a hundred films (fiction
and documentary) from Africa, Latin America and
Asia. It is one of the few festivals where genuine
discoveries may still be made. The Produire
Au Sud workshop created in 2000 takes place
during the festival and supports the creation of
a network of young producers from Asia, Africa
and Latin America, laying foundations for lasting
cooperation between European film professionals
and emerging professionals from the South
– Nov.*

**Festival du Cinema International en Abitibi-
Temiscamingue**, 215 Mercier Ave, Rouyn-
Noranda, Quebec J9X 5WB, Canada. Tel: (1 819)
762 6212; e: info@festivalcinema.ca; web: www.
festivalcinema.ca. *The festival presents nearly
150 International shorts, medium and full-length
features; animation, documentary and fiction
from more than thirty countries – late Oct./early
Nov.*

Festival du Nouveau Cinema, 3805 Boulevard
St-Laurent, Montreal, Quebec, Canada H2W 1X9.
Tel: (1 514) 282 0004; e: info@nouveaucinema.
ca; web: www.nouveaucinema.ca. *The festival
celebrated its 40th edition in 2011 and is known
for highlighting new trends in cinema and new
media, providing a showcase for new, original
works, particularly in the fields of independent
cinema and digital creation. The festival welcomes
Quebec, Canadian and international artists in
a convivial atmosphere that prizes public and
professional exchange – Oct.*

Filmfest Dresden – International Short Film Festival, Alaunstrasse 62, D-01099, Dresden, Germany. Tel: (49 351) 829 470; e: info@filmfest-dresden.de; web: www.filmfest-dresden.de. *Presents short animated and fiction films as well as documentary and experimental films from around the world. The centrepieces of the festival programme are the International and the National Competitions. Each year over 2,500 fiction and animated films from more than 80 countries are submitted for nominations to the competitions (must be no more than two years old and no longer than 30 minutes.) The festival also organises workshops and seminars for young filmmakers – Apr. 17–22, 2012.*

Filmfest Hamburg, Steintorweg 4, 20099 Hamburg, Germany. Tel: (49 40) 3991 9000-0; e: info@filmfesthamburg.de; web: www. filmfesthamburg.de. *In eight permanent and several temporary sections, Filmfest Hamburg shows around 120 national and international feature and documentary films as German, European or world premieres. The many facets of the programme range from sophisticated art house films to innovative mainstream cinema – late Sep./early Oct.*

Filmfest München, Sonnenstr 21, D-80331, Munich, Germany. Tel: (49 89) 381 9040; e: info@ filmfest-muenchen.de; web: www.filmfest-muenchen.de. *Germany's largest summer festival screening over 200 films from more than forty countries – Jun. 29–July.7, 2012.*

Florida Film Festival, Enzian Theatre, 1300 South Orlando Ave, Maitland, Florida 32751, USA. Tel: (1 407) 629 1088; web: www.floridafilmfestival. com. *This year we celebrate our 21st anniversary by bringing you more of the best. With over 160 cutting-edge films, 100 visiting filmmakers, plenty of special guests, and non-stop events, this festival will do everything to ensure 10-days of Film, Food, and Fun – Apr. 13–22, 2012.*

Fort Lauderdale International Film Festival, 1314 East Las Olas Blvd, Suite 007, Fort Lauderdale, FL 33301, USA. Tel: (1 954) 760 9898; e: info@fliff.com; web: www.fliff.com. *Screening features, documentaries and shorts from around the globe. Competitive – late Oct./early Nov.*

Fribourg International Film Festival, Ancienne Gare, Case Postale 550, CH-1701 Fribourg, Switzerland. Tel: (41 26) 347 4200; e: info@fiff. ch; web: www.fiff.ch. *The festival promotes and supports independent cinema and young filmmakers from Asia, South America and Africa. The core of the festival is the high level competition of feature-length fiction and documentary films, which attracts every year audacious, artistic and visionary pictures. This official selection is amended by a short film programme. Furthermore, special sections and retrospectives offer the possibility of going deeper into a cinematographic topic, genre or period – Mar. 24–31, 2012.*

Full Frame Documentary Film Festival, 324 Blackwell St, Suite 500, Washington Bldg, Bay 5, Durham, NC 27701, USA. Tel: (1 919) 687 4100; e: info@fullframefest.org; web: www. fullframefest.org. *Screening over 100 films as well as discussions, panels, and southern hospitality. Set within a four-block radius, the intimate festival landscape fosters community and conversation between filmmakers, film professionals and the public – Apr. 12–15, 2012.*

Future Film Festival, Via Pietralata, 65/2, 40122 Bologna, Italy. Tel: (39 051) 296 0672; e: ffinfo@futurefilmfestival.org; web: www. futurefilmfestival.org. *Dedicated to animation and special effects, and highlighting the changes in digital imaginary and the evolution of cinema and animation. Panels, international previews, special events and workshops – Mar. 27–Apr. 1, 2012.*

Galway Film Fleadh, 36D Merchants Dock, Merchants Road, Galway City, Ireland. Tel: (353 91) 562 200; e: info@galwayfilmfleadh.com; web: www.galwayfilmfleadh.com. *'The Galway Film Fleadh is a wonderful event. Might Rain. Doesn't matter!' – Anthony Minghella. The Galway Film Fleadh – Ireland's leading film festival takes place over six days in July. Now entering its 24th year, the Fleadh screens the best in Irish, European and World cinema through an all inclusive, educational, entertaining and enjoyable programme. The Fleadh is above all a film-lover's festival with numerous filmmakers on hand to discuss, debate and interact*

GET THE COMPLETE PICTURE!
24th GALWAY
FILM FLEADH
10-15 JULY 2012
WWW.GALWAYFILMFLEADH.COM

with their audiences through Masterclasses, Public Interviews, Tributes and Retrospectives. In addition, the Galway Film Fair, a transatlantic bridge for the European Film and Television Industry, hosts 600 one-on-one meetings for producers with projects and invited film financiers, seminars, networking breakfasts and other industry events – Jul. 10–15, 2012.

Galway Film Fleadh

Ghent International Film Festival, 40B Leeuwstraat, B-9000 Ghent, Belgium. Tel: (32 9) 242 8060; e: info@filmfestival. be; web: www.filmfestival.be. and www. worldsoundtrackacademy.com. *Belgium's most prominent annual film event which attracts an attendance of 132,000-plus and is selected by Variety as one of the 50 'must attend' festivals due to its unique focus on film music. This competitive festival awards grants worth up to $60,000 and screens around 100 features and 50 shorts, most without a Benelux distributor. Besides the official competition, focusing on the impact of music on film, the festival includes following sections: Festival Previews (World, European, Benelux or Belgian premières), World Cinema (films from all over the world,* mainly without a distributor), retrospectives, a programme of media art, film music concerts, seminars and a tribute to an important international film maker. The festival's Joseph Plateau Awards are the highest honours in Benelux. Presented for the first time in 2001, the festival also hands out the World Soundtrack Awards, judged by some 300 international composers. Every year the festival is the meeting point for film music composers and fans worldwide – Oct. 9–20, 2012.*

Glasgow Film Festival, 12 Rose St, Glasgow G3 6RB, UK. Tel: (44 141) 332 6535; e: boxoffice@ glasgowfilm.org; web: www.glasgowfilm.org. *The festival showcases a unique programme of feature films, shorts, special events and live and interactive happenings catering to an audience of more than 30,000 people across key city centre venues. The festival is committed to supporting Scottish talent and providing audiences with the opportunity to see the best of world cinema – Feb. 16–26, 2012.*

Glimmer: Hull International Short Film Festival, Suite 4 Danish Buildings, 44-46 High St, Hull, HU1 1PS, UK. Tel: (44) 01482 381512; e: office@hullfilm.co.uk; web: www.hullfilm. co.uk. *Celebrating its 10th edition, the festival is dedicated to showcasing the very best short films from across the world, of any genre that run up to a maximum of 45 minutes and were made after Jan. 1, 2010. The wide and diverse selection of films include dramas, documentaries, artist's film, video and animation with numerous competitions, masterclasses, and special programmes – Oct. 2012.*

Golden Apricot International Film Festival, 3 Moskovyan St, 0001 Yerevan, Armenia. Tel: (374) 1052 1042; e: info@gaiff.am; web: www. gaiff.am. *The festival takes place in the capital of Armenia, Yerevan, at the foot of biblical Mount Ararat. The theme of the festival is 'Crossroads of Cultures and Civilization' and the aim is to build cultural bridges and foster dialogue in this very complex corner of the planet. The festival includes two main competition sections: International Competition (Feature and Documentary) and*

Armenian Panorama National Competition. In each category there are two main prizes: one Grand Prize 'Golden Apricot' (together with a financial award) and one Special Prize 'Silver Apricot'. In 2012, a new short film competition section – 'Stone' – will be launched. Other festival sections are: Directors Across Borders Regional Competition, retrospectives, master-classes etc – Jul. 8–15, 2012.

2011 Golden Apricot International Film Festival opening ceremony with Serge Avedikyan, Fanny Ardant, Abbas Kiarostami and Harutyun Khachatryan.

Golden Carpathian Market and Film Festival, Strada Horatiu nr 12, Sector 1, Bucharest, Romania. Tel: (40) 31 405 61 65; e: radu.nicolae@ idea-zone.ro; web: www.goldencarpathian.com. *Showcases Eastern European productions with the affiliated Market providing film professionals the ideal forum in which to sell films and buy broadcast rights as well as providing networking opportunities for production and co-production deals – Aug. 23–26, 2012.*

Göteborg International Film Festival, Olof Palmes Plats 1, S- 413 04 Göteborg, Sweden. Tel: (46 31) 339 3000; e: info@giff.se; web: www.giff.

se. *Now in its 35th year, it is the leading festival in the Nordic countries and Europe's 5th largest public festival with around 200,000 visitors. With a large international programme screening some 450 films from around 70 countries and a special focus on Nordic films, including the Nordic Competition, the festival also features the Nordic Film Market, which showcases the newest Scandinavian films and aims to strengthen the position of Nordic films in the world. International seminars, master classes and parties – Jan. 27–Feb. 6, 2012.*

Guadalajara International Film Festival, Nebulosa 2916, Colonia Jardines del Bosque, Guadalajara, Jalisco, Mexico. Tel: (52 33) 3121 7461; e: info@festivalcinedgl.udg.mx; web: www.guadalajaracinemafest.com. *Offers recent Mexican and Ibero-American film productions, increasing the awareness of the world film industry to the work of noteworthy Ibero-American film directors and presenting other remarkable and innovative films by new filmmakers – Mar. 2–10, 2012.*

Heartland Film Festival, 1043 Virginia Ave, Suite 2, Indianapolis, Indiana 46203, USA. Tel: (1 317) 464 9405; e: info@heartlandfilmfestival. org; web: www.heartlandfilmfestival.org. *The festival screens independent films from around the world. The festival is comprised of student and professional films, a variety of special events and a one-of-a-kind experience in one of the Midwest's most inviting cities – Oct. 18–27, 2012.*

Helsinki International Film Festival – Love & Anarchy, Mannerheimintie 22–24, PO Box 889, FI-00101 Helsinki, Finland. Tel: (358 9) 6843 5230; e: office@hiff.fi; web: www.hiff.fi. *The largest film festival in Finland has found its place as the top venue for the new and the alternative in cinema and in popular culture. The festival has a memorable subtitle, 'Love & Anarchy', adopted from a Lina Wertmüller film from the 1970s. The subtitle Love & Anarchy has turned into a trademark of cutting edge films over the years: films with a spark of something different, fearlessly plunging into unexplored frontiers. During its 25-year lifespan, the festival has expanded from two theatres to 12 screens and* established itself as an 11-day homage to cinema. In 1988 the festival screened 26 films. Nowadays the programme consists of around 120 feature films and 80 short films from all over the world – Sep. 20–30, 2012.

Holland Animation Film Festival, Hoogt 4, 3512 GW Utrecht, Netherlands. Tel: (31 30) 233 1733; e: info@haff.nl; web: www.haff.awn. nl. *International competitions for independent and animation films; special programmes, retrospectives, exhibitions – Mar. 28–Apr. 1, 2012.*

Hong Kong International Film Festival, 21/F, Millennium City 3, 370 Kwun Tong Road, Kowloon, Hong Kong. Tel: (852) 2970 3300; e: info@hkiff.org. hk; web: www.hkiff.org.hk. *The festival screens over 300 titles from more than 50 countries in 11 major cultural venues across the territory and is one of Hong Kong's largest cultural events, reaching an audience of over 600,000, including 5,000 business executives who attend Hong Kong Film and Television Market (FILMART), which runs alongside the festival. Committed to discovering new talent, the festival premieres the breadth of Chinese cinema and showcases Asian talents. Festival-goers can enjoy world-class films, attend seminars hosted by leading filmmakers from around the world, visit film exhibitions, join celebration parties, and more – Mar. 21–Apr. 5, 2012.*

Hot Docs Canadian International Documentary Festival, 110 Spadina Ave, Suite 333, Toronto, Ontario, M5V 2K4, Canada. Tel: (1 416) 203 2155; e: info@hotdocs.ca; web: www.hotdocs. ca. *North America's largest documentary festival, conference and market, which presents a selection of more than 150 cutting-edge documentaries from Canada and around the globe – Apr. 26–May 6, 2012.*

Huelva Latin American Film Festival, Casa Colon, Plaza del Punto s/n, 21003 Huelva, Spain. Tel: (34 95) 921 0170; e: festival@festicinehuelva. com; web: www.festicinehuelva.com. *The festival reaches its 38th edition in 2012 and is one of the most important cinematographic contests of its kind. The most outstanding films from both shores of the Atlantic get together in one of the*

main Latin American cultural events. Due to its international vocation, the festival aims to open the European film market to up-and-coming talent from the Latin American sector. It also hosts the Latin American Co-Production Forum, where outstanding producers, directors and distributors meet. The best film is awarded a prize known as the Golden Colombus – Nov.

Huesca Film Festival, Calle del Parque 1, 2, 22002 Huesca, Spain. Tel: (34 974) 212 582; e: info@huesca-filmfestival.com; web: www.huesca-filmfestival.com. *Celebrating its 40th edition in 2012, the festival screens shorts and includes official competitive sections composed of the Iberoamerican, International Shorts and European Documentary contests. The winners receive the Award Danzante and the winners of the Award Danzante in the Iberoamerican and International contest automatically qualify to enter the Short Films category of the Academy of Motion Picture Arts and Sciences in Hollywood for the concurrent season – Jun. 8–16, 2012.*

Independent Film Week, 68 Jay Street Room 425 Brooklyn, NY 11201, USA. Tel: (1 212) 465 8200; web: www.ifp.org. *One-of-a-kind event that brings the international filmmaking community to New York City to celebrate, advocate and introduce new voices on the independent scene. The objective is to create a meeting place for emerging filmmakers and established producers selected for their strong new projects as well as individuals from companies, festivals and organisations, with the aim of helping the work get made and, ultimately, seen by public audiences. Annually, IFP invites approximately 125 new works-in-development. Projects are accepted into one of various sections: Emerging Narrative, No Borders, Independent Filmmaker Labs and Spotlight on Documentaries. Strategically positioned between the Toronto and New York Film Festivals, it is an efficient week for meetings, screenings and re-connecting with colleagues – Sep.*

International Film Festival Innsbruck, Egger-Lienzstrasse 20, A-6020 Innsbruck, Austria. Tel: (43 512) 571262; e: info@iffi.at; web: www.iffi.at. *Films about Africa, Latin America and Asia. Competitive – Jun. 5–10, 2012.*

International Leipzig Festival for Documentary and Animated Film, Grosse Fleischergasse 11, 04109 Leipzig, Germany. Tel: (49 341) 308 640; e: info@dok-leipzig.de; web: www.dok-leipzig.de. *The festival screens the best, most exciting, moving and artistically outstanding animated and documentary films from more than fifty countries. Competitive – Oct.*

International Short Film Festival Winterthur, Steiggasse 2, Postfach, CH-8402 Winterthur, Switzerland. Tel: (41 52) 212 1166; e: info@kurzfilmtage.ch; web: www.kurzfilmtage.ch. *Popular audience event and an important platform for European short films, attracting over 14,500 spectators. Over 200 films are shown from all over the world, with the core of the festival being the International and National Competition. In addition, the festival offers a rich and varied supporting programme that includes thematic film programmes, panel discussions, special events and concerts. At the Swiss Film School Day and the Producers' Day, filmmakers can meet important contacts from the film industry and participate at special industry events – Nov.*

Israel Film Festival, Israfest Foundation, 6404 Wilshire Blvd, Suite 1240, Los Angeles, CA 90048, USA. Tel: (1 323) 966 4166; e: meir@israelfilmfestival.org; web: www.israelfilmfestival.com. *The mission of the festival is to enrich the American vision of Israeli life and culture, to spotlight Israel's thriving film and television industry, and to promote cultural recognition of Israel through the powerful medium of film. It screens feature films, documentaries, television dramas and short films and is the largest showcase for Israeli films in the United States – 2012 dates: Mar. 15–29 in Los Angeles; Apr. 15–22 in Miami; May 3–7 in New York.*

Jameson Dublin International Film Festival, 50 Upper Mount St, Dublin 2, Ireland. Tel: (353 1) 662 4260; e: info@jdiff.com; web: www.jdiff.com. *Celebrating its 10th Anniversary in 2012, the festival is aimed squarely at the cinema-going public and presents over 120 films from around the world. Irish Film Talent is celebrated as an integral part of the JDIFF programme each year by presenting Irish film in all its forms, from archival and documentary to the very latest Irish feature films from first time directors – Feb. 16–26, 2012.*

Jihlava International Documentary Film Festival, Jana Masaryka 16, PO Box 33, 58601 Jihlava, Czech Republic. Tel: (420 7) 7410 1656; e: office@dokument-festival.cz; web: www.dokument-festival.cz. *The festival is a celebration of creative documentary film and shows work from around the world with screenings followed by after-film talks, plus an accompanying programme of workshops, panel discussions, theatre, authors' readings, concerts, and exhibitions – Oct. 23–28, 2012.*

Kaunas International Film Festival, V Putvinskio St 56, LT-44211 Kaunas, Lithuania. Tel: (370) 6550 6559; e: info@kinofestivalis.lt; web: www.kinofestivalis.lt. *The festival presents films that have been acclaimed worldwide, whilst also looking for new discoveries. The main priority of Kaunas IFF is a combination of the artistic and social statements in film and it continues its strategy of presenting exclusively Lithuanian or Baltic premieres – Sep. 26–Oct. 7, 2012.*

La Rochelle International Film Festival, 16 rue Saint Sabin, 75011 Paris, France. Tel: (33 1) 4806 1666; e: info@festival-larochelle.org; web: www.festival-larochelle.org. *Non-competitive, featuring over 250 original and new releases from all over the world to a large audience of very enthusiastic film buffs. The festival includes tributes to contemporary directors or actors, often in their presence; retrospectives devoted to the work of past filmmakers; Here and There, a selection of unreleased films from all over the world; From Yesterday till Today, premieres of rare films restored and re-edited; Carpets, Cushions and Video, video works projected on the ceiling above reclining spectators; Films for Children. The festival ends with an all night programme of five films, followed by breakfast in cafés overlooking the old port – Jun. 29–Jul. 9, 2012.*

Las Palmas de Gran Canaria International Film Festival, León y Castillo 322, 4ª Planta, 35007 Las Palmas de Gran Canaria. Tel: (34 928) 446 833;

e: coordinacion@festivalcinelaspalmas.com; web: www.festivalcinelaspalmas.com. *The festival is proud of its role as a defender of creative and independent productions from outside the mainstream. There are two main competitive sections: the Official Section, including art-house feature films and short films unreleased in Spain, and the New Directors Section – Apr.*

Leeds International Film Festival, The Town Hall, The Headrow, Leeds, LS1 3AD, UK. Tel: (44 113) 247 8398. e: leedsfilmfestpr@gmail.com. Web: www.leedsfilm.com. *Presented by Leeds City Council, the festival is the largest regional film festival in the UK. The programme will feature the Official Selection, Cinema Versa, Fanomenon, Thought Bubble, Short Film City and Cherry Kino programmes. In addition, Leeds Film organises a year-round exhibition with partner organisations in the city, education programmes and delivers the Leeds Young People's Film Festival – Nov.*

London Turkish Film Festival, 52B Beatty Rd, London, N16 8EB. Tel: (44 20) 7503 3584; e: vedide@ltff.org.uk; web: www.ltff.org.uk. *The festival provides a platform in the UK for a new generation of filmmakers of Turkish origin who live and work in Western Europe. It also features programmes of short films, giving an opportunity for the work of young feature and documentary film-makers to be widely seen – late Nov./early Dec.*

Ljubljana International Film Festival, Cankarjev Dom, Prešernova Cesta 010, 1000 Ljubljana, Slovenia. Tel: (306 1) 241 7147; web: http://en.liffe.si. *Provides an overview of contemporary world film production and shows over ninety feature films and 15 shorts films in more than 250 screenings. It also includes a film workshop, multi-media interactive projects, exhibition and other events. Competitive – Nov.*

Málaga Film Festival, Calle Ramos Marin 2, 29012 Malaga, Spain. Tel: (34 95) 222 8242; e: info@festivaldemalaga.com; web: www.festivaldemalaga.com. *The festival, together with the Goya prizes, have grown to become the two fundamental appointments for the whole audiovisual sector of Spanish Cinema. It brings together all the industry professionals, both to present their films and to debate questions affecting the industry – Apr. 21–28, 2012.*

International Filmfestival Mannheim-Heidelberg, Collini-Center, Galerie, D-68161 Mannheim, Germany. Tel: (49 621) 102 943; e: info@iffmh.de; web: www.iffmh.de. *The festival of independent new film artists presents around forty international new feature films in two main sections: International Competition and International Discoveries. The films are genuine premieres and have to be really outstanding new art-house films by new directors. The 'Mannheim Meeting Place' aims to support outstanding film projects via distribution or co-production. Furthermore, selected producers are invited to become potential co-producers of new film projects. More than 60,000 filmgoers and 1,000 film professionals attend – Nov.*

Margaret Mead Film & Video Festival, American Museum of Natural History, Central Park, West & 79th St, New York, NY 10024-5192, USA. Tel: (1 212) 769 5305; e: meadfest@amnh.org; web: www.amnh.org/mead. *The longest-running premiere showcase for international documentaries in the United States, encompassing a broad spectrum of work, from indigenous community media to experimental nonfiction – Nov.*

Melbourne International Film Festival, PO Box 4982, Melbourne 3001, Victoria, Australia. Tel: (61 3) 8660 4888, e: miff@miff.com.au, web: www.miff.com.au. *The longest-running festival in the southern hemisphere, showing more than 400 features, shorts, documentaries and new media works, presented in five venues. It has the largest and most diverse programme of screenings and special events in the country, in addition to the largest audience. There is also growing international regard for MIFF as a film market place, with a steady increase in the presence of sales agents – Aug. 2–19, 2012.*

Miami International Film Festival, 25 NE 2nd Street, Suite 5518, Miami, Florida 33132, USA. Tel: (1 305) 237 3456; e: info@miamifilmfestival.com;

web: www.miamifilmfestival.com. *The festival, presented by Miami Dade College, is considered one of the best Ibero-centric film festivals in the US. It is designed to introduce the finest selection of current films and filmmakers to South Florida's residents and visitors. The festival encompasses international film screenings, gala premieres, REEL seminars and the Miami Film Society, which offers Members an inclusive and rewarding range of year-round activities that investigate and celebrate the artistry and innovation of the world's most imaginative cinematic visionaries –* Mar. 2–11, 2012.

Midnight Sun Film Festival, Kansanopistontie 5, 99600 Sodankylä, Finland. Tel: (358 16) 614 522; e: office@msfilmfestival.fi; web: www.msfilmfestival.fi. *The festival is one of the most unique in the world, with internationally renowned film directors, young directors and an international audience meeting under the midnight sun, in the relaxed and informal 'spirit of Sodankylä'. The festival is informally divided in three sections: films by the most famous film directors of all time, pearls of the new cinema and silent movies with live music –* Jun. 13–17, 2012.

Mill Valley Film Festival, 1001 Lootens Place, Suite 220, San Rafael, CA 94901, USA. Tel: (1 415) 383 5256; e: mvff@cafilm.org; web: www.mvff.com. *Known as a filmmakers' festival, it offers a high profile, prestigious, non-competitive and welcoming environment perfect for celebrating the best in independent and world cinema. MVFF presents over 200 films from 50 countries featuring a wide variety of high calibre international programming, in beautiful Marin County, just across the Golden Gate Bridge. The festival includes the innovative Children's Film Fest, celebrity tributes, seminars and special events –* Oct.

Mipdoc, 11 rue du Colonel Pierre Avia, BP 572, 75726 Paris Cedex 15, France. Tel: (33 1) 4190 4580; e: info.miptv@reedmidem.com; web: www.miptv.com. *Specialist international screening marketplace and conference for documentaries –* Mar. 30–31, 2012.

Montpellier International Festival of Mediterranean Film (Cinemed), 78 Ave du Pirée, 34000 Montpellier, France. Tel: (33 4) 9913 7370; e:info@cinemed.tm.fr; web: www.cinemed.tm.fr. *The best recent production with more than 120 films previously unscreened films in the official selection, with cash, aid and services for the winners in the various competition sections. Comprising features, shorts, documentaries and experimental films –* Oct. 26–Nov. 3, 2012.

Netherlands Film Festival, PO Box 1581, 3500 BN Utrecht, Netherlands. Tel: (31 30) 230 3800; e: info@filmfestival.nl; web: www.filmfestival.nl. *Since 1981, the festival has presented the latest crop of Dutch feature films, documentaries, short films and television films to the Dutch public as well as an audience of international and Dutch-based professionals. Many of these productions are world premieres of which a selection compete for the grand prize of Dutch cinema, the Golden Calf for Best Film. During the festival each film genre is allotted its own special day. Retrospectives and special programmes offer audiences a chance to review films from previous years. Furthermore, the festival screens films made by talented young filmmakers from the Dutch audio-visual institutes as well as short and long films from neighbouring Flanders. Talkshows, workshops, parties and exhibitions make the festival complete. The Holland Film Meeting (HFM) is a sidebar of the festival that provides a series of business-oriented events for the international professionals in attendance. The HFM consists of the Benelux Screenings, the Netherlands Production Platform (NPP), professional workshops and panels, the Variety Cinema Militants Programme and the Binger-Screen International Interview –* Sep. 26–5 Oct., 2012.

New Directors/New Films, Film Society of Lincoln Center, 165 West 65th Street, 4th Floor, New York, NY 10023, USA. Tel: (1 212) 875 5610; e: festival@filmlinc.com; web: www.filmlinc.com. *One of the premiere international showcases for the work of emerging filmmakers. Non-competitive with no separate categories and no prizes awarded. Feature films and shorts are chosen according to quality from all categories:*

*animated, experimental, documentary, dramatic –
Mar. 21–Apr. 1, 2012.*

New York Film Festival, Film Society of Lincoln
Center, 165 West 65th Street, 4th Floor, New
York, NY 10023-6595, USA. Tel: (1 212) 875 5610;
e: festival@filmlinc.com; web: www.filmlinc.com.
*Celebrating its 50th Anniversary in 2012, the festival
will show new works by directors from around the
world, featuring inspiring and provocative cinema by
emerging talents and first-rank international artists,
whose films are often recognised as contemporary
classics – late Sep./early Oct.*

New Zealand International Film Festival,
Box 9544, Marion Square, Wellington 6141,
New Zealand. Tel: (64 4) 385 0162; e: festival@
nzff.co.nz; web: www.nzff.co.nz. *In 2009, the
Auckland and Wellington festivals dropped their
individual identities to become known as the
New Zealand International Film Festival. The
festival provides a non-competitive New Zealand
showcase and welcomes many international
filmmakers and musicians. Highlights of its
programme, brimming with animation, art-house,
documentaries and retrospective programmes,
tour to a further 14 New Zealand centres –
Auckland 12–29 Jul.; Wellington 19 Jul.–5 Aug.;
Dunedin 26 Jul.–12 Aug.*

Odense International Film Festival,
Kulturmaskinen, Farvergården 7, DK-5100
Odense C, Denmark. Tel: (45) 6551 2821; e:
filmfestival@odense.dk; web: www.filmfestival.
dk. *Denmark's largest international short film
festival invites the best short films with original
and imaginative content. Besides screenings of
more than 200 national and international short
films, the festival offers a number of exciting
side programmes consisting of retrospectives,
feature films screened at unusual venues, a
festival night club and viewing of all competition
films in the Video Bar. The festival hosts a range
of seminars for film professionals, librarians and
teachers, educates children and youth in the field
of forceful, alternative film experiences, and is a
meeting place for international film directors and
other film professionals in the field of short films
and documentaries – Aug. 20–25, 2012.*

Palm Beach International Film Festival, 6018
SW 18th Street, Suite C-7, Boca Raton, Florida
33433, USA. Tel: (1 561) 362 0003; e: info@
pbifilmfest.org; web: www.pbifilmfest.org.
*Committed to supporting emerging filmmakers
of today and tomorrow, and screens independent
features, shorts and documentaries from around
the world. Competitive – Apr. 11–19, 2012.*

**Palm Springs International Festival of Short
Films & Film Market**, 1700 E Tahquitz Canyon
Way, Suite 3, Palm Springs, CA 92262, USA. Tel:
(1 760) 322 2930; e: info@psfilmfest.org; web:
www.psfilmfest.org. *Competitive shorts festival
and market. Student, animation, documentary,
live action and international competition with
Audience and Juried Awards. Seminars and
workshops – Jun. 19–25, 2012.*

Palm Springs International Film Festival, 1700
E Tahquitz Canyon Way, Suite 3, Palm Springs,
CA 92262, USA. Tel: (1 760) 322 2930; e: info@
psfilmfest.org; web: www.psfilmfest.org.
*Celebrating its 23rd edition in 2012, the festival
is one of the largest in the US, hosting 130,000
attendees for a line-up of over 205 films from 69
countries at the 2011 event. Special sections of the
festival have included New Voices/New Visions,
Gala Screenings, Cine Latino, Awards Buzz (Best
Foreign Language Oscar Submissions), World
Cinema Now, Modern Masters and the True Stories
documentary section. The festival includes a Black
Tie Awards Gala on Jan. 7, 2012 – 2011 honourees
included Colin Firth, Natalie Portman, Robert Duvall,
Javier Bardom, Ben Affleck, Michael Douglas,
Carey Mulligan and Jennifer Lawrence. Festival
Director: Darryl MacDonald – Jan. 5–16, 2012.*

Pesaro Film Festival, Via Emilio Faà di Bruno 67,
00195 Rome, Italy. Tel: (39 06) 445 6643/491156; e:
info@pesarofilmfest.it; web: www.pesarofilmfest.it.
*The festival was founded in Pesaro in 1965 by
Bruno Torri and Lino Miccichè and since 2000
has been directed by Giovanni Spagnoletti.
The festival, in addition to being known for the
dynamic and original documentation it offers, is
synonymous with discoveries, with showcasing
emerging cinematographers, with re-readings,
with 'Special Events' – Jun. 23–Jul. 1, 2012.*

Philadelphia Film Festival, Philadelphia Film Society, 1600 North 5th Street, Philadelphia, PA 19122, USA. Tel: (1 267) 239 2941; e: info@filmadelphia.org; web: www.filmadelphia.com. *The 21st edition of the festival will screen over 140 International and USA features, documentaries, shorts and animation from thirty countries – Oct. 18–28, 2012.*

Raindance Film Festival, 6–7 Little Russell St, London, WC1A 2HR, UK. Tel: (44 20) 7287 3833; e: info@raindance.co.uk; web: www.raindance.org. *Raindance is one of Europe's leading independent film festivals and aims to reflect the cultural, visual and narrative diversity of international independent filmmaking, specialising in first-time filmmakers. The 20th edition in 2012 will screen around 100 feature films and 140 shorts as well as hosting a broad range of workshops, masterclasses and workshops – Sep. 26–Oct. 7, 2012.*

Rome International Film Festival, Viale Pietro De Coubertin 10, 00196 Rome, Italy. Tel: (39 06) 4040 1900; e: info@romacinemafest.org; web: www.romacinemafest.org. *The city of Rome provides a magnificent backdrop to the festival with the Auditorium Parco della Musica and the Cinema Village being the main nerve-centre. The festival provides films, retrospectives, meetings and major international stars, which attracts movie lovers is a great event for all those who work for cinema, show cinema and tell us stories through cinema. The festival has now established itself as a truly unique occasion, with over 600,000 visitors flocking to the events, exhibitions, encounters and screenings. The Business Street is a five day long Roman film market for industry professionals – late Oct./early Nov.*

Rotterdam International Film Festival, PO Box 21696, 3001 AR Rotterdam, Netherlands. Tel: (31 10) 890 9090; e: tiger@filmfestivalrotterdam.com; web: www.filmfestivalrotterdam.com. www.cinemareloaded.com and www.youtube.com/iffrotterdam. *With its adventurous, original and distinctive programming, Rotterdam highlights new directors and new directions in contemporary world cinema, exemplified by its Tiger Awards Competition for first and second feature films; the annual showcase of films from developing countries that have been supported by the festival's Hubert Bals Fund, supporting innovative and original film projects from developing countries; and CineMart, the international co-production market developed to nurture the financing and production of new cinema – Jan. 25–Feb. 5, 2012.*

St Louis International Film Festival, 3547 Olive St, St Louis, MO 63103-1014, USA. Tel: (1 314) 289 4150; e: mailroom@cinemastlouis.org; web: www.cinemastlouis.org. *SLIFF showcases the best in cutting-edge features and shorts from around the globe, with the majority of the 300 plus films screened receiving their only St Louis exposure at the festival. Competitive – Nov.*

San Francisco International Film Festival, 39 Mesa St, Suite 110, The Presidio, San Francisco, CA 94129, USA. Tel: (1 415) 561 5014; e: achang@sffs.org; web: www.sffs.org. *Founded in 1957, the festival is the longest-running film festival in the Americas. Held each spring for two weeks, the festival is an extraordinary showcase of cinematic discovery and innovation in the country's most beautiful city. It features some 200 films and live events, with more than 100 filmmakers in attendance and nearly two dozen awards presented for cinematic excellence. The festival attracts an annual audience of more than 75,000. Highly anticipated by its loyal and passionate audiences, championed by civic and community leaders, admired and adored by filmmakers and closely watched by industry professionals, SFIFF is one of the most important events in the Bay Area's cultural calendar and an important stop on the international festival circuit. Around $100,000 is awarded annually through special awards including the New Directors Award, the Golden Gate Awards and the FIPRESCI Prize – Apr. 19–May 3, 2012.*

Sarasota Film Festival, 332 Cocoanut Ave, Sarasota, Florida 34236, USA. Tel: (1 941) 364 9514; e: kathy@sarasotafilmfestival.com; web: www.sarasotafilmfestival.com. *Independent films and events in a beautiful and hospitable location; inquisitive audiences plus a well-organised and publicised programme – Apr. 13–22, 2012.*

Seattle International Film Festival, 305 Harrison St, Seattle, WA 98109, USA. Tel: (1 206) 464 5830; e: info@siff.net; web: www.siff.net. *The largest film festival in the US, SIFF presents more than 250 features, 50 documentaries, and 150 shorts annually. There are cash prizes for the internationally juried New Directors Showcase and Documentary Competition and for Short Films in the categories of: Live Action, Documentary, and Animation. Festival sections include: Alternate Cinema, Face the Music, FutureWave, Films4Familes, Contemporary World Cinema, Emerging Masters, Documentary Films, Tributes, and Archival Films – May 17–Jun. 10, 2012.*

Seville European Film Festival, Avenida del Cid 1, Pabellón de Portugal, 41004 Seville, Spain. Tel: (34 955) 115 586; e: info@festivaldesevilla.com; web: www.festivaldesevilla.com. *The festival is well established as a showcase for recent high-quality, but not always high-profile, European films. Already attracting an impressive critical mass of European industry figures, Seville has grown with each edition. As a result of the festival's international success, the European Film Academy (EFA) will once again hold the ceremony for announcing the European Film Awards nominations in Seville in 2012. The festival also has the support of the main European fund for aiding co-production, Eurimages, and participates in the Media Mundus Programme through the Eye on Films network. Along with the official and parallel sections of film screenings, the Festival continues to strengthen as a meeting place for industry professionals – Nov.*

AFI-Discovery Channel Silverdocs Documentary Festival, AFI Silver Theatre and Cultural Center, 8633 Colesville Road, Silver Spring, MD 20910, USA. Tel: (1 301) 495 6720; e: info@silverdocs.com; web: www.silverdocs.com. *SilverDocs encompasses a seven-day international film festival and five-day concurrent conference that promotes documentary film as a leading art form. SilverDocs takes place at the AFI Silver Theatre, one of the premiere exhibition spaces in the country, and the top art-house cinema in the Washington, DC region. Anchored in the US capital, where important global and national issues are the daily business, SilverDocs is marked by its relevance,* broad intellectual range, and wide public appeal. *Among its numerous special programmes is the Charles Guggenheim Symposium, which in 2011, honoured legendary film directors D.A. Pennebaker and Chris Hegedus – Jun. 20–26, 2012.*

Singapore International Film Festival, 554 Havelock Road, Suite 02-00A Ganges Centre, Singapore 169639, Singapore; web: www.siff.sg. *Celebrating its 25th Anniversary in 2012, SIFF has become known for its dynamic film programming and commitment to the development of film culture and local cinema. The festival screens over 150 films annually, with a focus on groundbreaking Asian cinema – 2012 dates to be confirmed.*

Slamdance Film Festival, 5634 Melrose Ave, Los Angeles, California 90038, USA. Tel: (1 323) 466 1786; e: programming@slamdance; web: www.slamdance.com. *The festival is organised and programmed exclusively by filmmakers for filmmakers, to nurture, support and showcase truly independent works. In doing so, Slamdance has established a unique reputation for premiering new films by first-time writers and directors working within the creative confines of limited budgets. This Academy qualifier also attracts and launches established artists, with world-class alumni including Steven Soderbergh, Christopher Nolan, Marc Forster and Jared Hess. The festival has helped hundreds of films find distribution, including The King of Kong, Weirdsville, Mad Hot Ballroom and breakout success Paranormal Activity. Slamdance adamantly supports self-governance amongst independents and exists to deliver what filmmakers go to festivals for – a chance to show their work and a launching point for their careers – Jan. 20–26, 2012.*

South by Southwest Film Festival, Box 685289, Austin, TX 78765, USA. Tel: (1 512) 467 7979; e: sxsw@sxsw.com; web: http://sxsw.com. *The festival explores all aspects of the art and business of independent filmmaking with emerging talent, new voices and all around exceptional films discovered at SXSW Film each year. The Conference hosts a five-day adventure in the latest filmmaking trends and new technology, featuring distinguished speakers and mentors – Mar. 9–18, 2012.*

Sundance Film Festival, Sundance Institute, 8530 Wilshire Blvd, 3rd Floor, Beverly Hills, CA 90211-3114, USA. Tel: (1 310) 360 1981; e: institute@sundance.org; web: www.sundance. org. *Long known as a celebration of the new and unexpected, the festival offers the best in independent film from the US and around the world. Audiences will discover the 125 feature films and 80 shorts that festival programmers have scoured the world to find. The critically acclaimed festival presents features and documentaries from the US and around the world, and competition films are combined with nightly premieres of works by veteran film artists for a programme that inspires, challenges, delights, startles and moves festival goers. Archival gems by early independent filmmakers, animation of every kind, cutting edge experimental works, midnight cult films, and a jam-packed schedule of panel discussions at Prospector Theatre, Filmmaker Lodge and New Frontier on Park, live shows at the Music Café and a host of spirited parties and events up and down historic Main Street make for a complete film experience that celebrates the art and community of independent filmmaking. Continuing the tradition of sharing the festival with online audiences, www.sundance.org/festival takes both original content and the nuts and bolts of festival going beyond the streets of Park City. With short films from the festival, filmmaker interviews, and breaking news, combined with film listings, box-office information and travel tips, Sundance Film Festival Online is a single online source for experiencing the festival both on the web and on the ground. John Cooper, Director of Festival Programming Department – Jan. 19–29, 2012.*

Sunny Side of the Doc, 21 Bis Quai Maubec, 17000 La Rochelle, France. Tel: (33 5) 4655 7979; e: info@sunnysideofthedoc.com; web: www.sunnysideofthedoc.com. *International documentary market – Jun. 26–29, 2012.*

Taipei Golden Horse Film Festival, e: info@ goldenhorse.org.tw; web: www.goldenhorse. org.tw. *The most prominent annual film festival in Taiwan comprised of two parts. The Golden Horse Awards Competition encourages the development of Chinese-language films. The international programme is intended to introduce excellent films from around the world to Taiwanese audiences in order to stimulate an exchange of ideas and inspire creativity – late Nov./early Dec.*

Taormina Film Festival, Via degli Zingari 11, 00184 Rome, Italy. Tel: (39 064) 86808; e: international@ taorminafilmfest.it; web: www. taorminafilmfest. it. *The festival has a strong identity as a Mediterranean festival with strong ties to the US and world cinema and has chosen to remain a boutique showcase for around 25 highly-selected films from the most recent production – Jun.*

Telluride Film Festival, 800 Jones Street, Berkeley, CA 94710 USA. Tel: (1 510) 665 9494; e: mail@telluridefilmfestival.org; web: www. telluridefilmfestival.org. *The festival keeps its programme a secret until opening day, drawing a crowd of adventurous cineastes vto the small town 9,000 feet up in the San Juan Mountains of Colorado. The 38th edition in 2011 screened 28 new feature films in its main programme, six rare revivals curated by Guest Director Caetano Veloso, 9 Backlot programmes, plus 11 restorations, 30 shorts and hosted 13 seminars and conversations. Student Symposium, City Lights and Film Lab brought 61 college and 15 high school students to see films and meet filmmakers. Screening in nine venues, the festival presentations meet the highest technical standards. Telluride is a non-competitive, non-profit festival. Complete programmes and the festival's 96-page magazine 'Filmwatch' plus video clips, information about attending, entering films students programmes can be found on the festival's website – Aug. 31–Sep. 3, 2012.*

Thessaloniki Documentary Festival, 9 Alexandras Ave, 114 73 Athens, Greece. Tel: (30 210) 870 6016; e: info@filmfestival.gr; web: www. filmfestival.gr. *The festival – Images of the 21st Century is Greece's major annual non-fiction film event. Its sections include 'Views of the World' (subjects of social interest), 'Portraits – Human Journeys' (highlighting the human contribution to cultural, social and historical developments) and 'Recording of Memory' (facts and testimony of social and historic origin). The festival also hosts* *the third largest documentary market in Europe, the Thessaloniki DocMarket – Mar. 9–18, 2012.*

Third Eye Asian Film Festival, Asian Film Foundation, Rajkamal Studio, Parel, Mumbai 400012, India. Tel: (91 22) 2413 7791; e: info@affmumbai.com; web: www.affmumbai.com. *Although Asian cinema has been winning accolades on the international film festival circuit, none of the theatres in India screen Asian cinema commercially. The festival promotes Asian cinema worldwide and aims to establish interaction amongst the Asian film fraternity and to create a dialogue with the West. The Asian countries share cultural similarities and a common socio-economic scenario being plagued by similar problems of poverty, illiteracy, population, lowly status of women. The festival was established to create awareness about each other, amongst Asian countries, with cinema as the common bond bringing people together and fostering understanding between varied cultures. Chairman: Kiran Shantaram. Director: Sudhir Nandgaonkar – Dec. 20–27, 2012.*

Tribeca Film Festival, 375 Greenwich St, New York, NY 10013, USA. Tel: (1 212) 941 2400; e: festival@tribecafilmfestival.org; web: www.tribecafilm.com. *The festival was founded in 2002 by Robert De Niro, Jane Rosenthal and Craig Hatkoff, to spur the economic and cultural revitalization of Lower Manhattan through an annual celebration of film, music and culture. The mission of the festival is to help filmmakers reach the broadest possible audience, enable the international film community and general public to experience the power of cinema and promote New York City as a major filmmaking centre. Since its founding, the festival has attracted over 3.5 million attendees from the US and abroad and has generated over $725 million in economic activity for New York City. The festival is anchored in Tribeca, with additional venues throughout Manhattan and includes film screenings, special events, concerts, a family street fair, and 'Tribeca Talks' panel discussions – Apr. 18–29, 2012.*

True/False Film Festival, 5 South Ninth St, Columbia, Missouri 65201, USA. Tel: (1 573) 442 8783; e: info@truefalse.org; web: www.truefalse.org. *International documentary festival screening some 50 films and including two shorts programmes. The festival highlights innovative work with a cinematic scope, creative takes on contemporary currents, and most of all work that provokes dialogue about its subject and the documentary form itself – Mar. 1–4, 2012.*

Uppsala International Short Film Festival, PO Box 2104, SE-750 02 Uppsala, Sweden. Tel: (46 18) 120 025; e: info@shortfilmfestival.com; web: www.shortfilmfestival.com. *Every year the festival shows more than 300 short films in five different sections exploring the diversity and richness of the short film – from new film to retrospective programmes, from fiction, documentary and experimental film to animation – Oct.*

Valencia International Action and Adventure Film Festival, Fundación Municipal de Cine, Plaza de la Almoina 4, Puertas 1, 2 and 3, 46003 Valencia, Spain. Tel: (34 96) 392 1506; e: info@mostravalencia.com; web: www.mostravalencia.org. *International showcase of the greatest action movies. It also pays tribute to the most successful action and adventure films of all time, through retrospectives of renowned artists who made these films an essential element for the development of the film industry – Apr.*

Vancouver International Film Festival, 1181 Seymour St, Vancouver, British Columbia, Canada V6B 3M7. Tel: (1 604) 685 0260; e: viff@viff.org; web: www.viff.org. *Both in terms of admissions and number of films screened, VIFF is among the five largest film festivals in North America, screening more than 350 films from 80 countries, with around 150,000 people attending. The international line-up includes the pick of the world's top film festivals and many undiscovered gems. Three main programming platforms make the festival unique: the largest selection of East Asian films outside of that region, one of the biggest showcases of Canadian film in the world and a large and important nonfiction programme. Founded in 1982, the festival's mandate is to encourage the understanding of other nations through the art of cinema, to foster the art of cinema, and to stimulate the motion picture industry in British Columbia and Canada – late Sep./early Oct.*

Victoria Film Festival, 1215 Blanshard St, Victoria, British Columbia, V8W 3J4 Canada. Tel: (1 250) 389 0444 389 0406; e: festival@victoriafilmfestival.com; web: www.victoriafilmfestival.com. *The festival screens 150 films at four central venues. It is Vancouver Island's biggest and longest-running film festival with the aim of exposing youth and adults to a broad range of cultural, artistic and philosophical ideas and lifestyles through the presentation of film, video, and new media in order to stimulate critical analysis and inspire an interest in using the medium as a creative tool – Feb. 3–12, 2012.*

Vila do Conde, Auditório Municipal, Praça da República, 4480-715 Vila do Conde, Portugal. Tel: (351 252) 646 516; e: info@curtas.pt; web: www. festival.curtas.pt. *The festival celebrates its 20th Anniversary in 2012 and includes National and International shorts competitions with special programme and retrospectives – Jul. 7–15, 2012.*

Vilnius International Film Festival (Kino Pavasaris), Gediminas Ave 50, Vilnius 01110, Lithuania. Tel: (370) 5249 7221; e: info@ kinopavasaris.lt; web: www.kinopavasaris.lt. *VIFF 'Kino Pavasaris' is the biggest and most important cinema event in Lithuania. Since 1995, the festival earned its reputation by showcasing the latest films, which are carefully chosen from other festivals. Serious discussion, the presence of respected filmmakers, events for industry guests and cheerful parties are essential part of the festival. In 2011 the festival presented more than 130 films with over 64,000 attendees. In 2012 the third 'International Film Festivals Forum' will be held. VIFF presents the annual competition programme 'New Europe – New Names'. The best debut films from Eastern and Central Europe compete for 'the Best Film Award, chosen by an International Jury – Mar. 15–29, 2012.*

Washington, DC International Film Festival (Filmfest DC), PO Box 5571, Washington, DC 20009, USA. Tel: (1 202) 717 0700; e: filmfestdc@ filmfestdc.org; web: www.dciff.org. *Competitive festival celebrating the best in world cinema from over thirty countries – Feb. 29–Mar. 4, 2012.*

ZagrebDox, Factum Centre for Drama Art, Nova Ves 18/3, 10 000 Zagreb, Croatia. Tel: (385 1) 485 4821; e: info@zagrebdox.net; web: www. zagrebdox.net. *International and competitive documentary film festival – Feb. 26–Mar. 4, 2012.*

Zlín Film Festival, Filmfest s.r.o., Filmová 174, CZ-76179 Zlín, Czech Republic, Tel: (420) 577 592275; e: festival@zlinfest.cz; web: www. zlinfest.cz. *The festival is the world's oldest and largest festival of its kind. The festival's core is its international competitions: feature films for children, feature films for youth, animated films for children, and European debuts. The main prize of Zlín's festival is the Golden Slipper. Aside from the competitions, the programme is made up of many non-competitive sections. Among its most significant are the presentations of cinema from European countries. Among the most notable supporting events are the Mini-salon of artistically rendered film clapperboards, the international festival of ethical advertising The Rainbow Marble, and a retrospective of the international festival of student films Zlín Dog. In the non-competitive informative section, feature-length films, short animations or documentaries will be screened – May 27–Jun. 3, 2012.*

Zurich Film Festival, Bederstrasse 51, 8002 Zurich, Switzerland. Tel: (41 44) 286 6000; e: info@zurichfilmfestival.org; web: www. zurichfilmfestival.org. *The festival screens film premieres from all over the world, offers cinematic treats to a fascinated national and international audience, and facilitates direct on-the-spot exchange with filmmakers. The International Competition forms the core of the festival. The competition will present films by young, aspiring filmmakers who will compete for the Golden Eye with their first, second or third directing works. All competition films are world, European or Swiss premieres. Films will be screened in the following three categories: International Feature Film Competition, German-Language Feature Film Competition, International Documentary Film Competition – Sep. 20–30, 2012.*

Index to Advertisers